Only the Ball Was White

by Robert Peterson

PRENTICE-HALL, INC., Englewood Cliffs, N. J.

"The other day Willie Mays hit his five hundred and twenty-second home run. He has gone past me, and he's pushing, and I say to him, 'Go get 'em, Willie.' Baseball gives every American boy a chance to excel. Not just to be as good as someone else, but to be better. This is the nature of man and the name of the game. I hope that some day Satchel Paige and Josh Gibson will be voted into the Hall of Fame as symbols of the great Negro players who are not here, only because they weren't given the chance."

From Ted Williams' speech
upon his induction into
the Hall of Fame
Cooperstown, New York
July 1966

PREFACE

This is a book about baseball but it is not a baseball book in the conventional sense. There are no thrilling stories of pennant fights decided on the last day of the season. There are few statistics, the lifeblood of the fascinating game of baseball. The reader will find no replays of epic games that held the attention of the nation, nor will he find the complete career records of renowned players.

This book is about Negro baseball and the men who played it. Young readers may pause at the term "Negro baseball" and wonder whether it was a game with special rules, perhaps some adaptation of the familiar sport played only in black communities. Let them be assured at once: Negro baseball was played by ordinary rules on ordinary diamonds by black men, some of them ordinary and some very extraordinary indeed.

Negro baseball grew out of the fact that for a long period, 1898 to 1946, black men were barred from the major leagues and the recognized minor leagues in organized baseball by a "gentleman's agreement," and so the black player with professional skill was forced to play only on all-Negro teams. Most of these black teams, some of major-league quality, played a majority of their games against white teams.

It was another, very different age—for America and therefore for baseball. Baseball was truly the national game. Every community, down to the crossroads we now whizz by on superhighways without knowing what we have passed, had a town baseball team with a fiercely partisan following. These teams played every Sunday and sometimes once or twice during the week, meeting teams from nearby towns. In the cities, white semiprofessional clubs flourished; some of these teams, such as the Bushwicks of Brooklyn, were only a step or two below major-league caliber.

Because baseball was everywhere, it was possible for a Negro player to scratch out a living, often precarious, by joining one of the black clubs that crisscrossed the nation from early spring to late fall, playing anywhere a game could be arranged. In the winter, many black players went to Florida, California or Latin America and played some more.

The aim of this book is to tell the story of Negro baseball: why and how it evolved after the Civil War, what it was like to be a part of it, how Negro leagues developed, and something about the great teams and players.

The obstacles to this enterprise are formidable. There are no record books for Negro baseball; black clubs were much too busy playing to have the time or the inclination for such niceties as record-keeping. The literature on the subject is scanty, consisting of a few pages in perhaps a dozen books and a score or two of magazine articles. Much of it is pretty fanciful stuff, a compound of fact and myth tempered by the writer's imagination.

To separate the fact from the myth and to trace Negro baseball history as accurately as possible, recourse was had to old sporting papers and to the Negro weekly press, primarily the *Chicago Defender* and the *Pittsburgh Courier,* the two papers which covered the game most completely, and to a lesser extent, the defunct *New York Age.* Many other publications are cited, but for the skeleton of this history I have relied chiefly on contemporary accounts in those papers.

Easily the most enjoyable part of the research, and probably the most fruitful part, too, was my conversations with men who played the game. Without exception, they gave unstintingly of their time and memory to tell what it was like. For periods ranging up to seven hours, they sat and talked about the glories and frustrations of baseball behind the color line while a tape recorder wound slowly on in the background. These men, several of whom fans of Negro baseball will recognize instantly, are Jimmie Crutchfield, Napoleon Cummings, Floyd (Jelly) Gardner, Arthur W. Hardy, Judy Johnson, Buck Leonard, Dave Malarcher, Jack Marshall, Ted Page, Jackie Robinson, Carter Wilson, and Bill Yancey. They are not to be blamed for any dubious conclusions I may have drawn from the evidence of their recollections, but if this book has value, much of the credit must be theirs.

Perhaps a hundred other persons have helped in one way or another and merit my gratitude. A list of their names would be wearisome reading and susceptible to omission. A handful of them, however, contributed much to the work, and I would be remiss not to mention them. They are Mrs. Elwood (Bingo) DeMoss and Mrs. John Henry Lloyd, widows of great players; Mrs. Annie Mahaffey and Mrs. Helen Dixon, sister and daughter of the incredibly powerful hitter Josh Gibson; the late Lee Allen, historian at the National Baseball Hall of Fame and Museum in Cooperstown, New York; Roy Campanella; Frank Forbes, New York State boxing official and a former Negro-league umpire and promoter; Earl M. Foster, son of Rube Foster, Negro baseball's preeminent figure; Whitey

Gruhler, retired sports editor of the *Atlantic City Press;* Horace G. Hall, former owner of the Chicago American Giants, and Joseph M. Overfield, Buffalo baseball historian.

Finally, I gratefully acknowledge the aid of Lawrence S. Ritter, author of a fine book on baseball's early days, *The Glory of Their Times,* whose continuing encouragement has been an inspiration during the preparation of this book. I am indebted to Mr. Ritter not only for his interest but also for sharing with me the tape recording of a lengthy interview he had with the Negro star Cool Papa Bell in the spring of 1968.

One summer day in 1939 a kid squatted on the bank behind home plate at Russell Field in Warren, Pennsylvania, fielding foul balls (which could be redeemed for a nickel each—no small consideration in those days), and saw Josh Gibson hit the longest home run ever struck in Warren County. It was one of many impressive feats performed by touring black players that excited the wonder and admiration of that foul-ball shagger. This book is the belated fruit of his wonder.

Robert Peterson

Ramsey, New Jersey

*This book is for
Steve and Tom,
who can go to the big leagues together*

Contents

Only the
Ball
Was White

PART I:

MINE EYES HAVE SEEN THE GLORY

1 THIS WAS NEGRO BASEBALL

Life in Negro baseball was tough. It was tough even in our Negro National League, and when you went down to that league [Negro Southern League] it was tougher.
  —BUCK LEONARD

They were saints and sinners, college professors and illiterates, serious men and clowns, teetotalers and Saturday night drunks. They were professional baseball players, some of them the equals of the greatest major-leaguers, with one other common tie: they were all Negroes.

For nearly a half-century, from 1898 to 1946, black men were barred from the organized leagues by an unwritten rule, and behind this color line there developed a uniquely American spectacle called Negro baseball. Each year, black teams took to the road in early spring, and from then until late fall, they played a ballgame almost every day, meeting black teams and white teams in farm villages and big cities, on sandlots and in major-league stadiums. In the winter they went to Florida or California, Cuba or Mexico, and played some more. Negro baseball was played the year-round.

Listen while a few of the men who played it tell about those years.

Arthur W. Hardy
(Topeka Giants; Kansas City, Kansas, Giants—1906–1912).

When I was barnstorming with the Kansas City, Kansas, Giants, we got around any way we could. I have ridden between towns, especially out in Kansas and Nebraska where they were off the railroads—there weren't any buses then—in a farm wagon. Any kind of transportation. I've ridden in a wagon fifteen or twenty miles and then slept all night in a railroad station to catch a train to get into the next place. We used

3

to carry our clothes in a roll, and whenever we got caught out, like in a railroad station or someplace, we'd unroll that for a pallet to sleep on, you see.

Our first problem was, what connections could we get? Now we tried for the most part to travel the railroads. Up through Kansas and up into Nebraska there were two main railroads. One was the Missouri Pacific and the other was the Burlington. Well, now, we tried to book games all along the railroads. But sometimes, here off maybe twenty-five or thirty miles, was a little town with a team that had a tremendous following, and we would make that town.

We'd have to make it by any transportation we could get. Sometimes we'd have delivery rigs; other times we'd have a hay wagon or just a plain dray with boards across it to sit on.

Later teams would travel in cars and rickety buses. A few—very few—would make long trips in major-league style in Pullman cars. But the black baseball player was nearly always a traveling man.

Bill Yancey
(Philadelphia Giants; Lincoln Giants; Hilldale Club; New York Black Yankees; Brooklyn Eagles; Philadelphia Stars—1923–1936)

Bill Yancey

On certain days our Negro National or Negro American League clubs could have been major-leaguers. If we played with Bill Holland pitching, we were major league. See, we all had a couple of great pitchers. With Smoky Joe Williams or Cannonball Dick Redding or Phil Cockrell or Nip Winters pitching, we could beat anybody. But if we had some other fella in there, we might be a Double-A club, because baseball is based on pitching.

If we could have selected the best of the colored leagues and gone into the major leagues, I'd say we could have won the championship. We could have selected maybe five clubs out of all the colored teams that would have held their own in the big leagues. Because in 1927 I was with Hilldale as a utility man and we played Connie Mack's Athletics intact and beat 'em! That's when they had Jimmy Foxx and Jimmy Dykes and Joe Boley and Max Bishop and Al Simmons—Simmons didn't play because he wouldn't play. We beat 'em!

And I got clippings from the Thirties that show we beat the Dean boys when they had the Brooklyn Bushwick club. And we went down and played the major-leaguers every fall in Baltimore. We went down there with two pitchers, Phil Cockrell and Leon Day. And we played seven doubleheaders and they won one ball game! They had Jake Powell and Bobby Estalella and Don Heffner; they had a major-league ballclub. And Clark Griffith, who owned the Washington Senators, used to come out there and shake his head.

Triumphs over big-leaguers were savored, recalled, elaborated upon. If black players could not play in the major leagues, they could show that they belonged there. And those lovingly remembered victories were Negro baseball, too.

Dave Malarcher
(Indianapolis ABCs; Detroit Stars; Chicago American Giants—1916–1935)

My mother, Martha Malarcher, was born in slavery, but she learned early to read and write. My father worked as a laborer on a big sugar plantation. He was the top workman on that plantation.

My father was a great big strong man, tall. My mother was short; I guess I got my height from her. And he worked all year, even in the off-season. He worked in the sugarfields, and then all summer he worked in the ditches—ditching and all that kind of stuff.

But he was lovely, and my mother was very, very fine. She loved education. Now one of the reasons for that—and this is quite interesting—I believe she learned to write early in her life, when she was just a child. It must have been in slavery or just shortly afterward. As she grew, she worked up in the big house —the plantation-owner's house—as a cook and nursemaid, and as she told us, she learned to write from some of the white children of the people she worked for. She never went to any kind of big school in her life, but she wrote all of her letters and she spoke good English and all of that.

She probably went to a small country school after slavery. You see, right after the Civil War, many white people from up in New England, Christian people, went South and founded schools. They founded my school, New Orleans University— Straight University, Talladega, Fisk—all those schools were

Dave Malarcher

founded by them. And then, of course, a few colored people that lived down in the cities where these schools were founded early learned to read and write and got a small amount of education, and they went out in the country and established "pay schools." A nickel a week, you know?

My sister, who had gone to New Orleans and gotten probably a grade-school education, came home and established a little pay school right in our house. That was the first school I went to. There were probably ten or fifteen children, paying a nickel a week. This was a very common thing throughout the country down there in Louisiana. The whites had public schools, of course.

The first regular school I went to was a little public school; this was a little later on after they'd established public schools for Negroes. I've never forgotten the man who taught there —William Bradley. He was quite a boy. Schools were different then. We had a hall—just one big room; there were no classes —and we had the primer, the first grade, second grade, third grade, all in this room. When we got ready to recite, he'd call out, "Second-grade spelling!" Everybody in the second-grade spelling group would march up to his desk and stand in a line before him, and he'd call them out, "Spell so-and-so! Spell so-and-so!" And if you couldn't spell it you had to hold out your hand. And he had a strap! It was not like today where they can't even look at the kids. Mr. William Bradley would lay that strap on you! And you learned your lessons the next day, I'm telling you!

The first baseball team I played with was called the Baby T's. That was in the country around Union, Louisiana, where I grew up. This was prior to 1907. It was a little boys' team and our mothers made suits for the kids. We played the boys about ten miles up from Union, and we played a team across the Mississippi River, and then another team across the river farther south. All these were different communities and each of them had their baseball team—little colored boys our age.

On Saturday afternoon in the summer, after we came out of the ricefields, we would play a game. Yes, we used real baseballs. We could get money, you know. When we were very small, the people that grew the rice down there would hire the little boys to go in the fields and pull the weeds out of the rice. I remember the little boys got forty cents a day and the big boys got fifty cents a day. I was one of the little boys.

On Sundays, when we were not allowed to play ball, we would steal away to these places and play match games. I was the catcher, and I remember the boy that was our pitcher—his name was Lawrence Henderson—he cried when I went down to New Orleans University to go to the elementary school on the campus in 1907. A lot of those people in the country were not like my mother. They didn't have the desire for education, and they didn't send their kids to New Orleans like my mother did; some of them did, but very few. This boy Lawrence's parents were ignorant and they didn't realize. But after I went—I've never forgotten this—he cried because he wanted to be down in New Orleans with me. And finally his parents sent him down there, and later he pitched on our school team at the university.

Now, as I said, we had this little boy's team, and then there was a team for bigger boys, and a men's team, all in this little community. Three teams, three different ages. My oldest brother played on the men's team, the Pelicans. And they had a good team! They had several fellas there that, when I think about them, were good enough for big-league teams because they really played a lot of baseball.

A Negro boy learned to play ball any way he could. In the South, during the early years of the century, he worked in the fields all day before turning to baseball and the southern Louisiana equivalent of a Negro Little League. In the cities of the North, he made his own baseball and joined a pickup game in a vacant lot.

Jack Marshall
(Dayton Marcos; Chicago American Giants; Philadelphia Stars; Cincinnati Clowns—1926–1945)

In 1929 I organized a troupe—ballplayers, show, and band —for a white Canadian named Rod Whitman out of Lafleche, Saskatchewan. He came to Chicago and he wanted two Negro ballclubs, he wanted a minstrel show, and he wanted a band. In Canada he had a midway or carnival, and he would show in different towns, so he wanted two ballclubs—specifically, he wanted one named the Texas Giants and one named the New York All-Stars. So I organized this group for him, and I got a five-piece band and six other people as the minstrel show.

We traveled from Fort Williams, Ontario, to Vancouver, British Columbia, as far north as Prince Albert and as far south as Medicine Hat. We had four trucks—they looked like old covered wagons. We had a tent where the performers lived. When we got into a small town, they'd set up a tent where the other tents were for the midway, and some of the performers would sleep there. Then, when we got into a town big enough to have a hotel, the ballclubs would stop in the hotel.

And at twelve o'clock every day, Rod would put up five hundred dollars to the local team to play the all-stars—a team that would be selected from the Texas Giants and New York All-Stars. And if they won the game, they'd get the five hundred dollars. Well, we never lost a game under those conditions because we had our own umpires. We weren't there to lose!

So he'd charge admission for that, and then, when the ball-game was over, he would open up his midway. At six o'clock the Texas Giants and the New York All-Stars would play a game, and that's another admission. Now, when this ballgame was over, then the midway would open up again. While the midway was open, he would put this colored minstrel show on. With the midway and the minstrel show going on at one time, this man is coining the money! Now, when the midway closes, then the band would play for the dance. That's another admission, and the dance would go till one o'clock. Damnedest operation you ever saw!

Whitman was just selling entertainment, no patent medicine or anything like that. All the ballplayers were semipros from Chicago. At that time, in 1929, you might call me a pro. Anyway, I organized the thing. We had a payroll of eighteen hundred dollars a month for twenty-four players.

We had thirty-eight people in the whole troupe. I got the band here in Chicago, too. I wasn't a musician, but I knew fellas that were connected with booking bands, and a fella in the band knew some troupers and got them for the show. They had a heckuva show, I'm telling you. People got a big kick out of it. And we spread a lot of good will up there.

Our biggest towns were Edmonton, Regina, Winnipeg, Saskatoon. The rest we played were small towns, but we'd draw from four and five hundred miles away. A lot of times we had to make up a ballfield. If we played near the midway, where the carnival was going on, we'd make up a ballfield, but most of the time the carnival would be set up close to the fairgrounds, where there was a ballfield.

Funny thing, the kids got a kick out of us because, you see, they knew there were colored people in Texas and so everybody was pulling for the Texas Giants. They weren't for the New

York All-Stars. So what we did, we took most of the dark-
complected players and put them on the "Texas" team and
the light-complected players we put on the "New York" team.
    We never played in the United States because Rod couldn't
get a license. There was too much stickup to it, see. Rod would
take *everything*! There wouldn't be anything left in the town
when he finished!

Few black teams were quite so closely allied with show business
as the Texas Giants and the New York All-Stars, but nearly all had
showmen. When a fan went to see a Negro baseball club, he expected entertainment. And he got it.

Judy Johnson
(Hilldale Club; Homestead Grays; Pittsburgh Crawfords—1921–
1937)

    On the Hilldale Club we didn't travel too much, because
around Philadelphia there were so many teams—white clubs

Judy Johnson

and leagues. We just traveled mostly around Pennsylvania. Maybe once or twice a season we'd go to Pittsburgh, and one year—my first year with Hilldale—we went to Chicago, Detroit, St. Louis, and back home. But we never traveled a lot. That was one thing I liked about Hilldale, you were home almost every night.

But when I went to Pittsburgh to play with the Homestead Grays, boy! I went to Pittsburgh in 1930 to manage the Grays, and we traveled in two cars—two brand-new Buicks. We would go down South to Hot Springs around the fifteenth of March and stay there for ten days and then we'd go to New Orleans. The first Sunday in New Orleans was a doubleheader, and every day from then on was a ballgame.

Both of those two new Buicks turned over on the same day, I remember. Down South on some of those dirt roads, you go straight for maybe ten miles, and then you make a turn and go across a railroad track, and away you go again. Well, the land is flat, so they pulled the dirt from each side to make the road high. And that would leave a ditch on the side. And the road-scrapers would go down one side of the road and back the other, leaving a knoll, like, in the middle.

This day we were racing down to Shreveport and we had nine men in each car. And we had a box on the back of the car with our suits and equipment and racks on the side for our clothes and luggage. Oscar Charleston was driving the lead car and we were trying to catch him in the second car. Well, the sun was just going down and we couldn't see very well. Our driver, Charlie Walker, who owned the Grays with Cum Posey then, didn't see the knoll in the middle of the road, and we hit it. Well, it pulled the wheel out of his hands, and here we go over on these two wheels. He straightened it out and came back and we went over on the other two wheels. I guess we went along like that for about a quarter of a mile, just flip-flopping back and forth, and after a while, we just bumped over. Brand-new car! So all of us got out and straightened her up again— it didn't even stop running—and the only thing mashed was a fender. So we straightened that out the best we could, and far down the road we could see a crowd around. Charlie Walker said, "There's some poor so-and-so has the same trouble we got."

And when we got there, it was our other car. Charleston had slid off the road and blew a tire. And the car went down in the ditch and rolled over three times. The cars had those old canvas tops then, and when those tops broke off, the men rolled out into the ditch. That's the only thing that saved their lives. Nobody got hurt! Nine men packed in there like sardines, and when the roof caved in they all just dropped out into the ditch. That was a miracle. And when Charleston got out he had a piece of the steering wheel—they were wood then—in each of his hands. Oh, he was powerful! And he was a great ballplayer! He played centerfield, and you couldn't hit a ball over his head. He was like Tris Speaker, you know. He could go back on a ball and it looked like the ball would wait until he would catch up with it. He was a great ballplayer—a great ballplayer!

Nine men in a car racing down a southern back road with the black Tris Speaker at the wheel—that was Negro baseball. And when they got to a hotel in Shreveport, everybody looked for a good room, and when they found one they liked, they would toss their hats on the bed, establishing residence. A hat on the bed meant the room was taken. That was Negro baseball, too.

Buck Leonard
(Brooklyn Royal Giants, Homestead Grays—1933–1950)

Buck Leonard

I was working in the railroad shops and playing semipro ball here in Rocky Mount. Then there was a cutoff in the railroad shops and I got cut off, so I went to Portsmouth, Virginia, and I was playing with a team called the Portsmouth Firefighters. I played there a couple of months and then the Baltimore Stars, with Ben Taylor managing, came through, so I left Portsmouth and went to Baltimore to play with the Stars. And we played around Baltimore until, I reckon, August. Then we decided to go to New York and play out of New York.

Well, at that time, Nat Strong was the booking agent around New York and he booked our team. At that time Nat Strong was charging ten percent for booking. And we weren't making enough, even though we were playing—well, we were making enough but we just didn't pay that ten percent. So he stopped booking us and we couldn't get any games. We had two cars that we were traveling around in, and the hotel man where we were staying sold both our cars right there in front of the hotel for his room rent.

So then we didn't have any way to travel. I went over to talk to Smoky Joe Williams and Dick Redding, and they said how about playing with the Brooklyn Royal Giants? Dick Redding was managing and pitching for the Royal Giants but Smoky Joe wasn't playing at that time. So I started playing with them in the latter part of 1933.

Then a fella named Ramirez from Puerto Rico asked me did I want to go to Puerto Rico for the winter of 1933 and play all winter on an all-star team, and I told him yes. So he said, "All right then, stick around here until the fifteenth of November and I'll take you to Puerto Rico." I hung around New York just working around wherever I could get a job or two. And the fella where I was rooming, I was helping him out to take care of my room rent, but I had to get my board the best way I could. So on the morning of the fifteenth of November, I came down to Ramirez's office with my bags packed all ready to go to Puerto Rico, and then he showed me a telegram where, instead of carrying fifteen players, he couldn't carry but twelve. That meant that I couldn't go.

Well, I had been in New York all that time since September without any money, so I didn't have enough money to come home to Rocky Mount. So he gave me five dollars to come home, but at that time the bus fare was $10.75. I messed around New York for a week or so and then I met a girl from Rocky Mount that I knew and she let me have the rest of the money to come home. That was in 1933.

In 1934 I went back to New York to play with the Brooklyn Royal Giants. I went over to talk to Smoky Joe Williams one morning in a bar where he was working on Lenox Avenue and he said, "Look, why don't you get with a good team?" I said, "Who you talking about?" And he said, "Go on out with the Homestead Grays." I said, "Where are they?" And he said, "They're in Pittsburgh. You want me to talk to Cum Posey about it?" So I said yes, and he said, "Well, all right then, I'm going to call him, be here tonight at twelve o'clock." So that night at twelve o'clock I was down there at this tavern and he called Cum Posey and told Posey that I was a prospect and looked good and what about sending me out there? So Cum Posey said, "All right, I'm going to send you the money, you buy him a ticket and send him out to Wheeling, West Virginia." That was where the Grays were training in the spring of 1934.

So a couple of days later he sent Smoky Joe Williams the money and told Smoky Joe not to give me the money but to buy my ticket and give me five dollars to eat on on the way out to Wheeling. So Smoky Joe did, and a fella named Tex Burnett—he was a ballplayer, too, a catcher—and I caught the bus in New York and went on out to Wheeling. When we got to Wheeling, the snow was on the ground about half-of-a-leg deep. So we messed around the hotel two, three days till the weather got better and then we started spring training. In the meantime, the Grays were supposed to get a first baseman from Fort Wayne, Indiana, whose name was Joe Scott. I was there on a look-see, and if I didn't make it they were going to get Joe Scott from Fort Wayne. But I guess I showed up all right, because anyway, Joe Scott never did come. And I played first base for the Homestead Grays for seventeen years after that.

Negro baseball was all that and more. It was the holiday spirit in a small midwestern town when a black barnstorming team arrived to play the local semipros and it was the roar of 50,000 people at a Negro all-star game in Comiskey Park, Chicago. It was made by men named Satchel Paige and Josh Gibson—names that even white fans recognized—and it was also made by men named John Henry Lloyd and Bingo DeMoss and Martin Dihigo and Willie Wells and Pete Hill. These men were the Willie Mayses and Henry Aarons and Bob Gibsons and Lou Brocks of their time, but they were unheralded except in the Negro press and mostly unknown to white baseball men except the major-leaguers against whom they often barnstormed.

Negro baseball was Josh Gibson standing loose and easy at the plate in Yankee Stadium and hitting the longest home run ever seen in the House that Ruth Built. And it was the touring Brooklyn Colored Giants arriving, broke and hungry, in a small Pennsylvania city where, because of a scheduling mixup, no game was arranged, and then playing a hastily called game with the local semipros so they could take up a collection for a meal and enough gas to get to the next town.

Negro baseball was at once heroic and tawdry, a gladsome thing and a blot on America's conscience.

2 PIONEERS IN BLACK AND WHITE

It is not presumed by your Committee that any club who have applied are composed of persons of color, or any portion of them; and the recommendations of your Committee in this report are based upon this view, and they unanimously report against the admission of any club which may be composed of one or more colored persons.
—NOMINATING COMMITTEE, NATIONAL ASSOCIATION OF BASE BALL PLAYERS, 1867

It began more than one hundred years ago, in December, 1867. The Civil War was two-and-a-half years in the past. Military governors ruled the old Confederacy, and black men, most of them former slaves, had just been given the right to vote.

Baseball was barely out of its swaddling clothes. Before the war, only a few gentlemen amateurs around New York City played baseball, but the game had spread rapidly in army camps and military prisons both North and South during the bloody years of conflict. By 1867 there were more than a hundred baseball clubs in the North, and the game's first league, the National Association of Base Ball Players, was nine years old. It was a loose confederation with the primary purpose of making rules for member clubs. On December 11 and 12, the NABBP held its annual convention in Philadelphia, with 237 delegates attending, some from as far away as Wisconsin. They could not be oblivious to the nation's moral dilemma—what to do about its four-and-a-half million new citizens, all of them black.

The NABBP addressed itself to the Negro question and came down on the side of repression, barring Negroes and the clubs to which they belonged from membership. The Association's nominating committee penned the first color line in baseball, unanimously calling for exclusion "of any club which may be composed of one or more colored persons." *Beadle's Dime Base Ball Player* of 1868 said the object was "to keep out of the convention the discussion of any subjects having a political bearing, as this undoubtedly had."

Political? Yes, the nation's black men were the hottest political topic in 1867. In the U.S. Senate and House of Representatives, gentle Charles Sumner and crusty, clubfooted Thaddeus Stevens were pleading and thundering in vain for justice for the former slaves. In the South, the notorious Black Codes, restricting the movements and rights of Negroes, were in force. The South was determined to reëstablish bondage for the blacks; they were called freed men but the title was a sham.

The Negro *was* a political subject in 1867, but politics was a secondary consideration for the NABBP. Simple prejudice brought baseball's first color line. The members of the Association were all Northerners, but most shared with Southerners the belief that the Negro was inferior and not fit company for white gentlemen.

The National Association of Base Ball Players was destined to survive only a few more years, because of growing professionalism in the game, but its ban on black men set the pattern for its successor, the National Association of Professional Base Ball Players, although not for all early leagues. Formed in 1871, the NAPBBP never had a written rule against Negro players. It did not need one, for there existed a "gentleman's agreement" barring Negroes from this first professional league and from its successor, the National League.

However, if Negroes could not play baseball with Association clubs, there was nothing to forbid them from playing among themselves. And they did. Nothing is known about the earliest Negro clubs, but by 1867 teams were sufficiently well-organized, at least in the North, to have challenge matches for supremacy.

A ballgame in those days (for both blacks and whites) was as much a social occasion as an athletic contest. Announcing plans for a visit by the Excelsiors of Philadelphia to play the Uniques and the Monitors in October 1867, the *Brooklyn Daily Union* commented:

> These organizations are composed of very respectable colored people, well-to-do in the world . . . and include many first-class players. The visitors will receive all due attention from their colored brethren of Brooklyn; and we trust, for the good of the fraternity, that none of the "white trash" who disgrace white clubs, by following and bawling for them, will be allowed to mar the pleasure of these social colored gatherings.

The *Daily Union* was less complimentary when the first of the games was played between the Excelsiors and Uniques, possibly because its sportswriter was insulted by one of the Philadelphia team's fans (whom he described as a "pretty rough crowd"). The Excelsiors of Philadelphia defeated the home team, 42–37, in a game marred by arguments and called after seven innings because of darkness. "The contest was in no way creditable to the organizations," the aggrieved writer reported. "In fact it put us in mind of the old style of nines which used to prevail among the white clubs."

That October, while the "colored championship" series was going on in Brooklyn, a thirteen-year-old boy was learning to play baseball in upstate New York. He was John W. (Bud) Fowler, who, five years later, would become the first black professional ballplayer.

Fowler, whose name at birth was John Jackson, was probably the best player ever born in Cooperstown, N.Y., where organized baseball maintains its museum and Hall of Fame, and where, faulty legend has it, the first baseball game was played in 1839. The late Lee Allen, museum historian, found that Fowler was born there in 1854. His parents are believed to have been itinerant hops-pickers, free Negroes who were then in Cooperstown.

Bud Fowler learned to play baseball around Hudson, N.Y., and, in 1872, he was on a white team in New Castle, Pennsylvania. He is thereby established as the first paid Negro player, according to Sol White, a black baseball pioneer whose *History of Colored Base Ball,* a little volume published in 1907, gives an invaluable though sketchy picture of early teams and players.

For the next twenty-five years, Fowler barnstormed around the country, from Massachusetts to Colorado, playing wherever Negro players were permitted. He played in crossroads farm towns and in mining camps, in the pioneer settlements of the West and in the cities of the East. These were the years of growth for the minor leagues, the foundation stones for organized baseball, and Fowler performed in several of them. He was the first of more than thirty Negroes who were in white leagues before the turn of the century, when baseball's leaders began to think of their structure as Organized Baseball in capital letters and when the long night of total exclusion lowered for the black man.

Like most of the peripatetic ballplayers of his day, Fowler could play any position, but it was as a second baseman that he excelled.

He was recognized by white sportswriters as the equal of any of his contemporaries at that position, but he had no chance to test his talents against them at the highest level, the National League.

Fowler's wanderings during his first twelve years as a professional are not recorded, but his career can be picked up in 1884 when a sprightly weekly called *Sporting Life* began publication in Philadelphia. It covered baseball, cricket, swimming, billiards, horse racing, music and drama, and quickly achieved a solid circulation among the sporting crowd for its extensive coverage of baseball and its penchant for the sardonic. Sample:

> Ike Carter, the best second baseman in the country and a member of the celebrated Black Stockings of St. Louis (a colored team), recently received a ball that was too much for him. It was made of lead. He turned burglar and was shot dead by a St. Louis man into whose house he broke.

In 1884 there were eleven leagues under the National Agreement; that is, professional leagues whose members agreed not to raid other teams covered by the Agreement. The four strongest were the National League, the two-year-old American Association, the Eastern League, and the Northwestern League.

Bud Fowler performed that year for the Stillwater, Minnesota, club in the Northwestern League. In May, *Sporting Life* reported, "The Stillwater club has a colored player named Fowler who pitches, catches, and plays left field in good shape." Fowler pitched Stillwater to its first victory and got a bonus of ten dollars and a suit of clothes as a result. The management got back the ten dollars in July when he was fined for a wild throw that let in two runs.

Minor-league players lived precariously in the 1880s. The leagues had a disconcerting proclivity for breaking up in the middle of a season as the hard facts of economics overcame civic pride and cities were forced to withdraw their teams. Bud Fowler's lot was doubly hard because he was black.

Take the year 1885, when Fowler was thirty-one years old and had been a professional baseball player for thirteen years. *Sporting Life* tells his story in bits and pieces:

> *May 13*: Fowler, the colored player who made quite a reputation in the Northwestern League last year, is now playing with Keokuk [Western League].

Bud Fowler with Keokuk of the Western
League in 1885. COURTESY OF LEE
ALLEN

June: The Western League broke up.

July 22: The Keokuk club disbanded last week. . . . Fowler, the crack colored player, is willing to manage and play with the Orion (Colored) Club of Philadelphia, but as yet is undecided as to what he will do. He is one of the best general players in the country, and if he had a white face would be playing with the best of them.

August 12: John W. Fowler, the noted colored player, late of Northwestern and Western League clubs, is in St. Louis without an engagement.

August 19: Fowler, the colored player, has signed with the St. Joseph, Mo., club.

August 26: Fowler, late second baseman of the Keokuks, has joined the Pueblos (in Colorado).

November 18: John W. Fowler, the famous second baseman, is now traveling through the Northwest, giving walking exhibitions against skaters, and running exhibitions. He is said to have walked a mile in 8 m., 30 s. and to have run a mile in 4 m., 56 s. He can be addressed care *Western Sport*, Denver, Colo.

December 30: Fowler, the crack colored second baseman, is still in Denver, Colo., disengaged. The poor fellow's skin is against him. With his splendid abilities he would long ago have been on some good club had his color been white instead of black. Those who know say there is no better second baseman in the country; he is besides a good batter and fine base-runner.

There are believed to have been one or two other Negro players on white teams during the late 1870s and early 1880s, but the next one who can be placed is a man of many parts named Moses Fleetwood Walker. Tall, slender, and handsome, Walker combined athletic talent with considerable intellectual capacity. By happenstance he became the first Negro major-league player and by exercising his diverse talents, Walker became a businessman, inventor, newspaper editor, and author. He attended integrated colleges and played professional baseball only on integrated teams, and the experience evidently so soured him that near the end of his life he was an advocate of complete separation of the races (separation by an ocean, for he called for emigration of Negroes back to Africa).

Moses Fleetwood Walker was born in Mt. Pleasant, Ohio, a village a few miles across the Ohio River from Wheeling, West Virginia. At his birth, on October 7, 1857, Mt. Pleasant was a way station on the Underground Railroad, which guided fugitive slaves to freedom in Canada. He was the son of a physician, Dr. Moses W. Walker, who moved his family to Steubenville, upriver from Mt. Pleasant, when Fleet was still a boy.

At twenty, Walker was at Oberlin, Ohio, a hotbed of Abolitionist sentiment before and during the Civil War and also a stop on the Underground Railroad. He was entered in the college preparatory course at Oberlin College in 1877 and 1878. For the next three years he was a student in the college, studying mathematics, Greek, rhetoric, mechanics, natural philosophy, French, civil engineering, zoology, chemistry, astronomy, German, botany, logic, and Latin. His marks were good though not exceptional.

In 1881, Walker's last year at Oberlin, a varsity baseball team was organized and he became the catcher. His brother, Weldy Wilberforce Walker, who was to become the second Negro major-leaguer, played right field. Weldy, three years younger than Fleet, was then enrolled in the college's preparatory school.

The Oberlin team played three games and won them all, the last against the University of Michigan, with Fleet starring as a hitter and receiver. It appears that Michigan thought highly of his talents, for he left Oberlin without taking a degree and was a student at Ann Arbor during the academic year of 1881–82. He earned no degree there, either, but he was the catcher for the team, winning

varsity letters in 1882 and 1883. Under the relaxed rules for inter-
collegiate athletics at that time, Walker was able to return to Oberlin
at commencement time in 1882 to catch one more game for the
old school.

In 1883 he became a professional baseball player, joining a white
teammate from Oberlin on the Toledo club of the Northwestern
League. His record and the testimony of sportswriters indicate that
Walker was a good journeyman catcher and an adequate batter.
Toledo won the Northwestern League pennant with Walker catching
sixty games and batting .251.

Weldy W. Walker

Moses Fleetwood Walker, the first Negro
major leaguer.

COURTESY OF OCANIA CHALK

The following year, Fleet Walker became the first Negro major-
leaguer when Toledo entered the American Association and he
went with the franchise. The AA was starting its third season, and,
although less prestigious than the older National League, it was
nonetheless recognized as a major league.

Walker's reception in the big league was mixed. If the other
players resented his presence, they gave no outward indication of
it, and spectators, on the whole, seemed favorably inclined toward
him except in the league's two distinctly southern cities.

According to the Toledo *Blade,* during Toledo's first appearance at Louisville, Walker was hissed and insulted because of his color:

> Walker . . . is one of the most reliable men in the club, but his poor playing in a City where the Color line is closely drawn as it is in Louisville . . . should not be counted against him. Many a good player under less aggravating circumstances than this, has become rattled and unable to play. It is not creditable to the Louisville management that it should permit such outrageous behavior to occur on the grounds.

Sporting Life's Louisville correspondent saw it differently. He reported: "Time works wonders. Walker, the negro [sic] catcher of the Toledo Club, who was several years ago forbidden to play on Louisville grounds on account of his color, was frequently applauded in that city last week for his fine catching."

Toledo fans, however, were *Blade* readers, and when Louisville next appeared there, the club was so roundly booed that the paper had to remind them that the players were "gentlemanly and honorable" and were not responsible for the conduct of their fans back in Kentucky.

In Baltimore three thousand people turned out to view the curious spectacle of a Negro playing with whites. "Every good play by him was loudly applauded," *Sporting Life* said. In Washington he made a "favorable impression," the paper reported.

Real trouble was promised for Walker if he appeared in Richmond. The Virginians had joined the Association after the collapse of the Washington franchise in midseason, and Toledo was scheduled for a series there Oct. 13–15. In September, Toledo manager Charlie Morton received a letter from Richmond:

> We the undersigned do hereby warn you not to put up Walker, the negro catcher, the evenings that you play in Richmond, as we could mention the names of 75 determined men who have sworn to mob Walker if he comes on the ground in a suit. We hope you will listen to our words of warning, so that there will be no trouble; but if you do not there certainly will be. We only write this to prevent much bloodshed, as you alone can prevent.

The letter was signed by "Bill Frick," "Jas. Kendrick," "Dynx Dunn," and "Bob Roseman," names which, according to *Sporting Life*'s Richmond correspondent, belonged to no one in Richmond.

If there was indeed a lynch mob waiting for Walker in Richmond, its resolve was not to be tested, for by October he was through for the season. He had suffered a broken rib when he was struck by a foul tip in mid-July (the chest-protector had not yet been introduced), and he played only sporadically after that. In late September, Walker was released, not without regret. The *Blade* called him "a conscientious player" and said he was "very popular with Toledo audiences." *Sporting Life's* Toledo reporter also spoke glowingly:

> To his fine work last year much of the success of the Toledo Club was due, as none will deny. This year, however, he has been extremely unfortunate, having met with several accidents which kept him disabled a large part of the time. During his connection with the Toledo Club, by his fine, gentlemanly deportment, he made hosts of friends who will regret to learn that he is no longer a member of the club.

The New York Metropolitans won the 1884 pennant. Toledo finished eighth in the twelve-club Association and in such financial trouble that no attempt was made to revive the team the next year. Walker's contribution to the Toledo cause included a .251 batting average in 46 games, with 4 doubles and 2 triples, and a fielding average of .888, twenty-sixth in the league for catchers.

Weldy Walker, Fleet's younger brother, entered major-league record books in 1884 because he was in the right place at the right time. In July, Toledo was crippled with injuries, to others as well as to Fleet. During a series in Indianapolis "the Toledos were short-handed and played Weldy Walker, a brother of the catcher; he played well," *Sporting Life* commented. Weldy was in six games with Toledo as an outfielder, batting .182.

In 1885 Fleet Walker and Bud Fowler were the only Negroes in organized white leagues, although Weldy Walker apparently was playing somewhere because, in a later report to the Oberlin College alumni office, he said he was in baseball that year. Fleet Walker started the season with Cleveland in the Western League. When that league folded in June, he went to Waterbury, Conn., in the Southern New England League. It, too, was a sick league, and Walker left it in early September and ended the season as a member of the Eastern League. In ten games with Waterbury in the Eastern League, Walker batted .160. Bud Fowler, as already mentioned, spent 1885 in close company with a railroad timetable, roving from Keokuk, Iowa, to St. Louis, to St. Joseph, Mo., to Pueblo, Colo., to Denver.

In the following year, the color line faded somewhat—though almost imperceptibly. Four Negroes are found on the rosters of important minor leagues in that year. Bud Fowler, for once, spent the whole summer with one club, batting .309 as the second baseman for Topeka, Kansas, in the Western League. Fleet Walker caught 35 games and hit .209 for Waterbury in the Eastern League. Joining Walker in that league was George W. Stovey, the first great Negro pitcher. A lefthander, Stovey was the top pitcher for Jersey City. *The Sporting News,* which published its first issue in 1886 and quickly became a rival of *Sporting Life,* called Stovey a "good one, and if the team would support him they would make a far better showing. His manner in covering first from the box is wonderful."

Reach's Official Base Ball Guide for 1887 gives no won–lost record for Eastern League pitchers in 1886, but it does show Stovey as the second most effective pitcher in the league in the matter of base hits yielded per batters faced. Stovey faced 1,059 batters and gave up only 177 hits for a percentage of .167.

The fourth Negro in organized baseball in 1886 was a cherubic twenty-year-old named Frank Grant, who was probably the best of the black players who appeared in white leagues during the early years. He was a strong hitter, and his play at second base earned him the sobriquet "the Black Dunlap," a signal compliment, because Fred Dunlap, the St. Louis second baseman and the first player to reach the $10,000-a-year salary level, was regarded as the best at the position.

Like the other Negro baseball pioneers, Frank Grant was a Northerner. He was born in Pittsfield, Massachusetts, in 1867, and at seventeen he was a pitcher for the Graylocks of Pittsfield. The next year he was catching for a club in Plattsburg, N.Y., and demonstrated his eagerness by once shinnying eight feet up a telegraph pole to catch a foul fly—or so one legend has it.

Frank Grant entered organized baseball as an infielder with Meriden, Connecticut, of the Eastern League. When that club disbanded in July, he and two white teammates went to Buffalo of the International Association. In reporting his signing by the Bisons, the Buffalo *Express* described Grant, whose color was light, as a "Spaniard."

He had a fine year in 1886, batting .325 in 33 games for Meriden and .340 in 45 games for Buffalo, best on the club and third in the league. The Buffalo correspondent of *Sporting Life* described him as

> a great all-around player; he can fill creditably every position on the diamond, but his speciality is second base. Some consider him rather weak in touching base-runners, but I think he is fully as quick in that respect as any other guardian of "the key to the diamond." He is a very accurate thrower, and withal swift. He is exceedingly hard to fool at the bat . . . and his shots are generally long. . . . I think I can say that Grant is the best all-around player Buffalo ever had.

The season of 1887 dawned full of promise for Negro players in organized baseball. Sol White said that twenty black men were on white teams, many apparently in small leagues, as only eight can be located with certainty. Bud Fowler, Fleet Walker, George Stovey, and Frank Grant were, of course, established players. All of them performed in the renamed International League; Fowler was with Binghamton, Walker and Stovey with Newark, and Frank Grant was again at second base for Buffalo.

Sol White himself entered organized ball in 1887 as a nineteen-year-old third baseman from Bellaire, Ohio, on the roster of the Wheeling club of the Ohio State League. Also in the Ohio league were Weldy Walker, who played briefly with Akron, and Richard Johnson, a catcher-outfielder for Zanesville. The eighth dark newcomer to the white leagues was Robert Higgins, a pitcher for Syracuse in the International League. Two other Negroes had brief trials that year, a player named Renfro with Binghamton and another named N. Higgins in the Ohio State League.

Exciting the fancy that more Negro players would gradually be absorbed into organized baseball's structure was recognition of the new League of Colored Base Ball Clubs as a legitimate minor league under the National Agreement. The clubs in this first Negro league were the Browns of Cincinnati, Capital Citys of Washington, Falls Citys of Louisville, Keystones of Pittsburgh, Lord Baltimores of Baltimore, Resolutes of Boston, Pythians of Philadelphia, and the Gorhams of New York.

Had the League of Colored Base Ball Clubs succeeded and remained a recognized part of organized baseball, it seems probable that eventually it would have become a feeder for major league teams. It is impossible to believe that as a legitimate minor league it could have been ignored completely as were the Negro circuits of a later era.

But it was not to be. The League of Colored Base Ball Clubs, collapsed after a week during which every team suffered financial disaster. But Sol White saw a ray of sunshine because, he said, "the short time of its existence served to bring out the fact that colored baseball players of ability were numerous."

Nobody rose to deny it. Frank Grant, called the most popular player on the Buffalo club by the *Express*, led his team to a second-place finish in the International League behind Toronto. He batted .366, tops among the Bisons. Despite his small stature (Grant was 5 feet 7½ inches tall and weighed 155 pounds), he was the leading slugger in the league, with 27 doubles, 10 triples and 11 home runs in 105 games. He also led the Bisons in base-stealing with 40 thefts. (If Grant's batting average and base-stealing record seem of superstar quality, it should be remembered that in 1887 the batter still received four strikes, a base on balls counted as a hit in the averages, and many more bases were stolen than in the modern game. The International League's batting leader that year had an average of .422, and the top base-stealer was credited with 112 steals.)

Bud Fowler batted .350 and stole 30 bases in thirty games for Binghamton, and Fleet Walker hit .263 and stole 36 bases as catcher and centerfielder for Newark in 69 games.

George Stovey won 33 and lost 14 in pitching Newark to a fourth-place finish. As was customary for pitchers, Stovey also played the outfield, acceptably if not brilliantly, and his batting average for 54 games was .255.

Bob Higgins, the other black pitcher in the IL, had a 20–7 won–lost record for Syracuse and compiled a .294 batting average in 41 games, some as an outfielder. His won–lost percentage was second best in the league.

In the Ohio State League, Sol White hit a solid .381 as Wheeling's third baseman for 45 games. Dick Johnson, alternating between catching and outfielding for Zanesville, had a .296 batting average. Weldy Walker played only four games and batted .250 for Akron before the club disbanded.

With all these players performing creditably (and some of them brilliantly) in 1887, there was reason to hope that more and more Negroes would enter organized white leagues. But prejudice against them was strong, and that season saw the first serious rumblings of player discontent that spelled the beginning of the end for Negroes in the early white leagues.

Trouble surfaced in early June on the Syracuse Stars. *The Sporting News* deemed the story newsworthy enough for the lead spot in its June 11 issue, which headlined:

Dug Crothers Suspended
HIS OFFENSE A REFUSAL TO SIT BESIDE
THE COLORED PITCHER

The Syracuse correspondent wrote:

> The Stars have broken out in a new spot. Manager Simmons last Saturday told the members of the club to put in an appearance Sunday morning at Ryder's photograph gallery to have a group picture taken. All the members reported except Pitcher Crothers and Leftfielder Simon. The manager surmised at once that there was a "nigger on the fence" and that those players had not reported because the colored pitcher, Higgins, was to be included in the club portrait.

Manager Simmons' surmise was correct. He suspended the recalcitrant pitcher, Douglas (Dug) Crothers, a native of St. Louis who later had a brief and undistinguished career in the majors, because, in addition to showing "impudence" to Simmons, Crothers also struck him; the two men were separated before Simmons "could get in his return work." The suspension was to be for a month but actually lasted only eight days. In any event, Crothers found it no hardship; he was making $25 a game pitching for amateur clubs around Syracuse.

A month later, on July 14, the International League's directors held a midsummer meeting in Buffalo at which white players' grumblings over the presence of Negroes were brought into the open. *Sporting Life* reported: "Several representatives declared that many of the best players in the League were anxious to leave on account of the colored element, and the board finally directed Secretary White to approve no more contracts with colored men."

So it was finally on paper. For the first time, a professional baseball league had drawn the color line officially; the five Negroes in the league were not ousted, but the handwriting was on the wall.

On the same day the International League's directors put up the color bar, the Newark *Evening News* announced that big George

Stovey would pitch an exhibition game against the Chicago White Stockings at Newark on July 19. As the ace of the Little Giants' staff, Stovey was a natural selection to face the White Stockings, who were led by Adrian Constantine (Cap) Anson, one of the greatest players in baseball's history, the Babe Ruth and John McGraw of his era.

Newark beat the vaunted White Stockings in that exhibition, but the Little Giants did it without the services of Stovey, who, said the *Evening News,* "complained of sickness." *Sporting Life's* Newark correspondent had nothing to say about Stovey's indisposition but commented, "There was not an objectionable feature during the game, and the 'champs' leave here with the best wishes of our people."

A year later *Sporting Life* admitted that Stovey's complaint of sickness was involuntary and that the real reason he did not pitch was because Anson refused to field his team if the Negro played. It was another first in organized baseball, this triumph of race prejudice determining a manager's judgment; it was not, however, the first—or last—attempt.

In 1883 Anson had tried to draw the line against Fleet Walker when the White Stockings played an exhibition in Toledo. But his bluff was called by Toledo manager Charlie Morton, who said that Walker would play or there would be no game. Anson played rather than lose his share of the gate receipts. "The joke of the affair," *Sporting Life* said several years later, "was that up to the time Anson made his 'bluff' the Toledo people had no intention of catching Walker, who was laid up with a sore hand, but when Anson said he wouldn't play with Walker, the Toledo people made up their minds that Walker would catch or there wouldn't be any game."

In his *History of Colored Base Ball,* Sol White indicted Anson as being almost solely responsible for imposing the color line. While Stovey was starring for Newark, White wrote, the New York Giants wanted to buy him,

and arrangements were about completed for his transfer from the Newark club, when a howl was heard from Chicago to New York. This same Anson, with all the venom of a hate which would be worthy of a [Senator Ben] Tillman or a [Senator James] Vardaman of the present day, made strenuous and fruitful opposition to any proposition looking to the admittance of a colored man in the National League.

If there was indeed a howl heard from Chicago to New York, it did not penetrate the offices of the leading sporting papers of the day, for no mention is made either of a prospective sale of Stovey to the New York Giants or of a subsequent furor.

That Anson did not like Negroes is undeniable. In his autobiography, *A Ball Player's Career*, published in 1900, Anson makes no mention of Negro ballplayers, but his references to a mascot who went with the White Stockings on a round-the-world exhibition trip in the winter of 1888–89 make clear his contempt for Negroes. The mascot was a talented singer-dancer named Clarence Duval, who entertained before games, and Anson refers to Duval as the "little darky," the "chocolate-covered coon," and the "no-account nigger."

Sol White was puzzled by Anson's bias.

> Just why Adrian C. Anson, manager and captain of the Chicago National League Club, was so strongly opposed to colored players on white teams cannot be explained. His repugnant feeling, shown at every opportunity, toward colored ball players, was a source of comment throughout every league in the country, and his opposition, with his great popularity and power in base ball circles, hastened the exclusion of the black man from white leagues.

Anson's attitude *was* strange. He was the first white child born in Marshalltown, Iowa, and his early playmates were Pottawatomie Indians whose tepees still dotted the land around the Anson family's log cabin in the 1850s. His whole baseball career of a record twenty-seven years in the major leagues was spent in northern cities. For twenty-two years he was the idol of the sporting world in Chicago, which, until the 1890s, was considered a racially liberal city.

Whatever its origin, Anson's animus toward Negroes was strong and obvious. But that he had the power and popularity to force Negroes out of organized baseball almost singlehandedly, as White suggests, is to credit him with more influence than he had, or for that matter, than he needed. For it seems clear that a majority of professional baseball players in 1887, both Northerners and Southerners, opposed integration in the game.

In September 1887, two months after Anson's triumph in barring Stovey from the field at Newark, the St. Louis Browns, champions of the American Association, refused to play an exhibition game against the all-Negro Cuban Giants at West Farms, N.Y. The game had been widely advertised, and 7,000 fans were on the grounds when the Cuban Giants got a telegram from Chris Von der Ahe, owner of the Browns, saying that his club was badly crippled and would not be able to play.

The real reason, however, was that the night before, in Philadelphia, Von der Ahe had been handed a message from eight of his players which read:

> We, the undersigned members of the St. Louis Base Ball Club, do not agree to play against negroes tomorrow. We will cheerfully play against white people at any time, and think, by refusing to play, we are only doing what is right, taking everything into consideration and the shape the team is in at present.

Of the eight players who signed, four were native to the North; a fifth was born in Canada.

The attrition of Negroes in the International League's ranks began before the 1887 season was over. In July, Binghamton released Bud Fowler on condition that he sign with no other IL club, and the veteran thereupon joined the Cuban Giants, the best all-Negro team of that era.

At the end of the season, Newark put Fleet Walker on its reserve list of players for 1888 (indicating its intention to sign him) but, curiously, did not reserve George Stovey, the 33-game winner with a pleasingly wild fast ball against which no batter dared dig in. (Newark dropped out of the league later that fall, and Walker was signed by Syracuse.) Frank Grant was reserved by Buffalo and Bob Higgins by Syracuse, but hanging over the heads of Walker, Grant, and Higgins that fall was the threat of expulsion from the league during the winter meetings.

The editorial guns of the press were unlimbered on behalf of the black men. The Syracuse *Standard* advised: "The Star directors should at once take steps toward the rescinding by the International League of the rule forbidding the employment of colored players," which, the *Standard* added, was a "shameful regulation."

The Newark *Call* expressed its scorn in more vigorous language:

> If anywhere in the world the social barriers are broken down it is on the ball field. There many men of low birth and poor breeding are the idols of the rich and cultured; the best man is he who plays best. Even men of churlish disposition and coarse

hues are tolerated on the field. In view of these facts the objection to colored men is ridiculous. If social distinctions are to be made, half the players in the country will be shut out. Better make character and personal habits the test. Weed out the toughs and intemperate men first, and then it may be in order to draw the color line.

Whether because of the press' interest or for some other reason, the International League directors stepped gingerly around the color issue that winter. In November, they met in Toronto and took no action. At their February meeting, *Sporting Life* said that

> there was some informal talk regarding the right of clubs to sign colored players, and the general understanding seemed to be that no city should be allowed to engage more than one colored man. Syracuse has signed two (Walker and Higgins) whom she will undoubtedly be allowed to keep. Buffalo has signed Grant, but outside of these men there will probably be no colored men in the league.

The Ohio State League, which had three Negroes in 1887, also wrestled with the color question that winter. Accounts of the league's action differ. *The Sporting News* reported, "The rule that no colored players be hired was repealed," while *Sporting Life* said, "The law permitting colored men to sign was repealed." From other evidence it seems likely that *The Sporting News'* version was correct and that the league rescinded a rule passed earlier that year forbidding the signing of additional Negro players. In any case, Richard Johnson was back with Zanesville in 1888.

Weldy Walker, who was a *Sporting Life* reader, was outraged after seeing its account of the league's action and vented his frustration in a letter to league president W. H. McDermitt. His letter is perhaps the most passionate cry for justice ever voiced by a Negro athlete:

> The law is a disgrace to the present age, and reflects very much upon the intelligence of your last meeting, and casts derision at the laws of Ohio—the voice of the people—that say all men are equal. I would suggest that your honorable body, in case that black law is not repealed, pass one making it criminal for a colored man or woman to be found on a ball ground.

There is now the same accommodation made for the colored patron of the game as the white, and the same provision and dispensation is made for the money of them both that finds its way into the coffers of the various clubs.

There should be some broader cause—such as lack of ability, behavior and intelligence—for barring a player, rather than his color. It is for these reasons and because I think ability and intelligence should be recognized first and last—at all times and by everyone—I ask the question again, "Why was the law permitting colored men to sign repealed, etc.?"

The question went unanswered, because it was unanswerable. Weldy Walker knew the bitter truth. There would be Negroes in white organized leagues in 1888 and after, but the truth was plain for all who wished to see it: Jim Crow was warming up.

3 EARLY BLACK PROFESSIONAL TEAMS

The Cuban Giants, the famous baseball club, have defeated the New Yorks, 4 games out of 5, and are now virtually champions of the world. The St. Louis Browns, Detroit and Chicagos, afflicted with Negrophobia and unable to bear the odium of being beaten by colored men, refused to accept their challenge.
—INDIANAPOLIS FREEMAN, *1888*

While Bud Fowler, Frank Grant, and Fleet Walker were maintaining a shaky toehold in organized baseball, scores of other accomplished black ballplayers were being paid to play on all-Negro teams. Just when the first Negro team began paying its players cannot be determined, but it must have been in the early 1880s, perhaps even in the late Seventies.

Sol White said the first Negro professional team was the Cuban Giants, formed in 1885 at a Long Island summer resort. This may well have been the first *salaried* Negro team, but it is certain that other teams were paid to play before then.

In 1882 the *Cincinnati Enquirer* noted, "Philadelphia has a nine of colored professionals." This probably was the Orions, one of the strongest teams in Philadelphia at that time. And *Sporting Life*, in its inaugural year of 1884, referred to several other Negro clubs as if they were professional, or at least semipro. Among them were the Black Stockings of St. Louis, the Mutuals of Philadelphia, and the Atlantics of Baltimore. In August 1884, *Sporting Life* reported that the Atlantics beat the Mutuals, 30–5, at Baltimore, then "failed to pay their unfortunate brothers from Philadelphia their share of the gate receipts, and the latter had to walk home."

Whether or not they were the first fully professional Negro team, there is no doubt that the Cuban Giants dominated black baseball in its infancy. They were so popular, in fact, that their name was appropriated with variations by other teams. In 1896 the owner of the Cuban Giants brought suit against the Cuban X Giants, but the X Giants' owner replied: "We are informed legally that the name of the Cuban X Giants is not incorporated, and that we have a perfect right to the use of same."

The original Cuban Giants were the creation of Frank P. Thompson, headwaiter at the Argyle Hotel in Babylon during the summer of 1885. Sol White said that Thompson formed the team from among his Negro waiters to provide entertainment for the resort's guests.

The Argyle was a huge, rambling frame building surrounded by rental cottages and looking out over the Atlantic Ocean on Long Island's South Shore. Hundreds of affluent New Yorkers took the hour-long train trip to spend their summers away from the city, and they were entertained with nightly orchestral music, riding stables, full-dress balls on festive occasions, and Frank Thompson's baseball club. The team, which was called the Athletics, won 6, lost 2, and tied 1 during that summer. The evidence is strong that Thompson picked his waiters more for their baseball skills than for their plate-balancing talents, because several of the players were well-known in professional baseball long after that first season; none seems to have been native to Babylon.

When the Argyle closed on October 1, the Athletics took to the road as full-fledged professional ballplayers under the management of John F. Lang. Like many later Negro baseball entrepreneurs, Lang was a white man. His club was an immediate artistic success. Babylon's weekly newspaper, the *South Side Signal*, said on October 10:

> The colored base ball team who during the summer played many excellent games on the Argyle grounds, have, since leaving Babylon, tried conclusions with several of the leading clubs. They were victorious in every game, and encouraged by their success, on Monday played the celebrated Metropolitan team, and were badly beaten. The score was 11 to 3 in favor of the "Mets."

The New York Metropolitans had finished seventh in the American Association that year, but still, they *were* a big-league team, and so Lang was emboldened to tackle other big-leaguers. A few days later, the Negro club met the Philadelphia Athletics, fourth-place finishers in the AA. They lost, 13–7, but on the testimony of *Sporting Life*'s observer, the Philadelphians needed help from the umpire: "Lack of experience, weak attempts at running the bases, and the umpire's very partial decisions, contributed to the defeat of the colored aggregation."

While they were in Philadelphia, the Babylon team played the Orions, and after beating them, Lang compounded the injury by signing the Orions' three best players, Shep Trusty, a pitcher, shortstop Abe Harrison, and George Williams, second baseman and captain. By this time it was clear that a strong Negro club was a good gate attraction. Among those who saw the point was Walter Cook, whom Sol White identified as "a capitalist of Trenton, N.J." Cook became the financial angel, installed S. K. Govern, a Negro, as manager, made Trenton home base, and gave the club its counterfeit but utilitarian name of Cuban Giants. The origin of the name is uncertain, but the intent is clear: the players hoped to avoid, at least to some degree, the onus of being American Negroes in their native land. In 1938 Sol White told *Esquire* magazine that he had heard this version of the Giants' christening: When the Babylon club

> began playing away from home, they passed as foreigners—
> Cubans, as they finally decided—hoping to conceal the fact
> that they were just American hotel waiters, and talked a gibberish to each other on the field which, they hoped, sounded
> like Spanish. The New York Giants were even then baseball
> idols, and so the name, Cuban Giants, was settled upon for the
> new club.

"When Mr. Cook signed his men for the following season of 1886," White wrote in his short history, "they were the happiest set of men in the world. As one of them told the writer, not one would have changed his position with the President of the United States." Pitchers and catchers were paid $18 a week, plus expenses; infielders got $15, and outfielders, $12.

Only third baseman Ben Holmes and centerfielder Ben Boyd remained from the club that had started out from Babylon the previous fall. The other Cuban Giants were the cream of the Negro crop in 1886, except for Grant, Fowler, and Fleet Walker. Among the Giants were two players who are mentioned among the all-time Negro greats: pitcher Billy Whyte and catcher Clarence Williams. At the start of the season, they also had George Stovey, but he spent most of that year with Jersey City in the Eastern League.

The Cuban Giants' record for that first full season is not known, but clearly they caught the fancy of fans and sportswriters. Sol White wrote:

> Their games attracted the attention of the base ball writers all over the country, and the Cuban Giants were heralded everywhere as marvels of the base ball world. They were not looked upon by the public as freaks, but they were classed as men of talent. . . . They closed the season of '86 with a grand record made against National League and leading college teams.

The Cuban Giants went their independent way in 1887, declining to join the short-lived League of Colored Base Ball Clubs and even rebuffing a bid to join a white league. In late July, the Giants were elected to membership in the Eastern League, but they declined because it would mean they could not play profitable Sunday games in Brooklyn and Hoboken, New Jersey.

The Cuban Giants took on all comers, playing (and nearly always beating) minor-league clubs and teams from colleges and universities as well as semipro clubs. Yale, Amherst, Princeton, and Penn appeared on the long schedules of the Cuban Giants during the late Eighties. Their big game of the 1887 season was a heart-breaking loss to the world-champion Detroit Tigers, who had won the National League pennant and gone on to rout the St. Louis Browns, 10 games to 5, in a World Series that was played like a road show. Ten different cities enjoyed games in that World Series.

Sol White said that the Cuban Giants led the Tigers, 4–2, in the eighth inning when their defense fell apart and four errors let in four runs for Detroit. "Luck played a prominent part," White sadly editorialized.

By the late 1880s, Negro teams were established all over the eastern part of the nation, even in the Deep South. "Most country towns and crossroads had baseball teams from the Gulf of Mexico to the Mason-Dixon line," Edwin Bancroft Henderson says in *The Negro in Sports*. "Negro players took to baseball with the vim they had gone in for boxing for the best part of a century. . . . In the past ages of hard work and colorful religion, nothing meant so much to the life of an impoverished people after a week of toil as the scene and setting of the country-side baseball game."

It was still possible for Negro teams in the South to play against whites. Beginning a report on such a game in New Orleans in 1888, *The Sporting News* noted:

> A few years ago, a white base ball club could not be paid to play against a colored club, but yesterday a large crowd of both complexions sat in inclement weather and watched a fine game between the Pinchbacks, the colored champions, who recently made a tour of the North, and the Ben Theards, champion white amateur nine.

The Pinchbacks, named for P. B. S. Pinchback, a Negro who sat in the Louisiana governor's chair and in the U.S. Senate during the Reconstruction years, were the best black team in Louisiana. The white club beat the Pinchbacks that day, but another game was scheduled for a side bet of $100 and all the gate receipts. The result of that game is not recorded.

As the last decade of the nineteenth century neared, all-Negro baseball teams were commonplace. The only effort to found a Negro league had foundered, but at least two clubs from that league, the Keystones of Pittsburgh and the Gorhams of New York, survived the debacle. Also operating in the East, besides the Cuban Giants, the preeminent team in Negro baseball, were the Orions and Mutuals of Philadelphia, the Atlantics and Remsens of Brooklyn, the Atlantics of Baltimore, the New York Colored Club, and the Long Island Alpines.

In the South there were the St. Louis Black Stockings, the Red Stockings of Norfolk, the Pinchbacks of New Orleans, and clubs in Atlanta and Savannah which had played for the championship of Georgia as early as 1884.

Negro baseball west of the Alleghenies was naturally slower in developing since only a tiny fraction of the nation's Negro population was outside the South and Northeast. It was not until 1890 that the first professional team was formed in the "West"—that part of the nation beyond Pittsburgh and north of St. Louis. The club was started in Lincoln, Nebraska, and, according to Sol White, it compiled an enviable record against semipros and clubs in organized baseball. It lasted for only two seasons, but it left an enduring legacy in Negro baseball—its name. That first pro team in the "West" was called the Lincoln Giants.

There was considerable optimism about the future of Negro baseball during the years up to 1890. White referred to these years of beginning as "the money period." Players' salaries were low—probably in the range of $10 to $20 a week for a season of five-and-a-half months—and winning teams were assured of financial stability. Attractions like the Cuban Giants had no trouble booking 150 games, most of them against white teams. They traveled widely and apparently without crippling discrimination. In 1887, for example, the Cuban Giants made a long western trip, playing the major-league clubs in Cincinnati and Indianapolis as well as minor-league teams along the way. In Wheeling, West Virginia, they were lodged at the best hotel in town, a phenomenon that only a few years later would be regarded as inconceivable.

The better players in the late 1880s were able to make a living at baseball almost the year-round by barnstorming in the South and West after the regular season in the North. In 1889, the Cuban Giants spent the winter at a resort hotel in Jacksonville, Florida, where they supplemented ballplaying with waiting on tables to earn their board. *The Sporting News* could not resist punning: "They can handle codfish balls with ease, serve fouls 'as you like 'em,' will take to their base on tips, and only draw the line on flies on the tables."

Sol White did not exaggerate in his insistence that these early Negro clubs were not just novelties; clearly they were superior clubs. Even white sportswriters, on the rare occasions when they saw Negro teams play, recognized their worth.

In 1888, after watching a tournament involving the Cuban Giants, the Red Stockings of Norfolk, New York's Gorhams, and the Keystones of Pittsburgh, *The Sporting News'* New York correspondent was moved to write: "There are players among these colored men that are equal to any white players on the ballfield. If you don't think so, go and see the Cuban Giants play. This club, with its strongest players on the field, would play a favorable game against such clubs as the New Yorks or Chicagos."

The Reconstruction years were history by the late 1880s. And gone with them was the hope of immediate equality for black men. But there was still faith in a steady advance toward equal treatment, and in baseball, Negroes could still point to three black players in the highest minor league. An optimistic view was rational, if not realistic.

Baseball has an adage that goes, "The ballgame is never over till the last man is out." But in 1888 no Negro could be sure of the count, or even what inning it was.

4 JIM CROW SCORES ON THE SQUEEZE PLAY

It was hard picking for a colored player this year. I didn't pick up a living; I just existed. I was down in the lower Illinois country and in Missouri, cross-roading with teams in the little towns. . . . My skin is against me. If I had not been quite so black, I might have caught on as a Spaniard or something of that kind. The race prejudice is so strong that my black skin barred me.
—BUD FOWLER, *1895*

Here is the way it was for the three Negroes in the International League in 1888:

Frank Grant led the Buffalo club in batting—but the other Bisons refused to sit with him for the team photograph.

The Syracuse Stars, International Association champions in 1888, with pitcher Robert Higgins, seated on floor at left, and Moses Fleetwood Walker, catcher, standing at left. COURTESY OF PAUL C. FRISZ

Bob Higgins grew so discouraged over discrimination and taunts that he became "homesick" and threatened to leave the Syracuse club in midseason.

Only Fleet Walker got through the year without incident.

Perhaps that season can best be summed up by quoting extensively from an unsigned story that appeared in *The Sporting News* in the spring of 1889. The story does not refer merely to the 1888 season, but from the facts available, it seems to catch the spirit of '88:

There are only four or five colored professional baseball players who have gained any prominence on the diamond. What fame they have won has been made in the face of very disheartening circumstances. Race prejudice exists in professional baseball ranks to a marked degree, and the unfortunate son of Africa who makes his living as a member of a team of white professionals has a rocky road to travel.

The rest of the players not only cut him in a social way, but most of them endeavor to "job him" out of the business. He gets the wrong instructions in coaching, and when a field play comes up in which he is interested, an effort is always made to have an error scored against him.

An International League player, talking to the writer the other day, said, "While I myself am prejudiced against playing in a team with a colored player, still I could not help pitying some of the poor black fellows that played in the International League. Fowler used to play second base with the lower part of his legs encased in wooden guards. He knew that about every player that came down to second base on a steal had it in for him and would, if possible, throw the spikes into him. He was a good player, but left the base every time there was a close play in order to get away from the spikes.

"I have seen him muff balls intentionally, so that he would not have to try to touch runners, fearing that they might injure him. Grant was the same way. Why, the runners chased him off second base. They went down so often trying to break his legs or injure them that he gave up his infield position the latter part of last season and played right field. This is not all.

"About half the pitchers try their best to hit these colored players when (they are) at the bat. I know of a great many pitchers that tried to soak Grant. . . . One of the International League pitchers pitched for Grant's head all the time. He never put a ball over the plate but sent them in straight and true right at Grant. Do what he would he could not hit the Buffalo man, and he (Grant) trotted down to first on called balls all the time."

Two years later *Sporting Life* credited the invention of baseball's first shinguards to Frank Grant rather than Bud Fowler. In that story, Ed Williamson, a retired big-league shortstop, said Grant not only used the first shinguards, which he described as looking like nail kegs, but that the young Negro was indirectly responsible for the invention of the feet-first slide.

You may have noticed in a close play that the base-runner will launch himself into the air and take chances on landing on the bag. Some go head-first, others with the feet in advance. Those who adopt the latter method are principally old-timers. . . .

Frank Grant, probably the best of the Negro pioneers in white leagues, in the uniform of Buffalo. COURTESY OF JOSEPH M. OVERFIELD

They learned the trick in the East. The Buffaloes . . . had a Negro for second base. . . . The haughty Caucasians of the association were willing to permit darkies to carry water for them or guard the bat bag, but it made them sore to have the name of one on the batting list.

Players on opposing teams, Williamson explained,

made it their special business in life to spike this brunette Buffalo. They would tarry at second when they might easily have made third, just to toy with the sensitive shins of the second baseman. . . . To give the frequent spiking of the darky an appearance of accident the "feet-first" slide was practiced.

When Grant took to wearing wooden armor on his legs, Williamson added, the whites filed their spikes and the first man on base went to second and usually split the shinguards. And that, Williamson concluded, is how ball players learned to slide.

This explanation for the invention of the feet-first slide seems fanciful. Historian Harold Seymour writes in *Baseball, the Early Years*, that sliding was becoming common in the 1870s, although at that time "it was thought best to run around the waiting fielder, bend, and touch the base from the rear." During the 1880s, he adds, "most runners used the 'Kelly spread,' a contemporary version of the modern hook slide."

But if the slide was not developed with the purpose of maiming Fowler and Grant, it seems likely that some players perfected the art with that aim in view. Whether or not International League players actually chased Grant into the outfield with their spikes, it is true that he was an outfielder during most of the 1888 season. The change of position had no deleterious effect on his batting eye, for he led the Bisons with a .326 average in 95 games, was second on the club in doubles with 19, third in triples with 6, and second in homers, 11. He was also second in stolen bases with 26.

Fleet Walker caught 77 games for Syracuse and batted .170. Bob Higgins pitched in 25 games and batted .225. By mid-August, Higgins evidently had had enough. The year before he had been humiliated when two teammates refused to sit with him for the club portrait. This season was no better. *The Sporting News* reported: "Robert Higgins, the colored pitcher . . . is in a state of insubordination. He is tired of baseball, and after failing to obtain his release decided to desert the club, give up his $200 a month, and return to his barbershop in Memphis, Tenn." Higgins was fined $100 and threatened with suspension after failing to appear on time for a road trip, but he finished the season, described as "the very much homesick colored pitcher."

Frank Grant and Fleet Walker were on the reserve lists of their clubs after the season of 1888. Bob Higgins was not; now the list of Negroes in white leagues was down to three: Grant, Walker, and Dick Johnson.

There were further rumblings in the International League that winter. The Buffalo *Express* said Grant, who was touring in Florida with the Cuban Giants, was holding out for more money, and a Syracuse paper predicted a strike by the Bisons if he was on the team again. The Buffalo management denied it.

By mid-April 1889, when training was to begin, Grant was still a holdout. *The Sporting News* reported:

> Grant played with the Cuban Giants in Washington yesterday, and in reply to an inquiry said he would sign only for $250 a month. This is considered too high, and the other members of the team threaten to rebel if he plays. Last year they refused to have their picture taken on Grant's account and objected to traveling with him. The boys acknowledge that he is a good player, but they are in rebellion just the same. Their sentiment is that colored men should not play with white men.

Their sentiment prevailed; Grant was not signed, and he played out the season with the Cuban Giants.

And now there were two—Walker and Johnson, who spent 1889 with Springfield in the Central Interstate League. Of the five Negroes who had been in the International League in 1887, only Fleet Walker remained as the 1889 season opened. The least talented of the five, Walker ended his career as he had begun it in Toledo six years earlier, the only Negro in a white league. He caught fifty games, batted .216, and rated twentieth among 21 catchers for fielding. He was not on the Syracuse reserve list for 1890; Fleet Walker, the first Negro major-leaguer, was through in baseball, and the most receptive of the early leagues to black men was through with them. More than a half-century would pass before the next Negro would step onto an IL diamond.

Walker stayed in Syracuse after his retirement from baseball, supporting his family by working as a railroad mail clerk. In April 1891 he was accosted on the street by several men who came out of a saloon in what *Sporting Life* described as "a low district of the city." Walker became angered "and applied insulting epithets to them." A thug named Patrick Murray, a convicted burglar, hit him in the face. Thereupon, "Walker drew a knife and made a stroke at his assailant. The knife entered Murray's groin, inflicting a fatal wound. Murray's friends started after Walker with shouts of 'Kill him! Kill him!' He escaped but was captured by the police, and is locked up."

Early accounts of the fight said that Walker was drunk and that when he sobered up, he asked police, "Who was that fellow I hit? He made a bad move when he came for me." But the ballplayer's friends were quick to come to his defense, claiming that what appeared to be a drunken stupor was actually the staggering effects of being struck on the head with a rock in the fray.

Whatever his degree of sobriety during the fight, there is no doubt that public feeling was with Walker, who was, by all accounts, a man of considerable charm as well as intelligence. When in June a jury found him not guilty of second-degree murder, "immediately a shout of approval, accompanied by clapping of hands and stamping of feet, rose from the spectators," the Syracuse correspondent for *Sporting Life* wrote.

Some time after his acquittal, Fleet Walker went home to Steubenville, where, with his brother Weldy, he managed a hotel. Later he was owner and manager of several motion-picture houses; during this time, he said later, he was credited with several inventions useful to the movie industry. Around the turn of the century, he turned to journalism as editor of a newspaper called *The Equator* in Steubenville. Again his younger brother was at his right hand.

In 1908, Fleet Walker published a 47-page booklet on the Negro problem. He was fifty-one years old, a distinguished-looking man who was at home in a top hat and swallow-tailed coat when the occasion demanded it.

In his book, entitled *Our Home Colony—A Treatise on the Past, Present and Future of the Negro Race in America,* Walker proved himself to be a precursor of the modern militant Negro, alienated in his native land.

Dean Carl F. Wittke of Oberlin College in 1946 described *Our Home Colony* as the work of "a man of considerable learning and

intellectual capacity." Walker characterized the years after Eman-
cipation in 1863 as the "colonial period" in the American Negro's
development—a time when the "American people were in no way
prepared to accept the Negro with full equality of civil and political
rights."

Walker rejected the usual suggestions for dealing with the race
problem, including education, religion, and improved economic
position, and he had no faith in eventual intermarriage as a solution.
The old ballplayer looked to Africa, the ancestral home of America's black citizens, for the answer. He believed America's Negroes
should emigrate and establish new Liberias there; in fact, he believed
force should be used to make them leave this country if that should
prove necessary. "Nothing but failure and disappointment" awaited
them in America, wrote Fleet Walker. It appears that to implement
his idea he may have established an office in Steubenville, because his
brother Weldy described his own occupation in 1908 as "general
agent for *Our Home Colony* and Liberian emigration."

Fleet Walker died in retirement in Cleveland on May 11, 1924,
but not before adding a puzzling piece to the jigsaw of his life as
athlete, intellectual, businessman, journalist, and knife-wielder. In
1922, Oberlin College sent a questionnaire to all its former students
in preparation for a report on the successes of its alumni. Among the
questions was, "What has been the influence of Oberlin on your life?"
From this intellectual forebear of Stokely Carmichael and H. Rap
Brown, Oberlin, a citadel of white liberalism, might have expected a
tirade. Walker simply wrote "Excellent" and underlined the word.

He went to his grave in Steubenville's Union Cemetery without
ever having seen Africa. His brother Weldy, who had joined him in
his abortive movement, died in Steubenville in 1937.

In 1889, while the International League's door was closing to
black men, others were opening. A Negro named R. A. Kelly covered first base for Danville of the Illinois–Indiana League in 1889,
and Dick Johnson was with Springfield in the Central Interstate
League. More significantly, the first all-Negro teams appeared in an
organized league.

The Gorhams of New York and the Cuban Giants, who had declined a bid to enter the Eastern League two years before, joined the
Middle States League. The Cuban Giants represented Trenton, N.J.,
but played many of their games in Hoboken. Other clubs in the MSL
were Harrisburg, Lancaster, Reading, York, and a team called the

Philadelphia Giants. (A little more than a decade later there would be an outstanding Negro team with that name, but in 1889 it was a white club.)

Harrisburg won the pennant that year amid protests from the Cuban Giants. Forfeits and disputed games were common in baseball's early days, and the Cuban Giants claimed that two games had been awarded unfairly to Harrisburg. There was no suggestion of racial bias, however, in the league president's ruling that awarded the pennant to Harrisburg.

The Middle States League shuffled franchises and reorganized in 1890, changing its name to the Eastern Interstate League despite the fact that all teams were in Pennsylvania cities; however, league games were often played in cities outside the circuit and occasionally even outside the state. The Gorhams did not enter the Eastern Interstate League, but the Cuban Giants were back, this time as representatives of York, Pennsylvania. The Giants were without the services of Frank Grant and third baseman-catcher Clarence Williams, both of whom had been signed by Harrisburg. The signing of Grant was evidently a thorny issue, as it went to court; the judge awarded his contract to Harrisburg.

In July, after 65 games had been played, the Cuban Giants (who were now called the Monarchs of York) enjoyed a one-game lead over Harrisburg when the latter club jumped to the faster Atlantic Association, breaking up the Eastern Interstate.

The record of the short-lived Eastern Interstate League is especially interesting because the only batting averages extant for the pioneering Cuban Giants were recorded in that league. *Sporting Life's Official Base Ball Guide* for 1891 listed them as follows: George Williams, c-1b-3b, .371 (second in the league); Sol White, 2b, .358 (fifth in league); William Selden, p-of, .326; Arthur Thomas, 1b-of, .317; Jack Frye, 1b, .303; Andrew Jackson, 3b, .295; Billy Whyte, p-of, .291; Abe Harrison, ss, .267; Ben Boyd, of, .267; William Jackson, of, .247; Oscar Jackson, of, .247; William Malone, p-of, .215; Terrill, ss, .143.

Frank Grant batted .325 for Harrisburg in the Eastern Interstate and .328 when the club moved to the Atlantic Association. Clarence Williams' average as Harrisburg's third baseman was .256.

Although the Interstate league's breakup was disappointing, the season seems to have been a pleasant one for the Negro players. Sol White commented, "It can be said for the management of the Harrisburgs, that although fighting the colored team (Monarchs of York) by every conceivable manner on the ballfield, they never drew the color line in any of the league meetings. They would not enter unless their colored player, Frank Grant, was allowed to play."

Things were not quite so pleasant for Grant in the Atlantic Association later that season, although the unpleasantness was not the work of his teammates or opponents. *Sporting Life* reported in August that Grant had been barred from the Clayton House in Wilmington, Delaware, because of his color.

> The same team was here a few days ago and all the members, including Grant, the Negro player, were quartered at the Clayton. Grant took his meals in the dining room with the rest of the guests, and was assigned a sleeping apartment in the guests' hall. The boarders protested against being obliged to eat in the same dining-room with a colored man, and threatened to leave the house unless the dusky-hued ball player was turned out. Mr. Pyle, however, allowed him to stay with his fellow players while they remained here. This morning the club returned and with them Grant. They applied at the hotel for board, and Proprietor Pyle informed them he would accommodate all but the colored man. The white players determined to stick by their sable-hued companion and all marched out of the hotel in high dudgeon over the refusal to accommodate Grant. Another hotel was sought, where the players were given rooms with the understanding that Grant must eat with the colored help or get his meals elsewhere. He accepted the latter alternative.

In 1891 Grant returned to the Cuban Giants, who were back in organized baseball. They were under new ownership, were called the Big Gorhams, and represented Ansonia in the Connecticut State League. They had no happy time of it, for in June *Sporting Life* noted: "They are making themselves unpopular by misbehavior and may be fired from the league." Sol White jumped from the Giants to Harrisburg early in the year and evidently took other Negroes with him, because sportswriters were soon calling Harrisburg the "Polka-Dots."

The Connecticut State League broke up in midsummer, and the Cuban Giants-Big Gorhams went back to their wandering ways, never again to appear in organized white leagues. They won 41 straight games, but *Sporting Life* reported that "the games were mostly with weak amateur and semiprofessional teams." According to Sol White, their record for that year was 100 victories and 4 defeats. The club included the best of the original Cuban Giants, plus George Stovey, Frank Grant, and Clarence Williams.

R. A. Kelly, who had been with Danville in 1889, was in his second year with Jamestown, N.Y., in the New York and Pennsylvania League in 1891. He was apparently accepted as just another player in that league, because the Jamestown *Evening Journal* never referred to his color. When the Elmira *Advertiser* noted that "Jamestown's first baseman is a colored man, despite the fact that his name is Kelly," the *Journal*, which often printed such notes from other papers, did not deign to pick it up.

The winds were blowing cold on black players in organized baseball in 1891, just as they were on integration in all phases of American life. The South's Jim Crow laws, which legalized many excrescences of racial segregation, were well established; the North, which had no Jim Crow laws, nevertheless reflected much of the southern view of the Negro in its social mores. From 1892 to 1895 there were no Negroes in organized white leagues. Even segregated baseball seems to have been in a decline. The Cuban Giants, owned and managed by J. M. Bright, were the only black professional team from 1892 to 1894. An attempt to start a club in Boston during 1893 failed within a month.

Two years later interest in Negro baseball was revived with the organization of the Page Fence Giants in Adrian, Michigan. In the process, Negroes were again briefly allowed in a white league. The Page Fence Giants were formed by Bud Fowler, now the elder statesman of Negro ballplayers, and Grant (Home Run) Johnson, one of the best of the pioneers. They were backed by three white men from Adrian and offered a judicious blend of showmanship and good baseball. They traveled in a private railroad car, and before every game the Giants paraded through the streets on bicycles to drum up interest in the contest.

Adrian was also represented by a club in the Michigan State League, which, in 1895, was involved in a tight race with Jackson for the pennant. For at least one series, the white club signed five players from the Page Fence Giants, once again giving black players exposure in organized ball. In addition, Sol White played with Fort Wayne, Indiana, in the Western State League until it broke up in June. He then joined the Page Fence Giants and may have been one of the five from that club who appeared with Adrian.

No league was open to Negroes for the next two years. Then, in 1898, a young all-Negro team wrote the final chapter to the story of black men in white leagues during baseball's early days. The team was organized by a brash white man named Harry Curtis, who promised that "we will have the strongest colored club in America, if we are the youngest." Curtis named his team the Acme Colored Giants and placed it in the Iron and Oil League, representing Celeron, N.Y.

Celeron was a village on Chautauqua Lake, about three miles west of Jamestown in southwestern New York, whose sole claim to attention was a big amusement park. The village was near the Chautauqua Assembly, a collection of summer schools offering education and entertainment. Chautauquans who wearied of the cultural life could go down the lake by steamboat and enjoy the more plebeian amusements at Celeron, including the Acme Giants.

They opened the season in Warren, Pennsylvania, in early May and promptly lost three straight games, setting a pattern which was to persist. They appear to have been well received, however, for the Warren correspondent of *Sporting Life* wrote after that first series: "The Celerons drove home from here Saturday night, and leaving town they enlivened the air with singing and they can sing as well as they can play ball . . . The negroes are a jolly, gentlemanly crowd, and an honor to the league."

The Acme Giants opened the local season in Celeron a few days later and continued their losing ways, being trounced by Bradford, Pennsylvania, 15–4. The Spanish-American War was at its height, and the headline writer for the Jamestown *Evening Journal,* overcome by the war fever, headed the story of the game:

Celerons Bombarded, Their Fleet
Sunk, and Their Forts Demolished—

DISCOURAGING BEGINNING
OF THE SEASON

The *Journal* said the fans were

> prepared to shout, but it was impossible to get up any enthusiasm for the team that represents Celeron. It did not seem like a home team because all members were strangers. Still all this would have been excused if a strong game had been put up by the Celeron Acme Giants. It cannot be said that they put up a strong or fast game, however, in any respect, and they failed entirely to meet the expectations of the Jamestowners.

The next day the Giants "won praise and admiration" by beating Bradford, 7–6. The *Journal* commented: "The strength of the

Celeron players lies largely in their batting and while this does not appeal strongly to many baseball enthusiasts, it certainly is an attractive feature to the average attendant at ball games."

Although the Giants were occasionally referred to in newspaper reports around the league as "darkies" and the "Celeron Chocolates," they do not seem to have suffered much discrimination on or off the field. By early July they were planted solidly in the league's cellar and they were losing money; prospects were dim for improvement on the field or in the box office.

On July 5 the Acme Giants lost to Warren, 12–4. The next day they defeated a team of Jamestown amateurs, 7–5. And the day after that, the young Acme Giants were broken up by Harry Curtis. None ever appeared later with a major Negro team. Their final record in the Iron and Oil League was 8 victories, 41 defeats. A team of white players, hastily recruited from the Louisville club of the recently disbanded Southern League, immediately replaced the Acme Giants in Celeron, but because of waning attendance in other member cities, the Iron and Oil League broke up two weeks later.

Indomitable Harry Curtis was only temporarily discouraged. He wrote to *Sporting Life*: "I have just returned from Jamestown, N.Y., where I was located with my Acme Colored Giants in the Iron and Oil League wherein (despite all reports to the contrary) we were third at the time we quit." Evidently responding to complaints from a couple of players that they had not been paid, Curtis lamented, "I myself am out of pocket over $600." But he bounced back like the born promoter he was: "I have a complete outfit and I am prepared to furnish a first-class team, either colored or white, to play independent ball, or will go in any league." There were no takers.

On this opportunistic note, an era ended. It had been a time when more than thirty Negroes had been given the chance to match their skills against whites in organized baseball (although the majority were on all-Negro teams). They had not had equal opportunity, since Frank Grant, Bud Fowler, and George Stovey were unquestionably of major-league star calibre and were barred by the unwritten color line. But at least they had been a part of organized baseball's rollicking, uncertain beginnings as the national sport. Now all that was ended.

Another age was starting, almost a half-century when black players, some of them the peers of the greatest major-league stars, would spend their talents in the obscurity of Negro baseball.

PART II:

WAY DOWN IN EGYPT LAND

5 GIANTS IN THOSE DAYS

The St. Louis Giants, a black baseball team, have easily beaten everything in town but the Browns and the Cardinals, and neither of these latter will play them. The Chicago Giants, all alligator bait, have done the same thing in that city, and there are no end of people up there willing to wager that they can beat either the White Sox or the Cubs. . . . It requires some courage to predict that colored baseball, like colored pugilism, is to supersede the white brand, but someone has to think ahead and indicate whither we drift, and we therefore wish to go on record as having said that it will. If the Browns and Cardinals will admit the St. Louis Giants to a three-cornered series for the local championship this fall it will begin in St. Louis right away.
—ST. LOUIS POST-DISPATCH, *1912*

On Sept. 18, 1895, the thirty-nine-year-old president of Tuskegee Institute stood on the speaker's platform at the Cotton States Exposition in Atlanta and delivered an address that was to become famous as the "Atlanta Compromise." He was Booker T. Washington, born in slavery, a tall, brilliant, commanding man whose address that day made him the unchallenged spokesman for the nation's Negroes for two decades and set the tone for their treatment that was to persist even longer.

Said the great Negro leader to his audience of blacks and whites: "In all things that are purely social we can be as separate as the fingers, yet one as the hand in all things essential to mutual progress."

This acceptance of social inequality reflected the national consensus—of whites and most Negroes—as the Reconstruction era came to a close in the last decade of the nineteenth century. Jim Crow was entrenched in the South; the last nails were being driven into an elaborate structure of segregation laws. A year after Washington's speech, the Supreme Court, in *Plessy vs. Ferguson*, wrote segregation into the national law.

Organized baseball was in step with the times as the new century began. There were no black players in the white leagues, but segregation in baseball was not yet so deeply ingrained that the idea of Negroes playing with whites was unimaginable.

And, in fact, it *was* imagined more than once during the early 1900s. The man with the most frequent vision was a fiery competitor named John J. McGraw whose exploits as a battling third baseman and manager were to earn him a place in baseball's Hall of Fame. In his autobiography, McGraw put forth no opinions about the talents of Negro players, or about their desirability as social companions, but it is clear that he would cheerfully have played a black man on his club.

In 1901 he almost did. McGraw was managing the Baltimore Orioles in the new American League and was sorely in need of good ballplayers. In March he had the Orioles in training in Hot Springs, Arkansas, based at the Eastland Hotel. One of the bellboys at the Eastland was Charles Grant, who had been second baseman for the Columbia Giants, a Chicago Negro team, the previous year.

Grant and several other employes of the hotel idled away their free time playing ball on the grounds around the building, and McGraw, watching them, saw that Grant had major-league ability. How to sign him without outraging the color-consciousness of the league?

In *The American League Story,* Lee Allen tells of McGraw's answer to this dilemma:

> One day, while examining a large wall map just off the lobby at the Eastland, he was seized with an inspiration. Calling Grant over to him, he said: "Charlie, I've been trying to think of some way to sign you for the Baltimore club and I think I've got it. On this map there's a creek called Tokohama. That's going to be your name from now on, Charlie Tokohama, and you're a full-blooded Cherokee."

"Tokohama" was described by *Sporting Life* as "a phenomenal fielder. . . . He is between 21 and 23 years of age, and weighs about 160 pounds, and is of about medium height. His position is second base, where he has been thoroughly tried out on the lawn surrounding the hotel. He is, moreover, a good batter."

Charlie Grant, John McGraw's "Tokohoma," who edged up to the major-league color line in 1901 in the guise of an Indian. COURTESY OF LEE ALLEN.

This is Charlie Grant fielding a ground ball. COURTESY OF LEE ALLEN

But his disguise was thin. The first to penetrate it was Charles Comiskey, president of the Chicago White Sox after long years of stardom on the field and in the dugout, who said:

> I'm not going to stand for McGraw ringing in an Indian on the Baltimore team. If Muggsy really keeps this Indian, I will get a Chinaman of my acquaintance and put him on third. Somebody told me that the Cherokee of McGraw's is really Grant, the crack Negro second baseman from Cincinnati, fixed up with war paint and a bunch of feathers.

Sporting Life commented that Comiskey was objecting "facetiously" to McGraw's intention to play Grant, and indeed Comiskey had himself played against at least one Negro without recorded complaint. He was the St. Louis Browns' first baseman in the American Association in 1884, when Toledo had Fleet Walker.

"Tokohama" stoutly maintained that he was an Indian, or at least a halfbreed. He said his father was a white man and his mother a Cherokee. Furthermore, he said, McGraw could get proof of his origin, because his mother was still living in Lawrence, Kansas. Mc-Graw backed up this version, saying. "He is a real Indian and not the Negro Grant as alleged." But it was all in vain.

Grant was actually the son of a Negro horse-trainer from Cincinnati. Whatever Comiskey's intent in exposing him, the effect was to kill Grant's chances in the American League. McGraw could not bear the obloquy that would be his if he signed the Negro. By late March he was quoted as saying that "Tokohama" still had a lot to learn, particularly about fielding ground balls. And by early April, when the Orioles' roster was announced, the list of players included neither "Tokohama" nor "Grant." Finally, in its April 20 issue, *Sporting Life* attached this postscript to the first serious effort to place a Negro on a big-league team since Fleet Walker in 1884: "McGraw's wonder, Tokohama, the Cherokee Indian, will play with the Columbia Giants, of Chicago, again this season."

Grant never appeared in a regular-season major-league game. He went back to the Columbia Giants and finished his ballplaying days in Negro baseball. In 1932, Grant was janitor for an apartment house in Cincinnati. He was seated out front one hot day in July when a passing car blew a tire, climbed the curb in front of the building, and killed him. His grave, in Cincinnati's Spring Grove Cemetery, is only a short distance from that of another second baseman, Miller Huggins, who rose to the pinnacle of baseball glory in the 1920s as manager of the New York Yankees.

John McGraw later expressed interest in other black players, among them the fireballing Cuban-Negro pitcher, José Mendez, and Andrew (Rube) Foster, who was at the height of his artistry on the mound during McGraw's early years as manager of the New York Giants. But he never again offended the sensibilities of organized baseball's leaders by going so far as to try to sign a Negro.

In 1906 there were again a few gentle waves on the placid surface of the big leagues over the color question. Sol White wrote, "on good authority," that a National League manager (it could have been McGraw, who was then leading the Giants) hoped to sign William Clarence Matthews, a Negro who had left Harvard University that spring to play with Burlington in the Vermont League, which was not a recognized minor league. Harvard was none too happy about it, and the university's correspondent for *Sporting Life* commented: "Harvard will learn with much regret that William Clarence Matthews, the famous colored shortstop, is to turn to the professional ranks." Matthews had earned his varsity *H* as a shortstop-outfielder

William Clarence Matthews, Harvard shortstop, later played in the Vermont League, an "outlaw" white league in 1906. Rumors that season that he would step over the major-league color line proved baseless. COURTESY OF HARVARD UNIVERSITY

in 1902, '03, '04, and '05, as well as a letter for football in 1904, and Harvard men simply did *not* become professional athletes.

But Matthews did, and immediately ran into difficulties over race. *Sporting Life,* which covered the Vermont League even though it was outside the pale of organized baseball, reported that his entry "threatens to disrupt the league." The other players "do not take kindly to this innovation" and "this has kicked up a big row, and the end is not yet." William Matthews never appeared in the major leagues or even in a recognized minor league; he went on to become a well-known lawyer and died in 1928.

Sol White, a congenital optimist, had not dared to believe that Matthews would be signed by the National League; but, he said, "when such actions come to notice there are grounds for hoping that some day the bar will drop and some good man will be chosen from out of the colored profession that will be a credit to all, and pave the way for others to follow."

Maybe. But after the middle 1890s the prudent Negro player wasted little time on such fragile hopes. He must find his bread and butter where he could, and that meant on Negro teams. In 1900 there were five black professional teams:

•The original Cuban Giants, now called Genuine Cuban Giants, whose home city varied from year to year, including at different times New York, Trenton, Hoboken, Johnstown and Gloversville, New York, Pennsylvania, and Ansonia, Connecticut.

•The Cuban X Giants of New York. Frank Grant was their second baseman.

•The Red Stockings of Norfolk, Virginia.

•The Chicago Unions, who had started as amateurs in 1886 and turned professional ten years later; they played in Chicago on Sundays and toured the hinterlands of Indiana, Illinois, Wisconsin, Michigan, and Iowa during the week.

•The Columbia Giants of Chicago. They were the former Page Fence Giants of Adrian, Michigan, who moved to Chicago in 1899 under the aegis of the Columbia Club, which Sol White described as "an organization composed of Chicago's best business and professional men." The Columbia Club did well by its team, for White calls the Giants the "best-equipped colored team" up to that time.

The pattern was already becoming apparent: Negro professional baseball on the highest level would be centered in the North, although in 1910 more than ninety percent of the nation's nearly nine

million Negroes still lived in the rural South. There would be professional teams in the South, and later even professional leagues, but
the greater freedom, opportunity, and prosperity in the North offered a more fertile seedbed for Negro baseball. And the game was
sprouting fast in the North's Negro communities right after the turn
of the century. In 1902 the Philadelphia Giants were organized by
Sol White and two Philadelphia baseball writers. Three years later, a
Brooklyn cafe-owner named J. W. Connor formed the Brooklyn
Royal Giants. By 1906 there were nine Negro professional teams
within 100 miles of Philadelphia, each of them bearing the name
"Giants." This predeliction evidently reflected the popularity of the
National League's New York club; whatever the cause, nearly all of
the Negro teams formed during this period used that name. Also
operating in the East were two authentic Cuban teams—the Havana
Stars and the Cuban Stars—the first professional fruits of the baseball mania in Cuba. As early as 1891 there were 75 clubs on the
island, and the fever was accentuated by visits by professional clubs
from the United States beginning in the 1890s. Big-league teams
often made postseason tours of Cuba in those years, and the original
Cuban Giants visited their namesake island in February of 1900.

The powerful Philadelphia Giants of 1906, probably the best black team in
the early years of this century. Seated in front are William Monroe, left,
and James Booker. Second row, from left, Home Run Johnson, Charlie
Grant, H. Walter Schlichter, owner; Rube Foster, and Pete Hill. Standing, unidentified man, unidentified player, Harry Moore, Sol White,
manager; Bill Francis, and Dan McClellan.

Since there was little color-consciousness in Cuba, those early Cuban teams were composed of both blacks and whites. Of necessity they played as Negro teams in the United States, and Cuban teams continued to be prominent in Negro baseball throughout its heyday in the Twenties, Thirties, and Forties.

Light-skinned Cubans had considerable mobility; they could move from Negro baseball into the white leagues and, occasionally, back again. In 1911 two former members of the Cuban Stars were signed by the Cincinnati Reds, creating a minor furor in the National League and raising new hopes among American Negroes for integration into organized baseball. Although outfielder Armando Marsans and third baseman Rafael D. Almeida were light-skinned, the Negro press saw their signing as a possible harbinger for the entrance of American Negroes. Here was the reasoning:

> Now that the first shock is over it would not be surprising to see a Cuban a few shades darker than Almeida and Marsans breaking into the professional ranks, with a coal-black Cuban on the order of the crack pitcher, [José] Mendez, making his debut later on. Manager McGraw of the New York Giants is

Advertisement in *The New York Age* August 8, 1907. NEW YORK PUBLIC LIBRARY

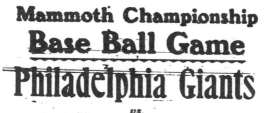

Mammoth Championship
Base Ball Game
Philadelphia Giants
vs.
Cuban Giants

for the benefit of

The **Colored Men's Branch**
Young Men's Christian Association

At American League Grounds
168th Street and Broadway

Saturday, August 24
at 3.00 p. m., sharp

Game to be umpired by "JACK" JOHNSON, the champion colored heavyweight, who is matched to meet "Tommie" Burns, champion heavyweight of the world.

Rare treat in store for all the "fans" who attend.   Reserved seats for ladies.

General Admission, 25cts.   Grand Stand, 50 and 75cts.

quoted as having said he would give a large sum of money for his release, and as quiet as it is kept, if McGraw did not think he would raise too much of a racket he would sign Mendez today. He is one manager who is not chuck-full of color prejudice, as he has shown by using Chief Meyers, the big Indian catcher. . . . With the admission of Cubans of a darker hue in the two big leagues it would then be easy for colored players who are citizens of this country to get into fast company. The Negro in this country has more varied hues than even the Cubans, and the only way to distinguish him would be to hear him talk. Until the public got accustomed to seeing native Negroes on big league (teams), the colored players could keep their mouths shut and pass for Cubans.*

But it was not to be. Almeida was in the big leagues for three years and Marsans for ten; no darker Cubans or American Negroes trailed in their wake.

The Cubans played ball the year-round, in the United States during the summer and back home in the winter. It was not long before they were attracting American-Negro stars to their winter leagues; by the 1920s, many Negro players were making an annual trek to Cuba a week or two after the end of the season in the United States. Later, Puerto Rico, the Dominican Republic, Mexico, and Venezuela were added to the migratory pattern.

With the proliferation of Negro teams shortly after the new century began, a second attempt was made, in 1906, to operate a league. This one, which was not a recognized minor league, was a good deal more successful than the abortive League of Colored Base Ball Players in 1887, since it lasted a full season. The new circuit was called the International League of Independent Professional Base Ball Clubs and included two white teams, the Philadelphia Professionals and the Riverton-Palmyra, Pennsylvania, Athletics. The black members that opened the season were the Cuban X Giants, Quaker Giants of New York, Cuban Stars, and Havana Stars. The Quaker Giants and Havana Stars dropped out in July and were replaced by the Philadelphia Giants and Wilmington Giants. Sol White said his Philadelphia Giants, who joined in August, won the pennant, but he did not explain the mathematics of winning the

---

* This comment was from a newspaper clipping in a player's scrapbook. Unfortunately, the source is unknown; it probably was the *New York Age*.

championship with less than a month's tenure in the league. The deciding game was played before 10,000 people, which White called "the largest crowd that ever attended a baseball game between colored teams," at the Philadelphia Athletics' park. This was the first recorded instance of Negro teams playing in a major-league park.

Four years later, in December 1910, by which time there were scores of Negro professional and semipro teams in the country, an effort was made to establish a truly national league. It was to include clubs from Chicago, Louisville, New Orleans, Mobile, St. Louis, Kansas City, Missouri, Kansas City, Kansas, and Columbus, Ohio. Meeting in Chicago, Negro baseball leaders agreed to pay $300 per franchise and to blacklist players who jumped from one club to another. In short, they hoped to create a league patterned after those in organized baseball. But the new league died without ever sanctioning a game, and it was to be ten more years before the first viable Negro league was established.

Between 1900 and 1920, many great Negro teams were born. Some of them, such as the Chicago American Giants, Lincoln Giants of New York, Bacharach Giants of Atlantic City, Homestead, Pennsylvania, Grays, Hilldale Club of Darby, Pennsylvania, and the Indianapolis ABC's, would continue into the 1920s and later and write their names large in the annals of Negro baseball. Others like Coogan's Smart Set of New York, the Dayton Giants, and the Lincoln Stars of New York lasted only a few seasons.

Player contracts were nonexistent, or at best informal agreements, usually verbal. As a result there was a great deal of shifting from team to team. It was not unusual for a player on the Brooklyn Royal Giants, for example, to appear with his club on Saturday in Brooklyn and then hop a train for Schenectady to play on Sunday with the Mohawk Giants. Because of this fluidity, the *Chicago Defender* always referred to black teams as semipro, even when they were playing 200 games a year, as some of them did about the time of World War I.

Negro baseball in the Chicago area was somewhat more stable than elsewhere, largely because of the influence of two men. The first was Frank C. Leland, who had been on the roster of the Washington Capital Citys of the ill-fated League of Colored Base Ball Clubs. When the Capital Citys disbanded after the league's sudden collapse, he went to Chicago and joined the Chicago Unions, managing them until 1900. The next year he started the Chicago Union Giants and ran them for three years; finally, in 1904, he formed the Leland Giants of Chicago. He did his work well, for ten years later all three teams were still in business.

The other man who brought stability to the Chicago baseball scene was Andrew (Rube) Foster, the dominant figure in Negro baseball from about 1910 until 1926. Foster came out of Texas in 1902 to begin a brilliant pitching career with the Chicago Union Giants, Cuban X Giants, the Philadelphia Giants, and, in 1910, as pitcher-manager of the Leland Giants in Chicago. By this time Foster was ready to step out as magnate as well as player-manager. And so in 1911 he organized the Chicago American Giants, who quickly became the strongest team in the Chicago area. Foster's stamp was imprinted so indelibly on the club that the *Defender* usually referred to the Giants as "Rube Foster's Giants."

During the second decade of the century there was a strong city league in Chicago, and the better Negro teams were members. (There were also a few Negroes on the rosters of white teams in the league.) The black teams did a good deal of traveling, but it was in this league that they made most of their money during the years around 1910.

An old ballplayer tells why:

> In Chicago I don't think they played over four games a week. But the Leland Giants and the American Giants were members of the city league with white teams like the Logan Squares and the Gunthers. Now those teams played on Saturdays and Sunday mornings. And they would draw 15 to 20,000 people out there for the Logan Squares, because you might go out there and here'd be Johnny Kling of the Cubs catching, Joe Tinker of the Cubs playing shortstop, or Johnny Evers—under other names, of course. But, you see, those big-leaguers didn't get the kind of money they're getting now, and if they could pick up a hundred or a hundred and fifty dollars a week extra, well, that was real money back in 1908, 9, 10. That would go a long way in those days. So they had a real following in that area, and that was where the Lelands and the Americans did most of their business.

This explanation was given by Arthur W. Hardy, now retired in Buffalo, N.Y., after long service as a YMCA official. He began his professional baseball career in 1906, primarily to finance his college education, as a pitcher on the Topeka, Kansas, Giants, the first full-time Negro semipro team in the Midwest. The Giants included

Hardy's fellow Topekans, second baseman Elwood (Bingo) DeMoss and pitcher Bill Lindsay, who were later to reach the heights of Negro baseball fame around Chicago.

The Topeka Giants were organized by Topeka Jack Johnson, a prizefighter and promoter who appropriated the name of the Negro heavyweight boxing champion of that era. Hardy recalls:

> We played baseball every day. We started in Topeka and we played up through Kansas, Iowa, and into Illinois and Chicago. And then we played back in those little country towns. Now that was a very interesting experience. We carried eight players and three pitchers. I pitched today; tomorrow I'd be on the gate; the day after that would be my rest day, or maybe I'd play in the outfield.

The ease with which teams and players shifted loyalties is illustrated by the metamorphosis of the Topeka Giants into the Kansas City, Kansas, Giants, one of the best-known teams around 1910. Hardy remembers:

> We used to go to Kansas City, Missouri, to play the original Kansas City Monarchs, who were composed largely of former college athletes—professional men like Dr. Tom McCampbell, Dr. Ernest McCampbell, Professor Gaitha Page, who was principal of one of the big schools there, and a number of other boys who were college athletes. In those days baseball was the big thing in college—football hadn't quite taken over.
>
> As the two cities were situated right next to each other, there was always a natural rivalry. So a bunch of doctors in Kansas City, Kansas, got together and decided they were going to get a team to beat the Kansas City Monarchs. The Kansas City, Kansas, doctors couldn't play baseball, but they wanted to see the Monarchs beaten, so they brought the Topeka Giants almost intact to Kansas City, Kansas, and we became the Kansas City Giants. That's all it was organized for; they didn't have any idea of developing the kind of team we became. That's the way the thing started, out of a little personal rivalry. But as it ended up, we brought all the good teams there —that is, from as far east as Chicago.

During the years of which Hardy speaks, Negro baseball fans took the game seriously. The Leland Giants had their own booster club, which met every Saturday night, and crowds of 4,000 to 10,000 were not uncommon for a game between two good black teams or between black and white teams.

The Negro press had a curiously ambivalent attitude toward the relationship of Negro teams—or rather, the lack of relationship—with organized baseball. In 1911 the militant *Chicago Defender,* whose editor, Robert S. Abbott, proclaimed, "I have made an issue of every single situation in which our people have been denied their rightful share of participation," printed the major-league standings and featured stories about big-league players side-by-side with a ringing cry for "all race loving and race building men and women" to support Negro teams.

While Chicago's Negro fans could see big-leaguers playing under assumed names against their favorites on weekends, they had to go to a big-league park if they wanted to watch the Cubs or White Sox in toto. Chicago's big-league teams shied away from direct confrontation with the American Giants, perhaps from the notion that they had very little to gain and a lot to lose. (In 1909 the Chicago Cubs had played a postseason series with the Leland Giants, winning three hotly contested games.)

The big-league teams in the East were much less reluctant to tackle Negro clubs. In 1915, for example, a year in which Rube Foster issued an unanswered challenge to Manager Joe Tinker of Chicago's Federal Leaguers, Negro teams in the East played eight games against big-league clubs, winning four of them. One of the victories for the Negro teams was a five-hit shutout of the National League champion Phillies by Joe Williams for the Lincoln Giants.

In 1915 the Great Migration of southern Negroes to the North was under way. Each year tens of thousands of black men and women, spurred by the promise of a better and freer life in northern cities, picked up their meager belongings and set out toward the promised land. As the black population swelled in the North, Negro baseball expanded. By 1916 there were Negro professional teams in nearly all the large cities of the North and West—as far west as Los Angeles, where the black White Sox played 36 games that year.

In the South there was little opportunity for the Negro ballplayer, and scores made their way to northern teams, even before the Great Migration began, including such fabled stars as Rube Foster (1902), John Henry Lloyd (1906), and Smoky Joe Williams (1910). At least one whole team joined the mass movement north. This club was the Duval Giants of Jacksonville, Florida, which, in 1916, left the South to become the Bacharach Giants of Atlantic City, New Jersey.

Napoleon Cummings of Atlantic City, who was born in Jacksonville in 1892, came north with the Duval Giants, and was the Bacharachs' first baseman until 1929, tells how it happened:

> We had this club—the Duval Giants—down in Jacksonville, Florida. It was pretty informal and we didn't make much—we just got peanuts. But we were working on other jobs too, you know; I had this job in a grocery store, but I wanted to be a ballplayer. In 1916 Tom Jackson and Henry Tucker—they were a couple of politicians around here in Atlantic City— brought us up here. They happened to see us down in Florida and brought us up here on behalf of the mayor. They got the name, the Bacharach Giants, from the mayor here, but he didn't put any money into the club. These colored fellas, Jackson and Tucker, got money from somewhere and helped us along, but we made our own way.

The Bacharach Giants began playing about three games a week around Atlantic City. They had "contracts" of sorts with Jackson, Cummings recalls.

> We got a contract for $250 or $300 a month, and you were supposed to get that money every thirty days. Well, at that time, sometimes you made the money and sometimes you didn't. Now we used to go New York to Dexter Park with a guarantee of five hundred or a thousand dollars—and we'd have a rain guarantee—and if we had two, three good days a week like that, we were sure of gettin' our money. See what I mean? But if rain hit us, we were behind the eightball.

Since they were not playing every day, the players got other jobs.

> Some of 'em come in here and got into politics and went from there. We were only here a few days before we got registered to vote. I been in politics ever since. [Cummings is employed in the prosecutor's office in Atlantic City.] We came here on the fifth of May, and we played our first game on the eighth, and I registered on the ninth.

It was, Cummings said, "quite an experience" to come North and play against white teams for the first time; but, he added, the Bacharachs had no fear of whites.

> You see, in the first place, we all had guts because we had a lot of experience down in Florida. We all worked downtown in Jacksonville, and we had a lot of experience during the Jack Johnson and Jeffries fight—there were thousands of whites in our part of town—and we had guts when we came up here. Of course, we had no chance to play baseball with whites down there, but we worked downtown with a whole lot of white fellas. And when we came up here and started playing ball with white boys, they were more scared of us than we were scared of them. Because we had such a hell of a ball club; we had a powerful ball club! There were other colored clubs here then but we broke 'em up, we were so strong, and everybody wanted to play the Bacharachs. We played so many ball clubs, and beat everybody, that people came all the way from Philadelphia to see who the Bacharachs were.

The two decades before the formation of the first sound and solvent Negro league were a period of great expansion for black baseball. Negro teams were no longer the novelties they had been in the 1890s. Although ownership of a club could still be a financial risk, the good teams made money, particularly in cities like New York and Chicago, where the burgeoning Negro populations insured a faithful nucleus of ardent fans.

Rivalries among teams were often intense, especially among the strongest clubs. Because there was no league or tournament to determine a champion, there was nothing to stop a good team from claiming to be "World's Colored Champions" except the certainty that the claim would be challenged. In 1903 the Philadelphia Giants advertised themselves that way, and E. B. Lamar, Jr., manager of the Cuban X Giants, promptly issued a challenge in the pages of *Sporting Life* in which he contemptuously referred to them as the "so-called colored champions" and charged that they were ducking the Cuban X Giants. The Philadelphia club rose to the bait, for Sol White records that the Cuban X Giants won five of seven games from his Philadelphia Giants and thereby earned the "colored championship of the world." In that series, incidentally, Rube Foster won four of the five games for the Cuban X Giants. The following year, Foster was pitching for the Philadelphia Giants and won both games as they took a best two-out-of-three series from the Cuban X Giants and thus retrieved the "world" title. These two teams dominated Negro baseball in the East in the years between 1900 and 1905. In the Midwest the honors rested with the Chicago Union Giants and the Leland Giants, except in 1903, when the Algona Brownies, representing the village of Algona, Iowa, and made up of former members of the Union Giants and Chicago Unions, were "western" champions.

Between 1906 and 1910, the Cuban X Giants and the new Brooklyn Royal Giants appear to have been the best in the East, while in the West the Leland Giants and the Chicago Giants were dominant.

From 1911 to 1915, many fine teams rose to compete for Negro supremacy. By all odds, Rube Foster's Chicago American Giants were most consistently superior, although they were often pressed by such clubs as the Indianapolis ABC's, managed by C. I. Taylor, whom some old baseball men consider the most astute of the Negro managers; the Leland Giants and Chicago Giants, and the Kansas City, Kansas, Giants.

In the East during this period, the Lincoln Giants of New York, the Lincoln Stars, a 1914 offshoot of the Lincolns, and the Mohawk

The Lincoln Giants, dominant eastern team in the pre-World War I era, shown in 1912. First row, from left, Ashby Dunbar, Louis Santop, Joe Williams, mascot, Dick Redding, Bill Pettus, and Charlie Bradford. Standing, Bill Francis, Pete Booker, John Henry Lloyd, George Wright, and Spot Poles. COURTESY OF BILL YANCEY

Giants of Schenectady led the field. The Lincoln Giants, one of the strongest Negro clubs in history, was formed in 1911 by Jess McMahon, a white boxing promoter, and his brother Rod. The lineup included pitchers Joe Williams and Cannonball Dick Redding, infielders Home Run Johnson and John Henry Lloyd, outfielder Spot Poles and catcher-outfielder Louis Santop, all of whom were among the all-time greats of Negro baseball. They played at Olympic Field at 136th St. and Fifth Avenue in Harlem, meeting semipro and major-league all-star teams several times a week before crowds that often numbered in the thousands.

Professional baseball was prohibited on Sundays in New York in that era. The Lincoln Giants got around the ban very neatly by admitting fans free and then selling them programs—50¢ a program for a grandstand seat and 25¢ for the bleachers. Somehow it happened that if a fan declined to buy a program, he found himself outside the park before the game began.

The Lincoln Giants was one of the first black teams to add burlesque to baseball. In pregame practice they juggled the ball, hid it, and performed all sorts of acrobatics in throwing and catching. In addition they had a pantomime act in which an imaginary ball flew from bat to glove and then went zipping around the infield. But once the game got under way, the Lincoln Giants were all business, and they were soon established as the best independent team in the East. Pitcher Joe Williams, who was called "Cyclone" with good reason, was the highest-paid player at $105 a month; the others made from $40 to $75.

During the World War I era, the number of first-rate teams multiplied. From 1916 through 1919, probably the best were the American Giants, Taylor's Indianapolis ABCs (in 1916 the ABCs split in a factional fight and there were two ABCs that year), and the Lincoln Giants and Lincoln Stars in New York. But there were many other outstanding clubs, notably the Bacharach Giants, Cuban Stars of New York, Long Branch, N.J. Cubans, Brooklyn Royal Giants, St. Louis Giants, Baltimore Giants, Chicago Giants, Havana Stars, Hilldale Club, and the Columbus Buckeyes.

Especially noteworthy during the war years was a club called the All Nations, which undoubtedly had the most complete racial mix of any team in baseball history. The club was organized by J. L. Wilkinson, a Kansas City white man who later operated the famed Kansas City Monarchs. Two of the greatest Negro pitchers, José Mendez and John Donaldson, were in the club at various times with several other black men and a Japanese, a Hawaiian, an American Indian, three

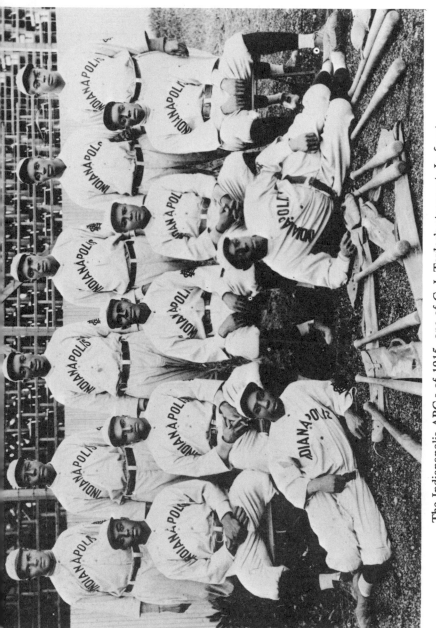

The Indianapolis ABC's of 1915, one of C. I. Taylor's strongest. In front, George Shively, left, and James Jeffries. Seated, from left, Oscar Charleston, Dicta Johnson, C. I. Taylor, manager, Jimmie Lyons, and Todd Allen. Standing, Russell Powell, Ben Taylor, Dick Redding, Bingo DeMoss, Morten Clark, and Dan Kennard. COURTESY OF BILL YANCEY white men, and one or two Latin-Americans. That the All Nations was more than merely a novelty may be seen in the fact that in 1916 the club won three out of four from Taylor's ABCs and split a series with the American Giants.

Many Negro players of big-league caliber started (and some finished) their playing days in the years between 1900 and 1920. Besides the men already mentioned in this chapter, there were players who would become legends in Negro baseball: pitcher Dan McClellan, who was the first black pitcher to twirl a perfect game, for the Philadelphia Giants in 1903; speedballer Frank Wickware; Bruce Petway, who was called the best catcher in baseball by a Pacific Coast League manager; outfielder Pete Hill; first baseman Ben Taylor; shortstop Dick Lundy of the Bacharach Giants, whom some old players offer the supreme compliment of favorable comparison with John Henry Lloyd (Lloyd himself was called the Black Honus Wagner, not without reason); pitcher Bullet Rogan; catcher George (Chappie) Johnson; spitballer Phil Cockrell, and Oscar Charleston, whom most Negro fans would argue belongs on *any* all-time team, black or mixed, as an outfielder. The careers of many of these stars will be dealt with in more detail in Chapter 16.

They left no enduring records to which fans can turn in dispute over their merits. But perhaps their quality can be demonstrated by citing a series that took place in Havana in the fall of 1910 for which batting averages are available. The Detroit Tigers, who had finished third in the American League that year, went to Cuba to play the clubs there, all of which starred American Negroes. The Tigers upheld the honor of the big leagues, winning seven, losing four, and tying one.

Ty Cobb, who had led the American League with a .385 average, continued to hit well in Cuba, compiling a .371 mark in five games. His teammate, Wahoo Sam Crawford, batted .360 for 12 games. Their averages were good enough for fourth and fifth place in the Cuban "league" that winter. Places 1, 2, and 3 were earned by American Negroes in the uniforms of Havana: John Henry Lloyd, who batted .500; Grant (Home Run) Johnson, .412, and Bruce Petway, .390.

Such demonstrations of ability were interesting but irrelevant so far as organized baseball was concerned, and the year 1920 arrived with the doors more firmly closed than ever against the Negro player. But it would be a year of considerable significance for Negro baseball, because it saw the birth of the first lasting Negro league.

The All Nations Club (about 1916) which included men of several races. Seated at center is John Donaldson, one of the greatest Negro pitchers. COURTESY OF GEORGE BRACE

6 THE BLACK WAGNER

I am honored to have John Lloyd called the Black Wagner. It is a privilege to have been compared with him.
—HONUS WAGNER

He was a tall, gangling man with a protruding jaw and hands like twin shovels. In Cuba they called him El Cuchara—the Shovel—

John Henry Lloyd in 1918.

because of his penchant for scooping up part of the infield in digging out ground balls; in the United States he was the Black Wagner.

His name was John Henry Lloyd. He played in top Negro clubs for twenty-five years, and through most of that period he was perhaps the most famous of the black stars. Toward the end of his career he was "Pop" Lloyd, the revered elder of Negro baseball. He loved the game with a fervor undimmed by the years and did not fully retire as a player until he was fifty-eight years old, although for the last ten years he was confined to the semipro lots near Atlantic City, N.J.

Such batting averages as are available suggest that during his prime he was a fairly consistent .400-plus hitter against good pitching. Unlike Honus Wagner, whom he resembled as a shortstop, Lloyd batted lefthanded. He held the bat in the crook of his left elbow and swung easily, gracefully, generating considerable power. He had a rather lumbering gait but it was deceptive; he took long strides and was sometimes referred to as one of the most dangerous baserunners in Negro baseball. Whitey Gruhler of the Atlantic City *Press-Union,* who covered many games in which Lloyd played, said, "If he was slow by stopwatch timing, he made up for it in the field by an instinctive ability to judge the direction of the hit as the batter began his swing. In other words, he got a big jump on the ball." Lloyd was big for a shortstop, standing 5 feet 11 inches and weighing about 180 pounds. He ranged wide in the field and, with his long arms and big hands, handled many balls that other shortstops could not reach.

Lloyd was born in the Negro section of Palatka, Florida, on April 25, 1884. His father died when he was an infant, and after his mother remarried he was given over to the care of a grandmother. As was usual for young Negroes in Florida before the turn of the century, he left school before completing the elementary grades and became a delivery boy in a store. After working hours he played ball with a local amateur nine.

While he was still in his teens, Lloyd went to Jacksonville and worked in a store and later as a porter for the Southern Express Company. There he began playing with a semipro club called the Young Receivers. Napoleon Cummings, who later starred with the Bacharach Giants, recalled that when he was a boy, the big, kindly John Henry Lloyd would get him into the ballpark by letting him carry his glove and shoes past the gate men.

In 1905, Lloyd was twenty-one years old and a professional ballplayer, catcher for the Macon, Georgia, Acmes. The club was too poor to have such luxuries as mask and chest-protector. Cary B.

Lewis, sports columnist for the *Chicago Defender,* told of the consequences years later:

> His team was playing against Augusta, Georgia, at Augusta, and the famous twirler "Georgia Rabbit" was on the mound. Lloyd was catching without a mask. In the third inning a foul tip pounced on his left lamp; the lid closed. He moistened his finger, rubbed the bruised member, and kept on. In the seventh inning another foul pounced on his right lamp; it sought redress in darkness. Lloyd, like a good sport, exclaimed: "Gentlemen, I guess I'll have to quit, I can't see the ball." Next day he purchased a wire paper basket, inclosed his mug, and finished the series.

The incident evidently ended his taste for catching, for when he showed up in Philadelphia the next year he was a second baseman. Why Lloyd happened to go north to find fame as a ballplayer is uncertain. Some authorities say that he was seen by E. B. Lamar, Jr., owner of the Cuban X Giants, while they were playing in the Florida winter circuit and doubling as waiters in resort hotels, and that Lamar paid his fare to Philadelphia. Lloyd's widow said he told her that he went north at the urging of his fellow porters in Jacksonville and that he arrived in Philadelphia with total assets of $1.50 and a pocketwatch and no assurance of employment. In any event, he started the season of 1906 as second baseman for the Cuban X Giants. In his first game he gave a preview of things to come when he hit the game-winning double in the tenth inning to beat Charles (Kid) Carter, one of the best black pitchers of that era, and the Wilmington Giants. Among Lloyd's teammates on the Cuban X Giants was Charles Grant, the "Tokohama" of McGraw's Baltimore Orioles in 1901.

For the following season, Lloyd moved to the X Giants' arch rivals, the Philadelphia Giants, as a shortstop. He played with that club for three years, leaving with several teammates in 1910 to join the Leland Giants in Chicago. The defection dealt a mortal blow to the Philadelphia Giants. Early that season, Sol White, who was the manager, had a falling out with the owner, a white sportswriter named H. Walter Schlichter, and organized his own club. But there was trouble in the "International League of Colored Base Ball Clubs," which was essentially a front for the booking office of Nat Strong, and the promoter declined to book games for White's new club. And so both the Philadelphia Giants and White's new team died on the vine.

In 1911, Jess and Rod McMahon selected White as manager of the new Lincoln Giants of New York, and he lured Lloyd and others who had gone to Chicago back to the East. Lloyd, now twenty-seven years old, was near his peak as a player.

In 1913 the Lincoln Giants reached a heady plateau when they beat the Philadelphia Phillies, 9–2, getting fourteen hits off Grover Cleveland Alexander, a 22-game winner in the National League that year. They had also treated Rube Foster's Chicago American Giants rudely, winning series both in New York and Chicago. Foster was not one to lose cheerfully, and the next year he stripped the Lincoln Giants of four of their top stars and put together a powerful team. From the Giants he took Lloyd, pitcher Joe Williams, third baseman Billy Francis, and outfielder Jude Gans.

"Wherever the money was, that's where I was," Lloyd would say later, and in 1914 the big money for black ballplayers was in Chicago on Foster's club. Lloyd stayed with the American Giants through 1917, playing alongside such stars as outfielder Oscar Charleston, second baseman Bingo DeMoss, catchers Bruce Petway and Louis Santop, and pitchers Dick Redding and Frank Wickware as well as Joe Williams. Lloyd probably earned about $250 a month during this period as cleanup hitter on the top Negro club of that age, if not of black baseball history.

In January 1918, Lloyd had a job in the Army Quartermaster's depot in Chicago, and he decided to stay there instead of traveling to Florida to play in the winter league with the American Giants. This appears to have displeased Foster, and by early spring the manager was singing the praises of a young shortstop named Bobby Williams, a slick fielder but no fence-buster at the plate.

Lloyd and Foster parted amicably; perhaps the shrewd manager saw that his veteran shortstop, now thirty-four, was a step slower in the field. Lloyd himself may have felt the weight of his years because when he went back east to become manager of the Brooklyn Royal Giants for the 1918 season, his first managerial job, he often placed himself at first base rather than shortstop.

From 1918 until his retirement from top professional teams in 1931, when he was forty-seven years old, Lloyd played first base as much as shortstop. During those years he managed and played for the Royal Giants, the Columbus, Ohio, Buckeyes, the Bacharach Giants, the Hilldale Club, and the Lincoln Giants.

Easygoing, slow-talking "Pop" Lloyd became like a father to the young players on those teams. He was a sound baseball man but not a disciplinarian in the Foster mold. "He was a great man and a great teacher," said Judy Johnson, who played under Lloyd with Hilldale in 1923. Lloyd was an exponent of the pat-on-the-back managerial method. "He put the confidence in you," Johnson explained, "and you had to do it—you just had to do it. I think that was one of the best years I ever had in baseball."

Despite his mild manner, Lloyd was a fierce competitor, both as player and manager. Cum Posey, who operated the Homestead Grays for thirty years and was one of the keenest observers of Negro baseball, called John Henry Lloyd "the Dr. Jekyll and Mr. Hyde of baseball." Off the field he was a pleasant, friendly man. "He was a very happy man," his widow said. "He laughed easily, and everybody was glad to see him."

Lloyd's long professional career blanketed an age when most ballplayers, both in the white and black leagues, were rough and tough, often hard-drinking and hard-talking. In contrast, Lloyd never drank or swore; his strongest oath was "Dad burn!" which he reserved for moments of crisis on the field. His only "dissipation" was an occasional fat cigar.

When he retired from big-time Negro baseball in 1931, Lloyd became a janitor in the post office in Atlantic City, where he had settled several years earlier. He declined offers to manage the Newark Eagles and the Baltimore Elite Giants and spent the rest of his life as a sort of foster father to the children of Atlantic City.

Lloyd had no children of his own, but he found ample opportunity to express his love for them. He left the post-office job in the middle Thirties and became a janitor in the Atlantic City school system. In that humble position he became a living legend to a couple of generations of schoolchildren. Whitey Gruhler described his hold over the children thus:

> The youngsters cluster about him between sessions. They call him "Pop" and love to listen while he spins baseball yarns of the past. Sometimes they refuse to break away from him and "Pop" has to pick them up bodily and carry them into their classrooms. He is their hero, this big, soft-hearted, soft-spoken, congenial man with a tired look in his eyes, but the bubbling spirit of youth in his heart.

Even in his late middle age, John Henry Lloyd was not through with baseball. He managed and played first base for semipro teams

in Atlantic City until 1942, when he was fifty-eight years old. Later
he served as the city's Little League commissioner for several years.

Unlike most of the other stars of Negro baseball, Lloyd achieved a
measure of enduring recognition in 1949 when the $150,000 ball-
park at a community recreation field was named for him. During
the dedication ceremonies, he was asked whether he regretted the
fact that his playing days were long past before the color line of
baseball was erased. Lloyd replied:

> I do not consider that I was born at the wrong time. I felt it
> was the right time, for I had a chance to prove the ability of our
> race in this sport, and because many of us did our very best
> to uphold the traditions of the game and of the world of sport,
> we have given the Negro a greater opportunity now to be ac-
> cepted into the major leagues with other Americans.

John Henry Lloyd died on March 19, 1965, of arteriosclerosis
after a two-year illness. His wife was his only close survivor, but he
left a host of friends in and out of baseball with dimming memories
of his grace at shortstop and his picture swing at the plate.

Do their memories deceive them? Just how good was John Henry
Lloyd? Few objective measures of his greatness are extant. Published
batting averages credit him with .475 in 1911, when he was twenty-
seven years old and at his prime, and with .418 twelve years later
against strong professional and semipro opposition. How reliable
those figures are, however, cannot be determined.

Old ballplayers and sportswriters who saw him during his glory
years are nearly unanimous in placing him at shortstop on any all-
time Negro team, and not a few of them call him the greatest player
in the annals of Negro baseball. There can be no doubt that he
would have been a major-league star had he been born forty years
later. Perhaps the best recommendations are the flattering comment
of Honus Wagner, and the reply of a white St. Louis sportswriter
when he was asked in 1938 who was the best player in baseball
history. "If you mean in organized baseball," the writer said, "my
answer would be Babe Ruth; but if you mean in all baseball, organized or unorganized, the answer would have to be a colored man
named John Henry Lloyd."

7 THE NEGRO LEAGUES

*There is nothing the matter with our
league and there will not be.*
— JUDGE W. C. HUESTON, PRESIDENT,
NEGRO NATIONAL LEAGUE, *1930*

*Negro leagues are in the zone of a
racket.*
— BRANCH RICKEY, PRESIDENT,
BROOKLYN DODGERS, *1945*

Tracing the course of the organized Negro leagues is rather like trying to follow a single black strand through a ton of spaghetti. The footing is infirm, and the strand has a tendency to break off in one's hand and slither back into the amorphous mass.

Leagues were born and died within a single season, franchises were often shifted from city to city in the middle of summer, and a number of teams had a brief fling at glory in the sun of big-time Negro baseball before returning to the scrubby obscurity of semipro lots. Many middle-aged fans, both black and white, will remember at least the names of the Kansas City Monarchs, the Homestead Grays or the Chicago American Giants. But how many remember the Cleveland Hornets or the Milwaukee Bears? They were in the Negro majors, too, each for a season during the Twenties.

Few generalizations are possible about the organized black leagues during the three decades in which they flourished so to speak. Perhaps three general statements might be advanced with some degree of temerity: (1) that the leagues (and most of the teams) were consistently underfinanced; (2) that, except for a brief period at the beginning, they lacked leadership; and (3) that, due chiefly to points 1 and 2, the Negro leagues never approached the level of white organized baseball in stability or discipline.

Beyond those propositions, the historian is on shaky ground in generalizing about the operation of Negro leagues. It is possible to say, as Judge Hueston did in 1930, that "there is nothing the matter with our league" and justify it by pointing to a certain league in a certain year (but there *was* a good deal wrong with the Negro National League in the year Judge Hueston spoke). It is also possible to say, as Branch Rickey did fifteen years later, that the Negro circuits were racket leagues dominated by promoters. Abe Saperstein and Eddie Gottlieb, whose business was sports promotion, *did* have a large stake in the two Negro major leagues in 1945, but that they were able to run the leagues as "rackets" is insupportable.

There is general agreement among men who played in the Negro major leagues that the level of play on the field was equal to that of Triple-A leagues, the highest minor leagues in organized baseball. Judy Johnson, who was at his peak as a star third baseman during the late Twenties, said the leagues were not of major-league quality:

> Not day in and day out. But of course you could have picked enough players then to put a team in each major league—a whole colored team in each league and they would have been the same calibre as the other big-league teams. The Hilldale Club that played in the (Negro) World Series in 1924 would have belonged in Triple A because there were a couple of positions where men would have had to be replaced. We had men in some positions who weren't major-league calibre.

Buck Leonard, whose career spanned the Thirties and Forties, agrees:

> We didn't have star men at every position. We didn't have —as the majors did—two good catchers and six or seven good pitchers and good infielders and outfielders. We had about four good pitchers and about two or three mediocre pitchers. We had pitchers that we would pitch in league games and we had pitchers that we would pitch against white semipro teams. Now that's the way we operated. We had pitchers that we never would have pitched in league games. Sockamayocks, we used to call 'em. Here's what I would say: In 1937, '38, '39, and '40—those were about the best teams for the Homestead Grays, and then we had another good team in 1945 when the fellas came back from the Army—I would say that we would have been a good Triple-A team for this reason—we didn't have the replacements that the major-league teams have. Those fellas I was talking about who weren't first-stringers,

they might be Class-B or -C or -D ballplayers. Our sockamay-
ocks might be Class-B or -D pitchers, and then our second-
string catcher might be Class B.

The story of organized Negro leagues properly begins in 1920, although due note should be made of the League of Colored Base Ball
Clubs, which lasted a week in 1887; the International League of Independent Professional Base Ball Clubs in 1906, which included both
white and black teams and struggled through one season; and a semipro Negro Texas League in 1919.

Andrew (Rube) Foster, manager of the American Giants, was
the unchallenged master of Negro baseball in the Chicago area in
1919. Indeed, his sway extended even to top white semipro teams
like the Logan Squares and Duffy Florals, whose games around Chicago were booked by him. Foster's American Giants were the pre-
mier attraction outside of the big leagues, and clubs that refused to do
business with him found themselves out of favor and thus unable to
schedule the American Giants or other top teams in the area.

The Chicago American Giants of 1921, a club that dominated the Negro
National League during its first three years. In front are, Tom Williams,
left, and Bobby Williams. Seated, from left, Christobel Torrienti, Tom
Johnson, Otis Starks, Jimmie Lyons, Jelly Gardner, and George Dixon.
Standing, Jim Brown, Dave Brown, Bingo DeMoss, Dave Malarcher,
LeRoy Grant, and Jack Marshall. COURTESY OF BILL YANCEY

He was a power, but he was also dissatisfied. In a series of columns titled "Pitfalls of Baseball" which he wrote for the *Chicago Defender* that winter, Rube summed up the troubles of Negro baseball. The chief thorn was piracy.

> If you have taken your club east, (and) win many games, the owners try to take the men away from you, bring dissatisfaction between you and your men; so much so you avoid going there. Ball players have had no respect for their word, contracts or moral obligations, yet they are not nearly as much to blame as the different owners of clubs.

In these columns, Foster proposed a Negro national association patterned after the big leagues. He suggested two leagues, one in the Midwest including Chicago, Indianapolis, Cincinnati, Detroit, St. Louis, and Kansas City, and one in the East made up of Pittsburgh, Cleveland, Washington, Baltimore, Philadelphia, and New York. The other owners were wary, moving Foster to complain in mid-January that "the get-together effort has been a failure." He was no man to assent to failure, though, and on February 13, 1920, the owners of the top Negro clubs in the Midwest gathered at a YMCA in Kansas City to hammer out a league. The *Defender* described them as "enthusiastic."

Foster had hardly been elected temporary president when he displayed to the startled owners a charter for a National Negro Baseball

Letterhead of the Negro National League in 1921. COURTESY OF LEE ALLEN

League incorporated in Illinois, Michigan, Ohio, Pennsylvania, New York, and Maryland. Only one eastern owner, W. A. Kelly of Washington, attended the two-day meeting, but Nat Strong of New York, the most powerful booker in the East, sent a telegram expressing support. It was the last kind word between Foster and Strong.

Dave Wyatt of the *Indianapolis Ledger,* Elwood C. Knox of the *Indianapolis Freeman,* Cary B. Lewis of the *Chicago Defender,* and Attorney Elisha Scott of Topeka stayed up all night to write the constitution for the National Association of Colored Professional Baseball Clubs and the Negro National League for approval on the second day of the meeting. It was signed by Foster for the American Giants, C. I. Taylor of the Indianapolis ABCs, Joe Green of the Chicago Giants, the other strong black club in Chicago; J. L. Wilkinson of the Kansas City Monarchs, Lorenzo S. Cobb of the St. Louis Giants, and J. T. (Tenny) Blount of the Detroit Stars, whom Foster had set up in 1919 as a baseball promoter in Detroit. John Matthews of the Dayton Marcos, who was ill and unable to attend, told the other owners he would agree to whatever was done. The Cuban Stars, who were represented at the meeting by Foster, became the eighth team in the league. Each manager paid $500 to bind him to the constitution.

If the owners had their own interests at heart in forming the league, they also realized that there had to be some semblance of balance among the teams, and so several player shifts involving some of the best players were made. Foster sent outfielder Oscar Charleston to Indianapolis and pitcher Richard Whitworth to Detroit; Kansas City got José Mendez (a former great pitcher who was a shortstop in 1920) and pitcher-outfielder John Donaldson from Detroit; outfielder Jimmie Lyons went from St. Louis to Detroit.

The owners announced that the league would not begin officially "until each city has a park, either leased or owned, and this will undoubtedly be by April 1, 1921." Evidently they changed their minds before the start of the 1920 season, because the first game in the Western Circuit, National Negro Baseball League, was played at Indianapolis on May 2 with the ABCs defeating Joe Green's Chicago Giants, 4–2.

In the larger cities of the circuit, attendance was good that first year, particularly on holidays and weekends. Crowds of 8,000 to 10,-000 were not uncommon in Chicago, Kansas City, and Indianapolis on a Sunday. The American Giants were awarded the pennant, although no final standings were published for the circuit, which in

A·B·C· 1921
BASE BALL CLUB
SUNDAYS AT HOME

JULY 3-4-10-17

AUG. 21

SEPT. 11-18

OCT. 9-16-23-30

WASHINGTON PARK INDIANAPOLIS

APRIL 24

MAY 8-15-22

JUNE 26

COURTESY OF LEE ALLEN

midseason was still being referred to as the "proposed" National League.

The first season had been a success overall, but the problem of shaky franchises was already arising. For the 1921 season, the Dayton franchise was shifted to Columbus in the first of a long series of changes. Over the twelve-year life of this first Negro National League only the American Giants were members continuously. The league was always represented in St. Louis, too, but the St. Louis Stars took over the Giants' franchise after the 1921 season.

In 1921 two Eastern clubs became "associate members" of the year-old National Association of Colored Professional Base Ball Clubs. In accepting association, the two clubs—the Bacharach Giants of Atlantic City and Hilldale of Darby, Pennsylvania—agreed to schedule games with league teams when they visited the East and to refrain from raiding their rosters. This practice of giving associate memberships continued for many years because it had value for both league and nonleague teams. For one thing, it curbed to some extent the predatory instincts of clubowners who coveted players on rival teams; for another, it assured league clubs of a full schedule of games when they were in the territory of an associated team.

The scheduling problem was paramount during the early years of Negro organized baseball and would remain troublesome as long as there were leagues. It was due in large part to the fact that few Negro clubs owned parks. In 1921, for example, when the Negro National League was in its second season, no club owned a park and grounds outright. Foster's American Giants owned the grandstand but not the grounds for their park, and St. Louis and Detroit had leases which permitted them to use stadiums whenever they wanted, but the five other league clubs were at the mercy of white clubowners. Three teams—Kansas City, Indianapolis and Columbus—used the stadiums of clubs in the white American Association; one—the Chicago Giants —was a road club, playing its "home" league games in whatever town offered the prospect of a good gate; and the Cuban Stars, who had also been a road club in 1920, spent 1921 at Redland Field in Cincinnati, the first Negro club to become a regular tenant of a big-league team. The season lease cost $4,000, and the Cincinnati Reds made sure of getting their money by taking twenty percent of the gate receipts until the full amount had been paid.

By the terms of their rental arrangements with American Association clubs, Kansas City, Indianapolis, and Columbus had to use the parks whenever the white clubs were out of town. As a result, the Monarchs, ABCs and Buckeyes often had to make long jumps to get back home when the Association teams were leaving, and vacate the stadiums for other parts when they returned home.

With this mishmash of field arrangements, it was nearly impossible to make a schedule that would be equitable for all league clubs. The reader who checks the final standings for all Negro major leagues through 1950 (in Appendix A) will be struck by the fact that rarely did all teams play the same number of league games. In 1921, for example, when the American Giants won the pennant for the second time, they played 62 games, the second-place Kansas City Monarchs played 81, and the last-place Chicago Giants played only 42.

While the NNL was still struggling to find a firm base for a stable league, a second major league was beginning to shape up in the East. It was formalized on December 16, 1923, at a meeting of representatives of five clubs in Philadelphia. The Brooklyn Royal Giants, Lincoln Giants of New York, Bacharach Giants, Baltimore Black Sox, and the Hilldale Club formed the Mutual Association of Eastern Colored Baseball Clubs, which would be known as the Eastern Colored League. They added Alex Pompez's eastern Cuban Stars to make a six-team league. (The NNL's western Cuban Stars were owned by Augustin Molina.)

The league elected no president but was ruled by six commissioners, one from each team, with Edward H. Bolden of Hilldale as chairman. The real power, however, was Nat C. Strong, the New York booking agent who owned the Royal Giants and controlled the scheduling arrangements for nearly all black clubs and most of the white semipros in the New York metropolitan area. The *Chicago Defender* noted caustically that five of the six league clubs were booked by him. It was hinted that the league's prime purpose was to strengthen Strong's control over the clubs and thus ensure the continued flow of ten percent of their gate receipts into his coffers.

The Eastern Colored League opened in 1923 and, like the NNL, had a reasonably successful first season. Hilldale played the most league games, 49, and won the pennant.

The Negro National League was well aware of the Eastern League's existence, but there was too much enmity between owners to allow for an agreement between the leagues, and in 1924 "war" started. Foster's dream of a single national association was buried by that war. The eastern clubs as a whole were more affluent than the western, and players began jumping in bunches. Hardly had the new league been formed when the great lefthander, Dave Brown, jumped from the American Giants to New York's Lincoln Giants. Others followed him east during that season, and in 1924 the Indianapolis ABCs were literally destroyed, no fewer than ten ABC players making the trek east. An uneasy peace was established late that year (in fact, the first Negro World Series was held between the two leagues), but throughout their short lives, both circuits were often shaken by threats of player wars and, occasionally, the start of one.

Both leagues were weak structurally. The Eastern Colored League was a flimsy federation of owners who felt free (and sometimes exercised that freedom) to decide whether or not their teams would play scheduled games. In its second year, Nat Strong declined to have his Royal Giants play some games on the league schedule. James Keenan, business manager of the Lincoln Giants, led a movement to oust him, but of course with Strong's clout as the booking agent for most of the teams, it was doomed to failure. As W. Rollo Wilson noted in the *Pittsburgh Courier,* "Nat Strong is more than a name in the Eastern League, and . . . he will get out only when it suits Nat Strong to do so."

In the Negro National League, the situation was different—much different. Rube Foster *was* the league during the early years. It was a product of his imagination and foresight, and he ruled with an iron but usually benevolent hand. Until he was incapacitated by mental illness in 1926, Foster was NNL president and secretary, and the league office was wherever he happened to be.

His hold over league affairs is illustrated by the story, possibly apocryphal, that at a league meeting after the 1920 season, John Matthews, owner of the Dayton Marcos, indulged in a catnap and awoke to find that he had lost his franchise and his players, whom Rube had distributed among other teams. Whether true or not, the tale reflects the reality; it is a fact that Dayton was not in the league in 1921. Reporting a later league meeting, a *Pittsburgh Courier* correspondent wrote: "The writer was much impressed with the actions of the various owners of the league clubs. Some of these owners have as much to say at a league meeting as the editor of the *Negro World* has to say concerning the policies of the *Atlanta Constitution.*"

But if he was stern and domineering, Rube Foster was also a responsible businessman, and there is no question that his efforts alone kept the league afloat during its infancy. He shored up shaky franchises with his own money, paid transportation costs for some clubs, and guaranteed hotel bills for teams stranded far from home because games were rained out and they had no money.

In return, Rube Foster expected compliance with his will, and, although there were frequent mutterings about his high-handedness, there was never serious mutiny. In early 1925 the mutterings grew too loud for Foster to ignore and he offered his resignation. The other owners, feeling the lash of his wrath and knowing that if Foster didn't run the league they would have to take a hand in it, backed off and gave Rube a unanimous vote of confidence. Foster's hospitalization the following year forced them to act, but their unwillingness to assume responsibility almost ended the league then. It managed to stumble on to an inglorious finish after the 1931 season.

For his leadership, Foster exacted a price besides instant obedience to his wishes. He drew no salary from either of his league offices, but he got five percent of the receipts from all league games. This was not clear profit, since he had to pay his office costs and a stenographer's wages from it, but it was enough to sour owners who were having poor seasons at the gate. It is impossible to calculate how much the five percent actually meant to Foster, because, as with nearly everything else about the operation of the Negro leagues, the financial picture is muddy.

For one season (1923), some financial data on the Negro National League was published. Attendance at league games that year was 402,436, an average of about 1,650 per game. Total receipts were $197,218. This would indicate that Foster's percentage was $9,860.90 for running the league. But the probability is that in addition to paying his office costs, Rube also chipped in toward some of the other expenses, which were as follows: players' salaries, $101,-000; rail fares, $25,212; board and streetcar fares, $9,136; baseballs, $7,965; umpires, $7,448; club advertising, $7,500; other expenses, $4,164. The total of expenses was $162,425, so for that year the league operated at a profit of $34,793, which was split among the seven clubs still operating at the end of the season.

This suggests that Negro baseball was fairly profitable, and it was for only a few owners. But a big problem was an imbalance of strength among the teams; for the whole twelve-year life of the first Negro National League, only three teams won pennants—the American Giants, Kansas City Monarchs, and St. Louis Stars. These teams were the drawing cards and thus the big moneymakers. Over the first six years, the American Giants averaged $85,000 a year from league games and the Monarchs $41,000. Tailenders, on the other hand, might expect an income of only $10,000 or $15,000 a year as their share of the gates of the league games.

A similar imbalance in strength prevailed in the Eastern Colored League, where only two teams—Hilldale and the Bacharach Giants —won championships before the league crumbled early in the 1928 season. But Eastern League teams played fewer league games and more independent ball. Therefore, the variance in strength of the clubs was not reflected quite so much in their financial standing, because they did not depend so heavily on the league for games.

The eastern circuit was reorganized in 1929 as the American Negro League but it lasted only that season, with the Baltimore Black Sox winning the pennant. Meanwhile, the Negro National League was disintegrating under the leadership of Judge W. C. Hueston, an attorney and Negro lodge panjandrum who had been elected to the presidency in 1927 after Foster was hospitalized. Evidently he was paid an honorarium for his services (which appear to have been confined mostly to optimistic statements about the health of the league), but the amount was never announced.

It is likely that no one could have saved the Negro National League after Foster's departure, because he was its foundation, and even during his reign it was troubled. Besides the problems of scheduling, insufficient finances, and player raids by eastern clubs, the league also had troubles with umpiring and player conduct.

When the league began it had no staff of umpires. The home club furnished the umpires—often white—and this led to charges of favoritism and lack of race pride. Even Foster, who clearly hoped for and expected the advancement of Negroes in baseball and in the nation's life generally, hired white umpires for his games.

It was not until the league's third season that W. W. (Billy) Donaldson, a Negro, was put under contract as the first league umpire. Five other black men were soon hired, but the league found that because their transportation bills had to be paid, it cost $4,000 more a year to have a staff of umpires than to hire them by the game in each city. In addition, there were frequent blasts at the competence of the Negro arbiters (and sometimes the white ones, too), and in 1925 four of the six black umpires were discharged for incompetence. Negro umpires predominated during the later years of the Negro leagues, however, although there was not always a traveling staff that worked full-time in the leagues.

As might be expected, the behavior of players both on and off the field mirrored the strength of the league leadership. While Rube Foster was in charge, discipline was good, but when he passed from the scene restraints on players' actions on the field were eased because the men knew that retribution was unlikely. Rowdyism, sometimes involving fans, was rampant during the late 1920s (in the East as well as the West) as the two leagues floundered toward extinction.

Candy Jim Taylor, a player and manager over almost the whole span of Negro organized baseball, had this to say about league conditions in 1930:

> The clubowners fail to cooperate in the establishment of ball clubs in each city. Limiting the number of men a team can carry to fourteen is bad. Umpires who do not give fair decisions and who are paid by the club instead of the league; dirty parks and unclean players' uniforms, and the failure of the clubs to give their teams good publicity, these are bad. The season of 1929 was the poorest from the standpoints of both playing and attendance since the beginning of the National League in 1920, mainly because no club in the league was able to put a club on the field each day in condition to play.

The picture did not get better that year or the next, and in 1932, for the first time since 1920, by late summer no major Negro league was functioning.

That year marks the nadir of organized black baseball. It was also the harbinger of a new era, a period that would see the emergence of strong personalities in the Foster mold as leaders of realigned leagues. Aided in no small measure by the nation's gradual recovery from the Depression, these leagues were more firmly grounded and prosperous than the old. Had these strong men been able to work for the common good, it is likely that organized Negro ball would have become as stable as its white counterpart.

The first of the strong men was Cumberland Willis Posey: he led the Homestead Grays almost from their start to a position of eminence in eastern baseball. The Grays were the impressive offspring of the Blue Ribbon nine, which was organized about 1900 by Negro steelworkers in Homestead, Pennsylvania, a grimy town in the shadow of a huge mill of the Carnegie Steel Corporation (now U.S. Steel), on the Monongahela River, just east of Pittsburgh. Cum Posey, born in Homestead on June 20, 1891, had already made a name as a basketball player at Duquesne and Penn State when he joined the club, then called the Murdock Grays, about 1911. A year later the team became the Homestead Grays. Posey, an outfielder, was named manager in 1916, and within the next decade he had established the Grays as a top-ranking team in eastern Negro baseball. During the Grays' formative years, incidentally, they were occasionally integrated to the extent of having one or two white players.

Cum Posey favored Negro leagues in principle, but he was harsh in his criticism of the two major leagues during the Twenties and he was slow to join them. The Grays did not enter an organized league until 1929, when they finished third and fourth in the split-season schedule of the American Negro League.

In 1932, Rube Foster's Negro National League was dead. His old club, now owned by Chicago businessman Robert A. Cole and called Cole's American Giants, was in the Negro Southern League, as was the Indianapolis ABC team, another charter member of the NNL. There had been no eastern league for two years.

Cum Posey was ready to step out as more than merely the proprietor of one of the most successful clubs in black baseball. Characteristically, his plans were ambitious. He envisioned a strong, tightly knit league of teams in the major cities of the East playing league games almost every day. His East-West League was born at a meeting in Cleveland in January. Besides Posey's Grays, the league included the Baltimore Black Sox, Cleveland Stars, Alex Pompez's Cuban Stars, Hilldale, the Newark Browns, and the Detroit Wolves, who were also controlled by Posey.

Posey's ambition exceeded the economic realities in 1932, a year in which the nation's business and industrial life was near standstill, and the East-West League barely made it off the ground. By early June the Detroit Wolves had disbanded, the schedule was curtailed, players took drastic salary cuts, and the league's staff of umpires was let go. A few weeks later, the East-West League was moribund. It did not survive the summer. The Grays went back to barnstorming, the trade they knew best, and Cum Posey retired for a time from league leadership. But his Grays would become the dominant team in the second Negro National League, and he would remain one of the real powers of Negro baseball until his death on March 28, 1946.

The second of the strong men who picked up Rube Foster's mantle was W. A. (Gus) Greenlee, a Pittsburgh numbers king and tavern operator whose other interests included a boxing stable which boasted John Henry Lewis, the light-heavyweight champion. Unlike Foster and Posey, Greenlee had no background in baseball when he began organizing the Pittsburgh Crawfords in 1931. The name "Crawfords" was borrowed from a semipro team in Pittsburgh (which in 1928 and 1929 had featured a young slugger named Josh Gibson), but there was nothing semipro about Greenlee's Crawfords. With his bulging pocketbook, Greenlee soon had a lineup of many of the great names of black baseball: Satchel Paige, Gibson, Oscar Charleston, Judy Johnson, Cool Papa Bell, Ted Page, Leroy Matlock, Jimmie Crutchfield.

In 1933, Greenlee put together the second Negro National League. The league opened with his Crawfords, the Homestead Grays, Robert A. Cole's American Giants of Chicago, the reorganized Indianapolis ABCs, the Detroit Stars, and the Columbus Blue Birds.

By the end of the first half of the split-season schedule, the Homestead Grays were out (charged with raiding other clubs), and so were the Indianapolis ABCs. They were replaced by the Nashville Elite Giants and the Baltimore Black Sox. The American Giants edged the Crawfords for the first-half championship. The second-half schedule was not completed, and the American Giants, as first-half winners, claimed the pennant. Several months after the season ended, Greenlee, as league chairman, announced that the American Giants had not won the pennant after all. The real winners, he said, were his Crawfords.

Despite this tainted start, Greenlee had laid the foundation for a league that would survive, but with many changes, until 1948. During its first four years, the Negro National League included cities in both the East and Midwest, but with the formation of the Negro American League in 1937, the NNL became an eastern circuit. The Negro American League was formed under the leadership of H. G. Hall, then president of the Chicago American Giants, with franchises in the Midwest and South. The keystones were Chicago, Kansas City, and Birmingham. Other franchises rotated among Memphis, Cincinnati, Detroit, Indianapolis, St. Louis, Atlanta, Jacksonville, Cleveland, Louisville, and Houston. After the dissolution of the Negro National League in 1948, the NAL absorbed some of the eastern clubs and managed to stagger on, a shadow of its former self as a major circuit, until 1960.

Unlike Rube Foster's first Negro National League and the Eastern Colored League of the Twenties, the second NNL and the NAL were on reasonably firm financial ground in the late Thirties and early Forties. Most clubs managed to break even, at least; and during the World War II years, organized Negro baseball grew to the stature of a two-million-dollar-a-year business, probably the single biggest black-dominated enterprise. It was not, however, stable enough to inspire much confidence in the heart of a conservative businessman. Few clubs owned parks (Greenlee's Crawfords were one of the few), and many of them depended upon their share of the gate receipts from the annual East-West all-star game to break even for the year. More will be said about the East-West game later.

Like the early leagues, the two major circuits of the Thirties and Forties suffered from lack of central authority. Both were run by the most powerful owners with an assist from booking agents, who had a considerable voice in league affairs because they could give or withhold the blessing of a full schedule of games for league teams playing in their domains.

Gus Greenlee's NNL made a couple of half-hearted attempts to put its house in order by hiring a commissioner who was, in theory, independent of the clubowners, but in the end, self-interest triumphed over the weak impulse for discipline in league affairs. The first commissioner was W. Rollo Wilson, a highly respected Philadelphia newspaperman and perhaps the most knowledgeable and fair-minded man available. He was hired in 1934, soon after Greenlee had awarded the 1933 NNL championship to his Crawfords. Wilson settled several disputes about the ownership of players during the season, once even ruling against Greenlee without retribution, and it appeared that he might become a fixture and bring order out of chaos. Unfortunately, however, he had to make a ruling on a protest of a game in the championship playoff between the Philadelphia Stars and Robert A. Cole's American Giants. He ruled for Philadelphia, and Cole, who was league treasurer, expressed his displeasure by declining to sign the commissioner's paycheck until well into the following winter.

The following year the Negro National League elected Ferdinand Q. Morton, a New York City Civil Service official, as commissioner, but he was rarely called upon to do anything except appear at league meetings. When in 1938 he called a league meeting on his own authority, Gus Greenlee told the other owners not to bother appearing, and they did not. Later that year, the league, meeting over Greenlee's Crawford Grill in Pittsburgh, abolished the commissionership. There was no further nonsense about an authority independent of the dominant clubowners until 1947, when the Rev. John H. Johnson of New York, an Episcopal clergyman, was elected to head the league with the title of president.

The Negro American League had a figurehead commissioner, Maj. R. R. Jackson, from 1939 to 1941. When he was not rehired for

1942, Jackson promptly formed the Negro Baseball League of America, but the new circuit did not last the season. The reluctance of owners in both leagues to submit to the discipline of a strong central office was damaging, since it weakened public confidence in the circuits and made it difficult for a fan to take them seriously. Almost every season began with the Negro press enthusiastic about the prospects and with full reports and complete standings of the leagues. But by mid-August, because games were canceled without notice and because clubs often failed to turn in results of games they had lost (few games were covered by the press), the newspapers were carrying diatribes against the owners in place of standings. Frequently, at the end of the season, a fan would be hard put to figure out who had won the pennant, much less what the final standings were.

Inevitably the looseness of the league structure was reflected on the field. It was not unusual for a player to attack an umpire with his fists and get off with a slap on the wrist. On occasion, it was worse than that. In 1938, umpire James Crump was assaulted on the field during a game in Baltimore. Crump promptly levied a $25 fine on a Baltimore Elite Giants player. The next day he got a telegram from the Negro National League's ruling board dismissing him. One of the three members of the ruling board was Tom Wilson, Elite Giants' owner.

With this sort of permissiveness prevalent on the field, it did not take the players long to figure out that the owners were worrying about Number One, not about the league. As a result, contract-jumping was common, both in the early leagues and later. The leagues had a standard contract that included a reserve clause binding the player to the same club the following season, similar to the one used in organized baseball. All players on league clubs were supposed to sign a contract, and in fact almost all of them did. Bill Yancey, who played with several league teams, recalled:

> They were regular contracts. But we didn't pay much attention to them. You signed up for a year. All right, you played that year but if you felt like jumping the next year, you jumped. There was a reserve clause in it, but it was disregarded; that's the reason I played for so many clubs. If I was unhappy I said the hell with this and I jumped.

Many players did not wait for the end of the season to jump from one team to another. Particularly during the sporadic wars between eastern and western leagues in the mid-1920s and the late 1930s, players shuttled back and forth between East and West seeking the best deal for themselves. Clubowners often wrangled over ownership of a player, but jumping was a two-way street. If Club A lured away one of the stars of Club B, obviously the proper response was for B to take one of A's stars. As a rule, peace was restored in the league family on the basis of you-scratch-my-back-and-I'll-scratch-yours.

When a player war had run its course and several owners had been badly hurt, an accommodation would be reached between leagues, but it rarely included return of the jumpers. This could be costly to a clubowner who wanted to get a jumper back. In 1925, for example, the Kansas City Monarchs of the National League had to trade Oscar (Heavy) Johnson, a hard-hitting infielder-outfielder, to the Baltimore Black Sox to get back outfielder Wade Johnston, who had jumped to Baltimore during the war of 1924.

A few players had no contracts at all, if, as sometimes happened, the club was living on hope alone. Jimmie Crutchfield, an outfielder who became one of the stars of the powerful Pittsburgh Crawfords, said that in 1931 he had only a verbal agreement with the Indianapolis ABCs. The ABCs were barely making expenses and

> we weren't being paid. That would go on maybe for two months till we had a good gate. Then perhaps you got some of your back pay. Maybe one or two of the fellows would be getting something under the table, but most of us weren't being paid. So we were going to Pittsburgh to play, and when we got there the Crawfords gave me $25 or $50, so I stayed. That's how I went to the Pittsburgh Crawfords.

The problem of players jumping from club to club plagued all the major leagues throughout their existence; while it was not condoned by the owners, it was accepted as a hazard of the business. Much more serious from their viewpoint were raids that took players out of the country. A boys-will-be-boys attitude could be sustained when a player jumped from one club to another in the Negro leagues; it was, after all, within the family. But when entrepreneurs from Latin America enticed American Negro stars, it was another matter entirely, because their loss was felt not only by their clubs but by the whole league.

Black players had played winter ball in Cuba and other Latin countries long before Negro leagues began, but they had always returned to the United States for the baseball season here. In 1937, however, Satchel Paige led a contingent of Americans to the Dominican Republic for the summer in the first serious exodus from the country during the regular season. Nine of the eighteen stars who were lured to Santo Domingo that year were from the Crawfords, and their leaving wrecked the club. The Crawfords stumbled on for several more years, playing in Toledo and Indianapolis, but they were never again a power in Negro baseball.

A few years later, Mexico was the mecca for black ballplayers, and many stars, including Josh Gibson, spent several summers as well as winters there. Immediately after World War II, when Jorge Pasquel was waving the big peso in front of white major-leaguers as well as blacks, Negro league players were like so many Mexican jumping beans in their haste to get over the border. White big-leaguers like Mickey Owen, Danny Gardella, and Tommy De La Cruz may have been the names captured in Pasquel's forays into Norte Americano, but the heart of his Mexican League was its Negro contingent, American and Cuban.

The Latin lure was, of course, money. Baseball-mad Mexico was willing to double or triple the salaries players were earning in the Negro leagues. There was another attraction, too—an unaccustomed freedom. Willie Wells, who over a span of twenty years was the best shortstop in Negro baseball, commented while he was playing in Mexico,

> Some people look at my situation simply from the standpoint of money. But there is more to it than that. In the first place, I am not faced with the racial problem in Mexico. When I travel with the Vera Cruz team, we live in the best hotels, we eat in the best restaurants, and can go anyplace we care to. . . . Players on teams in the Mexican League live just like big-leaguers.

The Negro leagues reacted to the threat of ruin from abroad in characteristic fashion, enacting bans ranging from one to five years against jumpers and then failing to enforce them when the players returned. If a player was unhappy in Latin America, he might rejoin his old club in midseason and any talk of outlawing him for a period from league play was promptly forgotten because, as the players well knew, the leagues needed them more than they needed the leagues.

During the Mexican League madness, Negro stars who stayed behind also profited from the Latin threat. They found they could hold

up the owners of league clubs for considerably more money by re-
minding them of the welcome awaiting them South of the Border.
This threat, plus the fact that during World War II attendance in the
Negro leagues soared on the wings of prosperity, pushed salaries to
previously unheard of levels. An average player during and immediately after the war might make $400 or $500 a month, and a star of
the magnitude of Buck Leonard could command $1,000 a month—
a far cry from the $150 to $200 that was common during the early
days of the Negro leagues.

By 1945 the organized Negro leagues had reached a plateau of
stability and efficiency unknown to the early leagues. For three years,
each league had had only one franchise change. Attendance was excellent, most clubs were prospering, player salaries were good, and
schedules were completed as advertised.

The story of their decline properly belongs to a later chapter, but
before leaving the subject of organized Negro baseball, two adjuncts
should be mentioned. One was the Negro World Series, which usually was not much more than a glorified barnstorming tour and
never developed even proportionally the appeal of the white major-
league Series; the other was the annual East-West game, an all-star
contest that became the biggest Negro sports event of the year.

Eleven World Series were played over the three decades of Negro
major league operations. The first four were from 1924 through 1927
when Foster's Negro National League and the Eastern Colored

Scene at the first Negro World Series in 1924. Photo was taken before fifth game at Kansas City's Muehlenbach Park. COURTESY OF BILL YANCEY

League were operating. The other seven belong to the era of the 1940s and pitted the second National League against the Negro American League.

World Series games were not especially big draws. In the first Series, in 1924, for example, when the Kansas City Monarchs, National League champions, defeated Hilldale, the Eastern League's winner, 5 games to 4, total attendance was 45,857. And that was for *ten* games, one a tie game called because of darkness after thirteen innings. One Series game, at Baltimore, attracted only 584 fans, and the deciding game, played in Chicago, drew only 1,549. During the regular season, Kansas City could expect to attract 10,000 for a Sunday doubleheader against the American Giants.

The Monarchs and Hilldale staged a repeat the next year, with Hilldale winning, 5 games to 1. Attendance averaged less than 4,000 a game. For the 1926 series, it was even worse, with crowds of under 2,000 a game for a Series in which the Chicago American Giants beat the Bacharach Giants of Atlantic City, 5 games to 3. Frank A. Young of the *Chicago Defender,* calling the Series a "joke," wrote in 1926 that "the ballplayers would rather barnstorm against the big-leaguers or other league clubs than to win a league championship to enter a world series as handled the past three years." He noted that for the 1925 Series, the world champion Hilldale players made only about $80 for the 12 days the Series lasted; the losing Monarchs got $57.64 each. Although when the World Series was resumed during the 1940s and the players could expect a good deal more, it was never much more attractive than a barnstorming tour with major-leaguers would be.

Only one of the eleven World Series was played entirely in the home cities of the contesting teams; that was in 1925, when the six games were played in Philadelphia and Kansas City. Usually four or five cities were covered. The record for a wandering World Series was set in 1943, when the Homestead Grays defeated the Birmingham Black Barons, 4 games to 3, in six cities: Washington, Chicago, Columbus, Indianapolis, Birmingham, and Montgomery, Alabama.

Joke or not, the World Series did have the virtue of establishing an undisputed champion of Negro baseball. And so, for the record, here are the winners: 1924, Kansas City Monarchs; 1925, Hilldale; 1926 and 1927, Chicago American Giants; 1942, Kansas City Monarchs; 1943 and 1944, Homestead Grays; 1945, Cleveland Buckeyes; 1946, Newark Eagles; 1947, New York Cubans, and 1948, Homestead Grays (the reader will find fuller details in Appendix A).

Overshadowing the World Series, and, in fact, every other Negro sports event, was the East-West Game, which brought together the greatest stars in Negro baseball. It was a production worthy of the major leagues and never attracted less than 20,000 fans; in 1943, the East-West game drew 51,723, the biggest crowd ever to attend a Negro sports event up to that time. It was played each year at Comiskey Park, home of the Chicago White Sox. (In 1946 a second East-West game was played at Griffith Stadium in Washington.)

The East-West game had a twofold importance for Negro baseball: first, it was a showcase for black talent, the one occasion when the white press took notice of the players of major-league talent who were destined to obscurity; and second, it was a financial boon to clubs with insecure financing. Many teams depended upon their share of the East-West game receipts to pay off their players and give them a small reserve with which to open the next season.

Gus Greenlee fathered the East-West game, promoting the first one in 1933 in cooperation with Robert A. Cole of the American Giants. The idea for the game came from Roy Sparrow, one of Greenlee's employes, who dreamed it up in 1932, the year before the first major-league all-star game, which was played in Chicago under the auspices of the *Chicago Tribune*. Greenlee handled the promotion and took ten percent of the East-West game receipts until he had a falling out with the other owners and resigned the presidency of the National League in 1939. There was grumbling about that ten percent and also about the five percent Abe Saperstein got for several years for handling publicity for the East-West game. For the first few years the players got nothing extra for appearing, and once a strike was threatened. It did not materialize, and during the 1940s, players chosen for the East-West game got from $100 to $200 each out of the gate.

Except for one or two years, players for the East-West game were elected by the fans, with the result that often the lineups were heavily loaded with players from the home cities of the *Chicago Defender* and *Pittsburgh Courier,* the biggest Negro papers. In the first game in 1933, seven of the nine West players were from the Chicago American Giants and nine of the fourteen men on the East team were stars on the Pittsburgh Crawfords and Homestead Grays. Eligibility was not restricted to league teams when there was only one league; in fact, in that first game only three teams represented *were* in the single operating league that year—the Negro National League. They were the Crawfords, the American Giants, and the Nashville Elite Giants. The other teams that sent players to the East-West game were the nonleague Philadelphia Stars, the Grays, the New York Black Yankees, and the Cleveland Giants.

Later, when the Negro National and American leagues were fairly well stabilized, the East's players came from the NNL and the West's from the NAL. [Boxscores of all East-West games are in Appendix B.]

Negro league baseball was not confined solely to the major circuits covered in this chapter. After 1920 there were several leagues, most of them in the South and a bit above the semipro level. The first and most important was the Negro Southern League, which was organized in 1920, one month after Rube Foster's Negro National League. It operated sporadically through the Forties. The Southern League was generally regarded as a minor league, but it never had an agreement with any of the major circuits. In fact, there was occasional friction when clubs from the major leagues approached its players. Like the major circuits, the makeup of the Southern League varied from year to year, but franchises were usually held by the Atlanta Black Crackers, New Orleans Crescent Stars, Montgomery Grey Sox, Jacksonville Red Caps and the Memphis Red Sox, Birmingham Black Barons, and Nashville Elite Giants until the latter three clubs joined the western major league.

From 1929 to 1931, two other leagues were centered in the South. One was the Texas-Oklahoma-Louisiana League, with teams in

Shreveport, Dallas, Houston, Tulsa, San Antonio, Oklahoma City, Fort Worth, and Wichita Falls. The other was made up of small towns in Kentucky and western Tennessee. Both leagues succumbed to the Depression. In the late 1930s, there was a Midwest League composed of teams from small cities and another, the Negro International League, in Virginia and the Carolinas.

Some inkling of the financial picture of black baseball at this level may be gleaned from these facts about the Southern League, the top "minor" circuit, in 1936. A league franchise cost $100, the weekday guarantee for a visiting club was $25, the Sunday guarantee was $50, and the rain guarantee was $12.50. It would appear that Southern League clubs were operating on about $200 a week, out of which came transportation costs, meals, and the salaries of fourteen players. Out of the hard-scrabble life of the Southern League with its rickety parks, its hot-dog breakfasts, and its bedding down in the bleachers at the ballpark when the club had no money for even a fifth-rate hotel came some of the great names of Negro baseball: men like Satchel Paige, Mule Suttles, and Turkey Stearns.

If a player could survive the Southern League, it was all downhill in big-time black baseball.

8 RUBE FROM TEXAS

*Rube Foster is a pitcher with the tricks
of a Rusie and with the coolness and
deliberation of a Cy Young. What does
that make him? Why, the greatest
pitcher in the country; that is what the
greatest baseball players of white persuasion that have gone against him say.*
—CHICAGO INTER-OCEAN, *1907*

If the talents of Christy Mathewson, John McGraw, Ban Johnson,
and Judge Kenesaw Mountain Landis were combined in a single
body, and that body were enveloped in a black skin, the result would
have to be named Andrew (Rube) Foster. As an outstanding
pitcher, a colorful and shrewd field manager, and the founder and

Rube Foster in 1924. COURTESY OF WILLIE FOSTER

stern administrator of the first viable Negro league, Foster was the most impressive figure in black baseball history. From about 1911 until 1926, he stood astride Negro baseball in the Midwest with unchallenged power, a friend of major-league leaders, and the best-known black man in Chicago.

Rube Foster was an unlettered genius who combined generosity and sternness, the superb skills of a dedicated athlete and an unbounded belief in the future of the black baseball player. His life was baseball. Had he chosen otherwise, baseball would have been the poorer.

He came out of Texas shortly after the turn of the century as a crude pitcher of obvious potential. Within a few years, by studious application to the intricacies of baseball, he was perhaps the most accomplished hurler in the game. From then until he was struck by mental illness in 1926, his fame and power soared.

Foster was born September 17, 1879, in Calvert, Texas, a farming-center village southeast of Waco. His father, Andrew, was the presiding elder of Calvert's Methodist Episcopal Church, and Foster carried a Puritan heritage into manhood. He never drank and never allowed intoxicants in his house, although he tolerated drinking elsewhere by others.

Even as a youth, Foster showed promise as organizer and administrator, operating a baseball team in Calvert while he was still in grade school. He quit Calvert's Negro school after the eighth grade to try to make a living at baseball. By 1897, when he was seventeen years old, Foster was the righthanded pitching ace of the traveling Waco Yellow Jackets, whose territory was Texas and its bordering states. Touring with the Yellow Jackets was no bed of roses for the minister's son. Many times, he said later, the players "were barred away from homes . . . as baseball and those who played it were considered by Colored as low and ungentlemanly."

Baseball was taking root in the growing black community in Chicago at about this time, and Foster was first noticed by clubs from a big city while the Yellow Jackets were playing in Hot Springs, Arkansas. In the spring of 1902, W. S. Peters, owner of the Chicago Unions, invited Foster to join them. Young Foster agreed but, because Peters sent no money for transportation, he stayed home. At the same time, Frank C. Leland, a veteran on the Chicago baseball scene, was forming the Chicago Union Giants to challenge the Unions, and he also invited Foster, warning him that he would be put to a severe test, because the Union Giants intended to play all the good white clubs.

Foster wrote back, "If you play the best clubs in the land, white clubs, as you say, it will be a case of Greek meeting Greek. I fear nobody." And so, packing a pistol in the best Texas tradition, Rube Foster went north, brash, big (he stood 6 feet 4 inches tall and weighed well over 200 pounds), with unlimited confidence in his strong right arm.

He pitched a shutout in his first game for the Union Giants but was not especially impressive later during a barnstorming trip, according to a teammate, Dave Wyatt. In midseason, Foster and Wyatt quit the Union Giants to join a white semipro team in Otsego, Michigan. He was no worldbeater with that club either. Wyatt, who became a sportswriter after leaving baseball, said that Foster lost the first five games he pitched for Otsego. "But I told them that Foster was just a wild young fellow right out of Texas, and if they would give me a chance to smooth the rought spots down he would yet surprise them." Evidently Wyatt was successful in the smoothing operation, because Foster subsequently defeated all the clubs in the white Michigan State League.

He could not, however, take the measure of the Big Rapids, Michigan, Negro team, which was made up of former stars of the old Page Fence Giants of Adrian, Michigan, perhaps the strongest club in the Midwest during the late 1890s. "Foster would engage in personalities while pitching," Wyatt said, "and they always took him for a ride. Foster had a reputation as a gunman and was never seen without his Texas pistol. All the colored players formed a decided dislike for Foster and declared he couldn't pitch."

When Otsego's season ended, Foster headed East and joined the Cuban X Giants, the best of the eastern black teams, in Zanesville, Ohio. "At that time, he had as much speed as Amos Rusie and a very good curve ball," according to Giant manager E. B. Lamar Jr. But in his first game in the New York City area, when he was pitted against Hoboken, one of the best white semipro clubs in the East, he suffered a 13–0 lacing. "He depended on his windup and speed to win games," Lamar explained years later. "Foster thought he knew more than anyone else and would take that giant windup with men on bases. They ran wild and that taught Rube a lesson. From then on he made a study of the game, and every chance he got he would go out to the big-league parks and watch the big clubs in action."

Foster learned quickly and the next season he was the best pitcher in black baseball. The brashness was gone, but the confidence was still there, and he won 4 of the Cuban X Giants' 5 victories in a series against the Philadelphia Giants for the 1903 "colored championship of the world." The next year, Foster jumped to the Philadelphia Giants and led them to the title, earning both of the Philadelphia club's victories in a three-game series against the Cuban X Giants. He struck out 18 batters in the first game and pitched a two-hitter in the third; Foster also led Philadelphia at bat in that series with a .400 average.

When he was uncertain that his fastball and curve were sharp enough to get out of a tough inning, Rube Foster relied on his brains. Dave Malarcher, third baseman on Foster's American Giants during the 1920s and his successor as manager, remembers a story Rube told about those days with the Philadelphia Giants. Malarcher said:

> They were playing one of the big white teams, and Topsy Hartsel was on it; he was a great hitter then. Rube was pitching, and he was beating everybody in the East.
>
> Hartsel was at the bat, three men on the bases, and Rube's team is leading the white boys. So Rube calls out his catcher, James Booker, and says, "Now you stand out of the box like I'm going to walk him—like I'm afraid of Hartsel and I'm going to walk him. And then I'm going to throw the fast one right through the middle. So you be ready."
>
> Rube went back, and Booker stood out of the box, and then Rube cut loose with his fastball, right through the middle. And Booker jumped over and caught it. The umpire says, "Strike one!"
>
> Everybody in the grandstand was saying, "What's going on?" Then Rube goes back to the box and he throws over to first base several times. And then he throws to second base and then he walks around a while. He fools around so long that people in the grandstand started hollering, "Make the big smoke pitch! Make him pitch!" Rube was working on Hartsel, see? So then he calls out Booker and says, "The same thing again." So Booker goes back and steps out of the catcher's box and calls to Rube, "Be sure this time!" And Rube cuts loose with his fast one again, right down the middle! Strike two!
>
> Rube figured he couldn't fool Hartsel that way the last time. So he goes back to the box and stalls around a little more. He was quite a showman, you know. Then he gets in the box and he looks at Hartsel. Hartsel's rarin', because he's got those two strikes on him.
>
> Then Rube calls, "Look out, ump, he's standin' on the plate!" Hartsel looked down, and as he looked down—right through the middle with it! That was it! O, he was marvelous.

It was during this period that the nickname "Rube" was attached to the young pitcher. Legend has it that his teammates began calling him Rube after he defeated George E. (Rube) Waddell and the Philadelphia Athletics, 5–2, in a game in New York. The name stuck. On Negro National League letterheads, and on his tombstone, which he himself chose long before his death, he is A. R. (for Andrew Rube) Foster.

The Philadelphia Giants had been formed in 1902 by Sol White and H. Walter Schlichter, a white sportswriter for the *Philadelphia Item*. They played second fiddle to the Cuban X Giants until Foster joined them and provided the pitching strength to tip the balance. Also on the club were several of the legendary figures of black baseball, plus Jack Johnson, who became heavyweight boxing champion in 1908. Johnson played first base in 1903 and 1904. By 1906 the Giants were without question the strongest black team in the country, boasting stars like shortstop Grant (Home Run) Johnson, outfielder Pete Hill, second baseman Charlie Grant (John McGraw's "Tokohoma"), and pitcher Dan McClellan.

But, Foster said later, "The whole team was making only $100 out of Sunday games and a proportionate amount for other games. In spite of the fact that we were the best colored team in baseball, that was all Walter Schlichter, the owner, could or would do for us." At the end of the 1906 season, eight of the Giants, led by Foster, decided to go West.

Joining the Leland Giants of Chicago in 1907, they found the pickings there just as lean. Frank C. Leland, proprietor of the Giants, could command only $150 for a July 4 doubleheader. Foster's native business acumen was outraged by such paltry finances, so he persuaded Leland to let him do the booking and immediately demanded forty percent for the club. "After some argument," Foster said, "we got it and made over $500 that day instead of the piffling $150. From then on, every team Rube Foster played on got a fifty-fifty split of the gate until the formation of the Negro National League."

During his three seasons with the Leland Giants, Foster pitched against a major-league club for the last time. In a post-season game in 1909, he lost to the Chicago Cubs, 6–5, when the Cubs staged a ninth-inning rally good for 4 runs. On this occasion, his war-of-nerves strategy backfired; the winning run was scored by Joe Tinker while Foster, the umpires, and some Cubs were in an argument that began when the Cubs accused him of stalling. The Leland Giants played two other games against the Cubs that October, losing both,

4–1 and 1–0. Both times the winning pitcher was Mordecai (Three-Finger) Brown, who, like Tinker, is in baseball's Hall of Fame.

In 1910, Foster was managing the Leland Giants. It appears that he and Frank C. Leland had a falling out, because in April of that year, Leland was managing the Chicago Giants and had gone to court to try to restrain Foster from using the name "Leland Giants." He was unsuccessful, and Foster's 1910 Leland Giants, whom Rube later called the greatest team ever assembled, black or white, finished the season with a record of 123 victories and 6 losses. The club included Frank Wickware, Pat Dougherty, Bruce Petway, Pete Hill, John Henry Lloyd, and Home Run Johnson, all of whom are often mentioned among the all-time greats of Negro baseball.

With his first experience in field and business management behind him, in 1911 Rube Foster was ready to embark upon his career as magnate as well as player and manager. His partner was John M. Schorling, a white tavern-owner who had been operating sandlot clubs in Chicago for several years. Schorling had leased the grounds of the old White Sox park on 39th Street after the White Sox moved north to 35th Street to occupy their new stadium. The White Sox had torn down their old grandstand before leaving, so Schorling built a new one, a wooden stand with bleachers, seating about 9,000. He then approached Foster with an offer of partnership. "When he wanted me," Foster declared, "he said, 'I am fixing to invest lots of money in baseball. I want you with me. Name the terms.' I told him. He said, 'If that's what you want you must be worth it.' That was our last business talk." Foster and Schorling agreed verbally on a fifty-fifty split of receipts. In an association that lasted until Foster's hospitalization in 1926, they never had a disagreement over money, but the lack of a written contract is an unaccountable lapse in a man of Foster's shrewdness.

And so in 1911 the American Giants were born, and the signs were auspicious. They had the most of the best players from the Leland Giants. They had Foster, probably the best field manager in black baseball and still a formidable pitcher. And they had a sound financial base. Under Foster's leadership, the American Giants quickly became the most famous independent team in the Midwest, the idols of Chicago's black community, and the envy of other clubowners. On one Sunday in their first season, they drew 11,000 fans, more than either the Cubs or White Sox that day. The dropout from a segregated southern grade school was soon dealing in hundreds of thousands of dollars with equanimity. Rube Foster became the respected and trusted friend of major-league managers, especially of John McGraw, who often dropped by to talk baseball and watch the American Giants, He was the darling of Negro baseball fans; he returned their favor by addressing everyone, male or female, as "Darlin," in his Texas drawl.

Foster played fairly regularly until about 1915. After that he put himself into games only occasionally, sometimes as a first baseman. When his playing days ended he was still one of the American Giants' major attractions, because he was a dominant figure even while on the bench. Many fans came out to watch him, as well as the game. And they were not disappointed. An inveterate pipe-smoker, Rube sometimes sat on the bench and gave signs with his pipe.

"One day he'd take his pipe out of his mouth for a steal, or motion this way with his hand," said Floyd (Jelly) Gardner, who starred in the outfield for the American Giants beginning in 1920. "Most of the time he'd give signs with his head, like he'd be talking with some people and he'd nod his head a certain way and that would be a sign. Sometimes he'd give signs by puffing on his pipe— a couple of puffs might mean steal."

Like many colorful white baseball stars of his time, Rube Foster even tried a vaudeville turn. In 1919 he was on the Klein circuit, appearing in Columbus, Ohio, with an act evidently based on baseball. Cary B. Lewis of the *Chicago Defender* described Rube's short-lived theatrical career thus:

> When he approached the middle of the stage, a voice sang out from the audience, "Take him out!" Uncle Rube mistook the occasion and thought he was on the ballfield. He forgot the footlights and approached the audience in a manner similar to one when he was manning the Giants. He forthwith stepped directly into the band pit, plunged through the bass drum, doing $200 damage to the drummer's outfit. Rube returned to Chicago the next morning.

Arthur W. Hardy, who pitched for Foster in Cuba in 1910, remembers Rube as stern but fair:

> I wouldn't call him reserved, but he wasn't free and easy. You see, Rube was a natural psychologist. Now he didn't know what psychology was and he probably couldn't spell it, but he realized that he couldn't fraternize and still maintain discipline. Rube was a strict disciplinarian. He wasn't harsh, but he was

strict. His dictums were not unreasonable, but if you broke one he'd clamp down on you. If he stuck a fine on you, you paid it—there was no appeal from it. He was dictatorial in that sense.

Rube Foster was indeed a practicing psychologist, and he sometimes made his point in parables with roots in his memory of boyhood in a Texas farming village. If one of Foster's players was giving less than his best, Dave Malarcher said, Rube would tell him this little story:

Once there was a donkey and an ox that were teamed to work on a farm. They worked hard, and one day the ox decided to stay in his stall and take a rest. So he did. When the donkey came back to the barn that night after work, the ox asked, "What did the boss say about me?" "Didn't say nothing," the donkey replied. So the next day the ox decided he'd stay in his stall all day again and eat, and he did. When the donkey came back that night, the ox asked again, "What did the boss say?" "Didn't say nothing," the donkey answered, "but he visited the butcher." Well, the next day the ox came out bright and early and backed right into the traces. The farmer told him, "You might as well stay in the stall." "Oh, no," said the ox, "I'm ready to go today." And the farmer said, "You might as well stay, because I've sold you to the butcher."

Malarcher said this tale had an energizing effect on any of Foster's ballplayers who had a tendency toward casualness on the field.

As a field manager, Rube Foster manipulated his players like robots. In a close game, pitchers were signaled what to pitch and where, and even with what motion. Batters were often instructed to take two strikes before swinging to tire the opposing pitcher. Foster once explained his system thus:

If you let a player make the pitcher pitch four and five balls to him, he will tire around seven innings, and if you can hit him at the beginning you can hit him when he is weaker and less effective. It is at this point I always center my attack. In most cases it is successful. On the other hand, if you allow your players to make a few runs at the beginning of the game they become careless. Should these few runs be overtaken they are in most cases beaten. That is why I vary my attack in the field. . . .

He was a strong advocate of the bunt and the steal, and his players were expected to be adept at both. A player literally had to be able to bunt the ball into a hat to play for Rube Foster. He developed to a high art the hit-and-run bunt in which the runner on first raced for second on the pitch and went on to third as the play was made at first on the bunter.

Foster brooked no disobedience to his orders. Earl M. Foster, Rube's son, remembers, "One time Jelly Gardner was sent up to bunt and he tripled. He came back and sat down on the bench. The old man took that pipe he smoked—he always had it—and he popped him right across the head. And he fined him and told him, 'As long as I'm paying you, you'll do as I tell you to do.' "

In the view of Dave Malarcher, Foster was the greatest manager of all time, black or white. In what respect was he better than his big-league contemporaries, John McGraw and Connie Mack?

Malarcher explains:

> In that he directed his team wholly, and he made the kind of plays they didn't make. For example, I say that Ty Cobb was the only white ballplayer that we observed who played somewhat like we played on the American Giants. None of the teams in the major leagues in those years—and up to now—really concentrated their attack against the opposition. The batters come up and they swing away and okay, it's a double play or a triple play—or a home run. But so often they fail.
>
> Now one of the things Rube taught was that you win the ball game in one or two innings, you don't win it over a long period. Once in a while, you'll see a game when they make one or two runs in the first inning, two more later, and so forth, but in most cases the game is won in one rally. That means when you get the opportunity to win it, you'd better win it now and not throw it away by doing the wrong thing.
>
> Here's what Rube said: "*Now* is the time." Rube used to say—and I followed it when I became a manager, "You don't have to get three hits every day for me. You don't have to get even two. But I want one at the *right* time."
>
> Now I'm a small man and I couldn't hit the ball to the fences, but I became a good hitter in the pinches because that

was our principle: *Now* is the time, and when you're in the crisis you must deliver. Rube used to say, "You must hit that ball, and you must hit it hard where I want it hit." And that's what we attempted to do.

And so I developed this strategy against pitchers: I became a very good waiter. If I went to bat with nobody on the bases, I never hit anything but the third strike—I never hit at the first nor the second. But when I came up with men on the bases, I hit the first good thing that came in there because of Rube's principle, "Now is the time." Why? Because when I came to bat with men on the bases, the pitcher would figure I was going to wait anyway and he would give me that pitch right down the middle, belt high, and that's when I would hit it. So that's why I was called a great clutch hitter. It wasn't because I was a great hitter at all; it was because they pitched good balls to me at the times I really needed to hit.

Foster was feared and respected by his players and was on the whole a generous and benevolent employer, but he did have occasional troubles. In 1921, for example, he was traveling through the South with his club when he was taken off the train in Atlanta and arrested on a complaint by several players that he owed them money. After putting up $500 bond, Foster continued his trip. The wage dispute apparently was settled amicably.

Two years later, there was grumbling among the American Giant players that they weren't getting enough money. Some players wrote letters to newspapers hinting that the reason the American Giants didn't win the Negro National League pennant that year was that they weren't paid enough. Foster indignantly produced contracts showing that the lowest-paid player earned $175 a month from May to October 1, an excellent wage for black ballplayers of that time. Furthermore, he said, his men always got bonuses, some as high as $3,000 a season.

During their early years the American Giants played all over the country, although most of their regular-season games were in Chicago. For long trips they traveled in big-league style, renting a private railroad car. During winter they often were on the Pacific Coast or in Florida. Usually they made one trip East during the summer, except for the five years between 1914 and 1919 when the antipathy between Foster and Nat Strong, the white booking agent who controlled the schedules of most eastern black teams, was at its height.

Foster was becoming a booking power in the Midwest by this time; the peace between these two lords of black baseball was best maintained when each stayed in his own fief.

When the American Giants did go East in 1919 it was by necessity rather than choice. They were in Detroit in August when a race riot ripped Chicago, leaving twenty-three Negroes and fifteen whites dead. They were due to come home to play the Bacharach Giants on August 3, but their park was occupied by soldiers and so the American Giants traveled East for games.

That fall, Foster began his campaign through the pages of the *Chicago Defender* for an organization of Negro clubs—in effect, for the formation of one or two Negro leagues. The evidence is scanty, but in view of his emphasis on the need to end player raids as the best reason for leagues, it appears that some of the eastern clubs must have tried to raid his club on that trip. In any case, he made much of the need for owners to cooperate rather than cut each other's throats in player raids. He also foresaw the possibility that the champion of the black leagues might play the winner of the white major leagues in a real world series.

It is impossible to say whether his motives extended beyond the altruistic aims he outlined. There were skeptics. Among them was Al Monroe, who wrote in 1932, two years after Foster's death, that his real goal had been to enlarge his hegemony over Negro baseball in the Chicago area to a much greater range. "He was determined to extend his booking agency as far west as Kansas City and as far south as Birmingham, and the only way to perform this miracle was to form a Race baseball league," Monroe wrote in *Abbot's Monthly*. The sportswriter added that the NNL's constitution gave Foster the power to tell any club in the league where it should play, regardless of the schedule, and that all balls, bats, and uniforms must be purchased through him.

Monroe said that Foster's power over league clubs went beyond their finances. "Many a time have I sat in his offices and observed him direct managers in other cities of the league as to the proper pitchers to assign to certain games. No star twirler was used to the limit before a small Saturday crowd, with prospects of a good Sunday attendance, while Rube was bossing baseball."

Another view was articulated by Frank A. Young, who was for many years the *Chicago Defender's* sports editor. He saw Rube Foster's purpose in forming the league as an effort to keep Nat Strong from controlling all Negro baseball. Young feared that Strong eventually might dominate black baseball all across the country as he did in the East.

Also in defense of Foster is the opinion of Dave Malarcher. "Rube Foster was too great and too big a man to stoop to petty and selfish ambition such as perpetuating a booking agency," Malarcher says.

Whatever his motives, Rube Foster worked long and hard to keep the young Negro National League afloat. His son Earl remembers that more often than not Rube was in his office from eight-thirty every morning until eleven or twelve o'clock at night, with breaks for lunch and supper at home, during the time he was running both the American Giants and the league.

He had ambitious plans. Earl said that in 1926 his father met with John McGraw and Ban Johnson, president of the American League, to concoct an agreement by which the American Giants would play any big-league club which had an off-day in Chicago. The plan never reached fruition because soon afterward Rube Foster, perhaps driven by overwork, was committed to a state mental institution at Kankakee, Illinois.

"What his trouble was I don't know, but he was off and he never did get back to normal," Earl Foster said. "It could have been a borderline case. He wasn't dangerous or anything like that, but he couldn't be at home. Sometimes he'd recognize you and sometimes he wouldn't."

Foster spent the last four years of his life in the mental hospital while his beloved Negro National League skidded precipitously toward oblivion. His failure to make a written contract with his partner, John Schorling, cost his wife dearly. She was completely ignorant of his business arrangements and realized nothing from the club he had built. Schorling ran the American Giants until the spring of 1928, when he sold the club to a white florist, William E. Trimble, charging that he had been squeezed out because other owners conspired to keep the best teams away from Chicago. During the early 1930s, under the leadership of two Chicago Negro businessmen, Robert A. Cole and Horace G. Hall, and later under Dr. J. B. Martin, the American Giants reached some semblance of their former glory but they were never again the powerhouse they had been under their founder.

Andrew Rube Foster died on December 9, 1930. Baseball men, remembering their debt to him, sent impressive floral pieces to the funeral. The NNL's directors offered a 200-pound baseball made of white chrysanthemums with roses for the seams. The American Giants Boosters Association sent a giant baseball diamond made of flowers with Foster's initials in the center and crossed bats and a ball above it. Thousands of Chicagoans viewed the body, and the congregation for the funeral service was estimated at 3,000.

Assessing Rube Foster's contributions to black baseball is easy. He was far and away the most important influence in raising the game to respectability, both artistic and financial. Although his league never achieved his dream of parity with the majors, it did provide a measure of stability and permanence to many black teams which, before him, had been little more than loosely organized groups of barnstormers.

Rube Foster's stature as a player is often forgotten by baseball men in the light of his accomplishments as a manager and league operator. Honus Wagner, who faced the best major-leaguers over a 21-year span, called him "one of the greatest pitchers of all time. He was the smartest pitcher I have ever seen in all my years of baseball." His view was echoed in 1939 by Pittsburgh Pirate coach Jewel Ens, who said, "Foster pitched with his brains as well as his arm. He never did the wrong thing. Rube Foster would have been a sensation in the big leagues."

He would indeed. Rube Foster: pitcher, manager, league president, major league in everything but name.

9 ON THE FIELD AND OFF

Oliver Marcelle—the Ghost, we called him. He was out of Louisiana. What got him out of baseball, he and Frank Warfield had a fight in Cuba and Warfield bit his nose off. He was a proud, handsome guy, you know, and then he used to wear a black patch across his nose and he got so he couldn't play baseball anymore.
—BILL YANCEY

Negro baseball was baseball for keeps. It was tough on the field as well as off.

When two black clubs tangled, no quarter was asked and none was given. For a game against a white semipro team, a Negro club might clown a bit, perhaps switch positions, and to enliven the generally one-sided game, whip the ball all around the infield before retiring the batter at first on a hard-hit ground ball to third. A game against white semipros was a holiday after the rigors of a Negro league contest.

Prudent infielders wore shinguards as protection against flying spikes. Bill Yancey recalls:

We had these little felt things that went from your ankle up to your knee. Because some of them guys would jump on you trying to get safe. Now you see ballplayers sliding all around— you never see anybody getting spiked, and if they do it's an accident. But them guys would deliberately jump on you. Oh, rough!

Buck Leonard also remembers those small wars between infielder and baserunner: "Chaney White was one of those baserunners that a fella was afraid to tag," he said. "He came in pretty high. Oscar

116

Charleston did, too. They needed those shin guards with Charleston and Chaney White running."

Daring baserunning was always a feature of Negro baseball. The advent of Babe Ruth as a slugger of prodigious home runs changed the face of major-league baseball, bringing a souped-up, lively ball to meet the demands of the fans for longer drives, and with the lively ball came caution on the basepaths. Why risk being thrown out trying for an extra base when the next batter might well hit one into the seats?

While the baserunning art was languishing in the big leagues, it continued to flourish in the Negro leagues, although, said Buck Leonard, "we never did have a Ty Cobb. Cool Papa Bell was about the best, and he was over the hill when I came up."

Bell was a swift chop-hitter who played more than twenty years in the Negro leagues, and, when he was in his forties, he was still one

Cool Papa Bell, who may have been the fastest man ever to don spikes, in a characteristic scene at Griffith Stadium, Washington. Flagging him down at third base is veteran manager Candy Jim Taylor.

of the base-stealing leaders. Bill Yancey remembers Bell in his prime during the 1920s and early Thirties:

> I haven't seen anybody yet could run with Cool. When I was on the Lincoln Giants, we played in a little park in New York called the Catholic Protectory up in the Bronx. That was our regular home field. Judy Johnson had been telling me about this guy that came to Cuba every winter, and Judy told me, if this guy hits the ball on two hops on the ground you won't be able to throw him out from shortstop. Now I could throw, and I said nobody can outrun a baseball.
>
> So the first time Cool Papa came to New York with the St. Louis Stars, he hit a ball into right field. Chino Smith was out there, and he could field a ball, and if you made a wide turn at first base he could throw you out trying to hustle back. I went out to get the throw, and when I looked up Cool Papa was slowing up going into third. And I said to myself, That sonofagun didn't touch second. Next time up he hit another one about the same place. Now, *nobody* got a three-base hit in that little park, I don't care where they hit the ball. And I watched this guy run. Well, he came across second base and it looked like his feet weren't touching the ground!
>
> And he never argued, never said anything. That was why they called him Cool Papa; he was a real gentleman.

Like infielders, pitchers fought a constant battle for survival. Because a Negro club played nearly every day with a small staff of pitchers, they were rarely rested; and so, many of them relied on guile when their arms were too weary to whip a real fastball or break off a curve. Spitballs, shine balls, and emery balls were among their weapons long after such trick pitches had been officially outlawed in the Negro leagues. According to Buck Leonard:

> We also had some fellas that did what we called cuttin' the ball. They'd put a little burr on the ball. Some of them used a pop-top—the top of a soda bottle—or some other player on the team had one, and they'd put a little burr on the ball with it. If the pitcher turned that little burr up and threw sidearm, the ball would go down. And if they turned that little burr down, the ball would go up. They were what we called cut-ball pitchers.

Roy Campanella, a Negro league veteran before he went on to become one of the greatest major-leaguers, put his experience in catching these trick deliveries to good use as a Brooklyn Dodger star. The Dodgers had a very effective lefthander during the early 1950s named Preacher Roe, who confessed—after his retirement— that his best pitch was a dipping, darting spitball. Roe told *Sports Illustrated* in 1955 that when he developed his spitter, Campanella expressed no concern about his ability to catch the unpredictable pitch. "I caught spitters in the Negro league for years," Campanella said. Roe continued:

> It didn't take me long to find out that Campy wasn't just bragging. He was great at catching it. He'd handle most of them just as smooth as if I was throwing a fastball. Once in a while, one of them would do a whole lot and get away from him. But Campy was always ready. He figured the umpire would ask for the ball, or the batter would call for the umpire to look at it. Campy'd toe the ball, sly, like, as he bent over to pick it up, and that would roll it dry. He'd do that if nobody was on base. If there were men on, he'd step on it, and grind it into the dirt, hard, like, where he could grab it if he had to.

Campanella earned his skill over nine seasons in Negro baseball, all but one of them with the Baltimore Elite Giants. (He spent the summer of 1943 in the Mexican League after jumping his contract with the Elite Giants.) Campanella had started playing for pay as a fifteen-year-old off Philadelphia's sandlots with the Bacharach Giants, which, in 1937, was a semipro club based in his home city. The original Bacharach Giants, one of the strongest teams of its era, had died in the Depression depths after the 1929 season.

Campanella's discovery by the Baltimore Elite Giants while he was with the Bacharachs was fairly typical. Young Negro ballplayers who lived in or near cities which the top clubs called home stood a good chance of being seen and invited to try out. But scouting was at best haphazard. If a young player was with an amateur or semipro club far from one of the league cities, his best hope for advancement was to have a good day when a big club barnstormed through his town. There were no paid scouts beating the bushes for talent, simply because there was no money for such frills.

Since the top Negro clubs did so much barnstorming and played so many games outside the league, it may seem unlikely that many good black players missed a chance to become full professionals for a lack of efficient scouting. But Buck Leonard, who was to become a nearly unchallenged choice as the all-time Negro first baseman, was twenty-five years old before he was seen by a big club.

He had been playing for years on the semipro sandlots around Rocky Mount, North Carolina, with only local recognition when he decided to go north. "I had almost given up baseball," Leonard said. "I had gotten too old to play around here. I had just about decided I wouldn't play anymore because twenty-five is a pretty good age around here on the semipro lots."

When a young player was invited for a trial with a big Negro club, he knew that he had to make good right away or it was back to the semipros. There was no place else to send him, for Negro clubs could not afford a farm system. Leonard recalled:

> We did have a farm team one year at Chattanooga, but it was just a semipro team. They were called the Chattanooga Black Lookouts. If we had a young boy who wasn't quite good enough for the Grays, we sent him there, but he wouldn't stay. Life in Negro baseball was tough. It was tough even in our league, and when you went down to that league it was tougher. They would try to pay a salary but they couldn't. So they would just give the player some money once in a while. We sent two players down there and both of them left and went home, said they couldn't make it. So we never did get any players from down there on the Grays.

As a rule, the big clubs in Negro baseball paid a guaranteed salary after about 1920. (Before that time, only a few were affluent enough to be certain of meeting a regular payroll.) But even during the Twenties and Thirties, some major teams paid their players on the "co-op plan." Under this system, the team owner took a certain percentage of the receipts after expenses had been paid and the players divided what remained.

Negro baseball, which always operated close to the vest, was very sensitive to the country's economic position, and particularly to the economic status of the Negro population. Salaries tended to follow closely the barometer of gate receipts. This is obviously also true for organized baseball (or any other business enterprise), but because most black clubs had a precarious financial standing to begin with, it was even truer for Negro baseball.

Satchel Paige was in a class by himself in the matter of finances, as in so many other respects. As Negro baseball's greatest attraction, Paige made from $30,000 to $40,000 annually during the boom years of segregated baseball. Trailing him, but by a considerable margin, was Josh Gibson, who was paid somewhat more than $1,-000 a month at his peak earning period during the early Forties. Satchel's secret was in his drawing power as a master showman as well as perhaps the best pitcher of his time. He was able to negotiate bonuses and special deals because the announcement that he was to appear in a game was worth an additional five to ten thousand spectators.

Such high finance was just a dream when the first stable Negro leagues were born in relative poverty during the early 1920s. Judy Johnson, who was destined to become one of the greatest Negro third basemen, was signed by the Hilldale Club in 1922 for $135 a month, an average salary for a young player at that time. By the late Twenties, the salary level had reached $250 a month for a good journeyman player on a Negro league club. Although this was paid only during the playing season of about six months, it put the ballplayer on an elite economic plane in the Negro community, espe cially since he could augment his earnings by playing ball all winter long in Florida, California, or Latin America.

In 1934, when the Negro National League was reorganized after its collapse in the Depression, salaries had dropped to the original scale. A promising rookie could expect to make $125 to $150 a month on one of the top clubs. At a time when millions of Americans were unemployed and when a good weekly wage for anyone, white or black, was $20 a week, this was big money.

Like their counterparts in organized baseball, Negro league players received expenses for board and lodging, at least while on the road. Buck Leonard remembers that this was handled differently on the two Pittsburgh clubs in 1934:

> On the Grays we had to pay our own expenses at home, and when we were on the road we were getting 60¢ a day on which to eat. Every morning they would give you 60¢—a half-dollar and a dime. And we could eat two good meals in 1934 with 60¢ Ham and eggs, toast, and coffee, cost you about 20-25¢; dinner would cost you about 30 or 35¢. So when we were on the road they paid our lodging in a hotel and gave us that 60¢. Now all of us maintained a room in Pittsburgh and later in Homestead when they made us move there because we weren't behaving ourselves in Pittsburgh. I was paying $6 a week for my room in Homestead. Sometimes we would leave Homestead and be gone three weeks, and when we got back I would still owe because I had kept the room.

Later on they went up to 75¢ a day for meal money, then a dollar, then they went to a dollar and a half per day, and the last year the Grays played in 1950 we were getting $2 a day on which to eat.

Now there were some fellas on the Pittsburgh Crawfords who used to get $80 a month, but they got their expenses at home *and* on the road. But with us, I was getting $125 but I had to pay my expenses while I was at home.

Hotels were almost universally segregated during Negro baseball's peak years, and so black ball clubs had to stop at Negro hotels, many of them aptly described as fleabags. Even this luxury was beyond the means of some Negro Southern League teams. Often players in that league spent the night sleeping in the ballpark where they were to play the next day, because the club had no money for any kind of lodging.

There were exceptions. The Monarchs of Monroe, Louisiana, lived fairly well due to the beneficence of the owner, a white drilling-company operator, J. C. Stovall. He built a fine ballpark with an adjoining swimming pool and dance pavilion for Monroe's Negroes because he felt that since he made his living in part from the city's black population it was only right that he offer them free recreation. Stovall also built a strong club, and the Monarchs were Negro baseball powers in the late Twenties and early Thirties. Their stadium was equal to most good minor-league fields of that time, and after the Negro club was disbanded the park was leased to the white Monroe team in the old Cotton States League, a Class-D circuit.

The playing fields of Negro baseball varied from sandlots in farm villages to major-league stadiums. When they were barnstorming, black teams played on whatever field their hosts offered, which, in a small town, might be a rock-strewn cow pasture or a miniature Yankee Stadium. For their home field, most of the big clubs rented a park, often one owned by a club in organized baseball.

One of the most successful teams, the Homestead Grays, never owned a park. Until 1937 they played their home games in Pittsburgh at either Greenlee Field, owned by Gus Greenlee, or at Forbes Field, home of the Pirates. Later they represented Washington as the Washington Homestead Grays and played three times a week at Griffith Stadium when the Senators were out of town.

As noted in Chapter 7, in 1921 the western Cuban Stars became the first regular tenants of a major-league team. Soon a number of black clubs were calling big-league parks home. Among the last of the major-league teams to succumb to the lure of Negro league dollars was the New York Yankees. It was not until June 1930 that the first Negro game was played in the storied confines of Yankee Stadium. The Lincoln Giants beat the Baltimore Black Sox in a benefit game for the Brotherhood of Sleeping Car Porters before 18,000 fans, a few of them whites. Colonel Jacob Ruppert, the Yankees' owner, permitted use of the stadium without charge for that game. The Yankees were not so generous in subsequent years, however, and by 1945 they were making $100,000 a year from rentals and concessions at the Stadium and their minor-league parks in Newark, Kansas City, and Norfolk, Virginia.

Rental of a big-league park by Negro teams was not always presumed to include use of the locker rooms and showers. Ted Page, an outfielder who played for several big clubs, remembers that often when they were to play in a big-league park, the players had to dress at their hotel or a YMCA.

Strong black clubs that owned their own parks (or had leases permitting use whenever they wanted) were obviously better off than renters, because they could control their schedules completely. One of these was the Hilldale Club, which had started as a boys' team in Darby, Pennsylvania, about 1910. By 1920 it had developed into a powerful club with a big following in the Philadelphia area. Ed Bolden, the business manager, incorporated the club, and with the proceeds of a stock sale he bought a field and built a wooden grandstand seating about 5,000. The Hilldale third baseman, Judy Johnson, remembers:

> We usually filled it. Mr. Bolden told me one Decoration Day that we had already made enough money to pay off our salaries for the rest of the year. So what we made from Decoration Day on was velvet.
>
> We had the best infield that the big-league players had ever played on—that's what they told us. The dirt—I don't know what it was, but it shone something like silver. And it could rain for an hour like everything and if you sat around for half an hour you couldn't see a bit of water anyplace. The dirt looked like ground isinglass. A ball would very seldom take a bad hop unless someone dug a hole with his spikes. You could just smooth it over and you wouldn't have any trouble.

The big-league boys always liked to come out there and play because they could make big money. They would never take a guarantee. They'd take sixty or forty percent—sixty for winning, forty for losing. They were willing to take it because of the crowds we were having. One year I remember we played the Athletics intact and the field was so crowded we had to have special ground rules. You couldn't get a home run unless the ball went out of the park, because the people were so crowded in the outfield. They were up so close the centerfielder was almost playing second base. That's a fact!

Most weekday games during the early years of Negro baseball were played in late afternoon or early evening so that fans who had worked all day could attend. When lighting systems were advanced to the point where it was possible to play night baseball, Negro clubs, due to economic necessity, were quick to exploit the lights. They found that while baseball under those primitive lights might be tough on the players, the fans would flock to see it.

Early lighting systems were portable and had to be set up for each game. Power was furnished by a generator run by a 250-horsepower engine housed in a truck that was parked in the far reaches of the outfield during the game. Trucks carried the light poles and banks of lights, three or four on a pole, from city to city.

Night baseball was often an engima to the spectators, because if the generator's engine coughed during the game, the lights dimmed until the outfielders were barely visible from home plate. The pitcher could not see his catcher's ordinary finger signs in the gloom, so special signals had to be developed based on the position of the catcher's mitt. To give batters at least an occasional glimpse of the ball, a big piece of canvas was stretched in centerfield to provide a light background in the blackness of full night beyond.

The Kansas City Monarchs had the first portable light system in Negro baseball in 1930. The Monarchs would often have a game in the afternoon and another at night, frequently in different towns. Three games a day were not unusual for the Monarchs when they took to the barnstorming trail with the portable lights in their van.

The Monarchs, who had won the Negro National League pennant in 1929, went East with their lights in July 1930 for a series with the Homestead Grays. Six night games were played in Pittsburgh and nearby small cities; the Grays won five of them including the first night game ever played at Forbes Field, an attraction that drew a crowd of more than 30,000. It was during this series, incidentally, that Josh Gibson made his debut as an eighteen-year-old catcher with the Grays.

In early August the Grays went West with the Monarchs to mine some more of the gold newly discovered in night baseball. The highlight of that trip was a twelve-inning pitcher's battle in Kansas City between the Grays' Smoky Joe Williams and the Monarchs' Chet Brewer in which there were 46 strikeouts.

Smoky Joe, who was fifty-four years old then, fanned 27 men and gave up only 1 hit in winning, 1–0. Brewer allowed 4 hits and struck out 10 men in a row beginning in the seventh inning.

As if the dim illumination weren't handicap enough for the batters, Williams and Brewer resorted to emery cloth to make the ball do tricks. Said the *Pittsburgh Courier:* "The opposing pitchers were cheating without a question of a doubt. An emery ball in daylight is very deceptive, but at night it is about as easy to see as an insect in the sky."

The Monarchs toured with their lights for several years, but, as lighting methods were improved, the vogue for night baseball led to permanent lights in many parks, particularly those used by minor-league and semipro clubs. By the late Thirties, most weekday games in the Negro leagues were being played at night. Sunday games, almost always doubleheaders, were played in daylight.

Spring training in Negro baseball was not the leisurely, slow-paced conditioning process, interspersed with intrasquad games, that big-leaguers enjoyed. On some Negro clubs, the day the players appeared at the training site was the day serious baseball began.

In his autobiography, *It's Good to Be Alive,* Roy Campanella says:

> Training in Nashville, or anyplace else with the Elites, was nothing like my Dodger days at Vero Beach. In the big leagues the first week and more is spent pretty much just loosening the winter kinks and getting your arms and legs in shape. But that's not how it was—ever—in the Negro leagues. No sooner did you pull on your uniform than you were in a game, playing before paying customers.
>
> *Play* yourself into shape! That was the only way the Negro leagues got on the ball. Man, we didn't just sop up sun and

orange juice and run laps and play "pepper" and listen to theory on the "pickoff play" those first few days after reaching camp. No sir—regular exhibition games with the hat being passed. And often as not, those old boys were hard as iron and limber as a rubber tube right from the gun. The reason for that was because they'd never stopped playing ball, really, from the season before!

Not all the Negro clubs had quite the rigorous spring-training schedule of the Elite Giants. The Homestead Grays, who usually trained in Orlando or Daytona, Florida, might spend five or six days getting in shape before beginning exhibition games. But once they started there was no stopping. They would barnstorm through the South, playing black clubs every day, always pointing toward Pittsburgh, or later, Washington, and arrive home about April 25, a few days ahead of the Negro leagues' opening day. Sometimes two Negro clubs would train in the same city for a few days and then barnstorm together up through the South, playing each other every day to defray expenses.

Bill Yancey recalls that he never went South at all. On the clubs he played with, the players trained for a week or two in the club's home city before beginning season's play.

> I've played in the snow flurries in the early spring. But, you see, I always played basketball and I was always in good shape; I never had to worry about getting into condition. And remember, most of the ballplayers would go to Cuba and play all winter and they'd come home and rest a while. They were in pretty good shape, because they were all good ballplayers and they could go places to play ball.

There was no time during spring training for instructing young players. The Negro ballplayer learned as he played, because there was no other way. The big Negro teams rarely had coaches, and the manager was usually a player himself with little time to spend drilling young rookies on the fine points of baseball.

"We were playing what they call strongarm baseball," Buck Leonard said. "That means: Do what you know and that's all. What I'm saying is that we did not know the fundamentals of baseball." Leonard explains further:

> We did not know about backup plays or pickoff plays or how valuable they were. We weren't told the certain positions

you were supposed to get in for certain plays. We did know a few, but the few we knew we picked up ourselves. We weren't told on our beginning teams where you were supposed to be on certain plays—how you are supposed to back up plays or how an outfielder is supposed to relay the ball to an infielder, and how the infielder is supposed to stand in line with the throw to keep the hitter from advancing an additional base. We didn't know all that; how we learned was by playing. After playing so many years we found out that was the best.

And we didn't have time to teach that to young ballplayers coming up. Every day we went out there to play, and we didn't have coaches. We just had pitchers who pitched the day before to coach at third and first. We didn't have paid coaches and all like that, and the manager was playing in the outfield or some other position. He wasn't sitting on the bench until our later years.

And when we'd go in the clubhouse to have a meeting, here's what we'd talk about: The manager would go over the players on the other team and say that we were going to try to make so-and-so hit to right field or so-and-so hit to left field, we were going to pitch so-and-so high inside or low outside, or we were going to throw so-and-so curve balls because we didn't think he could hit them.

Or maybe we were going to slow the ball up on so-and-so. That was my weakness. Everywhere that I would go to play, I'd know that the pitcher was going to slow the ball up on me because I was a fastball hitter. And I got to looking for that change-of-pace. Consequently, I learned how to hit the change-of-pace. But there was nobody to tell me how to hit it, like in the major leagues, where they got coaches that take you out in the morning and give you extra batting practice. Or like in the majors and in the minors, coaches that would take the time to drill you on tossing the ball to the pitcher covering first base or drill you on throwing to second base. We had to play until we learned it. Now that was what we used to call inside baseball. We weren't taught that; we weren't taught the fundamentals.

We *did* try to tell the batters how to bat. But nowadays you don't tell the batters how to bat. You just confuse a batter if you tell him how to stand at the plate and how to bat. If he's doing all right the way he's doing it—whether it's "right" or "wrong"—they let him continue. But with us, when you came up to a big team, whether you were getting results or not, if you were "wrong" they would tell you you had to correct it then and there. But now, if a ballplayer is getting results—say, for instance Stan Musial, the way he used to crouch at the plate —they let him go because of the way he hit the ball. Take Reggie Smith of the Boston Red Sox right now, how he stands at the plate. When I first came up they wouldn't let me stand like that even if I was hitting the ball. When I came up I used to hold my hands apart, and they told me you couldn't hit a curve ball—you couldn't hit anything going down with your hands apart. They wouldn't even let you begin that way.

When I first came up, I couldn't throw the ball to the pitcher covering first base. I threw too low, too high, behind him, in front of him. I had never practiced that. Down here in Rocky Mount I would always try to beat the runner. I would always play close to first and try to beat the runner to the bag, but after I got up there I played further away from the base and I was able to field more balls. Then I had to start tossing the ball to the pitcher. You can imagine how many games I messed up trying to learn it through playing.

They told me: "Look, you don't come up here to learn, you come up here to improve on what you know."

Now in the minors they'll take you out in the morning and give you an hour's batting practice or an hour's fielding practice. We didn't do that. You had to learn the best way you could down here in the lower semipros. And then when somebody would see you down here, you would go on up to a big team up there, green as a goose so far as fundamentals are concerned.

You were *strong!* But fundamentals? You didn't know them. We just didn't have time to teach anybody anything. We played every day unless it rained.

10 THE TRAVELIN' MAN

A bunch of the fellows get in a barber session the other day and they start to arguefy about the best pitcher they ever see. Some says Lefty Grove and Lefty Gomez and Walter Johnson and old Pete Alexander and Dazzy Vance. And they mention Lonnie Warneke and Van Mungo and Carl Hubbell, and Johnny Corriden tells us about Matty and he sure must of been great and some of the boys even say Old Diz is the best they ever see. But I see all them fellows but Matty and Johnson and I know who's the best pitcher I ever see and it's old Satchel Paige, that big lanky colored boy.
—DIZZY DEAN

Mention Negro baseball during a hot-stove-league discussion and the average white fan (and most Negro fans) will murmur, "Oh yes . . . Satchel Paige." During the late 1930s and through the middle Forties, Satchel Paige dominated Negro baseball as Babe Ruth had dominated the major leagues earlier—and for similar reasons. Both displayed awesome abilities on a baseball field, but they had something more. There was an aura of excitement about them that drew fans through the turnstiles by the thousands. They were larger than life, men of whom the extraordinary was expected as a matter of course.

Even when he struck out, which was often, Babe Ruth looked prodigious. To most fans he was more impressive when he swung and missed than another player was in rapping a three-base hit. In the same way, the anticipation that something fantastic would happen when Satchel Paige was scheduled to pitch would swell the crowd. Just the sight of him strolling languorously toward the mound—an improbable figure rising high on pencil-thin legs—was enough to send waves of excitement coursing through the ballpark.

129

Satchel in action for the Cleveland Indians. COURTESY OF ARTHUR M. CARTER

He did not pitch a no-hitter or call in his outfield in every game, even on the barnstorming trail. He did not even win every game (although he probably won more than any other pitcher in history), but the thought that today he just *might* do something wondrous made him for a long period the biggest attraction in Negro baseball. And, after the color line fell in the major leagues, his debut as an ancient rookie drew record crowds there, too.

Paige's appeal transcended race. Bill Veeck, who brought Satchel to the big leagues with the Cleveland Indians in 1948, observed that Paige is interracial and universal. And yet Paige never forgot (nor was allowed to forget) that he was a black man; he was no modern militant, eager to do battle over every slight or insult, whether real or imagined, but in his own way he broke ground toward integration long before the world had ever heard of Jackie Robinson, by refusing to pitch in towns where he could not lodge or get a meal in a restaurant.

Just how good was Satchel Paige? Dizzy Dean, who barnstormed against Satchel during the early 1930s, called him the best he ever saw. Similar tributes came from Joe DiMaggio, Charlie Gehringer, and a number of other major-league stars who faced Satchel in all-star barnstorming games of that era.

Was he as good as Walter Johnson, who was winding up his career with the Washington Senators when Paige was starting as a professional in 1926? As good as Lefty Grove, whose prime coincided with Paige's? Or Bob Feller, against whom he pitched (and usually won) in post-season tours during the 1940s?

Certainly Paige should be ranked with these men, although his major-league record cannot be compared with theirs. He had pitched for twenty-two years behind the color line before he entered the major leagues as a forty-two-year-old rookie, the oldest in history, and his record in the big leagues is only 28 victories and 31 defeats.

Was he then the best pitcher in Negro baseball history? In 1952 the *Pittsburgh Courier* asked thirty-one men who had been closely connected with Negro baseball during its best years to select an all-time team. Naturally Satchel Paige was chosen as one of the pitchers; it would have been unthinkable not to have included him. But the pitcher who led the balloting was Smoky Joe Williams, who got twenty votes to Satchel's nineteen. In the judgment of men who were there, Satchel Paige was certainly one of the great ones but not necessarily the best.

Whatever his standing on any all-time list, there can be no doubt that Negro baseball owed a large debt to Satchel Paige. Even as a young pitcher, he *was* the franchise for some clubs. During the Forties, before he went to the majors, Paige's drawing power was the difference between red and black ink on the ledgers of marginal Negro clubs. And years later, even when he had officially turned sixty, Satchel Paige could still fill a small-town park if he were advertised to pitch a couple of innings against the locals. As recently as 1968 he was hired as a pitching coach and (perhaps) pitcher by the Atlanta Braves, ostensibly so that he could complete five full years in the major leagues and qualify for a big-league pension. The suspicion remains, though, that the Braves were not moved solely by humanitarian motives; Satchel Paige is still a name.

As befits a living legend, there is considerable haziness about how old the ageless Satchel Paige really is. The *Baseball Register,* relying on a birth certificate for a LeRoy Paige issued in Mobile, Alabama, says he was born July 7, 1906. Bill Veeck is skeptical. So skeptical, in fact, that when he brought Paige to Cleveland, he hired a private detective to inspect Mobile's birth records. On the basis of the detective's findings, Veeck announced that Paige could not have been born later than 1899.

But since it has been established that Paige first pitched as a professional in 1926, the year 1906 seems more likely for his birth.

It is impossible to believe that his fastball could have been kept under wraps until he was twenty-seven years old.

Paige was born and grew up in a "shotgun house" (because its four rooms were a straight shot from front to back) in Mobile's black ghetto. He was the seventh of eleven children born to John Paige, a gardener, and Lula Paige. Life was hard for a black family down by the bay in Mobile, and at the age of seven he was put to work toting bags at the railroad station after school (which he rarely attended anyway). In the process, LeRoy Paige was given the nickname that became his trademark. After a day or two of carrying bags for a nickel or a dime each, the young Paige put his ingenuity to work and rigged up a pole and ropes to make a sling that enabled him to carry three or four bags at a time. His income soared, but the other budding redcaps snorted, "You look like a walking satchel tree." Satchel he became, and the name, which most people thought referred to his size-12 feet, seemed so appropriate that even when he had been a professional ballplayer for four years he often appeared in boxscores as—simply—Satchel.

As a member of a gang of hookey-players who sometimes got into rock-throwing fights with white boys, Paige was often in trouble with the police. In 1918, when he was twelve (give or take a couple of years), LeRoy Paige was committed to the reform school for Negro boys at Mt. Meigs, Alabama, for the theft of a handful of toy rings from a store. It was, Paige would say later, a break for him, because it got him away from Mobile's street gangs, it gave him regular meals and a warm place to sleep, it gave him some schooling, and most important, it gave him a chance to play baseball.

Satchel Paige had started playing on his school team back in Mobile, but it was during his five years at Mt. Meigs that he learned something about pitching. In December 1923, LeRoy Paige was released from the reform school and went home to Mobile. He was seventeen years old, 6 feet 3½ inches tall and weighed 140 pounds. Although he would add forty pounds in later years, he never lost the long, skinny look of his youth.

Satchel Paige played his first game for money in the spring of 1924, pitching for the Mobile Tigers, a black semipro club. He earned a dollar a game when the collection was good, a keg of lemonade when the game receipts didn't match expenses. He played for several semipro teams around Mobile during the next couple of years and finally, during the 1926 season, he got an offer from the Chattanooga Black Lookouts of the Negro Southern League for

$50 a month. He jumped at it, and for the next two years, Satchel Paige bounced around the Negro Southern League, trekking from town to town in ancient buses, sleeping in the ballpark when his club had no money for even a fifth-rate hotel. His pay rose to $200 a month, a big salary for the Southern League, and during those two years he rarely lost a game.

In 1928 he was sold to the Birmingham Black Barons of the Negro National League and was given a contract for $275 a month. There he played under Bill Gatewood, a veteran pitcher who had started with the Cuban X Giants in 1905. Satchel had no curve, no change-of-pace—just a fastball. But what a fastball! There is some difference of opinion about his control during this period, although none at all about it a few years later. Paige claims that even as a boy he had pinpoint control, so good that on his first day with Chattanooga in 1926 he could throw his bee ball (it hummed) over a handkerchief time after time.

One player remembers it differently. Floyd (Jelly) Gardner, an outfielder on the Chicago American Giants in 1928, said, "It was worth half your life to hit against him when he came up. One time at you, one time behind you, the next time at your feet. You had to be an acrobat when he first came up. And I saw him the first day he was in the ballpark at Birmingham. The American Giants were down there then."

Paige stayed with Birmingham through the 1930 season, but his nomadic instinct was already appearing. He had jumped Chattanooga in 1926, his first year as a pro, to play briefly with the New Orleans Black Pelicans when they offered him his first car, an aging jalopy, and in 1930 he had a short stay with the Baltimore Black Sox.

But he was officially a Black Baron from 1928 through 1930, and he was becoming a big attraction in the Negro leagues. Jimmie Crutchfield, who joined Birmingham as a nineteen-year-old outfielder in 1930, recalls, "With the Birmingham ball club, the only big thing we had was Satchel. Everybody in the South knew about Satchel Paige, even then. We'd have 8,000 people out—sometimes more—when he was pitching, which was something in Birmingham."

In 1931, Satchel Paige was sold by the Black Barons to the Nashville Elite Giants. Owner Thomas T. Wilson moved the club to Cleveland that spring because it had not drawn well enough the previous year to hold its franchise in the sinking Negro National League. Playing as the Cleveland Cubs, Wilson's team struggled through mid-season, playing in a tiny stadium in the shadow of the Cleveland Indians' League Park before disbanding.

It was a break for Satchel. W. A. (Gus) Greenlee was forming the Pittsburgh Crawfords that summer, and as soon as he heard that Wilson's club was folding, he sent a hurried call for Paige. The lanky pitcher responded for $250 a month and joined a team that Paige calls the best he ever saw, black or white. The Crawfords started Paige's march toward national fame.

Greenlee, a numbers operator, had a fat bankroll and a determination to assemble a great ball club. He did. In 1932, the Crawfords won 99 and lost 36 with such stars as Oscar Charleston, Judy Johnson, Josh Gibson, outfielders Rap Dixon, Cool Papa Bell, and Jimmie Crutchfield, pitcher-catcher Ted (Double Duty) Radcliffe, and pitcher Sam Streeter. They belonged to no league but barnstormed against the best black and white clubs they could find. Satchel won 23 and lost 7 for them that year. When he was not pitching for the Crawfords, Gus Greenlee hired him out to semipro clubs who wanted a star pitcher for an especially important game, giving him a chance to earn an extra $100 to $500 here and there. With those windfalls and his salary from the Crawfords, Paige was undoubtedly the highest-paid black player.

The following year his record with the Crawfords was 31–4 and he continued to pitch independently with semipro clubs. He stayed with the Crawfords through the 1934 season; he was the winning pitcher in the East-West game that year, a 1–0 duel won by the East when Jud Wilson of the Philadelphia Stars singled in the eighth inning, scoring Cool Papa Bell of the Crawfords from second base. In the fall of 1934, Satchel Paige got married, and, finding that matrimony had a way of diminishing his wallet, he asked Greenlee for more money. Greenlee refused and Satchel quit in a huff. When he got an offer of $250 a month to finish out the season with a white semipro club in Bismarck, North Dakota, he accepted, jumping a two-year contract he had just signed with the Crawfords.

Greenlee, who was then president of the second Negro National League, was so miffed that he had Paige barred from the league for 1935, and Paige spent that summer with Bismarck, too. Chester Williams wrote a tentative, premature obituary in the *Pittsburgh Courier:* "The champ of today may be the chump of tomorrow. So it may be with Paige. The league helped to make him and now the league may be the medium to break him."

But in 1936, Paige went back to the Crawfords and was again their ace and chief drawing card. In 1937, while he was at spring training with the Crawfords in New Orleans, Satchel heard the soothing rustle of dollars. This time the call came from the Dominican Republic through an emissary of President Rafael L. Trujillo. El Presidente, who was sovereign of the most absolute dictatorship then existing, was unaccountably being opposed for reelection and his opponent had imported a ball club that was beating everybody in Dominica and thus spreading his name among the volatile, baseball-mad Dominicans. There was only one thing to do—assemble a team that could beat them. Trujillo's lieutenants naturally went to the top—Satchel Paige.

Cool Papa Bell, Satchel's teammate on the Crawfords, recalls what happened:

> They liked baseball down there. They had a championship series set down there, and they said if Trujillo would win they would put him back in office: he was pretty near out of office then. So they got guys from Cuba, Panama, and guys out of the Negro leagues—they had a lot of boys from the States. And they wanted Satchel. He was down in New Orleans training with the Crawfords, and he didn't want to go. So they trailed Satchel to a hotel in New Orleans. Someone told them Satchel was in there. So two of them went in to look for him, and Satchel slipped out the side door and jumped in his car and tried to get away from them, but they blocked the street and stopped him.
>
> These were men from Santo Domingo who were looking for ballplayers to take down there. Now Satchel was the type of guy that if you showed him money—or a car—you could lead him anywhere. He was that type of fella. He did a lot of wrong things in baseball, but he was easily led. So they said they wanted him to go down there, and he said, "I don't wanna go."
>
> He had been out in North Dakota already and run off from our team. And we bought a boy from St. Louis named Vincent, and we swapped Vincent out in North Dakota to bring Paige back to the league. So when Vincent went out there and Paige came back to the league, he didn't want to jump again. That's why he was ducking those people. But when they offered him a big salary, then he jumped again and went down there.
>
> But they needed some more ballplayers down there, so they sent back to get them. They already had from our league a boy

named Griffith, Perkins—a great catcher—and Andrews. Most of the rest of the players were Cuban. But they had Orlando Cepeda's daddy—he was from Puerto Rico and he was playing.

In that year, Gus Greenlee, who was in the numbers racket, had lost a lot of money. He had a little old boy working for him, sweeping around where they counted the numbers money, and he was tipping off the detectives whenever they was counting the money. Gus didn't know just why, but everywhere they would move the detectives would be there. So Gus Greenlee had lost so much money and he was giving the ballplayers a tough way to go. So a lot of the boys on the Crawfords were ready to go quick. Some of the boys got a job in Pittsburgh in a mill where they had a team, and I had an application in there. I was going to quit as soon as I had a job. Some of the boys was jumping the league—it was going bad again. So Satchel called from down in Santo Domingo and got in touch with Leroy Matlock, Harry Williams, and Sam Bankhead.

That phone call had a distressing ring for the Pittsburgh Crawfords, because nine men from the club, including Bell, went to the Dominican Republic. Nine other Negro League players also jumped in the first serious defection from the Negro leagues during the regular season.

Paige and his Trujillo Stars won the tournament in Santo Domingo under very close chaperonage. They lived in a private club, which was constantly under armed guard, and the games were played under the eyes of a large part of Trujillo's army, with the sun glinting off long knives and bayonets. Satchel, who got $30,000 for himself and the other Crawfords, could not leave Trujillo land fast enough after that series.

He and a few of the other refugees from Santo Domingo went back to the Crawfords for the 1938 season, paying a fine of one week's salary to the league for jumping, but the season had not begun before Satchel was on the run again. He and Gus Greenlee could not come to terms. Greenlee's offer was $450 a month, and Paige told him, "I wouldn't throw ice cubes for that kind of money." Driven beyond endurance, Greenlee sold Paige to the Newark Eagles, who were owned by Abraham Manley and his beautiful wife, Effa. (Effa, a lady of positive opinions, was one of the most colorful of the clubowners. She was prone to offer unsolicited advice to other owners in league meetings and sometimes took a hand in the proceedings on the field. Buck Leonard of the Homestead Grays remembers, "Sometimes she'd tell the manager who to pitch. Once we were playin' 'em and she had her club members in the grandstand, and she sent word down to pitch Terris McDuffie because she wanted her club members to see him.")

The sale price for Paige was reported to be $2,000 to $3,000, a bargain-basement figure for the most famous personality in the game. There was to be no confrontation between Effa Manley and Satchel Paige, a meeting that would have enriched baseball's annals. Even a restraining order the Manleys got against the footloose Paige could not stop him. This time he was on his way to Mexico.

The Negro National League promptly banned Satchel "for life." Cum Posey, operator of the Homestead Grays and secretary-treasurer of the league, wrote a wistful bon voyage in the *Pittsburgh Courier:*

> We think Satch would have drawn many customers to the league parks this season. Some owners and fans are genuinely glad to have Paige leave. Others are sorry. Negro baseball has been very good to Paige. His phenomenal, well-publicized pitching ability could not be expressed in terms of finance. No colored club drew enough cash customers to pay him a salary commensurate with his ability. Then again, his unreliability was a factor which at all times kept him from being really a valuable asset to any team. Personally we never considered Paige as good a pitcher as Joe Williams, Dick Redding, or Jesse Hubbard, in their prime.
>
> To punish him severely by baseball law or by civic law is like chastening a child who has been brought up wrong.

Paige pitched the 1938 summer season in the Mexican League (which had several other American-Negro players), and there he developed his first sore arm in twelve years as a professional, pitching summer and winter, sometimes every day for a month. Paige blamed his troubles on his delicate stomach, which could not handle the spicy Mexican food. The miseries spread from his digestive tract throughout his body, finally engulfing the fabulous right arm. By late summer, he could not lift it above his head. Returning to the States, he was told by a physician that he would never pitch again.

It appeared that Satchel Paige was through at thirty-two. No Negro league clubowner seemed to want him even as a manager or coach; those he approached for a job remembered too well his casual approach to contracts. But late that winter he was offered a job as pitcher and first baseman for the Kansas City Monarchs' second team, a barnstorming club that traveled through the Northwest and into Canada from spring to fall. J. L. Wilkinson and Tom Baird, Monarchs' owners, believed that Paige could still draw crowds even if he couldn't pitch; in addition, they were noted for going out of their way to help fading Negro stars.

The great Satchel Paige, a pathetic replica of the long, lean hurler with the whiplike right arm, spent the early part of the 1939 season painfully blooping pitches plateward in ballparks all over the Northwest. The traveling club was rechristened Satchel Paige's All-Stars, and day after day its namesake pitched an inning or two in small-town parks against semipros who, a year or two earlier, would have hesitated to go to the plate against him. Then one day the miracle occurred. The miseries were gone and the fastball was back. Satchel was promptly recalled to the big club of the Monarchs. It was a reprieve for Paige, a second chance at an age when most pitchers are thinking of retiring. Satchel made the most of it.

From 1939 through 1942, the Monarchs won the Negro American League pennant each year with Paige as their mainstay. In 1942, the first Negro World Series since 1927 was played between the Monarchs and the Homestead Grays, champions of the Negro National League. The star was, of course, Satchel Paige.

He won 3 of the Monarchs' 4 straight victories. There was one slight delay in the Monarchs' march to Series triumph, though. After the Monarchs had won the first three, the Grays imported pitcher Leon Day and two other players from the Newark Eagles, plus one from the Philadelphia Stars, and beat Satchel and the Monarchs, 4–1. The Grays claimed that Kansas City had given them permission to use the ringers because their lineup was riddled by injuries, but the Monarchs denied it. Their protest was upheld and the game was thrown out. Thereupon Satchel beat the Grays in the official fourth game for his third victory in the Series.

His contract-jumping days over, Satch settled down contentedly with the Monarchs for the next five years. He was used more as a nomadic independent attraction, hired out by Wilkinson and Baird to pitch for semipro clubs, than as a regular with the Monarchs. In 1944, for example, the first year in which an independent agency kept official statistics for the Negro American League, Paige appeared in only eight games for the Monarchs, working 48 innings, winning 4 and losing 2, and compiling an 0.75 earned-run average. The following year he pitched in only six games in the NAL, working 33 innings. His won-lost record was 2–2. In 1946, though, he was used considerably more and won about 20 games as the Monarchs took the NAL pennant and then lost the World Series to the Newark Eagles.

In 1948, Satchel Paige was still with the Kansas City Monarchs. A former teammate on the Monarchs, Jackie Robinson, had broken the color line in the major leagues the year before with the Brooklyn Dodgers. In the American League, Larry Doby, formerly of the Newark Eagles, was a star in the Cleveland Indians outfield after becoming the American League's first Negro player late in 1947. In 1948 the Indians were making a run for the pennant, and Bill Veeck, the president, sought some pitching insurance. With the help of promoter Abe Saperstein, he found it in Satchel Paige. On July 9, 1948, two days after his more or less official forty-second birthday, Satch became the first Negro ever to pitch in the American League, making a two-inning relief appearance against the St. Louis Browns in Cleveland. Pitching in 21 games, the venerable rookie won 6 and lost only 1 as the Indians won the pennant in a tight race that went down to a playoff game against the Boston Red Sox. Cleveland won the World Series, too, beating the Boston Braves in six games, but Paige was used in only one inning.

Satchel was with the Indians again in 1949, but he was let go after the season, having won 4 and lost 7. He went back to barnstorming for any club that would meet his price. In 1951, Veeck, then president of the St. Louis Browns, brought him back to the big leagues. He stayed with the Browns through 1953, his last full season in the majors. (Satchel made a three-inning appearance with the Kansas City Athletics in 1965.)

After being released by the Browns, Paige drifted back into Negro baseball and the barnstormer's life. The ubiquitous Veeck rescued him again in 1956, hiring him for Miami in the International League. Paige stayed there through 1958. In 1961, he pitched briefly for Portland in the Pacific Coast League. But during most of these latter years, Satchel was on the rickety bus circuit, an elderly, bespectacled gentleman pitching an inning or two for various barnstorming clubs. In 1967 he toured with the Indianapolis Clowns for a reported $1,000 a month, plus a $250 bonus for the Clowns' occasional appearances in big-league parks. He spent the off-seasons in his Kansas City home and sometimes worked as a sheriff's deputy. He ran unsuccessfully for the Missouri legislature in 1968 before being taken on as a coach by the Atlanta Braves.

Satchel Paige's unbelievably long career spanned several eras of the eve of his 60-home-run season. Walter Johnson, Ty Cobb, and Tris Speaker were still active. During the early 1930s, when he was the greatest pitcher in Negro baseball, only Lefty Grove, Dizzy Dean, and Carl Hubbell could be mentioned as worthy rivals of Satchel Paige. When the big-league color line was finally broken, Satchel was there. And when Negro baseball was dying during the 1950s, he was still pitching.

The essence of Satchel Paige cannot be captured by dry statistics, and besides, most of the available figures are somewhat elusive, like the man himself. Nevertheless, for what it is worth, here is a summary:

• In 1961 he estimated that he had pitched in more than 2,500 games, winning about 2,000. Since he was still barnstorming through 1967, perhaps a hundred games should be added.

• From 1929 through 1958 he played both summer and winter, taking the sun after the summer season from California to Cuba and points south. He claims to have pitched 153 games in a single year.

• His estimate of the number of his no-hit, no-run games is 100. His victims were Negro-league and semipro teams.

• He pitched for about 250 teams, most of them, of course, on a one-game basis. Before going to the majors he had been on the rosters of the following Negro professional clubs: Chattanooga Black Lookouts, New Orleans Black Pelicans, Birmingham Black Barons, Baltimore Black Sox, Nashville Elite Giants (called Cleveland Cubs in 1931), Pittsburgh Crawfords, and Kansas City Monarchs. He had pitched occasionally for several other black teams for a game or two, particularly after his comeback in the early 1940s.

• He earned three to four times as much money as any other player in black baseball. Estimates of his top salary range from $22,-000 to $40,000 during his years with the Kansas City Monarchs. (Paige himself was quoted at various times as putting his top salary at $22,000 and $37,000.)

• He was the oldest rookie in major-league history. For his first three starts in the big leagues, he drew 201,829 fans, setting night-game attendance records in Cleveland and Chicago.

• His best strikeout mark for a game appears to have been 22, reached several times, including one game against major-league barn-stormers in 1930.

Behind these assorted figures lie two factors: a blazing fastball, and showmanship. Of the two, the fastball was the more important.

Biz Mackey, one of the greatest catchers of Negro baseball, once described Paige's fastball thus:

> A lot of pitchers have a fastball, but a very, very few—Feller, Grove, Johnson, a couple of others besides Satchel—have had that little extra juice that makes the difference between the good and the great man. When it's that fast, it will hop a little at the end of the line. Beyond that, it tends to disappear. Yes, disappear. I've heard about Satchel throwing pitches that wasn't hit but that never showed up in the catcher's mitt nevertheless. They say the catcher, the umpire, and the bat boys looked all over for that ball, but it was gone. Now how do you account for that?

Paige called his fast one variously a bee ball, jump ball, trouble ball, and Long Tom, and he depended on it and his exquisite control until he had been around for some years. He developed a curve ball during the 1930s (although Bill Veeck claimed he never really learned to throw a good curve until he was with Miami in the International League in 1956). Only when the Long Tom became less overpowering during the 1940s did Paige begin leaning heavily on the curve and an assortment of other pitches. It was also about this time that he worked out his hesitation pitch, which was nothing more than a perceptible pause in his motion just as his left foot hit the ground. The effect was so devastating to a batter's timing, though, that the American League banned it in his first year in the major leagues.

Paige began as an overhand fireballer, but as he grew older he began using several motions, varying all the way from directly overhead to a submarine delivery. He pitched without windup or stretch at times, with a full corkscrew windup at others.

Satchel Paige's penchant for showboating appeared early and grew out of his unswerving confidence in his pitching arm. He was still in semipro baseball in Mobile when he first called in his outfielders and pitched without them. This became a fixture in his performances on the mound, although he did not do it unless the game was safely in hand. Occasionally he would promise to strike out the first six or the first nine men in a game—and deliver.

Off the field, Satchel Paige went his own way, unfettered by the calendar and clock of lesser mortals. He is remembered with affection and respect by teammates and opponents alike among old Negro ballplayers. Three of them speak. Here is Jimmie Crutchfield, Satchel's teammate on the Birmingham Black Barons and the Pittsburgh Crawfords during the early Thirties:

Satch never had too many friends. He didn't ever seek too much friendship, but he had a fondness for Gus Greenlee. For some reason he liked Gus, and he stuck pretty close to our ballclub.

Satchel was always a restless guy. He would pitch for us on Sunday—he'd shut some team out in Yankee Stadium, and we wouldn't see Satchel maybe until the following Sunday. Maybe we'd be playing in Cleveland or some other big city. We'd leave the hotel, go to the ballpark—no Satchel. Fifteen minutes before gametime, somebody would say, "Hey, Satchel just came in the dressing room." He was always full of life. You'd forgive him for everything because he was like a great big boy. He could walk in the room and have you in stitches in ten minutes' time. He'd warm up by playing third base or clowning with somebody and then he'd go out and pitch a shutout. How could you get mad at a guy like that?

Buck Leonard of the Homestead Grays:

I was down in Puerto Rico the winter of 1940 playing with a Puerto Rican team, and Satchel was pitching for another team down there. In the first inning we got three men on base and nobody out, and a boy named Bus Clarkson [a hard-hitting shortstop then with the Newark Eagles] came to bat. So Satchel told the catcher he was going to walk him intentionally. So the catcher told him, "Don't you know the bases are loaded? Don't you know you're going to walk a run home?" Satchel said, "Well, I'd rather walk one run home than have him hit three or four home."

So Satchel walked Bus Clarkson and walked a run home. Then he said, "Well, that's all y'all goin' to get now." And that's the only run we got. Satchel could tell you he was going to do something and do it. I don't mean against mediocre teams—I mean against good teams! Very few folks got ready for his fastball—very few. The ball used to come up to the plate and rise a little.

Jack Marshall of the Chicago American Giants:

When Satchel Paige had his all-stars they wouldn't play in a town if they couldn't lodge there. Wilkinson owned the ball club, and if Satchel Paige couldn't sleep where they played or eat where they played, they wouldn't play there. He'd just tell the Chamber of Commerce, no soap. They were warned beforehand, so they didn't have any trouble; the Chamber of Commerce made the arrangements.

Did you know that Satchel Paige is the cause of ballplayers wearing plastic helmets today? In 1936 we had a Negro National League all-star team we took to Denver to play in the Denver *Post* tournament. I played third base, Chester Williams played shortstop; Sammy T. Hughes played second base, Buck Leonard first base, Josh Gibson and Hardy was catching, Raymond Brown, Sam Streeter, and somebody else was pitching—and Satchel. And Wild Bill Wright, Cool Papa Bell, and another boy in the outfield. That was the team we had. We didn't lose a game. We won 7 straight games. And when we came up to play Borger, Texas, a white team—we were the only colored team in the tournament—these boys sent back to Borger, Texas, and had these helmets made to go around in their caps because they didn't want to get hurt with Satchel's speed. And that was the very first time anybody ever put any kind of protection on their heads in baseball. That was in 1936. Satchel must have struck out about 21 men and never threw a ball higher than the person's belt line. Well, for three innings he called in the outfield!

Satchel threw his first curve ball in 1936. Now if he got by with a straight ball from '28 to '36, he must have been a great man! Then when he came in with his curve ball he was even greater.

He was the fastest I ever saw. He was so fast you couldn't bunt him. Was he faster than Bullet Rogan? Oh God, yes! When Satchel came up, it was nothing but fire! Bullet was throwing curve balls, which made his fastball look very fast. And after Satchel came in with his curve ball it made his fastball look even faster. He didn't throw what you call a heavy ball like Bullet. Satchel would throw a light ball.

As the elder statesman of the major leagues when he was almost fifty years old, Paige was often asked for his prescription for eternal youth. A sportswriter who heard him discourse on the subject set down the essence of Satchel's rules as follows:

Avoid fried meats, which angry up the blood.

If your stomach disputes you, lie down and pacify it with cool thoughts.

Keep the juices flowing by jangling gently as you move.

Go very light on the vices, such as carrying on in society—the society ramble ain't restful.

Avoid running at all times.

And don't look back. Something might be gaining on you.

The last of those rules, Paige said, was the most important. His autobiography, published in 1961, is titled *Maybe I'll Pitch Forever,* surely the quintessence of a forward-looking view of life. And maybe he will.

11 PODUNK TODAY, HICKORY SWITCH TOMORROW

The Grays traveled all season long. Every day you were going, you'd go and ride over those hills. Every two hours you had to average a hundred miles. With nine men in the car! That's what we averaged. The cops all knew us; we had "Homestead Grays" on the sides and they'd call, "Hey, Homestead Grays!" and we'd be going like a bat out of hell. We never got stopped once until we got in the South. We were treated pretty rough down there at times.

—JUDY JOHNSON

C. I. Taylor, in right front seat, taking several of his Indianapolis ABCs on a tour of Washington in 1918 just before they joined the Army. The passenger on the windshield was apparently a passerby who was induced to pose, not a mascot. COURTESY OF DAVE MALARCHER

145

Barnstorming and Negro baseball were practically synonymous in the minds of fans, and with good reason. Clubs in the organized Negro leagues were not, strictly speaking, barnstormers, since they played a formal schedule with several series a year against other teams in the league. But more than half their 200-odd games a year (sometimes two-thirds) were outside the league; Negro clubs kept promoters around big cities busy booking them for their days off from league play, usually with white semipro teams in towns within driving distance of the city where they happened to be stopping for a day or two. "Driving distance" was very liberally interpreted; for some clubs, a jump of 200 miles, a ball game, and another 200 miles back to their base was all in a normal day's work.

Barnstorming in Negro baseball goes back to 1887, when Bud Fowler organized a traveling club soon after his release by Binghamton of the International League. Periodically until about 1900, Fowler formed barnstorming teams whenever he was without a job. Probably the most colorful of them was a team he gathered in 1899, called the All-American Black Tourists. They traveled in their own railroad car, and every game was preceded by a street parade with the players outfitted in full-dress suits with black pants and white vests, swallow-tail coats, opera hats, and silk umbrellas. "By request of any club," Fowler announced, "we will play the game in these suits."

As Negro baseball began to mature in the years around 1910, most of the better clubs would spend at least a part of each winter barnstorming either in California or Florida. (The annual treks to Cuba and other parts of Latin America did not start until somewhat later for most players.) Rube Foster took his Chicago American Giants to California almost every winter during this period. In 1916 they shuttled between California, Florida, and Havana, Cuba, drawing well as Negro baseball's biggest attraction. Later, the American Giants were engaged for several winters to provide entertainment for the guests at the Royal Poinciana Hotel in Palm Beach, Florida. They played a series of games with the Lincoln Giants, who represented the Breakers Hotel in Palm Beach, through the winter, assuring themselves of a steady income and keeping in shape for the summer season back in Chicago.

Chicago's rabid baseball fans were able to follow the fortunes of the American Giants wherever they were through the pages of the *Defender*. The fans got a scare in April 1914, when the front page blazed with a 60-point headline, "Rube Foster's Team Starving in Oregon." The correspondent wrote that the presence of the black club had created ill-feeling in the winter league on the West Coast and that some Coast League clubs had refused to play them. The headline was justified in the last few paragraphs of the story, where it was reported that the American Giants had trouble finding a place to eat in Medford, Oregon. After prolonged argument, the proprietor of a Japanese restaurant opened up his establishment and fed them cheese and crackers for breakfast. "This cool reception caused considerable indignation among the players," the *Defender* noted.

Securing food and lodging was not always a problem for touring Negro clubs. The degree of difficulty depended upon the time and the place. Arthur W. Hardy, who toured with the Topeka Giants in the Midwest in 1906 and 1907, remembers:

> We had no trouble whatever up in that territory about getting meals or board. Not a bit. Now you take some towns in Kansas like Smith Center, Clay Center, Phillipsburg, we'd always book a series of games in those towns. Well, the local team would put us up in the hotel. We had no trouble.
>
> I guess it was good management on the part of Topeka Jack Johnson, our manager. He knew his territory. I suppose there were trouble spots that he just avoided. Then, along the railroad high line in Nebraska—of course, Nebraska has always been a fairly liberal state on the race question anyhow—we played all those little towns like Superior, Nebraska, and Red Cloud, and others along the high line on the way to Denver, and into Chicago. That was ideal. We used to play three games in Superior, maybe three games in Red Cloud, three or four games in Franklin or someplace like that, all going in a straight line. Well, after a series, we could leave the next morning and take the local train that went through there which would put us in the next town in plenty of time for the game. We always liked to get into town at least by the middle of the morning for advertising purposes. As a rule, when we went into a town, we would placard it and uniform up and go out and practice so the people could get it noised around that we were in town.
>
> Sometimes they set up a parade. Both teams paraded. That was in Smith Center and Blue Rapids and Frankfort, Kansas. That was the regular program. They had very good bands.

Most of those little towns had a municipal band, you know—the band concert once a week was a big event then—and they would lead the parade and we'd march out to the baseball park.

Those games in the little towns had to be played before harvest, because everybody was working during harvest season. Then after harvest they would come back at it. So during the harvest season we would be in Chicago. We scheduled it so that by the time the harvest season began we had played in Iowa maybe a couple of weeks run over into the harvest season. And, of course, we'd be losing money because the people were busy and just didn't come to a baseball game. But we'd get them on the way back.

During that month or so, we'd play around Chicago. We played all the teams in the city league and we played the Cuban Stars—the *real* Cubans, whose headquarters was in Chicago—we played them two or three different series. Then we'd start back and get back home around Labor Day in time to get hooked up with Johnny Kling of the Chicago Cubs and his all-pro gang for a series of games around Kansas City. Sometimes we'd make almost as much in those six or seven games with Johnny Kling as we would pretty near all summer. I've gotten as much as $700 or $800—and this was in 1910 and 1911 dollar values—for six or seven games. That would see me through pretty near two years of college.

But in those little towns, we would average $15, $20 a man for a game. The admission charge was 50¢ or 75¢, kids a quarter. They paid it; they'd turn out to see us. And expenses were at a minimum. In those days you could get a good meal for 25¢, and you could get lodging for 50¢.

They'd turn out for our games. In a small town—say, Superior, Nebraska, which was largely a dairy center at the time and had, possibly, between 10,000 and 11,000 people—we would have 700 or 800 people out to the ballgame. Now those teams were very generous because we would get as much as seventy percent of the receipts, and the home team would pay all the expenses—advertising and everything else—so whatever we made was perfectly clear.

On the Topeka Giants we did some clowning on the field. But it was done like this: As you know, some people might resent what they might consider you making fun of them, and so Topeka Jack Johnson would always talk to the local people. He'd say, "Now what about your folks here? Do you want us to put on some kind of funny act? Or do you think they would resent it?"

Here was one of the stunts: The pitcher would throw the ball and maybe it would be a little low but the umpire would call it a strike; all right, you'd get down on your knees at the plate. Or some guy would hit the ball out of the park and run to third base and around the bases backward, that sort of thing.

Well now, unless the local people would approve, we would never do it. Johnson always insisted that we didn't want to humiliate anybody. After all, we were pros and the other teams were fellows who were playing once a week. Of course, if they wanted to come out and measure arms with us, all right!

But if the local people thought clowning would help any and add a little to it, okay, but not unless they gave their consent. And that's the way we handled it. Now, of course, the team that was noted for clowning a little later was the Indianapolis Clowns. That was part of their business, although most of their humor was directed at themselves.

We did have a little act on the Topeka Giants, though, that was in addition to baseball. We had four fellows who made up a topnotch quartet, and in the evenings, around the hotel, those guys would make $25 or $30 sometimes. They did especially well if they caught a bunch of traveling men coming in there, because, you know, there wasn't anything to do in those small towns; at that time, they didn't even have picture shows.

Even when the Negro leagues were functioning in later years there were still good black clubs that did nothing but barnstorm from spring to fall. Two of the best-known in the Midwest were Peters' Union Giants, whose territory was mostly confined to Illinois, and Gilkerson's Union Giants, who covered Illinois, Wisconsin, Iowa, Minnesota, North and South Dakota, and parts of Canada.

Carter Wilson, who played for both teams during the early Twenties, tells how it was to tour with Gilkerson's Union Giants:

Generally we were treated fine in that territory. Only once in a while did we have any real difficulty because Bob Gilkerson, the owner, would go ahead and make arrangements for stopping. I think the greatest difficulty we had was in a place in Iowa—a place called Hampton or New Hampton, I can't remember—but we had some games with them, and the arrangements they had were for us to stay in a bar. Some of the fellas had seen it and they didn't like it, and they decided they weren't being treated right. They said they weren't going to stay there, and some of them even wanted to get out without playing. But, of course, that couldn't happen—that would ruin everything, ruin Gilkerson and all. But New Hampton and another town about twenty miles away were great rivals. They had a little league around there, and I guess the New Hampton team had been getting the better of the other town. The other town's bettors wanted to get their money back, and they were supporting us. So they suggested that we could get good accommodations at the Y in their town. They told us to go ahead and play the game, and after the game we were sure to be treated fairly there. So that's what we did. We played Saturday and Sunday and we killed 'em! We probably put out a little extra effort. But generally our treatment in that section of the country was fine. Most of the time the home-club manager arranged for our lodging.

Gilkerson would make a skeleton booking for the whole season, covering Sundays and holidays, before the club started out in the spring. As he went along, he would fill in the other days. He had a letterhead and an ad which said, "Coming your way soon!" and he would write the managers of teams and tell them when we would be in their area. And, of course, because Gilkerson's Union Giants were an attraction he could easily fill in those other days. There were very few days when we didn't have a game.

We had some clowns on our team. There was one especially funny guy—Willis Jones. Sometimes he might go out to his position in the outfield with a newspaper and cut a little hole through and pretend he was reading it. And if a ball was hit to him and the game was lopsided in our favor, he wouldn't run after the ball. The centerfielder would have to go and get it.

Sometimes the clowning didn't have anything to do with the game. Once, a year or two earlier, for instance, the team was in a little place in Iowa. Hurley McNair was at bat; he was a little fella, a lefthanded outfielder who sometimes pitched, but he was a great hitter—he hit the ball hard. There was a high, three-story schoolhouse in right field—a good distance away, too. The bases were loaded, and McNair hit the ball up on top of the schoolhouse. It happened to have been the only ball they had, and the game had to be stopped until one of the young town boys went up on the roof and got it and threw it down. Now Bingo Bingham, who was coaching at first base, had a very loud voice—one of those stentorian voices—and when the ball came down, he said, "It's educated now!" in his big, deep voice. Bingo was a clown, too. Sometimes he would give a bouquet of weeds to a pitcher who had struck him out.

There were two schools of thought about clowning on the field. It was often good box office, particularly for white audiences, but base-ball purists frowned on it because they felt it degraded both the game and the players. Sometimes the humor was of the plantation or minstrel-show variety in which the white man's stereotypes of the lovable darky were pandered to—the Deep South Negro dialect, the grinning caricature of the happy-go-lucky, lazy fatback-and-grits Negro with which for decades, white America deceived itself.

Sol White, a dedicated baseball man, thought he saw signs as early as 1906 that clowns were becoming extinct in Negro baseball. He wrote:

> Where every man on a team would do a funny stunt during a game back in the Eighties and early Nineties, now will be found only one or two on a team who essays to amuse the spec-tators of the present day. Monroe, third baseman of the Royal Giants of Brooklyn, is the leading fun-maker of the colored profession of today. His comic sayings and actions while on the field, together with his ability as a fielder, hitter and runner, has earned for him a great reputation as a ball player.

Although there were fewer clowns in later years, White's predic-tion that they would soon go the way of the dodo never materialized. Many players who were not really clowns were noted for their showmanship in adding a touch of melodrama to every fielding play with some fancy glovework. Most of the good clubs concentrated on baseball, and the players were as mechanical and polished in their execution as major-leaguers.

Barnstorming during the Depression years was not much fun for clowns or anyone else. A dollar was hard to come by and barnstorm-ers chased it wherever the scent led. Buck Leonard, who was playing the outfield for the Brooklyn Royal Giants in 1933, recalls:

> We didn't have any home grounds. We played anywhere we could get a game. We didn't play much around Brooklyn. Sometimes we would go up in New Hampshire and play around those county fairs for two or three weeks. Playing over

at this fairgrounds this evening, going over to that fairground and sometimes getting $50, going to some other fairground tomorrow and getting $75, the next day going where they had one of those exhibition and amusement parks and passing the hat around. Things were *tough* in 1933. Fifty dollars was a lot of money for one whole baseball team to get for a ballgame.

As the nation's economy crept out of the Depression during the late Thirties, barnstorming became somewhat more profitable, especially for clubs playing against major-league all-star teams. During World War II, when pockets jingled with defense-industry earnings, black barnstorming clubs playing major-leaguers could do very well indeed. Here is Buck Leonard again:

> In 1943 I went to California and played with Satchel Paige's all-stars in the winter league, playing major-league stars out there until Judge Landis (the commissioner of baseball) quit us from playing. See, Satchel Paige had a team playing an all-star team of the major-leaguers—Peanuts Lowery and Lou Novikoff and Buck Newsom and Roy Partee and Metkovich and Priddy. And every Sunday we would play them a doubleheader in Hollywood.
>
> The first Sunday we played them, we split a doubleheader, and the next Sunday we beat them a doubleheader, and the next Sunday we split, and the next Sunday we split again. Then Judge Landis stopped us from playing the major-league all-stars. Then we started playing the Coast League stars.
>
> I don't know why he stopped us from playing the major-leaguers. Somebody said that the major-leaguers weren't organized and he didn't want an unorganized major-league team playing. That was one of the beginnings of having all major-league barnstorming teams be organized and be under discipline. Somebody had to be responsible for those fellas—they wouldn't let them abuse baseball, and Buck Newsom was kind of doing that out there.
>
> Now here's what he did one night. We were playing in Los Angeles, and Buck was getting $500 for pitching for the white team. A guy named Joe Perroni was the promoter out there. So Buck pitched two innings and the fog came in, and the fog got so we just had to call the game off. But Buck wanted his $500. And they wouldn't give it to him, told him we were going to play the next night. And Buck said he had made some commitments and he wanted his money. And Joe Perroni said,

"I'll give you the $500 if the other team will agree for me to pay you." And Buck said, "Well, I'll be back tomorrow night." And Perroni said, "Well, if the other team agrees for you to come back tomorrow night, all right." But we didn't agree for him to get his money, because we weren't getting ours. We had to come back the next night before we could get paid. So we think that was one of the beginnings of Judge Landis' rule—that argument we had out there.

Now we used to have 10,000, 12,000 out for those games. The first Sunday we played we made $106 apiece; the next Sunday we played we made $135 apiece; the third Sunday we made about $150 apiece; and the fourth Sunday we made a hundred and some dollars apiece. But when we started playing the Pacific Coast League stars, we didn't have those crowds and we weren't making that kind of money. We were making $60, then it got down to $40, and when it got down to $30 I left and came back home. I wasn't making expenses at $30 a week, see.

Setting the price for a barnstorming trip to play a white semipro club during the regular season was an exercise in financial acumen. An old player explains how the negotiations ran:

When a white ball club wrote and asked us for a game, they might offer us a $500-dollar guarantee. Well, if they offered a $500-dollar guarantee, you won't accept that; you want a percentage. But if they say they will give you sixty percent of the gate, *then* you ask for a guarantee. Simple as that!

If they want to give you a guarantee, you want a percentage; if they want to give you a percentage, you want a guarantee. Because when they want to give you a big guarantee, they *know* they're going to make it. And when they're not sure they're going to make it, they want you to take a percentage, so you want a guarantee.

During the Twenties and Thirties, traveling and living conditions for Negro barnstorming teams were rarely as pleasant as they were when Arthur Hardy was touring with the Topeka Giants soon after the turn of the century. Bill Yancey, who played with several clubs during the later period, remembers:

When I first started, if we were going any long distance we would go by train, but later on we used to travel by buses.

Because a lot of times you couldn't get trains to where we were going, you know. We'd take a train to go to Pittsburgh, and then we'd hire cars to go to Warren and places like that; we'd make Pittsburgh our home base. In a lot of towns they didn't even have places for us to dress. You'd dress in the hotel, and after the game you'd get in the car and come on back.

When I was playing with the Renaissance in basketball, sometimes we used to get treated something awful. We'd go in town and couldn't get any food, and then they'd expect us to let 'em look good! In baseball we didn't get bothered too much except in the South. In 1945 I managed the Atlanta Black Crackers, and we went over to a place called Rome, Georgia. Well, I'm the manager and I got to find out where you dress. So I asked this guy—he looked like a half-wit—who was taking care of the clubhouse, "Where can my boys dress?" He said, "Well, you niggers have to go down to some of those houses and get dressed." And that's what we had to do.

In the North we never had problems, not that you'd notice. Because the white ballplayers thought it was an honor to play against us. And the townspeople all liked baseball. Everybody likes baseball. If they didn't like baseball they couldn't draw like they do now because there's so many colored ballplayers, you know.

Oh, we used to have problems getting food in the North. The restaurants didn't want to serve us. That was general in the North, but we never had too far to ride. If we were going from New York to Philadelphia, how long is that going to take? And if you were going to Pittsburgh, you could stop at Harrisburg. There's always ways.

Our biggest problem was when we were on the road all the time, like when I was playing basketball. I'll never forget the time we went into West Virginia for the first time and there was no hotel at all where we could go. It took us maybe a couple of hours to find lodging for eight or nine fellas—one stay here, two stay here, like that.

Jack Marshall, an infielder who played both in the Midwest and East (with the Chicago American Giants and Philadelphia Stars) during the 1930s, recalls:

In the Negro American League, when we left Chicago to go to St. Louis and play, there was no place between here and St. Louis where we could stop and eat—not unless we stopped in a place where they had a colored settlement. From St. Louis to Kansas City, same thing. So many times we would ride all night and not have anything to eat, because they wouldn't feed you.

Going from Chicago to Cleveland, same thing. So the boys used to take sardines and a can of beans and pour them into one of those bell jars. They'd take some crackers, too, and that was their food—they'd eat out of that bell jar. That's the way they had to do it.

Out East we played mostly in the big towns. When we played in a small town, we'd just hook up after we finished the ballgame and go back to the big town because it was so close by.

But you kept playing so much baseball out there that you really didn't have time to sleep! On Sundays, they played four ballgames out there! On Sunday in Philadelphia we'd go to the YMCA at five o'clock in the morning to change clothes. We'd get into uniform and go up into Jersey and play a game at nine o'clock for some picnic or something. We'd leave from there and go to Dexter Park in Brooklyn and play the Bushwicks a doubleheader, and leave there and go out on Long Island and play a night game. It would be five o'clock the next morning when we'd get back to Philadelphia.

Black ballclubs got around on the barnstorming trail any way they could. They used farm wagons and drays, trains and cars, anything to get to the ballpark. By the 1930s, most were traveling in their own buses, which ranged from broken-down, battered, creaking little vehicles to the best conveyances that era had to offer, clean, brightly painted and reasonably roomy.

Negro baseball lived and died before the superhighways that now web the country had been built. Thirty-five to forty miles per hour was a good average for a long trip over the narrow, tortuous roads that wound through the Northeast and Midwest, where most of the best clubs barnstormed regularly. The memories of old ballplayers abound with tales of marathon trips, jouncing and bouncing over rough roads all night and all day until the passing countryside was a stupefying blur. Judy Johnson, for instance, vividly remembers a non-stop bus ride from Chicago to Philadelphia after a doubleheader, 800 miles of catnaps and sandwiches and soda-pop for breakfast, lunch, and dinner. When the bus pulled into Philadelphia, his ankles were about twice normal size. "And we played a doubleheader that afternoon in Connie Mack Stadium," Johnson said.

Once during the 1930s the New York Black Yankees had a shorter but similarly strenuous endurance test. They played a doubleheader in Pittsburgh one Sunday and were scheduled for another the next day in South Orange, N.J., 350 miles away.

The sixteen-man club left Pittsburgh in two cars loaded down with luggage and equipment about ten o'clock Sunday night and began pounding across the Allegheny Mountains toward New Jersey. Early Sunday morning, while the cars were chugging over the winding mountain roads, one of them broke down. The players tinkered frantically for a while and summoned help from a nearby garage, but it soon became clear that one car would have to go on with nine men aboard to make sure they would be on time for the first game in South Orange. So one full team boarded the serviceable car and resumed the trip, reaching the South Orange park twenty minutes before gametime. There was no time for lunch. The players dressed hastily and had five minutes to warm up.

A few minutes before the first game began, the second car with the rest of the Black Yankees pulled up to the park. The seven players in that car, who were luckier than their mates, stretched out in the dressing room and along the sides of the field and enjoyed a nap while the unlucky nine took the field and won the first game. The seven were then awakened and joined two of the yawning Black Yankees who had to play both games. They won the second game, too.

Perhaps the all-time record for a marathon between games was a bus ride taken by the American Giants in 1935. Dave Malarcher remembers that the team rode all the way from Monroe, Louisiana, to Winnipeg, Canada—a jaunt of some 1,700 miles—sleeping and eating in the bus all the way. Malarcher, who had come into professional baseball with C. I. Taylor's Indianapolis ABCs and played under Rube Foster, both of whose teams always traveled first class on railroads, left baseball because of trips like that. As American Giants' manager, he felt deeply the physical strain his players were enduring, and, he said, "they were conditions which I could not continue to bear."

There were white barnstorming teams during the age of Negro baseball, notably the bearded House of David club, based in Michigan. They traveled about as much as the Negro clubs, but they had a much easier time on the road because they had no trouble getting rooms and meals.

For fifty years the barnstormers, both black and white, brought good baseball to isolated farm towns and small cities. Their arrival in a small town generated a holiday atmosphere, a welcome respite from the narrow, daily routines of the burghers who, in the days before almost every family had an automobile, seldom ventured more than a few miles from home.

Even the smallest communities had semipro baseball teams, and, because there was very little other entertainment, these teams were loyally supported. The appearance of one of the big Negro clubs would be the highlight of the local season. In some mining towns around Pittsburgh, workers would get a half-holiday when the Homestead Grays arrived for a game with the town team. The town took on a festive air, and after the game, benches were set up along the main street and the townspeople and players got together for an outdoor supper.

Such occasions were welcome interludes in the drudgery of barnstorming. For a small-town baseball fan, white or black, barnstorming was a glamorous trade, redolent of faraway places and the lure of the road. For the black barnstormer, it was grueling labor mixed with the constant threat—and often reality—of insult, rebuff, and discrimination. But in Negro baseball, barnstorming was necessary for survival.

12 JOSH

There is a catcher that any big-league club would like to buy for $200,000. His name is Gibson . . . he can do everything. He hits the ball a mile. And he catches so easy he might as well be in a rocking chair. Throws like a rifle. Bill Dickey isn't as good a catcher. Too bad this Gibson is a colored fellow.

—WALTER JOHNSON

There is a story that one day during the 1930s the Pittsburgh Crawfords were playing at Forbes Field in Pittsburgh when their young catcher, Josh Gibson, hit the ball so high and far that no one saw it come down. After scanning the sky carefully for a few minutes, the umpire deliberated and ruled it a home run. The next day the Crawfords were playing in Philadelphia when suddenly a ball dropped out of the heavens and was caught by the startled centerfielder on the opposing club. The umpire made the only possible ruling. Pointing to Gibson he shouted, "Yer out—yesterday in Pittsburgh!"

Gibson fans of those years might concede that there was an element of exaggeration in the story, but not much. Josh Gibson was not merely a home-run hitter; he was *the* home-run hitter. He was the black Babe Ruth, and like the Babe a legend in his own time whose prodigious power was celebrated in fact and fancy. But while it is relatively easy to separate fact from fancy in Ruth's legend, Gibson's suffers from the paucity of certified records about the quantity and quality of his home-run production. Old-timers credit Gibson with 89 home runs in one season and 75 in another; many of them, of course, were hit against semipro competition.

Whatever the truth of these claims, a strong case can be made for the proposition that Josh Gibson, a righthand batter, had more power than the great Babe. The clincher in the argument is the

158

Josh Gibson, ready to unleash his awesome power. COURTESY OF BILL
YANCEY

generally accepted fact that Gibson hit the longest home run ever struck in Yankee Stadium, Ruth's home for twelve seasons.

Baseball's bible, *The Sporting News* [June 3, 1967], credits Gibson with a drive in a Negro league game that hit just two feet from the top of the stadium wall circling the bleachers in center field, about 580 feet from home plate. It was estimated that had the drive been two feet higher it would have sailed out of the park and traveled some 700 feet!

Some old Negro league players say that Gibson's longest shot in Yankee Stadium struck the rear wall of the bullpen in left field, about 500 feet from the plate. But Jack Marshall, of the Chicago American Giants, recalls an epic blast by Gibson that went *out* of the stadium—the only fair ball ever hit out of the Yankees' park.

> In 1934, Josh Gibson hit a ball off of Slim Jones in Yankee Stadium in a four-team doubleheader that we had there—the Philadelphia Stars played the Crawfords in the second game; we had played the Black Yankees in the first game. They say a ball has never been hit out of Yankee Stadium. Well, that is a lie! Josh hit the ball over that triple deck next to the bullpen in left field. Over and out! I never will forget that, because we were getting ready to leave because we were going down to Hightstown, N.J., to play a night game and we were standing in the aisle when that boy hit this ball!

Both Ruth and Gibson played before the era of the tape-measure home run when every long hit is carefully computed, almost to the inch. None of Ruth's towering smashes was ever officially measured, but the best guess of his longest is 550 feet. Only one of Gibson's home runs was ever measured. He was with the Homestead Grays in Monessen, Pennsylvania, one day in the late 1930s when he hit a homer of such impressive dimensions that the Mayor ordered the game stopped and a tape measure applied. The result: 512 feet.

Unlike Babe Ruth, whose swing was awesome and whose body wound up like a pretzel when he missed the ball, Gibson's power was generated with little apparent effort. Judy Johnson, who was Gibson's first manager, said:

> It was just a treat to watch him hit the ball. There was no effort at all. You see these guys now get up there in the box and they dig and scratch around before they're ready. Gibson would just walk up there, and he would always turn his left sleeve up, and then just before he swung he'd lift that left foot up.

And when Gibson raised his front foot, the infielders began edging backward onto the grass. If he met the pitch squarely and it came to them on one hop, they knew the ball would be in their glove before Gibson could drop his bat.

Josh Gibson was born December 21, 1911, in Buena Vista, Georgia, a village not far from Atlanta. His father scratched a bare living from a patch of ground outside the village. Josh, the first child of Mark and Nancy Gibson, was named Joshua after his grandfather.

At intervals of three years, two other children were born to the Gibsons: Jerry, who would follow Josh into professional baseball as a pitcher with the Cincinnati Tigers, and Annie. By 1923 the Gibson youngsters were growing up, and it became clear to Mark that if they were to have better opportunities than he had had he must join the swelling migration of black men to the North. And so, late that year, he went to Pittsburgh, where he had relatives, to find work. He quickly got a job as a laborer for Carnegie-Illinois Steel, which was later absorbed by U.S. Steel. In early 1924, Mark sent for his family. Josh was twelve years old when the Gibsons settled down in Pleasant Valley, a Negro enclave in Pittsburgh's North Side.

While equal opportunity was only a pleasant dream for a Negro boy in Pittsburgh, still, the change from the oppressive atmosphere of a southern small town was welcomed. "The greatest gift Dad gave me," Gibson said later, "was to get me out of the South."

Baseball was new to the migrant from Georgia, but he was soon the first one chosen for sandlot pickup games when he began demonstrating a talent for hitting the ball. He was always looking for a ballgame, to play or to watch, and he thought nothing of strapping on rollerskates and skating six miles downriver to Bellevue to see a game.

The young Josh did not care especially for football or basketball, the other neighborhood sports, but swimming caught his interest and as a teen-ager he brought home a number of medals from the city playground pools. At sixteen he was on his first uniformed baseball club—the Gimbels A.C., an all-Negro amateur team playing in Pittsburgh. He was already a catcher, as he would be throughout his career, except for an occasional game in the outfield.

His education was over. Josh had gone through fifth grade in the Negro school in Buena Vista and continued in elementary school in Pittsburgh. He dropped out after completing the ninth grade in Allegheny Pre-Vocational School, where he learned the rudiments of the electrician's trade. He immediately went to work as an apprentice in a plant that manufactured air brakes. But by this time it was clear that Gibson's vocation would be baseball. He was nearing his full size of 6 feet 1 inch and 215 pounds. He had a moon-round, trusting face, a friendly disposition, and the body of a dark Greek god. His broad shoulders sloped down to tremendous arms, thick with muscle, and his barrel chest tapered in the athlete's classic mold to a deceptively slim looking waist. Like his arms, Gibson's legs were heavily muscled.

For a Pittsburgh Negro boy who loved baseball, his goal would have to be the Homestead Grays. He could envy the Pirates' heroes of his youth—the Waners, Lloyd and Paul, and Pie Traynor and Burleigh Grimes and Rabbit Maranville—but he could not hope to step into their shoes. The next best thing was the Homestead Grays, who had started twenty years before in the steel town a few miles upriver and were beginning to emerge as a national Negro baseball power. They had Smoky Joe Williams and Johnny Beckwith and Sam Streeter and Vic Harris and Martin Dihigo—names that meant nothing to the typical Pirate fan but that loomed large in Negro baseball.

In 1929 and 1930, when the Grays were strengthening their position as one of the best Negro ball clubs in the country, Josh Gibson was catching for the Crawford Colored Giants of Pittsburgh. This was a semipro club that Josh had had a hand in organizing around a city recreation building in Pittsburgh's Hill District. The Crawfords (not to be confused with Gus Greenlee's powerhouse, which was formed in 1931) played other semipro clubs in and around Pittsburgh for a few dollars a game. No admission was charged for their games and the collection rarely brought in more than $50, although crowds of 5,000, attracted by the growing awareness of Gibson's power at the plate, were not uncommon.

The Grays, naturally, soon heard of the big, raw slugger. Judy Johnson, who managed Homestead in 1930, said:

> I had never seen him play but we had heard so much about him. Every time you'd look in the paper you'd see where he hit a ball 400 feet, 500 feet. So the fans started wondering why the Homestead Grays didn't pick him up. But we had two catchers. Buck Ewing was the regular catcher, and Vic Harris, an outfielder, used to catch if we were playing a doubleheader.

In late July the Kansas City Monarchs, Negro National League champions of 1929, came to Pittsburgh for a series with the Grays, bringing along their new portable lighting system. On July 25, the Grays and Monarchs were battling under these uncertain lights in Forbes Field. Johnson remembers:

> Joe Williams was pitching that night and we didn't know anything about lights. We'd never played under 'em before, and we couldn't use the regular catcher's signals, because if he put his hand down you couldn't see it. So we used the glove straight up for a fastball and the glove down—that was supposed to be the curve.
>
> Some way Joe Williams and the catcher got crossed up. The catcher was expecting the curve and Joe threw the fast ball and caught him right there, and split the finger. Well, my other catcher was Vic Harris and he was playing the outfield and wouldn't catch. So Josh was sitting in the grandstand, and I asked the Grays' owner, Cum Posey, to get him to finish the game. So Cum asked Josh would he catch, and Josh said, "Yeah, oh yeah!" We had to hold the game up until he went into the clubhouse and got a uniform. And that's what started him out with the Homestead Grays.

Gibson got no hits that night, but he made no errors, either, and that was strange, for he was still a raw-boned, eighteen-year-old and clumsy with the mitt. For the rest of that season, Johnson said, "Josh would catch batting practice and then catch the game, he was so anxious to learn. He wasn't much of a catcher then, but he came along fast."

Despite his shortcomings as a catcher, Gibson became an instant regular on the Grays, although he was often used in the outfield during his first year in top competition. His bat simply had to be in the lineup somewhere.

There remains a wide division of opinion among ballplayers who played with and against Gibson during his prime as to his skill as a catcher. Many maintain that he became a good receiver, but never a great one. They hold that he never learned to catch foul pop-ups, that his arm was adequate, but no more than that, and that as a receiver he was not in the same class with Bruce Petway, who threw out Ty Cobb twice trying to steal second in a series in Cuba in the winter of 1910, or Biz Mackey, whose career began in 1920 and spanned thirty years on top clubs, or Frank Duncan, Kansas City Monarchs catcher of the 1920s.

Walter Johnson's description of Gibson as a rocking-chair catcher with a rifle arm suggests otherwise. Joining Walter Johnson in his opinion that Josh was a superior catcher is Roy Campanella, who was beginning his career in professional baseball with the Baltimore Elite Giants in 1937, about the time Gibson reached his peak. Campanella said that Gibson was a graceful, effortless receiver with a strong, accurate arm. He was, said Campy, "not only the greatest catcher but the greatest ballplayer I ever saw."

The middle ground between these extreme opinions is held by Jimmie Crutchfield, an outfielder who was a teammate of Gibson on the Pittsburgh Crawfords from 1932 through 1936:

> I can remember when he couldn't catch this building if you threw it at him. He was only behind the plate because of his hitting. And I watched him develop into a very good defensive catcher. He was never given enough credit for his ability as a catcher. They couldn't deny that he was a great hitter, but they could deny that he was a great catcher. But I know!

In 1931, Josh Gibson was an established star on the Homestead Grays. He was credited with 75 home runs that year as the Grays barnstormed around Pennsylvania, West Virginia, Ohio, and into the southern reaches of New York State, feeding the growing legend about the young black catcher who could hit the ball a country mile. The next year he was lured to the Pittsburgh Crawfords by the free-spending Gus Greenlee to form with Satchel Paige perhaps the greatest battery in baseball history. Gibson stayed with Greenlee's Crawfords for five summers, his fame growing with each Brobdingnagian clout. In 1934 his record was 69 home runs and in the other years his homer production, although not recorded, was from all accounts similarly Ruthian. Or perhaps Gibsonian.

As Greenlee's dream of a baseball dynasty soured, Gibson jumped back to the Grays near the end of the 1936 season. In 1937 he was listed on the Crawford's spring roster, but by mid-March he was described as a holdout. John L. Clark, Greenlee's publicity man, wrote in the *Pittsburgh Courier* that Greenlee and Rufus (Sonnyman) Jackson, Grays' co-owner, were discussing a trade in which Gibson and Judy Johnson (who had been the Crawfords' third baseman since 1932) would go to the Grays for catcher Pepper Bassett and any infielder, plus $2,500. Here is a measure of Negro baseball's finances. The game's greatest slugger—who was also the

Murderer's Row for the Pittsburgh Crawfords in 1932. Manager Oscar Charleston talks to, from left, Rap Dixon, Josh Gibson, Judy Johnson, and Jud Wilson. COURTESY OF JAMES (COOL PAPA) BELL

paramount drawing card (always excepting Satchel Paige)—and
Negro baseball's most accomplished third baseman were to be traded
for two journeymen players and $2,500.

That the story was in part a ploy to bring Gibson to terms is
evident from Clark's faint praise of the slugger. He said that Gibson
was an asset to any club, "but not the kind of asset that more colorful
and less capable players might be. With all this ability, he has not
developed that 'it' which pulls the cash customers through the turnstiles—although he has been publicized as much as Satchel Paige."
Gibson's lack of color, plus a rumor that he had an offer to manage
an unnamed club at a higher salary than Greenlee would offer,
made it likely that a trade would be made, Clark wrote. Gibson did
not come to terms with Greenlee and a trade went through: Gibson
and Johnson for Pepper Bassett and Henry Spearman. No money
changed hands. Johnson did not report to the Grays.

And so Josh Gibson returned to the Homestead Grays, his first
team. Spring training had hardly begun when he heard the siren
call of the dollar to be made with Satchel Paige in the Dominican Republic. He heeded the call. The *Pittsburgh Courier* reported, most
improbably, that Gibson had gone to Trujillo land with the consent of
the Grays. In any event, he stayed only until July, returning in time
to help the Grays win their first Negro National League championship.

For the next two years, Gibson's big bat was the piledriving punch
on the strongest club in Negro baseball. Boasting Buck Leonard, Sam
Bankhead, Vic Harris, and other sluggers in addition to Josh, the
Grays dominated the league and toyed with their foes on the barnstorming trail. It was such a powerful and well-balanced team that
it could survive the loss of Gibson and continue its mastery over the
NNL in the 1940 and 1941 seasons after Gibson had jumped to the
Mexican League. He earned $6,000 a season with Vera Cruz, accord-
ing to the *Courier,* $2,000 more than he was paid by the Grays. If
Cum Posey and Sonnyman Jackson had looked on with favor when
he had gone to the Dominican Republic in 1937, they were not
pleased by his contract-jumping in later years. They won a court
judgment against Gibson for $10,000 and laid claim to his Pittsburgh
home. But when he signed with the Grays for 1942, all was forgiven
and they dropped the suit. Josh Gibson was at the height of his fame
and near the peak of his incredible power, envied but popular with
other Negro professional ballplayers, and the toast of Pittsburgh's
black community. There was nowhere to go but down, and the slide
would soon begin.

He had come into big-time Negro baseball twelve years before as a rookie of uncommon rawness, a young man so shy and retiring that when he visited in another player's home he spent the evening looking at his shoes. Now he was self-assured, the main attraction at any party, and he had developed a fondness for the bottle. Gibson's drinking never reached the point where he failed to show up for ball-games—or to hit with power—but in his final five seasons he was occasionally suspended for a few days for "failing to observe training rules," in Cum Posey's delicate phrase.

Another, more ominous, portent of the dark days ahead appeared when he began suffering from recurring headaches. On Jan. 1, 1943, he blacked out, lapsing into a coma that lasted all day and hospitalized him for about ten days. The diagnosis was a brain tumor. Doctors at Pittsburgh's St. Francis Hospital wanted to operate, but he would not permit it, according to his sister, Mrs. Annie Mahaffey. "He figured that if they operated, he'd be like a vegetable."

Gibson's knees, too, were giving him trouble, apparently the result of cartilage damage, and he was slowing to a snail's pace compared with his former speed. In his heyday, Gibson, despite his size, had been one of the fastest runners on the Grays. Yet, even while his troubles were pyramiding, Gibson was still the symbol of power. In 1944 he led the Negro National League in homers with 6 while batting .338 in 39 league games. The next year he was again home-run champion with 8 and boasted a league-leading .393 average in 44 games. As a matter of course, he was chosen as the East's catcher in the East-West all-star games in 1944 and 1946. He missed the 1945 all-star game because it was played during one of his periodic suspensions for violating training rules.

Josh Gibson had played baseball the year-round every year from 1933 through 1945, spending the winter seasons in Puerto Rico, Cuba, Mexico, and Venezuela. His greatest thrill, he said, had been winning the batting title and the most-valuable-player award in the Puerto Rican League in 1941. (He was without doubt the most valuable player in the Negro National League for several seasons, but no MVP award was ever given in the NNL.)

Now, in the winter of 1946, his headaches and blackouts were increasing in frequency and severity, and for the first time since 1933 he stayed home in Pittsburgh. Outwardly, he remained a cheerful, easy-going giant, gregarious and friendly, and only his increasing attachment to liquor betrayed his concern about his illness. "He never got drunk so that he was staggering or anything like that,"

Mrs. Mahaffey recalled, "but still it worried you, because he wasn't really a drinking man."

On the evening of Jan. 20, 1947, Josh came home and told his mother that he felt sick. He said that he believed he was going to have a stroke. Mrs. Gibson said, "Shush, Josh, you're not going to have no stroke," but she sent him to bed. The family gathered around his bedside and waited for a doctor while Josh laughed and talked. Then he sent his brother Jerry to the homes of friends to collect his scattered trophies and his radio and bring them home. "So Jerry came back about ten-thirty," Mrs. Mahaffey said, "and we were all laughing and talking, and then he had a stroke. He just got through laughing and then he raised up in the bed and went to talk, but you couldn't understand what he was saying. Then he lay back down and died right off."

There are those who believe his death was caused by his disappointment at being denied the opportunity to play in the big leagues. Ted Page, an outfielder who was Gibson's teammate on the Crawfords, said, "Josh knew he was major-league quality. We would go to a major-league game if we had a day off. He was never the kind of a guy to say, 'I'm the great Josh Gibson,' but if he saw a player make a mistake he would say what should have been done, or he might say, 'I would have been expecting that.' "

Page said that Gibson never complained about the hard lot of the Negro professional.

> He wouldn't have traded his life for anything. One weekend, I remember, we played a twilight game at Forbes Field in Pittsburgh. Afterward we jumped in two cars and drove the 600 miles to St. Louis for a 2 P.M. game the next day. And the next day we drove 350 miles to Kansas City for a doubleheader. It was 110 in the shade, but he loved it. That night Josh and I were sitting on the back porch of the hotel and we saw a kid ballgame and we went and joined it. That's the kind of guy he was.

By the standards of Negro baseball, Gibson was well-paid for such labors. During the boom of the early 1940s, he was, next to Satchel Paige, the highest-salaried performer in the game, earning about $6,000 from the Homestead Grays for a five-month season and adding perhaps $3,000 in winter baseball. (A journeyman black player made about $1,250 for the summer and considerably less during the winter, if he played at all.) While Gibson's salary was higher than that of the average major-leaguer during this period, it was nowhere near that of white stars of his stature like Joe Di-Maggio, Hank Greenberg, and Ted Williams.

Like them, he hit for a high average as well as for distance. Only for the last three years of his career are official records available, but they show him among the batting leaders in the Negro National League and suggest that in his prime he would have boasted a batting average not far below .400 against strong pitching.

As John L. Clark noted during Gibson's salary wrangle with the Crawfords in 1937, he was "colorless" in the same sense that Joe DiMaggio was. It was the colorlessness of perfection, the ability to do the difficult effortlessly. He loved the game and he played to win, but his performance excited only admiration and awe while Satchel Paige, with equally memorable though different skills, added to them a talent for showmanship. The result was that while hundreds went to the ballgame to see Gibson, thousands went to watch Paige.

Gibson died the year after Jackie Robinson had broken organized baseball's color line at Montreal and only months before Robinson would become the first Negro in the major leagues since Fleet and Weldy Walker in 1884. Gibson himself had had two tantalizing nibbles that suggested he might become the first to cross the line. In 1939, Wendell Smith of the *Courier* reported that Bill Benswanger, president of the Pittsburgh Pirates, had promised a trial for Josh and Buck Leonard, the Grays' slugging first baseman. Smith said Cum Posey had agreed to sell his two stars but Benswanger changed his mind. Benswanger's version was different. He said Cum Posey asked him not to sign Gibson because then other Negro stars would be taken and the Negro National League would be wrecked. In any case, no tryout was held.

A few years later, when the Homestead Grays were playing in Griffith Stadium regularly, Gibson and Leonard were called up to the Washington Senators' offices by Clark Griffith, the owner. "He talked to us about Negro baseball and about the trouble there would be if he took us into the big leagues," Leonard said. "But he never did make us an offer."

Griffith must have been sorely tempted to sign the two black men. His Senators were usually mired deep in the American League's second division, and when they were on the road he could look out of his office and watch Gibson and Leonard busting the fences in his park. In one game in 1943, Gibson hit 3 home runs there, one of them landing two feet from the top of the left-centerfield bleachers, 485 feet from the plate. For the season, he belted 11 home runs to left field, the deep field in Griffith Stadium, playing there only once or twice a week, reportedly more than were hit to left in all American League action in that ballpark.

That Josh Gibson would have been one of baseball's superstars if the color line had been lowered earlier is beyond dispute. It is likely that he would have posed the most serious threat ever to Babe Ruth's lifetime record of 714 home runs in the major leagues.

Gibson did achieve a considerable measure of fame, parochial as it was, as the greatest hitter in Negro baseball. After Satchel Paige, his was easily the most famous name among black players. He is remembered with admiration, affection, and even wonder by old teammates and opponents alike, no small legacy for any man. Since Josh Gibson was not a man to pine for what might have been, perhaps the most fitting epitaph that could be devised was pronounced by Ted Page: "He was a big, overgrown kid who was glad for the chance he had. He loved his life."

13 FRESHENING WINDS OF FREEDOM

I am an invisible man. No, I am not a spook like those who haunted Edgar Allan Poe; nor am I one of your Hollywood-movie ectoplasms. I am a man of substance, of flesh and bone, fiber and liquids—and I might even be said to possess a mind. I am invisible, understand, simply because people refuse to see me.
—RALPH ELLISON, *Invisible Man*

The two decades between 1900 and 1920—the period when Negro baseball was growing up—were a time when white America's racial attitudes were hardening. The Black Reconstruction had failed and ebbed into history; Jim Crow was firmly embedded, in fact if not in law, both North and South. Racial tensions exploded in 1906 in Atlanta, where ten Negroes and two whites died in a race riot, and in Springfield, Illinois, two years later when two Negroes and four whites were killed. The Great Migration of Negroes from South to North, beginning in 1915, was accompanied by a crescendo of race fury. During World War I race riots in East St. Louis, Missouri, and Houston, Texas, killed at least thirty-nine Negroes and twenty-five whites. After the Houston uprising, thirteen Negroes were hanged and forty-one imprisoned for life. Immediately after the war, in 1919, there were race riots in twenty-six American cities, the worst in Chicago, where twenty-three Negroes and fifteen whites died.

Riding the tide of race hate, segregation calcified during those two decades. But even during this harsh period for the nation's black men, there was still an occasional white voice raised in organized baseball on behalf of the Negro. In 1915, Walter McCredie, manager of Portland in the Pacific Coast League, tried to provide an opening wedge for Negroes by signing an outfielder of Chinese and Hawaiian parentage. His white players immediately rebelled and McCredie was forced to concede defeat. But, he said, "I

171

don't think the color of the skin ought to be a barrier in baseball.
. . . If I had my say the Afro-American would be welcome inside
the fold. I would like to have such players as Lloyd and Petway of
the Chicago Colored Giants . . ."

Black players also found a champion in *The Sporting News.*
In 1923 the baseball weekly (which, when integration finally arrived, was less than enthusiastic) bemoaned the exclusion of Negroes
from organized baseball. Calling racial prejudice a "hideous mon-
ster," the paper said that it is an "ivory-headed obsession that one
man made in God's image is any better than another man made in
the same image . . ."

Negro players of that day had little hope that black men would
ever play in organized ball. Napoleon Cummings, who began playing
with the Bacharach Giants in Atlantic City, N.J., in 1916, remembers,
"Yes, we talked about it. We talked about it years back, said there
would never be a Negro in the big leagues. But we always used to
talk about it among ourselves."

During the late Twenties such talk among players and fans generally receded. Memories that Negroes had once played in organized
baseball were dimming, and it seemed more and more the natural
order of things that whites played on their teams and Negroes played
on theirs. "We never thought much about it," said Bill Yancey,
whose career as a professional ballplayer spanned the years from
1923 to 1936. ". . . I remember Rojo [a Cuban-Negro catcher]—
he was funny. He didn't speak too much English. He'd see two white
kids throwing a baseball and he'd say, 'Byemby, s'ousands of dollars.' "

Rojo's wistfulness mirrored the belief of Negro players of the 1920s
that organized baseball, and particularly the big leagues, were forever
beyond their aspirations. That belief was reinforced during the care-
free years when America was careening on a headlong course toward
the Depression of 1929. Rarely was a white man's voice heard to
condemn segregation in baseball. In the early Thirties, when the
Depression was at its peak and Americans were blinded to social
justice by the pervasive, nagging struggle to put food on their tables,
Negro players became even more like Ellison's Invisible Man.

In *An American Dilemma,* Gunnar Myrdal put his finger on the
attitude of whites toward blacks during this period:

> The observer finds that in the North there is actually much
> unawareness on the part of white people to the extent of social

discrimination against Negroes. It has been a common experience of this writer to witness how white Northerners are
surprised and shocked when they hear about such things, and
how they are moved to feel that something ought to be done to
stop it. They often do not understand correctly even the impli-
cations of their own behavior and often tell the interviewer
that they "have never thought about it in that light." This
innocence is, of course, opportunistic in a degree, but it is,
nevertheless, real and honest too. It denotes the absence of an
explicit theory and an intentional policy. In this situation one
of the main difficulties for the Negroes in the North is simply
lack of publicity. It is convenient for the Northerners' good
conscience to forget about the Negro.

When the question of Negroes playing in the big leagues *was*
presented to them, most Northerners did seem to feel that "something ought to be done." In 1928 the New York *Daily News* Inquir-
ing Photographer asked six whites whether they would disapprove of
a black player in the big leagues. Four said they would not, and the
two who said they would gave as their reason a fear that the fans'
race prejudice would inflame the strong feelings aroused by competition on the diamond and possibly lead to riots in the stands. Typical
of the favorable replies was this one by a Bronx salesman: "Certainly
not. There shouldn't be any race prejudice. It isn't as bitter now as
it used to be, and I think prejudice is gradually dying out. Colored
men can enter almost any other field (sic). Why not baseball?"

Why not indeed? Years later, after the color line was finally ex-
punged, Judy Johnson became a scout for the Philadelphia Athletics
and a good friend of the A's venerable owner, Connie Mack. Johnson
recalls, "I asked him one day, I said, 'Mr. Mack, why didn't you
ever take any of the colored boys in the big leagues?' He said, 'Well,
Judy, if you want to know the truth, there were just too many of
you to go in.' As much as to say, it would take too many jobs away
from the other boys."

However, the Negroes who played in the Philadelphia area during
this time felt that Mack himself was prepared to accept Negroes if
his lodge brothers in the league would not protest too much.

Napoleon Cummings remembers talk around Philadelphia in 1929
that Connie Mack wanted to hire a couple of Negro players:

I remember when they played the '29 World Series, they were
short of ballplayers, and there was a rumor around here that

they wanted to get somebody from around Philadelphia to help them out because they were short. But they wouldn't let Negroes on that ballclub. I remember that, and I was at the World Series. Connie Mack was trying to get Biz Mackey and Santop and all them. No soap.

If Mack did try to hire Negroes for his Athletics, he did not make sufficient fuss about it for the story to break into print. Why didn't he just go ahead and do it? There was no written rule barring Negroes from organized baseball. What stopped him? Presumably the answer lies in the attitudes of the other major-league operators.

The reasons advanced during this period for baseball's color line (on the rare occasions when it was mentioned) were substantially the same as they were in 1946, when it was finally breached. They can be summarized thus:

(1) About a third of all major-league players were Southerners and they would not play with or against Negroes; (2) Negroes could not travel with a big-league club, because hotels would not accommodate them; (3) the clubs trained in the South, where Negroes and whites were forbidden by law to play together; (4) fans might riot in the stands if there was trouble on the field between a white and Negro player; (5) Negroes were not good enough to play in the big leagues anyway.

The first reason given was probably the most serious. It seems likely that some southern players would not have played on the same field with a Negro during the late Twenties and Thirties. But the evidence from the late Forties, when they *were* playing with Negroes, suggests that defections would have been few. Southerners, no less than Northerners, coveted the fame and fortune offered by major-league baseball.

Reasons 2 and 3 were evasions. Plenty of Negro players would have been perfectly willing to be Jim Crowed in hotels for a chance to play in the majors. As for spring training, Cuba and other areas of Latin America provided acceptable facilities, as the Brooklyn Dodgers would demonstrate when the color bar was crumbling.

Reason 4, the danger of racially motivated skirmishes in the stands, was a reasonable concern. But in retrospect it seems probable that if the way had been carefully prepared (as it was in Brooklyn), there would have been little trouble among the fans. In addition, some owners feared they would lose their white fans if they played Negroes. After all, organized baseball is a business; it cannot exist without paying customers.

Concerning Reason 5, the quality of Negro players, the testimony is mixed. Many white ballplayers and respected sportswriters believed that at least a few black players were of major-league calibre. Some baseball men were doubtful. In any case, this was not a very good reason, because, if Negroes were truly not ready for the majors, could they not have been initiated into organized baseball in the minors? (In fact, this turned out to be the way the color line was broken.)

Unspoken, but underlying all the stated objections, was the most compelling reason of all: baseball tradition. Organized baseball was steeped—perhaps a better word would be pickled—in tradition. Among the eternal verities were the sun's rising in the east, the sanctity of motherhood, and baseball's status as the National Pastime; and, since there had not been a Negro in the organized leagues in the memory of most baseball men, it must be part of God's plan that there should be none. Tradition is the father of inertia and the balm of the don't-rock-the-boat school.

By the early Thirties, gentle waves were washing against the stately hull of organized baseball. The Negro press had of course been running a low-keyed but persistent campaign to break down the bars for years, but the first powerful voice to raise the issue in the white press was Westbrook Pegler, who denounced baseball for its apartheid in 1931.

Jimmy Powers of the New York *Daily News* soon took up the cudgels and hammered at the ban for several years. In 1933 he conducted his own poll of the dignitaries at the annual Baseball Writers Association dinner on the question of admitting Negroes to the major leagues. Curiously, the only important baseball man who opposed the idea was John J. McGraw, who had tried in vain to sign Charlie Grant for the Baltimore Orioles more than thirty years earlier. Powers did not explain the basis for McGraw's opposition.

One of the problems in breaking down the color bar was the reluctance of baseball's leaders to admit officially that it even existed. John A. Heydler, president of the National League, could say without blushing in 1933, "Beyond the fundamental requirement that a major-league player must have unique ability and good character and habits, I do not recall one instance where baseball has allowed either race, creed or color to enter into its selection of players."

It was becoming increasingly difficult to sustain this sort of nonsense in the face of the performances against big-leaguers in post-season games by men like Satchel Paige, Josh Gibson, Buck

Leonard, Slim Jones, and Cool Papa Bell. In 1938, Clark Griffith became the first member of baseball's official family to admit to the possibility that Negroes might one day be in organized baseball. In an interview with Sam Lacy, an enterprising reporter for the Washington *Tribune,* a Negro weekly, Griffith said:

> There are few big-league magnates who are not aware of the fact that the time is not far off when colored players will take their places beside those of other races in the major leagues. However, I'm not sure that time has arrived yet . . .

Griffith predicted:

> A lone Negro in the game will face caustic comments. He will be made the target of cruel, filthy epithets. Of course, I know the time will come when the ice will have to be broken. Both by the organized game and by the colored player who is willing to volunteer and thus become a sort of martyr to the cause.

There was no shortage of willing volunteers among the black players. No one, not even Griffith, called for them, but the race question appears to have been on his mind as indicated by his talk with Josh Gibson and Buck Leonard in his office after he had watched the two black men belting the ball.

As the third decade of the century neared its close, powerful voices in the press were calling loudly for an end to baseball's discrimination against Negroes. In New York, Heywood Broun and Jimmy Powers were excoriating the major leagues. Shirley Povich of the Washington *Post* wrote after watching Negro clubs train in Florida:

> There's a couple of million dollars' worth of baseball talent on the loose, ready for the big leagues, yet unsigned by any major league. There are pitchers who would win 20 games this season for any big-league club that offered them contracts, and there are outfielders who could hit .350, infielders who could win quick recognition as stars, and there is at least one catcher who at this writing is probably superior to Bill Dickey. [The reference is to Josh Gibson.]

Only one thing is keeping them out of the big leagues—the pigmentation of their skin. They happen to be colored. That's their crime in the eyes of the big-league club owners. . . . Their talents are being wasted in the rickety parks in the Negro sections of Pittsburgh, Philadelphia, New York, Chicago and four other cities that comprise the major leagues of Negro baseball. They haven't a chance to get into the big leagues of the white folks. It's a tight little boycott that the majors have set up against colored players.

A magazine called *Friday* kept the pot simmering in 1940 by soliciting comments from a number of major-league players and managers on the quality of Negro ballplayers. The response of Gabby Hartnett, manager of the Chicago Cubs, is fairly representative: "I am not interested in the color of a player, just his ability," Hartnett said. "If managers were given permission, there'd be a mad rush to sign up Negroes."

Bill McKechnie, Cincinnati Reds manager, and Leo Durocher, then piloting the Brooklyn Dodgers, replied in a similar vein. Stars like Pepper Martin, Luke Hamlin, Bucky Walters, Johnny Vander Meer, and Carl Hubbell praised Negro players. So did William Benswanger, president of the Pittsburgh Pirates, who declared, "If it came to an issue, I'd vote for Negro players. There's no reason why they should be denied the same chance that Negro fighters and musicians are given."

Benswanger had no appetite for the role of pioneer, however, as he proved in 1942, when the *Daily Worker,* a Communist newspaper published in New York, put pressure on the Pirates. In his autobiography, Roy Campanella tells of being approached by a man from the *Worker* (which he did not know was a Communist paper) who said he had arranged a tryout with the Pirates for Campanella, Dave Barnhill, New York Cubans pitcher, and Sammy Hughes, second baseman for the Baltimore Elite Giants. Long afterward, Campanella got a letter from Benswanger saying that the Pirates would be glad to arrange a tryout, "but it contained so many buts that I was discouraged even before I had finished reading the letter." He replied that all he asked for was a chance. The Pirates did not answer his letter.

The *Worker* quoted Leo Durocher, manager of the Brooklyn Dodgers, as blaming the baseball commissioner's office for the color bar. Commissioner Kenesaw Mountain Landis reacted with stern words.

Negroes are not barred from organized baseball by the commissioner and never have been during the twenty-one years I have served. There is no rule in organized baseball prohibiting their participation and never has been to my knowledge. If Durocher, or any other manager, or all of them, want to sign one, or twenty-five, Negro players, it is all right with me. That is the business of the managers and the club owners. The business of the commissioner is to interpret the rules of baseball and to enforce them.

Negro players were not encouraged by the rising level of discussion about the injustice of the color line. Buck Leonard remembers:

We didn't think anything was going to happen. We thought that they were just going to keep talking about it, that's all. They'd talked about it all those years and there'd been nothing done. We just didn't pay it any attention. We'd say, well, if it comes, we hope to have a chance to play, but we just didn't pay it any mind.

Despite the Negro players' fatalism, the quickening tempo of talk about the color bar was significant; it told of subtle changes in America's racial attitudes. Segregation was still the rule, but it was becoming a shaky bulwark against the steady pricking of white America's conscience by the social and economic changes wrought by Roosevelt's New Deal, the Negro's improving educational and living standards, and perhaps most of all, by World War II. With American black men fighting along with whites in the far corners of the globe, it was no longer quite so convenient for whites at home to forget their black compatriots.

Whitey Gruhler, sports columnist of the Atlantic City *Press-Union* and one of the few white writers who had covered Negro baseball regularly, gave voice to the nation's moral crisis in July 1942, when America had been in the war for seven months. Gruhler had been calling in vain for the entry of Negro players into organized baseball for several years; now, with America fighting for its life, he found himself in the mainstream, articulating a thought that had growing echoes:

We are fighting a war—the most terrible war in all history. We are spending billions of dollars. Our youth is shedding barrels and barrels of blood. Every day is one of heartache and tragedy. And what are we fighting for? Freedom and democracy. But some of us seem to have forgotten that freedom and democracy are the human rights for which we fought the Civil War.

But baseball's conservatives were not yet ready for such a drastic step as removal of the color line. *The Sporting News* argued that Negroes were better off in their own leagues and that they were not ready or even willing to mingle with whites. The paper blamed "agitators" who "have sought to force Negro players on the big leagues, not because it would help the game but because it gives them a chance to thrust themselves into the limelight as great crusaders in the guise of democracy." After noting that some Negro baseball men were lukewarm to the idea of integration, *The Sporting News* concluded:

> Of course, there are some colored people who take a different view, and they are entitled to their opinions, but in doing so they are not looking at the question from the broader point of view, or for the ultimate good of either the race or the individuals in it. They ought to concede their own people are now protected and that nothing is served by allowing agitators to make an issue of a question on which both sides prefer to be let alone.

Larry MacPhail, president of the Brooklyn Dodgers, echoed this view. When a Brooklyn priest asked MacPhail whether the Dodgers would be willing to have Negro players, MacPhail replied that black players had their own leagues which would be wrecked if Negroes were in the majors. "Unfortunately," he added, "the discussion of the problem has been contaminated by charges of racial discrimination—most of it vicious propaganda circulated by professional agitators who do not know what they are talking about."

Other baseball executives, although uncertain that the time was yet ripe for introducing black players into organized baseball, saw that it was coming. Among them was William K. Wrigley, Jr., owner of the Chicago Cubs, who said he foresaw the day—"and soon." But, he declared, "there are men in high places who don't want it."

It was becoming apparent that the color question could not be kept submerged indefinitely, and in 1943 it surfaced in two places 3,000 miles apart. In Los Angeles that spring, Clarence (Pants) Rowland, president of the Pacific Coast League Angels, said trials would be given to three Negro players, Chet Brewer, Howard Easterling, and Nate Moreland. Two weeks later he reneged, apparently under pressure from other league operators, but his retreat brought a flurry of protests. The Los Angeles County Board of Supervisors and the huge local of the United Auto Workers union at North American Aircraft went on record opposing discrimination in the Pacific Coast League. The Angels' park was picketed on opening day.

There was trouble in Oakland, too, where Art Cohn, sports editor of the *Tribune,* scored the Oaks for not trying out Negroes. Oakland owner Vince Devincenzi ordered his manager, Johnny Vergez, to give trials to two Negroes, Chet Brewer and Olin Dial, but Vergez refused, despite the fact that most of the good Oakland players were in service.

Meanwhile, at the other end of the nation, Bill Veeck was trying to dig the grave of the color line. Veeck was a master showman and innovator who had been operating the Milwaukee Brewers of the American Association and who, after the war, would bring pennants to the Cleveland Indians and Chicago White Sox (and, incidentally, introduce the first Negroes into the American League). He also suffered the ultimate indignity of presiding over the St. Louis Browns.

Veeck's plan was to buy the sinking Philadelphia Phillies franchise and stock the club with Negro stars for the 1944 season. "With Satchel Paige, Roy Campanella, Luke Easter, Monte Irvin, and countless others in action and available, I had not the slightest doubt that in 1944, a war year, the Phils would have leaped from seventh place to the pennant," Veeck says in his book, *Veeck—as in Wreck.*

Jerry Nugent, president of the Phillies, was willing to sell and Veeck had lined up the necessary financing, but, Veeck says, "I made one bad mistake. Out of long respect for Judge Landis, I felt he was entitled to prior notification of what I intended to do. . . . Judge Landis wasn't exactly shocked but he wasn't exactly overjoyed either. His first reaction, in fact, was that I was kidding him."

The plan foundered soon afterward when Veeck learned that Nugent had turned the team back to the National League, and that Ford Frick, the league president, had arranged its sale to William Cox, a lumber dealer, "for about half what I was willing to pay." So that dream died.

The pressures against baseball's segregation were not building up in a vacuum. In 1941, under the threat of a "March on Washington" by thousands of Negroes, President Franklin D. Roosevelt had issued an executive order establishing a Fair Employment Practices Commission. That first FEPC was not a vigorous enforcement agency, but it did turn the spotlight on discriminatory hiring policies in industry, and it paved the way for state laws barring discrimination in employment.

In 1944 the New York State Legislature began considering the Ives-Quinn Bill to forbid discrimination in hiring on the basis of race, creed, color, or national origin. It was not aimed specifically at baseball's color line, but only the most myopic big-league operator could fail to see that it meant eventual legal challenge to the "gentleman's agreement." Given the increasing awareness of white Americans to the insults and outrages suffered daily by black citizens, there was not much question that it would be passed.

So the stage was being set for the climactic scene in the story of Negro baseball. Appropriately it was to be enacted in New York, the big town, which was represented in the six-club Negro National League in 1944 by the weak sisters of the circuit, the New York Black Yankees and the New York Cubans. If Harlem's fans mourned the lowly status of the Black Yankees and Cubans, it was not for long; bigger things were in the air than the final standings of the NNL's pennant race.

PART III:

AND THE WALLS CAME TUMBLING DOWN

14 EMANCIPATION PROCLAMATION

With us, the first man to break down the bars must be suited in every sense of the world. We can't afford to have any misfits pioneering for us, and for obvious reasons. Unwilling as they are to employ Negro players, they will be quick to draw the old cry: "We gave 'em a chance and look what we got."

—SAM LACY, AFRO-AMERICAN NEWSPAPERS, *1945*

The cataclysm of World War II was grinding inexorably toward its bloody end in the spring of 1945. Allied armies were mopping up remnants of the Nazi war machine in Europe; in the U.S., scientists were secretly preparing the first test of the atomic bomb, which, late that summer, would end the war in the Pacific in holocausts over two Japanese cities. In the little world of baseball, another evil was making its final stand that spring. The color line was being buffeted at every hand, but it appeared to be solid enough to stand another year or two.

The two men who would finally pierce it were half a continent apart and barely aware of each other's existence. The first was a twenty-six-year-old black man named Jack Roosevelt Robinson, the son of a Georgia sharecropper, who had just joined the Kansas City Monarchs as a shortstop. The second was a paunchy sixty-two-year-old white man named Wesley Branch Rickey, who, after a three-year career as a major-league catcher ending in 1907, had become the most successful front-office operator in baseball. He was president and general manager of the Brooklyn Dodgers. Before the year was out, their paths would converge and together they would write the beginning of the end for lily-white baseball.

Meanwhile, though, two sideshows were played as pressure against the color wall continued. Rickey himself was an unwilling actor in the first one, whose scene was the Dodgers' war-years' training camp at Bear Mountain, New York. One day during training, Joe Bostic, sports editor of the Negro *People's Voice* arrived unannounced with a photographer for the *Daily Worker,* Terris McDuffie, a thirty-six-year-old pitcher who had won 5 games and lost 6 for the Newark Eagles in 1944, and Dave (Showboat) Thomas, a thirty-nine-year-old first baseman of the New York Cubans. Bostic demanded a tryout for the two players. Rickey acceded and watched them perform for 45 minutes—the first time any Negro had worked out under the eyes of a major-league operator since Charlie Grant in 1901. Rickey was unimpressed by their talents and convinced that neither man was equipped for the role of pioneer in organized baseball.

For the second sideshow, the scene shifted to Boston, where two city councilmen had been pressing the Red Sox and Braves to hire black players. One of them, Isadore H. Y. Muchnick, whose constituency was largely Negro, had threatened to fight issuance of the annual permit for Sunday games unless the two Boston clubs ended the ban on black players.

Under Muchnick's pressure, the Red Sox and Braves finally agreed to a tryout for Negroes. Wendell Smith of the *Pittsburgh Courier,* who had been campaigning against the color line for several years, heard about the hassle in Boston and decided to capitalize on it. He called Muchnick and offered to furnish players of major league quality for the test.

So it was arranged. Smith brought Jackie Robinson from the Monarchs, Sam Jethroe, Cleveland Buckeyes outfielder, and Marvin Williams, Philadelphia Stars infielder, to Boston. The Braves were out of town and the Red Sox stalled the planned tryout for several days until Muchnick convinced them he meant business about fighting Sunday baseball. The trial was then scheduled for April 16.

Robinson, Jethroe, and Williams joined a dozen young white aspirants on the field at Fenway Park and began shagging for batting practice, making all the plays look easy. Then they were called in to bat and immediately all three began to demonstrate big-league hitting ability. Robinson recalls:

> In my view, nobody put on an exhibition like we did. Everything we did, it looked like the good Lord was guiding us. Every ball the pitcher threw up became a line drive someplace. We tattooed that short left-field fence—that is, Marv and I

did—and Jethroe was doing extremely well from the left side, too. And he looked like a gazelle in the outfield.

Manager Joe Cronin and Coach Hugh Duffy said they were impressed by the three Negroes. Duffy, who had hit .438 for Boston in 1894, told Smith, "There is no doubt about it that they are ballplayers. They looked good to me." But it was stated that the Red Sox would not hire them after such short tryouts. The players filled out application blanks and were told they would hear from the Red Sox, a polite brushoff meaning good-bye and good luck.

"That ended it," Robinson said. "We didn't go over to the Braves."

The trials for McDuffie and Thomas by the Dodgers, and Robinson, Jethroe, and Williams by the Red Sox, were not greeted with hosannahs in the Negro press. Frank A. Young of the *Chicago Defender* was critical, and Cum Posey, in the *Pittsburgh Courier,* called them "travesties." "It was the most humiliating experience Negro baseball has yet suffered from white organized baseball," he added.

The tryouts were, however, surface manifestations of the ferment in baseball. The major-league owners, spurred by the picketing of Yankee Stadium for the Yankees' home-opener against the Red Sox, appointed a two-man committee to study the color question. The two men were Branch Rickey and Larry MacPhail, Rickey's predecessor at Brooklyn, who was now general manager of the Yankees. In August, New York's Mayor Fiorello La Guardia added a subcommittee on baseball to his Anti-Discrimination Committee and got Rickey and MacPhail as members. Intensifying the squeeze on big-league owners was the statement by A. B. (Happy) Chandler, who was named baseball's commissioner after the death of Judge Landis in 1944, that he would not oppose the introduction of black players. "I don't believe in barring Negroes from baseball just because they are Negroes," the new commissioner said.

Beneath the visible turmoil, a plan was slowly reaching fruition. It was the work of the shrewd mind of Branch Rickey, who had demonstrated his far-sightedness before coming to Brooklyn by inventing the farm system, an innovation with which he established a pennant-winning dynasty for the St. Louis Cardinals. Now he was to lead the way again.

Born in 1881 to a devout fundamentalist family on a southern Ohio farm, Branch Rickey was successively schoolteacher, professional baseball player (who refused to play on Sunday), college baseball coach, and lawyer before entering baseball administration with the St. Louis Browns in 1913. By 1942, when he became president and general manager of the Brooklyn Dodgers, he was probably the best-known executive in baseball—certainly the most successful.

The Dodgers, who had won the National League pennant in 1941 and finished second in 1942, were aging. Looking toward the future after the war, Rickey talked with George U. McLaughlin, president of the Brooklyn Trust Co. (which had the controlling interest in the Dodgers), about mass scouting and signing of young players. "That might include a Negro player or two," he said.

McLaughlin replied that it sounded fine to him. "You might come up with something. . . . And if you don't, you're sunk," the bank president said.

And so the wheels were set in motion in 1943 to cross the color line. Rickey was not a simple man, and the decision was the product of the complex motives of a humanitarian who was also a hard-headed businessman. The Dodger president could think back to a vow made forty years earlier when he was baseball coach at Ohio Wesleyan University and his Negro catcher, Charles Thomas, was Jim Crowed at a hotel in South Bend, Indiana. He remembered Thomas' cry as he looked at his hands: "Black skin! Oh, if only I could make them white!" Rickey had promised himself that day he would do whatever he could to still that cry when the opportunity presented itself. The time was near to fulfill that vow, but it was by no means Rickey's chief purpose in his plan to end baseball's discrimination. In fact, says Arthur Mann, Rickey's biographer, although he had "firm beliefs about the equality of man . . . they were never a factor in his decision. The sole issue was a colored man's ability to play organized baseball."

Armed with the backing of the Dodgers' owners, Rickey's next step was to find the right black player. This was crucial to his plan, for he was well aware that the wrong man could set back the cause of the Negro player by years if not decades. The man he wanted had to be not only a potential star on the field but exemplary in his conduct off it. For two years he received reports from friends who checked on Negro players in Mexico, Puerto Rico, and Cuba, as well as the United States, but it was not until early 1945 that he went at it in earnest.

Because he was convinced that considerable flak would fly if he revealed his true purpose, Rickey disguised his scouting of Negroes by announcing that he intended to start a Negro team called the Brooklyn Brown Dodgers, who would play at Ebbetts Field when the Dodgers were away. The new team was to be entered in the United States Baseball League, which was set up in January 1945. The moving spirit behind the U.S. League was Gus Greenlee, who, after resigning as president and taking his Crawfords out of the Negro National League in 1939, had been rebuffed in all efforts to rejoin in subsequent years. At the start of the season, the league included Greenlee's Crawfords; the Brown Dodgers, who were managed by Oscar Charleston; the Chicago Brown Bombers, managed by Bingo DeMoss; the Toledo Rays; Philadelphia Hilldale Club, and the Detroit Motor City Giants.

Rickey threw his support behind the new league at a press conference following the tryout of Terris McDuffie and Showboat Thomas at Bear Mountain. The older leagues, he said, were merely fronts for monopolistic game-booking enterprises and were "in the zone of a racket." With his aid, Rickey told the press, the new league would be run on a businesslike basis and might eventually join organized baseball. (The United States League never became a serious threat to the Negro National or Negro American leagues and barely stumbled through the season before finally succumbing in 1946. But it offered Rickey an admirable screen for his scouting of Negroes.)

The camouflage was so effective that some segments of the Negro press bristled with indignation that another white man was moving in to try to control black baseball. Frank A. Young stormed in the *Defender* that Rickey was "trying to assume the role of an Abraham Lincoln in Negro baseball." Noting that Rickey, at his press conference, had refused to discuss the question of Negroes in the big leagues, Young wrote: "We want Negroes in the major leagues if they have to crawl to get there, but we won't have any major-league owners running any segregated leagues for us. We have enough 'black' this and 'brown' that in tagging ball clubs in various cities now and we don't need any more."

With the Brown Dodgers in business, Branch Rickey was able to turn loose his ace scouts—George Sisler, Wid Matthews, Tom Greenwade, and Clyde Sukeforth—ostensibly to find players for that club. Reports began to filter back to his office about Marvin Williams, Sam Jethroe, Showboat Thomas, Piper Davis of the Birmingham Black Barons, Satchel Paige, Silvio Garcia of the New York Cubans, Josh Gibson, and several others. But the name most often mentioned favorably was that of Jackie Robinson of the Kansas City Monarchs.

Robinson was in his first season in professional baseball, having joined the Monarchs in April 1945. He was born January 31, 1919, on a plantation near Cairo, Georgia, the youngest of five children of Jerry and Mallie Robinson. When Jackie was barely six months old, his father tired of sharecropping and left the family to make a new start in Texas. A year later, Mrs. Robinson, hoping for a better life for her children than Georgia offered, took her brood to California. Settling in Pasadena, she contended with poverty and racial hostility to raise her young family on her earnings as a domestic supplemented by welfare payments.

Jackie grew up in a mixed neighborhood with whites, blacks, and boys of Mexican and Japanese ancestry and quickly established himself as a versatile athlete. In high school, Pasadena Junior College, and at UCLA, he earned growing fame as a baseball player, track man, basketball player, and, especially, as a football player. By his senior year, 1941, he was widely acclaimed as the best all-around athlete on the West Coast, if not in the country.

After three years on limited service in the Army (because of bone chips in an ankle), Jackie Robinson was discharged as a second-lieutenant and joined the Monarchs with a verbal contract for $400 a month. In 41 games in the Negro American League that year he hit .345, with 10 doubles, 4 triples, and 5 home runs, and was the West's shortstop in the East-West game.

The other players in the NAL were not at first impressed by Robinson. Jimmie Crutchfield, who was with the Chicago American Giants in 1945, recalls:

> The first time I saw Jackie he was fat and I was of the opinion that the Monarchs just got him for his name. His first time at bat against us that spring—we were in Houston, Texas—he hit a ball just inside the bag and made it to second base easily. And the next night we were in Muskogee, Oklahoma, and I hit a ball through the box and across second base. It was an exhibition game early in the spring, and I wasn't putting forth my best effort, but the play was just like that—bang, bang!—at first base. Jackie raved and I told the umpire, "Throw him out of the ball game! He's just a young busher, he hasn't been up here two weeks." And boy, he left second base and started toward me, and I started toward him—but he was around 225 pounds then—and I started to laugh and he turned around and went back to his position.

The next night we were in Oklahoma City, and I hit one through the box again and the guy came up with the ball and I began to watch him. And I told the other guys on the team, "I'm surprised, this guy's got it." But no one else wanted to admit it.

As Crutchfield indicated, Robinson was a fierce competitor who put his heart and soul into the game. Off the field he was friendly and affable and, as a non-drinker and non-smoker, something of an oddity to the hard-drinking night owls on the Monarchs.

After his sham tryout with Jethroe and Williams in Boston, Robinson settled down to the nomadic life of a black ballplayer, enduring the constant travel by bus, the fleabag hotels and the scruffy playing conditions of Negro baseball. He was unaware that he was being carefully watched by Dodger scouts, who continued to send back glowing reports on this young man as a fine prospect for Rickey's Brooklyn Brown Dodgers.

By this time, Rickey had pretty well settled on Robinson as his candidate for pioneer. To make doubly sure that the Monarchs' shortstop could stand up to the abuse that inevitably would be heaped upon the first Negro in organized baseball in modern times, Rickey himself went to California to check Robinson's reputation there. The only criticism he found was that Robinson did not hesitate to stand up for his rights, either on or off the field, that he was not slow to protest when an attempt was made to Jim Crow him. It was a criticism that Rickey was glad to hear, for the pioneer had to be a man of courage as well as great baseball skills.

In late August, while the Monarchs were playing the American Giants at Comiskey Park in Chicago, Dodger scout Clyde Sukeforth visited Robinson and asked him to come to Brooklyn to meet Rickey. And so, on August 28, 1945, Jackie Robinson arrived with Sukeforth in the Dodgers' office, believing that he was going to receive an offer to play with the Brown Dodgers. That idea was quickly dispelled when Rickey said, "You were brought here to play for the Brooklyn organization—perhaps, as a start, for Montreal."

Thus began one of the most extraordinary interviews in sports history—a three-hour monologue by the bushy-browed, cigar-chomping president of the Brooklyn Dodgers. Rickey, with the flamboyant gestures of a Shakespearean actor and a voice to match, outlined in graphic detail the insults and abuse Robinson would face as the first man to step over baseball's color line in nearly a half-century.

Giving his thespian instincts free rein, Rickey played all the parts as he sketched for the ballplayer the confrontations he would have with Negro-hating players and umpires on the field and with hotel clerks and restaurant managers off it.

"Mr. Rickey," Robinson said, "do you want a ballplayer who's afraid to fight back?"

"I want a ballplayer with guts enough *not* to fight back," Rickey thundered. "You've got to do this job with base hits and stolen bases and fielding ground balls, Jackie. *Nothing else.*"

Finally, with both men emotionally drained by the marathon performance, Robinson agreed to play baseball in 1946 for the Montreal Royals, Brooklyn's top farm in the International League, with a bonus of $3,500 and a salary of $600 a month. Rickey pledged Robinson to secrecy, because he wanted to hold off announcement of the agreement until December to give the hot stove league something to chew over just before the Dodgers began spring training. Robinson went back to the Monarchs, informing only his mother and his fiancée about his fantastic day with Branch Rickey.

But events were conspiring to accelerate the announcement. All three big-league teams in New York were being urged by the new State Fair Employment Practices Commission to sign an agreement not to discriminate, and Mayor Fiorello La Guardia was publicizing the work of his Anti-Discrimination Committee in radio broadcasts and hinting that shortly baseball's color line would be overstepped because of it. About the middle of October, he asked Rickey if he could report to the people that organized baseball would soon begin signing Negroes. Rickey asked him to hold off the announcement for a week.

The Dodger president believed that it would be a mistake to permit an inference that he was hiring Robinson because of political and social pressures rather than because the Monarchs' infielder was a great athlete, so he determined to announce Robinson's signing quickly, thus putting an end to the possibility of making it a political football. He directed Robinson to fly to Montreal, and there on October 23, 1945, Jackie Robinson signed his contract to play the 1946 season with the Montreal Royals.

The announcement was easily the top sports story of the year, and the newspapers worked it over thoroughly, getting comments from almost everyone who conceivably could have an opinion about Ne-

Jackie Robinson signs his contract to play for the Montreal Royals in 1946. At left is Hector Racine, Royals' president; standing, Branch Rickey, Jr., head of the Brooklyn Dodgers' farm system.
WIDE WORLD PHOTOS

groes in general or Robinson in particular. On their editorial pages, the papers were in the main favorably inclined, even in the South.

White major-leaguers were either noncommittal or wished Robinson well, except most of those from the South, who predictably said Rickey's "experiment" would not work and that they certainly never expected to play on a club with a Negro. A few, like Bob Feller, the Cleveland Indians' ace pitcher, who had faced Robinson while barnstorming, said they doubted that he had major-league ability.

Judge William G. Bramham, head of the organized minor leagues, said that of course his office would approve Robinson's contract, since it was perfectly legal, but he had harsh words for Rickey:

Father Divine will have to look to his laurels, for we can expect Rickey Temple to be in the course of construction in Harlem soon. The Negro is making rapid strides in baseball, as well as in other lines of endeavor. They have their own form of player contracts, and, as I understand it, their organizations are well officered and are financially successful. Why should we raid their ranks, grab a player and put him, his baseball associates, and his race in a position that will inevitably prove harmful?

Bramham was not only intemperate, he was ill-informed about the Negro leagues' organizational strength. Almost immediately a debate broke out over whether Robinson had broken a Monarchs' contract to sign with Montreal. Tom Y. Baird, co-owner of the Monarchs with J. L. Wilkinson, maintained that he had a legal contract with Robinson. "We won't take this lying down," he said, promising to protest to Commissioner Chandler. But his partner and brother-in-law, who had founded the Monarchs twenty-six years earlier, was conciliatory:

Although I feel that the Brooklyn club or the Montreal club owes us some kind of consideration for Robinson, we will not protest to Commissioner Chandler. I am very glad to see Jackie get this chance, and I'm sure he'll make good. He's a wonderful ballplayer. If and when he gets into the major leagues he will have a wonderful career.

Robinson had, in fact, no written contract with the Monarchs, merely a verbal agreement to play so long as $400 was laid on the line each month. But Clark Griffith, owner of the Washington Senators, whose inept ballclub and conscience seem to have made him consider signing Negro players several years before, joined Baird and other Negro clubowners in protesting the signing of Robinson with no payment to the Monarchs. He urged the Negro leagues to go to Chandler and fight for their rights. Chandler told them he could do nothing.

Dr. J. B. Martin, president of the Negro American League and owner of the Chicago American Giants, foresaw great things ahead for Negro baseball. "I do not think this is going to hurt Negro baseball one bit," Martin asserted. "In fact, we may now be in a position to sell players to the major leagues. Robinson is a fine ballplayer and I'm sure he'll make good."

There was a considerable division of opinion in Negro player ranks, both about whether Negroes could get along with white players, particularly in traveling, eating, and lodging arrangements, and about Robinson's talents and the likelihood of his making good. Without exception they wished him well, but they knew that a hard road was ahead for him in the white league. As to his chances of making the majors, Buck Leonard said, "We didn't think he was going to get there. We thought we had other ballplayers who were better players than he. We thought maybe they were going to get there, but we didn't think he would." On the other hand, Jimmie Crutchfield recalls that when he was asked late that fall about Jackie's chances he said Robinson was "a cinch" and would "be in the major leagues in less time than two years and he will lead the league in everything." Then, contrary to Leonard's opinion, Crutchfield added that "we didn't have a lot of guys who were capable of playing that kind of ball. Most of the good ballplayers were over the hill."

The organized baseball establishment, which (except for the Dodger organization) was abysmally ignorant about the skills of most Negro players and the workings of the black leagues, tended to view Robinson's chances of making good even in the International League as remote. *The Sporting News* gave the establishment's view the week after Robinson's signing:

> Col. Larry MacPhail of the Yankees, who some time ago wrote a long report on the Negro-in-baseball question to the Mayor's Committee in New York, and Rickey himself, admit there is not a single Negro player with major league possibilities for 1946. Satchel Paige, of course, is barred by his age. Nor could he afford to accept a major contract, even if he were ten years younger. Robinson, at 26, is reported to possess baseball abilities, which, were he white, would make him eligible for a trial with, let us say, the Brooklyn Dodgers' Class B farm at Newport News, if he were six years younger. . . . The war is over. Hundreds of fine players are rushing out of service and back into the roster of Organized Baseball. Robinson conceivably will discover that as a 26-year-old shortstop just off the sandlots, the waters of competition in the International League will flow far over his head.

At the same time, *The Sporting News* rapped southern white players who had said they would never play with a Negro. " 'It's all right with me, just so long as Robinson isn't on our club'—the standard reply—is unsportsmanlike, and, above all else, un-American," the paper said.

The year 1945 ended with organized baseball resigned to at least token integration, the Negro press jubilant, and Negro baseball's controlling interests annoyed by what they considered Rickey's piracy, but optimistic that in the long run it might prove beneficial to their leagues.

15 THE NINTH INNING

*It has been exactly twenty years since
Jackie Robinson broke the color line
in major league baseball. Branch
Rickey signed Robinson as an infielder
to play at Montreal in the International
League in 1946 but it wasn't until
early in 1947 that Jackie came to the
Dodger training camp to tune up for
one of the most dramatic and fruitful
steps the American Negro had taken
since the Civil War toward social integration. That Jackie Robinson made
full use of the opportunity to break
through the big league color line is
now so deep in history that many forget how important he and Branch
Rickey were to the cause.*
   —SATURDAY REVIEW, *1967*

Organized baseball's wall against black men was cracked on April
18, 1946, when Jackie Robinson stepped to the plate at Jersey City's
Roosevelt Stadium in the first inning of the Little Giants' home-
opener against the Montreal Royals and grounded weakly to shortstop. It had been fifty-seven years since the last Negro had performed
in the International League and forty-eight years since a black man
had played anywhere in the recognized minor leagues.

Robinson's initial effort at bat was no ill omen of failure. Before
that opening day in Jersey City was over, he had gotten 4 hits, including a home run, he had stolen 2 bases, and his daring had so discon-
certed the Jersey City pitchers that twice he had been waved home
on balks. Afield as the second baseman, he had been flawless in the
Royals' 14–1 victory.

In the Montreal dugout was the second Negro in organized baseball in modern times, John Wright, a twenty-seven-year-old righthanded pitcher who had played with the Newark Eagles, the Crawfords, and the Homestead Grays. He had been signed by Montreal in
February after his discharge from the Navy.

The day the color line was crossed. Jackie Robinson scores after homering in his debut with the Montreal Royals at Roosevelt Stadium, Jersey City, on April 18, 1946. Congratulating him is teammate George Shuba.

Together, during spring training at Sanford, Florida, Robinson and Wright had endured Jim Crow living arrangements, removal from an exhibition game because of a local ordinance barring competition between whites and blacks, and the pressures of the national eye focused on them as pioneers in baseball's experiment in democracy. The stresses multiplied as the International League season got under way. In Baltimore, where racists threatened a boycott of the stadium if Robinson or Wright played, they suffered a barrage of racial abuse. As far north as the city of Syracuse, they were baited by the home club with the most vicious insults of any city in the league.

With his fiery temperament under tight rein and his lips sealed by Branch Rickey's admonition that he could fight back only with his bat, glove, and flying feet, Robinson stood up under the terrible strain. He was, in fact, goaded to put every atom of his being into his efforts on the field, with the result that he led the International League in batting with a .349 average, was second in stolen bases with 40, tied for the most runs scored (113) and had the best fielding average for second basemen (.985). He was also fourth in the league for the number of times he was hit by pitched balls.

John Wright succumbed to the terrible strain of pioneering. After only two appearances in relief for the Royals, he was optioned to Three Rivers, Quebec, in the Class-C Border League in May and finished the season there. He was released unconditionally by the Dodger organization that winter and went back to the Homestead Grays. Jackie Robinson says:

> John had all the ability in the world, as far as physical abilities were concerned. But John couldn't stand the pressure of going up into this new league and being one of the first. The things that went on up there were too much for him, and John was not able to perform up to his capabilities.
>
> In a number of cities, we had very little pressure. But there was always that little bit coming out. It wasn't so much based on race—I think most of the Negro players could have gone it as far as race. But because John was the first Negro pitcher, every time he stepped out there he seemed to lose that fineness, and he tried a little bit harder than he was capable of playing. He tried to do more than he was able to do and it caused him to be a lot less of a pitcher than he actually was. If he had come in two or three years later when the pressure was off, John could have made it in the major leagues.

That spring of 1946, while Robinson and Wright were under baptism of fire in the International League, the Dodgers signed Roy Campanella, veteran catcher of the Baltimore Elite Giants, and Don Newcombe, a nineteen-year-old pitcher who had played one season with the Newark Eagles. Both were assigned to Nashua in the Class B-New England League.

In May, after optioning John Wright, the Royals added Roy Partlow, a thirty-year-old Negro pitcher, to their roster. He, too, was optioned to Three Rivers later in the season, and Robinson finished the year as the only black man in the International League. In June, the sixth Negro entered organized ball when Manny McIntyre, a young shortstop with no experience in the Negro leagues, was signed by Sherbrooke, Quebec, a St. Louis Cardinal farm in the Border League.

Meanwhile, token integration was coming to Negro baseball, too. Eddie Klepp, a white pitcher, played with the Cleveland Buckeyes in the Negro American League that summer. Ironically, Klepp was a victim of Jim Crow, for he was forbidden to train with the Buckeyes in the South.

Although the Negro press' interest in how the black players in organized baseball were faring overshadowed their coverage of the Negro leagues, the leagues continued to enjoy prosperity during the 1946 season. Crowds of 12,000 to 15,000 were not uncommon at Negro National and Negro American League games, and the all-star East-West game attracted 45,474.

In the euphoria induced by clicking turnstiles and the success of black players in the organized minor leagues, Negro clubowners had visions of grandeur. Early in 1947 the Memphis Red Sox announced plans for a new $250,000 stadium, and the Negro National League, seeking stability and recognition by organized baseball as an affiliate, hired the Rev. John H. Johnson, a New York Episcopal clergyman, as president, the first league executive independent of clubowners since Ferdinand Q. Morton was bounced as commissioner in 1938. Despite this move to clean house, which was seen in part as an effort to break the hold of Eddie Gottlieb, a white booking agent and part owner of the Philadelphia Stars, over National League affairs, the NNL was never officially recognized as a minor league by organized baseball. (In 1949, however, the New York Cubans signed a working agreement with the New York Giants, making them the only black farm of a major-league team in history.)

The biggest sports story of 1947 was a two-sentence announcement by the Brooklyn Dodgers on April 10. The Dodgers, who trained in Cuba that spring in an obvious move to ease the path for Jackie Robinson, were playing the Montreal Royals in Panama. The announcement read: "Brooklyn announces the purchase of the contract of Jack Roosevelt Robinson from Montreal. He will report immediately."

Wily Branch Rickey had carefully paved the way for this announcement. During the winter he had met with leaders of Brooklyn's Negro community to ask their help in making Robinson's transition to the major leagues as easy and natural as possible. He had told them that there must be no gloating by Negroes when Robinson was brought up to the Dodgers, no "Jackie Robinson Days," no wining and dining of the young ballplayer until he was fat and futile on the field. He must be let alone to play baseball and nothing else. With his urging, the Negro leaders set up an informal campaign based on the slogan "Don't Spoil Jackie's Chances," which soon spread to other cities. Editorials in the same vein appeared in the Negro press.

During spring training, Rickey also had to deal with an incipient mutiny among Dodger players. He learned that a half-dozen players, most of them Southerners, were trying to get a general handshake agreement among the Dodgers that they would not play with the Negro. They were not really successful, since some of the players, including Pee Wee Reese and Gil Hodges, refused to have anything to do with the agreement, but Rickey was forced to act anyway. He quelled the mutiny in heated interviews with the players involved.

And so, on opening day, April 15, 1947, when the Dodgers met the Boston Braves at Brooklyn's Ebbets Field, their first baseman was the muscular, pigeon-toed former college football star and short-stop for the Kansas City Monarchs. Robinson's debut with the Dodgers was not auspicious—he got no hits—but the Dodgers won, 5–3, with Jackie scoring the fifth run for Brooklyn.

Robinson went to the plate twenty times in the Dodgers' first five games without a base hit, but even such a slump for a rookie trying hard to impress his manager and fellow players was not his most vexing trouble. He also had to contend with the animosity and verbal abuse of opposing teams. In the matter of scurrilous epithets and racial jockeying, the seventh-place Philadelphia Phillies led the league. Shouts of "Hey, nigger, why don't you go back to the cotton-fields where you belong?" and "Hey, snowflake" burned Robinson's ears when the Dodgers played the Phillies at Ebbets Field. Those taunts were heard by Eddie Stanky, Dodger second baseman and an Alabaman, who was outraged because Robinson could not answer and so answered for him. The slurs were also heard by newspapermen, who created a furor that led to a quasi-apology and an explanation by Ben Chapman, the Philadelphia manager and a native of Tennessee, that hard jockeying was the Phillies' style and that it was not reserved merely for Robinson.

Branch Rickey later said that Phillies president Bob Carpenter had told him before the Dodgers-Phillies series that his club would refuse to take the field if Robinson played. A similar threat by St. Louis Cardinals players was revealed in May by Stanley Woodward of the *New York Herald-Tribune*. Woodward wrote that the Cardinals had planned a protest strike when the Dodgers came to St. Louis and were in fact trying to foment a strike by all the teams in the National League because of Brooklyn's black player. League President Ford Frick clamped down quickly, according to Woodward, sending this message to the Cardinals:

> If you do this you will be suspended from the league. You will find that the friends you think you have in the press box will not support you, that you will be outcasts. I do not care if half the league strikes. Those who do it will encounter quick retribution. They will be suspended, and I don't care if it wrecks the National League for five years. This is the United States of America, and one citizen has as much right to play as another. The National League will go down the line with Robinson whatever the consequence.

The abortive strikes by the Phillies and Cardinals could not have come as a surprise to Branch Rickey. Speaking at Wilberforce University in 1948, he said that in early 1946, before Jackie Robinson had ever played a game in organized baseball, the other major-league executives had adopted unanimously a policy committee report "which stated that however well intentioned, the use of Negro players would hazard all the physical properties of baseball." He declared that after the owners had read it, all copies of the report were carefully collected by National League President Frick and that he had been unable to get hold of one later. Larry MacPhail, who was chairman of the major-league policy committee in 1946, vigorously denied that the twenty-page report had included an anti-Negro resolution or that there had been a vote against Negro players. The reason the copies were collected, he said, was that the report contained criticism of Commissioner A. B. Chandler that the commissioner felt was unfair and should not be publicized. Ford Frick had no comment on Rickey's charge. Other clubowners professed ignorance about my anti-Negro resolution in the report, and it was pointed out that because the resolution covered only half of one page in the twenty-page report on major-league policy, it was conceivable that they could have missed it.

For Jackie Robinson, the player, 1947 was beautiful. He batted .297, led the Dodgers in stolen bases with 29 and in runs scored with 125, and was tied for the club home-run leadership at 12 with Pee Wee Reese. The Dodgers won the National League pennant for the first time since 1941 and Dixie Walker, a Georgian who had been one of the ringleaders in the insurrection during spring training, voiced the general view that Robinson had done as much as any player to bring the pennant to Brooklyn. Although the Yankees beat Brooklyn in the World Series, this disappointment was tempered for Robinson by his selection as National League Rookie of the Year by *The Sporting News*. In making the choice, the weekly said it had

> sifted and weighed only stark baseball values. That Jackie Roosevelt Robinson might have had more obstacles than his first year competitors, and that he perhaps had a harder fight to gain even major league recognition, was no concern of this publication. The sociological experiment that Robinson represented, the trail-blazing that he did, the barriers he broke down, did not enter into the decision. He was rated and examined solely as a freshman player in the big leagues—on the basis of his hitting, his running, his defensive play, his team value.

For Jackie Robinson, the man, 1947 was a nightmare. He faced the usual strains of a rookie trying to make good in the big time; for the first black man in the major leagues in the modern era, these pressures were squared because he had to gain the acceptance of his white teammates, some of them initially sullen mutineers, and endure in silence the vilification of players on other clubs. But even that was not all. At home he found hate letters, some threatening him with death, the kidnaping of his infant son, Jackie, Jr., and assaults on his wife.

Robinson's triumph over these incredible pressures and his undeniable contributions to the Dodger pennant were sweet vindication
of Branch Rickey's judgment. The two pioneers—Robinson and
Rickey—could also take heart from the slowly growing acceptance of
other Negro players that summer. All told, sixteen black men appeared in organized baseball during 1947, about half of them on
minor-league clubs of the Brooklyn organization. In July, Larry
Doby, the hard-hitting twenty-two-year-old second baseman of the
Newark Eagles, was signed by Bill Veeck for the Cleveland Indians
and became the first Negro in the American League. He was the first
of several men to be taken directly from the Negro leagues into the
majors. A month later, two men from the Kansas City Monarchs,
infielder Henry Thompson and outfielder Willard Brown, were signed
by the St. Louis Browns. Both were released within a few weeks
and rejoined the Monarchs. (In 1949, Thompson went back to the
big leagues with the New York Giants and stayed eight years.)

For the Negro leagues, the season of 1947 was like the first
trickling pebbles of an avalanche to come. Six of the sixteen Negroes
who were in organized baseball that year were youngsters without
previous professional experience, and most of the Negro clubs still
had their top stars. But who cared? Baseball fans, and especially Negroes, had their gaze riveted on Brooklyn and Jackie Robinson, and,
to a lesser extent, on black players in the minor leagues. Attendance
was down alarmingly for Negro league games; to take a typical example, the Newark Eagles, who were playing their home games at
Ebbets Field in Brooklyn when the Dodgers were on the road, could
attract only 2,000 for a Sunday doubleheader in August. Curiously,
however, the 1947 East-West game drew 48,112, not far from the
record 51,723 in 1943. Perhaps the fans were hoping for a look at
some future major-league stars. If so, they were not disappointed,
because five men who played in that all-star game later played in the
major leagues: Monte Irvin, Minnie Minoso, Sam Jethroe, Quincy
Troupe, and the winning pitcher, Dan Bankhead, who was signed by
the Dodgers soon afterward and pitched in six games for Brooklyn
without a decision that year.

Nearly all the black teams lost money in 1947, including the New
York Cubans, National League champions and Negro World Series
winners, and the Cleveland Buckeyes, Negro American League winners. But if 1947 was a lean year, the following season was a disaster. Although the total number of black men in organized baseball
did not rise (remaining at about fifteen, including Josh Gibson, Jr.,

son of the great slugger, who played for a short time with Youngstown in the Middle Atlantic League), the Negro fan's interest increased tremendously. Robinson was joined on the Dodgers by catcher Roy Campanella, Larry Doby was coming into his own as a star on the Indians' world-champion team that year, and, significantly, Satchel Paige, the greatest star in Negro baseball, appeared on the big-league scene. Brought to the Indians in July by Bill Veeck, Paige won 6 games and lost only 1 to help the Indians to the American League pennant. Even at his official age of forty-two, Paige was black baseball's *pièce de resistance,* and his defection to the major leagues was the clap of doom for the Negro circuits.

Playing at Yankee Stadium or the Polo Grounds in New York, Shibe Park in Philadelphia or Comiskey Park in Chicago, the Negro league teams did well to draw 2,000 in 1948. Crowds as low as 700 were registered in big-league parks, and it was soon evident that Negro baseball no longer had the economic base for major-league pretensions. At the end of the season, the Homestead Grays, who won the Negro National League pennant and the Negro World Series, announced that they were folding. Rufus Jackson, co-owner, said the Grays had lost $45,000 in their last two years. (The Grays did, however, continue to operate through 1950, playing in the Negro American Association, which was made up of clubs in Virginia and North Carolina.) When the New York Black Yankees and Newark Eagles disbanded at the end of the 1948 season, the Negro National League died, ending sixteen years of continuous operation. The remaining clubs joined the Negro American League, which was split into two divisions for 1949.

Thirty-six black players were in organized baseball in 1949, fourteen with the Cleveland Indians and twelve with the Dodgers. A black face was no longer a novelty in the major leagues: the Dodgers had Robinson, Campanella, and Newcombe; the New York Giants had Henry Thompson and Monte Irvin; and in the American League, the Indians had Doby, Paige, Luke Easter of the Homestead Grays, and Minnie Minoso of the New York Cubans.

True integration of the national game was becoming a fact as the century reached midpoint, although the pace was not breathtaking. By 1950, when Sam Jethroe, the fleet outfielder of the Cleveland Buckeyes, joined the Boston Braves, only five major-league teams had been integrated—the Braves, Dodgers, Giants, Indians, and St. Louis Browns. Robinson was in his fourth season with the Dodgers, an established star and the most exciting player in the big leagues, and was well on his way to election to the Hall of Fame.

By 1953 there were twenty Negroes on seven major-league clubs; four years later there were thirty-six on fourteen of the sixteen major-league teams. Finally, in 1959, twelve years after Jackie Robinson's debut with Brooklyn, the last major-league club added a black player. Ironically, it was the Boston Red Sox, who could have been first with Jackie Robinson, Sam Jethroe, or Marvin Williams in 1945.

For Negro clubs, the signing of their young stars by teams in organized ball was both the kiss of death and their temporary salvation. By 1949 few black teams could make money, or break even, solely from gate receipts. To balance their ledgers, they sold young players to clubs in organized baseball. It was becoming clear that the only role remaining for them was as developers of young talent for the major leagues.

After the signing of Jackie Robinson by the Dodgers with no payment to the Kansas City Monarchs, Negro clubowners made sure that all their players signed legal contracts so that they could get some return on their investments, but sale prices were modest. For a journeyman player, a Negro club could expect to get $1,000 to $5,000. The top price paid by major-league teams during the early years of integration appears to have been $15,000. That figure was reported to have been paid by the Dodgers for Dan Bankhead, by the Red Sox in 1949 for Piper Davis (who played in Boston's farm system but did not make the majors), and by the New York Giants in 1950 for an exciting young outfielder on the Birmingham Black Barons named Willie Mays.

Inevitably, as full integration became a reality on organized baseball's player rosters, prospective stars were signed by big-league organizations directly out of high school and placed on their minor-league affiliates, thus eliminating the middle man—the Negro clubs. During the early Fifties, there were still some prime prospects in the Negro American League (notably Henry Aaron, bought by the Milwaukee Braves from the Indianapolis Clowns in 1952, and Ernie Banks, who went from the Kansas City Monarchs to the Chicago Cubs a year later), but their numbers were fast diminishing. The last black player who stepped directly from a Negro team into a major-league uniform was veteran New York Cubans' pitcher Pat Scantlebury, who pitched in eight games for the Cincinnati Reds in 1956.

Bereft of nearly all the young stars and drawing slim crowds, the Negro American League tried valiantly to stay afloat. Player salaries dipped to an average of $200 a month, about half of what it had been during the middle Forties. Most games were booked in small towns where the competition for the baseball fan's dollar was less intense but where the prospect of a large crowd was nonexistent.

To beef up anemic gates, some teams began adding novel attractions such as clowns and midgets to their entourage. Leading the way in this burlesque were the Indianapolis Clowns, lineal descendants of the Ethiopian Clowns, who had outraged many Negroes in the late Thirties and early Forties by wearing grass skirts, painting their bodies in a storybook approximation of cannibals and using such names as Selassie, Mofike, Wahoo, and—of all things—*Tarzan!* The Indianapolis Clowns reached the height of ingenuity in 1953 when they had a girl named Toni Stone as their second baseman. For a reported $12,000 a year, she played four to six innings in about fifty of the Clowns' 175 games. Miss Stone batted a creditable .243 in Negro American League competition.

But clowns, midgets, and even girls were not enough to save the NAL. In 1960 Dr. J. B. Martin, the president, said he was seriously considering an offer of a subsidy from an unnamed American League team in return for first call on all players in the league. Martin said he had turned down a similar offer the year before from a National League team because he didn't want to permit a monopoly. Only four clubs were left—the Kansas City Monarchs, Detroit-New Orleans Stars, Birmingham Black Barons, and the Raleigh, N.C., Tigers— and the Negro American League, last vestige of the great days of Negro baseball, died at the end of that season. A few teams continued barnstorming, but they found the pickings increasingly meager and one by one they disbanded. In 1968 only the Indianapolis Clowns, mixing comedy and baseball, remained in existence as a dim reminder of a world that was.

There are few to mourn at the grave of Negro baseball. Old-timers may wax nostalgic about the days when John Henry Lloyd and Smoky Joe Williams and Rube Foster and Oscar Charleston and Josh Gibson were kings on black diamonds, but their voices mix pride with sorrow that these men labored behind the lily-white curtain.

Here, in a sort of valedictory for Negro baseball, is Jimmie Crutchfield:

> I have no ill feeling about never having had the opportunity to play in the big leagues. There have been times—you know, they used to call me the Black Lloyd Waner. I used to think

about that a lot. He was on the other side of town in Pittsburgh making $12,000 a year and I didn't have enough money to go home on. I had to borrow bus fare to come home.

It seemed like there was something wrong there. But that was yesterday. There's no use in me having bitterness in my heart this late in life about what's gone by. That's just the way I feel about it. Once in a while I get a kick out of thinking that my name was mentioned as one of the stars of the East-West game and little things like that. I don't know whether I'd feel better if I had a million dollars.

I can say I contributed something.

PART IV:

OF THOSE WHO'VE
GONE BEFORE

16 LOST LEGENDS

In organized baseball there has been no distinction raised except tacit understanding that a player of Ethiopian descent is ineligible—the wisdom of which we will not discuss except to say that by such a rule some of the greatest ball players the game has ever known have been denied their opportunity.
— THE SPORTING NEWS, *1923*

Nothing is quite so irresistible to a baseball fan as arguing the merits of the game's outstanding players. Who was greater, Ruth or Cobb? Was Lefty Grove better than Sandy Koufax? Can Bob Gibson be compared with Christy Mathewson?

If it is a futile exercise to debate the comparative achievements of stars who left their imprint on major-league history, it is doubly so for the men who played out their careers behind the color line. For the latter, few records are available for ammunition, and most of those that do exist are suspect because there was no real effort to keep accurate statistics until the middle 1940s. During most of the long period of segregated baseball, a black player could not really be sure at the end of a season whether he had batted .200 or .400.

But the lack of hard data has rarely stopped an argument, and the names of about sixty men inevitably crop up in any discussion of the greatest players in Negro baseball. These are the lost legends, men who unquestionably would have starred in the major leagues. And it is easy to take the next step and say that perhaps eight or ten of these men, most of whom live only in the memory of those who saw them play, would have plaques on the walls of Baseball's Hall of Fame.

This chapter consists of brief sketches of the careers of the lost legends. It does not include men like Jackie Robinson, Larry Doby, Monte Irvin, Roy Campanella, and Don Newcombe, all of whom

are sometimes mentioned among the all-time greats of Negro baseball, because they played in the major leagues when the color wall
tumbled down. Nor does it include players of the nineteenth century
—men like Frank Grant, Bud Fowler, and George W. Stovey—because the sport of choosing all-time teams did not get under way for
Negro baseball until they were nearly forgotten.

The players are listed alphabetically by positions. The first group
for each position is made up of those most often selected as the best.
Following them is a second group of players who are occasionally
mentioned among the greats.

Dave Brown

Pitchers

Dave Brown

David (Dave) Brown was the ace lefthander of Rube Foster's American Giants from 1918 through 1922, boasting considerable speed and a good curve ball. He jumped to the Lincoln Giants during the player war of 1923 and pitched for them through 1924. Soon afterward he was sought in connection with a homicide in New York and dropped from sight. Brown had a previous history of lawbreaking, having been convicted of highway robbery even before joining the American Giants. Rube Foster put up a $20,000 bond to have Brown paroled to him even before he had "showed any real pitching ability," the aggrieved Foster said after Brown had jumped his club. During his relatively short career with top teams, however, Brown was often called the best lefthander in the game.

John Donaldson

A lefthander, John Donaldson was noted for his grace on the mound and a sharp-breaking curve ball that was faster than most pitchers' fastballs. He reached his peak just before World War I with the All Nations Club, which was made up of men of several races, once pitching three successive no-hitters for them. A native of Glasgow, Missouri, the tall, lean Donaldson started his professional career in 1912 with the Tennessee Rats, a ball club and entertainment troupe that barnstormed through the Midwest. In his years on top clubs stretching into the 1930s, Donaldson played for the Los Angeles White Sox, Kansas City Monarchs, Chicago Giants, Indianapolis ABCs, Brooklyn Royal Giants, Detroit Stars, and white semipro clubs in the Midwest and Canada. A strong and consistent hitter, he was used mostly as an outfielder during his later years with the Monarchs. J. L. Wilkinson, who owned both the All Nations and the Monarchs, called Donaldson the most amazing pitcher he had ever seen. At his best, Donaldson had near-perfect control and averaged 20 strikeouts a game. In 1917 the *Chicago Defender* reported that Donaldson was offered $10,000 by a New York State League manager to go to Cuba, change his name, and return as a Cuban to pitch for his club. Donaldson declined the offer. At about the same time, John Mc-

Graw said he would gladly have paid $50,000 for Donaldson's contract if he had been white. After the color bar fell, Donaldson became a scout for the Chicago White Sox. His home is in Chicago.

Andrew (Rube) Foster (See Chapter 8)

Willie Foster

Cum Posey, an astute baseball man, called Willie H. (Bill) Foster the greatest lefthander Negro baseball ever saw. Like his half-brother Rube, Willie was tall, and as a young pitcher during the 1920s he was noted for a burning fastball. As he grew older he turned "cute," saving his speed for times of real need. Bill Yancey remembers, "That guy would give you 10 hits and shut you out. He could really pitch!" Foster started pitching professionally in 1923 at the age of eighteen with the Memphis Red Sox. Toward the end of the season he joined the American Giants, with whom he was identified for many years, and won the only game he pitched for them that year. He was to win hundreds of others for the American Giants until 1937. Foster did not pitch for the American Giants throughout this whole period, however. In 1931 he was with the Homestead Grays and Kansas City Monarchs. In 1933 he played for a white semipro team in Jamestown, South Dakota, in a post-season tournament, losing to Satchel Paige and Bismarck, North Dakota, 3–2. Dave Malarcher, Foster's teammate and manager during most of his years with the American Giants, said:

> Willie Foster's greatness was that he had this terrific speed and a great, fast-breaking curve ball and a drop ball, and he was really a master of the change-of-pace. He could throw you a real fast one and then use the same motion and bring it up a little slower, and then a little slower yet. And then he'd use the same motion again, and Z-zzzz! He was really a great pitcher.

Foster spent his last year in baseball, 1938, with a white semipro team in Elgin, Illinois, and the Washington Browns, a Yakima, Washington, Negro team. During his tenure with the American Giants, he spent one year as manager, resigning in 1931 because he said he could not do justice to the manager's job and continue pitching. Foster is now dean of men and baseball coach at Alcorn College in Mississippi.

Willie Foster

José Mendez

José (Joe) Mendez was a very dark Cuban: had he been lighter, it is probable that he would have written several lines in the major-league record books. Born in 1888, he was at his peak as a pitcher about 1910. In 1908 and 1909, Mendez defeated Jack Coombs and Eddie Plank when the Philadelphia Athletics visited Cuba, and he split two games with Christy Mathewson and the New York Giants. John McGraw placed a value of $50,000 on Mendez if he could

José Mendez

play in the big leagues. Arthur W. Hardy, who batted against Mendez in his prime, said he was lean and rangy, with long arms and extremely long fingers. A righthander, Mendez was tremendously fast, and Hardy attributed much of his effectiveness to the fact that Mendez's long fingers permitted him to get great spin on the ball. He first came to the United States in 1908 with the Cuban Stars and played with them for several summers, in 1909 getting credit for 44 victories and 2 defeats. He joined the All Nations in 1912 and pitched for that club through 1916. About this time he was having arm trouble and stopped pitching regularly. In 1918 and 1919 he was a shortstop and outfielder for Foster's American Giants and the Detroit Stars. The following year he joined the new Kansas City Monarchs as manager and shortstop; and he was with that club, mostly as manager and infielder and occasionally as pitcher, until his last season, 1926. Mendez died in Havana on November 6, 1928. In his pitching prime, Mendez was very graceful. Hardy recalls:

> He threw the ball with such ease that it amounted almost to a change-of-pace. You couldn't gauge it and the ball came so fast that it was very deceptive. I would say that Mendez—and

this is just a personal judgment—I would say that Mendez was faster than Smoky Joe Williams.

Satchel Paige (See Chapter 10)

Cannonball Dick Redding

As his nickname implies, Richard (Cannonball Dick) Redding was noted for overpowering speed. A righthander, he was in his prime with the Lincoln Giants during the second decade of the century. Redding was born in Atlanta in 1891 and began pitching with small clubs in his home city as a youth. In early 1911 the touring Philadelphia Giants spotted him there and took him North. Late that season he went to the Lincoln Giants and promptly won 17 straight games for that powerful club. In 1912 he was at his peak as a fireballer, winning 43 games and losing 12 and pitching several no-hitters. Among his triumphs was a perfect game with 17 strikeouts

Cannonball Dick Redding

against the Jersey City Skeeters of the fast Eastern League. The same year he pitched a 3-hitter with 24 strikeouts against the "All Leaguers," a team made up of minor-leaguers. Three years later, when he moved to the Lincoln Stars, Redding blew his fastball past enough batters to win 20 straight games before being stopped by the Indianapolis ABCs. Among the victims of that string were several teams of major-leaguers. After Army combat service in France during World War I, Redding returned to baseball with the Chicago American Giants and the Brooklyn Royal Giants for the 1918 season. The next year he went to the Bacharach Giants of Atlantic City, pitching and managing them through 1922. In 1923 he went back to the Brooklyn Royal Giants and pitched and managed them until 1938. Long before Satchel Paige, Redding had developed a hesitation pitch, although it was different from Satch's. Redding would show the batter his back for perhaps two seconds while balancing on his right foot before letting go with his fastball. The fans loved this bit of showmanship and batters found that it did not detract from the speed of the pitch.

Bullet Rogan

Probably the most versatile black ballplayer (except for Martin Dihigo (see p. 243) was Wilbur (Bullet) Rogan. As a youth he was a catcher; as a professional he played every position except catcher and played them all well. Born in 1893 in Kansas City, Kansas, Rogan began as a catcher for the Pullman Colts in that city. He enlisted in the Army in 1911 and earned his first notices as a pitcher about 1915 with the Negro 25th Infantry team at Schofield Barracks in Honolulu. He served in the Army (with some time between hitches) until 1919. During one of his periods in civilian life he pitched for the Los Angeles White Sox. He was twenty-six years old when he joined the Kansas City Monarchs as a pitcher. To reach the club in Chicago, he rode trains for three days and nights, then jumped into uniform and pitched a 1-hitter against the American Giants. From that day until his retirement after the 1938 season, Rogan was the mainstay of the Monarchs, blowing his fastball and fine curve past the best hitters in Negro baseball and the best the white semipro teams of the Midwest and Far West could offer. He is generally regarded as the finest fielding pitcher in Negro baseball history. In one doubleheader he pitched, and played four other positions. Rogan was an

Bullet Rogan

excellent hitter, usually batting fourth, fifth, or sixth for the strong Monarchs. From 1920 to 1930, Rogan averaged 30 games a year in the box and, according to owner J. L. Wilkinson, was never once relieved. Rogan stood 6 feet and weighed about 180 pounds in his prime. The nickname "Bullet" was attached to him early in his career; toward the end he was sometimes called Bullet Joe. He was a friendly man and had leadership qualities, which he displayed as manager of the Monarchs during many of his later years with the club. After his retirement from the playing field, he had a civil-service job in Kansas City and umpired Negro National League games there for several years.

Smoky Joe Williams

Many men whose memory extends back fifty years or more regard Joe Williams as the greatest black pitcher, more remarkable even than the remarkable Satchel Paige. Certainly he rivals Paige in longevity on the mound, and there are those who say his fastball at its best could be compared only with that of Walter Johnson. A righthander, he did not arrive in big-time competition until he was thirty-four years old, having pitched for thirteen years on the scrubby diamonds of Negro baseball in Texas. He was born in Texas, probably in or near San Antonio, on April 6, 1876. Williams, whose mother was part Indian, had the facial structure of an Indian. He was pitching for the San Antonio Bronchos in 1908 when he was seen by Arthur W. Hardy, then with the Kansas City, Kansas, Giants. Hardy remembers:

> He was a great big tall guy—I think Joe must have been 6 feet 5 or 6. He threw overhanded and he had a terrific drop ball,

Smoky Joe Williams—COURTESY OF BILL YANCEY

and you never could tell whether the ball was going to drop or whether it was his fastball because he threw them both with the same motion—and that ball looked like a *pea* coming up there. Of course, after he went to Chicago and had been around sophisticated ballplayers, he got rid of his big overhand motion with a lot of show on it and used mostly a sidearm delivery with a semi-crossfire which was very effective. In his earlier days, when I first saw him, he tried to throw everything by you, but in his later days, particularly with the Homestead Grays, he had cut out all that stuff and had a fairly smooth delivery. His speed was not excessive then but it was not slow.

In 1909, while still with the Bronchos, Williams pitched against the Leland Giants in Birmingham, and although he lost, 3–2, he struck out 9 batters, prompting Rube Foster, manager of the Lelands, to invite him to Chicago. And so in 1910, Williams, who was then called Strikeout and Cyclone, joined the Leland Giants and began mowing down the best teams, both black and white, in the nation. From then until his retirement at the end of the 1932 season, he pitched for the Chicago Giants, Lincoln Giants, Homestead Grays, American Giants, Bacharach Giants, and the Brooklyn Royal Giants. Probably his finest season was 1914, when he was credited with 41 victories and only 3 defeats for the American Giants. Most of his best years as a strikeout artist, however, were spent with the Lincoln Giants from 1912 until 1923. A 20-strikeout game was not unusual for him during that period, and his record for a single daylight game appears to be 25 in twelve innings against the powerful Bushwicks, when he was with the Brooklyn Royal Giants in 1924. As noted in Chapter 9, Williams struck out 27 Kansas City Monarchs in a twelve-inning night game in 1930, but in that one he had considerable help from the weak wattage of the Monarchs' portable lights. From 1912 through 1918, Williams pitched twelve games against teams of major-leaguers, winning 6, losing 4, and tying 2. Among his opponents were Hooks Wiltse, Grover Cleveland Alexander, Rube Marquard, and Bullet Joe Bush. Probably the best of those games was a 3-hitter against Philadelphia, National League champions, in the fall of 1915, when he struck out 10 and won, 1–0. During the middle 1920s he became known as Smoky Joe, indicating that he still had his fast ball even though he was approaching his fiftieth birthday. In 1925 he joined the Homestead Grays and stayed with them until he retired in 1932, still winning consistently against the best black clubs and the strongest of the white semipro teams within 300 miles of the Grays' Pittsburgh base. In 1928, when he was fifty-two years old, he had enough on the ball to throw a no-hit no-run game against a strong Akron, Ohio, semipro club, the last of what probably numbered several score of no-hitters. His last manager, Cum Posey of the Grays, said only Walter Johnson, and perhaps Lefty Grove and Satchel Paige, could match Williams' fastball.

Also . . .

Pat Dougherty

A lefthander, Charles (Pat) Dougherty earned the soubriquet "the Black Marquard" while pitching with top Chicago area teams from 1909 to 1915. He was with the Leland Giants in 1909-10 and the American Giants through 1914. His last year in fast competition was 1915, when he pitched for the Chicago Giants. In 1909 he lost a 3-hitter to the Chicago Cubs and Three-Finger Brown, 1–0. He was born in Summershade, Kentucky, in 1879, and died July 12, 1940. Despite his brief career, he is remembered as a great hurler.

Dizzy Dismukes

William (Dizzy) Dismukes grew up with Negro baseball, his career spanning the period from 1913 to the 1950s and all phases from the playing field through business management. He was a well-known manager and coach for much of that period, but he earned his first fame as a pitcher for the Philadelphia Giants, beginning in 1913. Over the next eighteen years, Dismukes, a righthander, pitched for the Brooklyn Royal Giants, Mohawk Giants of Schenectady, Indianapolis ABCs, American Giants of Chicago, Dayton Marcos, Pittsburgh Keystones, Memphis Red Sox, St. Louis Stars, and Cincinnati Dismukes. He later was involved in business management (and sometimes field management, too) of such clubs as the Detroit Wolves, Homestead Grays, Columbus Blue Birds, and, for a long period, the Kansas City Monarchs.

Bill Jackman

William (Bill) Jackman is not often mentioned among the select few, but there are men like Bill Yancey who consider him the best of all. A Texan, the righthanded Jackman was a towering submariner with unusual control. He spent much of his career with the Philadelphia Giants, who were touring New England during the 1920s, when he was having his best years. He had started with the Lincoln Giants in 1925 but was released when he injured his arm. Jackman also pitched for the Brooklyn Eagles and ended his career with the Boston Royal Giants in the short-lived Negro Major Baseball League of America in 1942.

Slim Jones

Stuart (Slim) Jones, a towering lefthander with a blazing fastball, had a short but impressive career in big-time baseball. Standing 6 feet 6 inches and weighing 185 pounds, he was the ace of the Philadelphia Stars' staff from 1934 through 1938. Born in Baltimore on May 6, 1913, he broke into baseball with the Baltimore Black Sox in 1932. In his first year with Philadelphia, he won 32 and lost only 4. In that year, and again in 1935, Jones was the East's starting pitcher in the East-West game.

Dan McClellan

Danny McClellan was noted not only as an effective righthanded pitcher around the turn of the century but also as a shrewd developer of young talent. He has the distinction of having pitched the first perfect game for a Negro team, turning the trick in 1903 for the Cuban X Giants against the Penn Park Athletic Club of York, Pennsylvania. Subsequently, he pitched for the Philadelphia Giants, Coogan's Smart Set of New York, and the Lincoln Giants before retiring as a player on top clubs in 1912. His career as a manager extended into the early 1930s.

Theodore Trent

Theodore (Ted) Trent, a righthander, was the mainstay of the pitching staffs of the great St. Louis Stars' teams of the late 1920s and the Chicago American Giants of the Thirties. While with the Stars from 1927 through 1931, he is reported to have struck out Bill Terry, the New York Giants' slugger, four times in an exhibition

Theodore Trent

game. Trent also pitched for the Detroit Wolves and Homestead Grays. His last year was with the American Giants in 1938.

Frank Wickware

A righthander with great speed, Frank Wickware was a contemporary of Smoky Joe Williams, Cannonball Redding, and Pat Dougherty. He was born in Coffeyville, Kansas, in 1888 and got into big-time baseball with the Leland Giants in 1910. A fondness for the bottle evidently made him the despair of managers, for he spent the next ten years shuttling between the St. Louis Giants, Philadelphia Giants, Mohawk Giants, Lincoln Stars, American Giants, Brooklyn Royal Giants, Chicago Giants, and the Detroit Stars. After 1919 he was mostly in less formidable competition, although he was

Frank Wickware—COURTESY OF
BILL YANCEY

on the roster of the Lincoln Giants in 1925. His most memorable
games were pitched against Walter Johnson, with whom he matched
arms three times in 1913 and 1914, winning 2 and losing 1.

Nip Winters

Jesse (Nip) Winters was the lefthanded ace of the strong Hilldale
Club during the 1920s. Born in 1899, he grew up in Washington and
started pitching with the Norfolk Stars in 1919. He performed for the
Bacharach Giants, Philadelphia Stars, Norfolk Giants, and Harris-
burg Giants before signing with Hilldale in 1923. For the next sev-
eral years he was the most effective pitcher in the Eastern Colored
League. He later pitched for the Lincoln Giants and again with the
Bacharachs until 1933.

Catchers

Josh Gibson (See Chapter 12)

Biz Mackey

Perhaps the best testimonial to the abilities of Raleigh (Biz) Mackey was given by Cum Posey in 1944. Naming his all-time team that year, Posey, who had owned and managed the great Josh Gibson, selected Mackey as his No. 1 catcher. Said Posey: "A tremendous hitter, a fierce competitor, although slow afoot he (Mackey) is the standout among catchers who have shown their wares in this nation." Mackey, who was born in San Antonio in 1897, was one of a number of black players whose playing days extended well into their fifties. He started as a professional with the San Antonio Giants in

Biz Mackey—COURTESY OF ARTHUR M.
CARTER

1918 and was still playing quite regularly thirty years later. There is little disagreement among men who saw him at his best that he was the finest catcher Negro baseball produced. He owned a powerful arm, strong enough so that he could throw harder to second base from a squatting position than most catchers could standing up. Roy Campanella, who broke in with the Baltimore Elite Giants under Mackey's management, credits the old catcher with teaching him most of what he knew about catching. The evidence is somewhat mixed about his hitting talents. On the one hand, Bill Yancey and Judy Johnson, both of whom were his teammates on the Hilldale Club, agree that the switch-hitting Mackey was not in a class with Josh Gibson or Campanella. "He'd sting the ball, but the pitchers didn't fear him. They wouldn't walk him to get to somebody else," Johnson said. On the other hand, Mackey was credited with an average of .423 with Hilldale in 1923, and in the 1925 World Series he led Hilldale with .375. As late as 1945, when he was forty-eight years old, Mackey had an official average of .307 with the Newark Eagles of the Negro National League. Over his long career, Mackey also played with the Indianapolis ABCs and the Philadelphia Stars. As manager of the Newark Eagles he aided in the development of Larry Doby, Monte Irvin, and Don Newcombe, all of whom starred in the majors when the color bar toppled.

Bruce Petway

Like Mackey, Bruce Petway was renowned as an outstanding receiver and thrower who was an excellent hitter, although not with Gibson's power. He is said to have been the first catcher who often threw to second base without rising from his haunches. Petway was born in Nashville in the late 1880s. While attending Meharry Medical College in Nashville, he broke into professional baseball in 1906 with the Leland Giants and Brooklyn Royal Giants. After giving up medicine in favor of baseball, he was with the Philadelphia Giants in 1909 when he joined the exodus to Chicago to play under Rube Foster on the Leland Giants and, beginning in 1911, with Foster's American Giants. He was with Foster's powerhouse until 1919, when he went to the Detroit Stars. Petway was Detroit's catcher and manager until his retirement in 1925. In a series in Cuba against the Detroit Tigers in 1910, when he was playing with the Havana Reds, he is reputed to have thrown out Ty Cobb twice in attempts to steal. Petway died in July 1941.

Louis Santop

Louis (Top) Santop Loftin, who dropped his last name for his baseball career, was a lefthanded power hitter and a skilled catcher. During the Twenties, when he was with Hilldale, he was reported to be earning $500 a month, a fabulous salary for that era. His longest drive was a home run that cleared a fence 485 feet from the plate in Elizabeth, New Jersey, in 1912. Santop was born in Tyler, Texas, in 1890 and began playing for pay with the Fort Worth Wonders in 1909. In a career that lasted until 1926, he was with the Oklahoma Monarchs of Guthrie, Oklahoma, Philadelphia Giants, Lincoln Giants, American Giants, Lincoln Stars, Brooklyn Royal Giants, and Hilldale. He gained his greatest fame with the Lincoln Giants and Lincoln Stars from 1911 to 1916 and with Hilldale from 1918 until his release in 1926. Santop was a showman and sometimes called his home-run shots à la Babe Ruth. He died in Philadelphia in January 1942.

Louis Santop

Also . . .

Frank Duncan

A native of Kansas City, Missouri, Frank Duncan spent most of his long playing and managing career with the Monarchs, joining them in 1922 after two years with the Chicago Giants. From then until the late Forties, he was with the Monarchs, except for brief stop-overs with the New York Black Yankees, Pittsburgh Crawfords, Homestead Grays, New York Cubans, and Chicago American Giants, and a trip to Japan to play there in 1927. He was an excellent catcher and a good, but not devastating, right-handed hitter. Duncan was born in 1903. He was manager of the Monarchs when Jackie Robinson left the club to sign with the Montreal Royals. Duncan lives in Kansas City.

Chappie Johnson

Arthur W. Hardy, who played against George (Chappie) Johnson about 1910, calls him the smoothest catcher in baseball at that time. Hardy said Johnson was a coach for the young catchers of the St. Paul club in the white American Association during spring training in the years from about 1907 to 1912, although he was not officially on the Saints' roster. He started as a first baseman for the Columbia Giants of Chicago in 1899. In a career as player and manager going into the Twenties, Johnson was with the Chicago Union Giants, Brooklyn Royal Giants, Leland Giants, Chicago Giants, St. Louis Giants, Dayton Chappies, Custer's Baseball Club of Columbus, Philadelphia Royal Stars, and Norfolk Stars.

First Basemen

Buck Leonard

Josh Gibson and Walter F. (Buck) Leonard were the Ruth and Gehrig, the Mantle and Maris of Negro baseball. From 1937 until Gibson's last season in 1946, they were the most feared No. 3 and 4 batting combination in black baseball. A lefthanded hitter standing 5 feet 11 inches and weighing 185 pounds, Leonard had a smooth, powerful stroke which produced both a high average and home-run production only slightly less than Gibson's. He usually compiled an average in the high .300s, occasionally topping .400, and, during the Forties, when he was around the forty-year mark, Leonard was still among the home-run leaders of the Negro National League. He was born in Rocky Mount, North Carolina, on September 8, 1907, and learned baseball while earning a living as a shoeshine boy and railroad-yard worker. He was twenty-five years old before he began playing professionally with the Baltimore Stars and Brooklyn Royal Giants. From 1934 until their breakup in 1950, Leonard was the smooth, sure-handed first baseman of the greatest Homestead Grays' teams. A lefthanded thrower, he had a strong, accurate arm and a reputation for never throwing to the wrong base. After the collapse of the Grays, Leonard went to Mexico and played in Mexican leagues until 1955, when he was forty-eight years old. He was also a home-run leader in those leagues several times. During black baseball's boom period in the middle 1940s, Leonard was probably the third-highest-paid player at $1,000 a month, trailing only Satchel Paige and Gibson. Leonard is now assistant probation officer for the city of Rocky Mount and operates a real-estate business. He is also vice president of the Rocky Mount club in the Class-A Carolina League.

Ben Taylor

Buck Leonard's first professional experience was under Benjamin H. Taylor, the only other first baseman who is frequently mentioned as Leonard's peer. Taylor was managing the Baltimore Stars when Leonard joined them in 1933. The youngest of four brothers famed in black baseball, (C. I., Steel Arm Johnny, and Candy Jim were the others), Ben Taylor was born in Anderson, South Carolina, in 1888. He started his career with the St. Louis Giants in 1911, but he reached his prime with his brother C. I. Taylor's Indianapolis ABCs from 1915 to 1922. Like Leonard, he batted and threw lefthanded and was highly regarded as both hitter and fielder. During a career that lasted until the late 1930s, Ben Taylor played with the American Giants, Bacharach Giants, Washington Potomacs, Harrisburg Giants, and Baltimore Black Sox. He managed several of those clubs and was an East-West League umpire in 1932.

Also . . .

Mule Suttles

George (Mule) Suttles, who played both first base and the outfield, was not noted for his defensive skills but for his big bat. A righthanded hitter and thrower, Suttles generated nearly as much power as Josh Gibson but was not a high-average hitter. Born in Brockton, Louisiana, on March 31, 1901, Suttles stood 5 feet 11 inches and weighed 195. He broke in with the Birmingham Black Barons in 1918 and played with the St. Louis Stars, Detroit Wolves, Washington Pilots, Chicago American Giants, Newark Eagles, and New York Black Yankees through 1943. His eleventh-inning home run brought victory to the East in the 1935 East-West game.

Mule Suttles

Second Basemen

Newt Allen

A wide-ranging second baseman and a consistent hitter from either side of the plate was Newt Allen, who was identified with the Kansas City Monarchs through most of his career. He started with J. L. Wilkinson's All Nations Club in 1922, switching to Wilkinson's Monarchs late that same season. A native of Texas, Allen played with the Monarchs until 1943, with occasional seasons elsewhere— St. Louis Stars, Detroit Stars, and Homestead Grays. He stood 5 feet 7½ inches and weighed about 170. Allen was generally regarded as the slickest second baseman during the 1920s and early Thirties.

Newt Allen

Bingo DeMoss

Elwood (Bingo) DeMoss began a playing career in 1905 that lasted twenty-five years, and he managed top clubs for about fifteen years after retiring as a player. He began as a shortstop with the Topeka Giants, but after weakening his arm in pitching one game in an emergency, he shifted to second base and made his name there as the finest second baseman in black baseball from 1915 to the early 1920s. During his prime, DeMoss was with the Indianapolis ABCs and the American Giants. An old teammate, Jelly Gardner, remembers:

Bingo DeMoss—COURTESY OF OLD BALL
PLAYERS CLUB OF CHICAGO

He could make all the plays at second. He was a good hitter and a good sacrifice man. He batted second and I led off for the American Giants, and I could run anytime I wanted to with him at bat. He'd save you. If he thought you'd be out trying to steal, he'd foul off the pitch if he couldn't hit it well. He could hit 'em anywhere he wanted to. He often went to right field, but he could pull 'em if he wanted to.

DeMoss was born in Topeka, Kansas, on September 5, 1889. He played with the Kansas City, Kansas, Giants, the Oklahoma Giants, and the Detroit Stars, in addition to Topeka, Indianapolis, and Chicago. He managed Indianapolis, Detroit, the American Giants, and Chicago Brown Bombers. A holler guy and a righthanded line-drive hitter, DeMoss is mentioned most often by old-timers as the best second baseman. He died in Chicago on January 26, 1965.

Sammy T. Hughes

Already a veteran on the Baltimore Elite Giants when a young catcher named Roy Campanella joined the club in 1937 was Sammy T. Hughes. That same year, Cum Posey, who had seen all the great ones since 1912, called Hughes the best second baseman in Negro baseball history. His description: "a good hitter, crack fielder, and real baserunner." Hughes, a righthanded batter, started with the Louisville White Sox in 1931. Two years later he joined the Elite Giants, who then represented Nashville. He went with them during their travels of the next few years to Columbus in 1935 and Washington in 1936 before they settled on Baltimore as home. Like Campanella, he spent the 1941 season in Mexico, returning to the Baltimore club for the 1942 season. His last year was 1946, the year that saw Campanella enter organized baseball as one of the first three black men to step over the color line.

Also . . .

William S. Monroe

Rube Foster called William S. (Bill) Monroe, a second baseman who started just after the turn of the century, the greatest ballplayer who ever lived. John McGraw of the New York Giants did not go quite that far but he agreed that Monroe would have starred in any league. He began with the Philadelphia Giants in 1903. He subsequently played second base for the Quaker Giants of New York and the Brooklyn Royal Giants before joining Foster's American Giants in 1912. For three years he was the keystone man (in both senses of the word) on a club that included John Henry Lloyd, Pete Hill, Bruce Petway, Frank Wickware, and Joe Williams. Monroe died March 16, 1915.

George Scales

One of the strongest hitters among black second basemen, and a good fielder who compensated for lack of speed with intelligence and alertness, was George Scales, a versatile player who was also at home at third base and in the outfield. Scales, a righthanded batter, started with the St. Louis Giants in 1921. After spending the next year with the St. Louis Stars, he joined the Lincoln Giants in 1923 and was a fixture of that club's infield for seven years. During the Thirties, Scales played for the Homestead Grays, the New York Black Yankees, and the Baltimore Elite Giants, managing the latter two clubs. After retiring as a player-manager in 1944, Scales spent four years as road secretary of the Elite Giants.

Frank Warfield

Frank Warfield was an aggressive, smart second baseman and a fair righthanded hitter. Born in Indianapolis in 1895, he began playing professionally with the St. Louis Giants in 1916. As player and manager he served with the Indianapolis ABCs, Hilldale, Detroit Stars, Kansas City Monarchs, and the Baltimore Black Sox. Warfield died in July 1932 while playing manager of the Washington Pilots.

Shortstops

John Beckwith

John Beckwith was a very versatile performer who could handle any position acceptably, but it was as a righthanded power hitter that he made his name. He was the first player, black or white, to hit

John Beckwith

a ball over the left-field fence at the Cincinnati Reds' Redland Field, turning the trick as a nineteen-year-old with the Chicago Giants. During his best years he was credited with 72 home runs in 1927 and 54 in 1928. Beckwith, born in 1902, began playing in Chicago's Sunday school leagues; he started as a professional with the Chicago Giants in 1919. He went to Foster's American Giants in 1921 and stayed there three years, catching, playing shortstop, first base, third base, the outfield, and even doing some pitching. In 1924 he went East and spent the rest of his career with the Baltimore Black Sox, Homestead Grays, Harrisburg Giants, Lincoln Giants, New York Black Yankees, and Newark Dodgers. His last year with a big club was 1934. Beckwith hit consistently as well as powerfully; he was the second-leading batter in the American Negro League in 1929 with a .443 average.

Home Run Johnson

Grant Johnson earned the nickname "Home Run" by his powerful righthanded swing in the dead-ball era. He was born in Findlay, Ohio, in 1874 and began a career in 1895 that took him to the best clubs of the early years of this century. He played with the Page Fence Giants of Adrian, Michigan, Columbia Giants of Chicago, Cuban X Giants, Philadelphia Giants, Brooklyn Royal Giants, Lincoln Giants, and Lincoln Stars up to 1916. He joined the Pittsburgh Colored Stars and stayed with that club when it moved to Buffalo. Johnson continued playing in the Buffalo area with the Buffalo Giants until he was fifty-eight years old. His most notable accomplishment came in 1910 when he outhit Ty Cobb and Wahoo Sam Crawford of the Detroit Tigers in a twelve-game series in Cuba while he was with the Havana Reds.

John Henry Lloyd (See Chapter 6)

Dick Lundy

A shortstop with a wide range and a storm arm was Richard (Dick) Lundy, who emerged as the best shortfielder in black baseball in the 1920s. Lundy was born on July 10, 1898, in Jacksonville, Florida, and began playing professionally as a third basemen with the Duval Giants of his home city in 1915. He came North with the club the next year when the Duval Giants became the Bacharach Giants of Atlantic City. In his years as a player and manager until 1948, Lundy was with the Lincoln Giants, Hilldale, Baltimore Black Sox, Philadelphia Stars, Newark Eagles, New York Cubans, and Jacksonville Eagles. A switch-hitter, he was a steady .300 batter with power. He was 5 feet 10 inches tall and weighed about 180 pounds. No holler guy, Lundy rarely opened his mouth during a game except when, as manager, he gave instructions. In common with most players of his era, he had a cavalier attitude toward contracts. In 1920 he signed three of them—with the Bacharach Giants, the New York Bacharach Giants—who split from the Atlantic City club in 1919—and Hilldale. A court in Philadelphia awarded him to the New York Bacharachs. Napoleon Cummings, Lundy's teammate at Atlantic City, regards him as the peer of John Henry Lloyd or any other shortstop in history.

Willie Wells

Succeeding Lundy (who had succeeded Lloyd) as the recognized master at shortstop was Willie Wells, whose career as a professional began in 1923 and extended into the late Forties. A stocky 5-foot-7-inch 160-pounder, Wells used his speed, good hands, and an accurate

Willie Wells—COURTESY OF ARTHUR M. CARTER

though not strong arm to achieve preeminence as a shortstop. "He didn't have a strong arm," Buck Leonard remembers, "but he could always get that man at first—he would toss you out, the boys used to say." Wells was a master at going back for Texas-Leaguers, enabling outfielders who played behind him to position themselves deeper than normal. He was a righthanded batter who rarely hit a long ball but whose average was usually above .320. Wells was born in Austin, Texas, on October 10, 1905, and broke in with San Antonio in 1923. The next year he went to St. Louis to play with the Giants and then with the Stars. He stayed with the Stars until their breakup after the 1931 season. Subsequently, Wells played with the Detroit Wolves, Homestead Grays, Kansas City Monarchs, Chicago American Giants, New York Black Yankees, Newark Eagles, Indianapolis Clowns, and Memphis Red Sox until 1949. He also played three years in Mexico during the early Forties. His stature as a shortstop is indicated by the fact that Arthur W. Hardy, who played against John Henry Lloyd in his prime, calls Wells the greatest at the position.

Also . . .

Sam Bankhead

The eldest of five ballplaying brothers—one of whom, Dan, made the major leagues after the color line was crossed—Sam Bankhead starred as shortstop, second baseman, and outfielder for the Pittsburgh Crawfords and Homestead Grays from the middle 1930s. He boasted a powerful arm and a batting average of about .290. Bankhead started in 1930 as a wild righthanded pitcher for the Birmingham Black Barons. After settling down as infielder and outfielder, he played for the Nashville Elite Giants before moving to Pittsburgh. He was playing manager when the Grays disbanded in 1950.

Bill Yancey

A superior shortstop with a strong, accurate arm was William J. (Bill) Yancey, who was also one of the stars of the Renaissance basketball team, the contemporary and rival of the white Original Celtics. In a baseball career spanning 1923 to 1936, Yancey starred with the Philadelphia Giants, Hilldale, Philadelphia Tigers, Lincoln Giants, New York Black Yankees, Brooklyn Eagles, and Philadelphia Stars. He was a good righthanded hitter, fast, and a sparkplug in the field. He lives in Moorestown, N.J., and is a beer salesman and major-league scout.

Third Basemen

Ray Dandridge

Raymond (Hooks) Dandridge came tantalizingly close to major-league stardom after a lifetime in Negro baseball. He was a veteran of sixteen seasons in black baseball when he and New York Cuban

Ray Dandridge—COURTESY OF ARTHUR M.
CARTER

pitcher Dave Barnhill were signed as the first Negroes on the Minneapolis Millers of the Triple-A American Association in 1949. He
was then about forty; had he been just a few years younger, there is
little doubt that he would have become a big-league star. He was
still a sure-handed fielder with a powerful arm, and he raked American Association pitching in his first year for a .362 average. The
following year, batting .311 for the Millers, he was named the
league's most valuable player. He was also the roommate of a young
black outfielder named Willie Mays. Dandridge ended his career
with the Millers in 1951 with a hefty .324 batting mark. He was
noted primarily as a third baseman, but he was at home also at second
base and shortstop. He started with the Detroit Stars in 1933 and the
next year moved to the Newark Dodgers. He remained with the
Dodgers and their successors, the Newark Eagles, throughout most
of his career, except for several seasons in the Mexican League.
Cum Posey placed him among the all-time greats of Negro baseball
in 1944 with the comment that "there simply never was a smoother-
functioning master at third base than Dandridge, and he can hit that
apple, too." Dandridge lives in Newark and is a scout for the San
Francisco Giants.

Judy Johnson

A wiry, 5-foot-11½-inch 145-pounder, William J. (Judy) Johnson was a fixture on the great Hilldale teams of the Twenties and the Pittsburgh Crawfords of the Thirties. He was regarded as one of the smartest players in the game, with sure hands and a great arm at third base. Johnson was a line-drive hitter with fair power and a batting average usually around .300. He was born on October 26, 1900, in Snow Hill, Maryland, but grew up in Wilmington, Delaware, and, as a boy, played baseball and football on integrated teams. In 1918 he attracted the attention of the Bacharach Giants and began playing with them on Sundays for $5 a game. A year later he added Darby, Pennsylvania, to his itinerary, taking the streetcar from Wilmington to Darby each Thursday to play with Hilldale and going to Atlantic City on Sundays for Bacharach games. In 1920 he was with the semipro Madison Stars in Philadelphia when he was sold to Hilldale for $100. He stayed there through 1929, leaving to manage the Homestead Grays. He returned to Darby in 1931 to manage the Darby Daisies, Hilldale's short-lived successor, and from 1932 until his playing days ended in 1937 he was one of the key men in the potent attack of the Pittsburgh Crawfords. In the first Negro World Series in 1924, Johnson led Hilldale's hitters with a .341 average, and five years later he had the most hits of any batter in the American Negro League. Johnson lives in Marshallton, Delaware, and is a major-league scout.

Dave Malarcher

Like Marcelle a native of Louisiana, and like Judy Johnson a smart, smooth-fielding third baseman, David J. (Gentleman Dave) Malarcher was a mainstay on the American Giants' teams which dominated the Negro National League in the early 1920s. He succeeded Rube Foster as manager in 1926 and quickly established himself as one of the best strategists in the game. Malarcher was a speedy switch-hitter with an average usually in the .300 range and was noted as especially dangerous in clutch situations. He was born in the hamlet of Whitehall, Louisiana, on October 18, 1894, the youngest of ten children of a plantation laborer. In 1916, while attending New Orleans University and playing with the university team and the semipro New Orleans Eagles, Malarcher was picked up

Oliver Marcelle

by the Indianapolis ABCs. He played the outfield, second base, and third base for the ABCs for two years, leaving in 1918 for Army service. In 1919, returning to civilian life, he joined the Detroit Stars. After a year with the Stars he went to the great American Giants and was with that club as player and manager through most of the years until 1935. Malarcher, who earned a real-estate broker's license in 1928, continued in the real estate business after his retirement from baseball. He lives in Chicago.

Oliver Marcelle

A Creole and native of New Orleans, Oliver H. (Ghost) Marcelle (also Marcel, Marcell) was possessed of an ungovernable temper and all the skills needed by a third baseman. He came North in 1918 to join the Brooklyn Royal Giants and was soon recognized as the most accomplished third baseman in black baseball. Judy Johnson remembers Marcelle as his superior defensively but not with the bat. Marcelle, a righthanded batter, was a slash hitter and at his best in the clutch. Most of his best years were spent with the Bacharach Giants, but he also played with the Lincoln Giants, the Detroit Stars, and the Baltimore Black Sox, in a career in top competition which ended in 1930. His violent temper often had him in hot water with umpires. Whitey Gruhler, retired sports editor of the

Atlantic City Press, recalls a game there during which Marcelle became so incensed over a rhubarb that he belted Oscar Charleston over the head with a bat. Marcelle went West after retiring from big-time baseball and lived in Denver for the last fifteen years of his life. He died there in 1949.

Also . . .

Jud Wilson

Judson (Bojung) Wilson was not in the same class with Dandridge, Johnson, Marcelle, or Malarcher as a defensive third baseman, but as a hitter he had few peers during his long career. Jimmie Crutchfield remembers, "He was not a good third baseman, but he could play enough third base not to hurt you, and he could hit everything in sight." A lefthanded batter, Wilson feared no pitcher and was especially strong in the clutch. In 1945, his twenty-second season with top clubs, he hit Negro National League pitching for a .288 average as a pinch-hitter for the Homestead Grays. He started in 1924 with the Baltimore Black Sox and later played with the Philadelphia Stars and Pittsburgh Crawfords as well as the Grays.

Outfielders

Cool Papa Bell

James (Cool Papa) Bell was probably the fastest runner who ever played baseball. He was so fast that opposing players had trouble believing their eyes when they saw him run. Jimmie Crutchfield recalls that when "Bell hit one back to the pitcher, everybody would yell, 'Hurry!' " And Judy Johnson said that when Bell was at bat with no one on base, the infielders moved in as if a man were on third with one out. "You couldn't play back in your regular position or you'd never throw him out," Johnson said. A lefthanded thrower who started as a righthanded batter, Bell taught himself to switch-hit to make the most of his speed. The result was a batting average in the high .300s, usually near the .400 mark. Although he had little power, he accumulated a high total of doubles and triples be-

Cool Papa Bell, just before he joined the
St. Louis Stars in 1922

cause of his speed. On a sacrifice bunt, Bell often went from first to
third, and in one game against a major-league all-star team, he
went all the way home when he saw no one covering the plate as he
rounded third. In 1945, when he was forty years old, he was still
one of the base-stealing leaders of the Negro National League. Bell
played such a shallow centerfield that occasionally he was able to
sneak in behind a runner at second base and trap him while the
first- and third-base coaches were watching the infielders. His
arm was mediocre, but he overcame this weakness by getting rid of
the ball quickly. Bell was born in Starkville, Mississippi, on May 17,
1905. He went to St. Louis in 1920 and joined four of his brothers
on the Compton Hill Cubs, an amateur team. A rail-thin 5-foot-11-
inch 135-pound pitcher, he went to the semipro East St. Louis
Cubs in 1922 and left them during the season to start his pro
career with the St. Louis Stars. He pitched and played the outfield
for most of two seasons before he was made a full-time outfielder.

Bell was with the Stars, Homestead Grays, Detroit Wolves, Kansas City Monarchs, Pittsburgh Crawfords, Memphis Red Sox, and Chicago American Giants until 1946, his last year in top competition. He spent four of his peak years in Mexico. He later was player-manager for the Monarchs' traveling team, a training ground for the big club. The nickname "Cool Papa" was not, as it sounds, an attachment of his later years. It was given to him by the St. Louis Stars when he was a nineteen-year-old pitcher and coolly struck out Oscar Charleston in the clutch. The Stars began calling him Cool; manager Bill Gatewood, deciding that the nickname sounded incomplete, added the "Papa." Bell lives in St. Louis and is a guard at City Hall there.

Oscar Charleston

If an old Negro ballplayer is asked to name an all-time team, the odds are good that the discussion will start with Oscar Charleston. Built like Babe Ruth with a barrel chest and spindly legs, Charleston

Oscar Charleston in 1949—COURTESY OF
ARTHUR M. CARTER

combined speed, power at the plate, a strong arm, and an unerring sense of where a ball was hit in the outfield. From 1915 until about 1930, Charleston, a lefthanded thrower and batter who was just under six feet tall, was recognized as the best outfielder in the game. When he grew heavier and lost his speed, he moved to the infield and became a superior first baseman. His batting eye, which earned him a .396 average in 1929 in the American Negro League, was still sharp when he was around forty years old. Jimmie Crutchfield, who played under Charleston on the Pittsburgh Crawfords, remembers:

> We were playing a major-league all-star team one night in Des Moines, Iowa—Bob Feller, Gus Suhr, Ival Goodman, Al Todd, Jimmy King, Big Jim Weaver, Johnny Mize, Jim Winford—oh, they had a heckuva club! Now this was in 1936 when Charleston was big and fat. I heard him on the bench saying "I just don't get a thrill out of batting anymore unless there's someone on the bases." He had popped up a couple of times. Sure enough, we got two men on against Big Jim Weaver, and Charleston said, "Now this is what I've been waiting for." And he doubled against the left-centerfield wall and waddled into second base. That's the kind of guy Charleston was. If I had to pick the best player I saw in my time, it would be hard to pick between Charleston and Josh Gibson. When the chips were down and you needed somebody to bat in the clutch—even at his age he was as good as anybody playing baseball.

Charleston was born in Indianapolis in 1896, and as a youngster he was batboy for the ABCs. At fifteen he ran away from home and joined the Army. While serving in the Philippines he played ball for the Negro 24th Infantry and ran on the track team, setting a mark of 23 seconds for the 220-yard dash. In 1914, while still in the Army, he played ball in the Manila League, the only Negro in the circuit. He was mustered out in 1915 and joined the ABCs. By 1923 he was one of the highest-paid players in black baseball, earning $325 a month with the ABCs. During his playing days, Charleston was also with the Lincoln Stars, American Giants, St. Louis Giants, Harrisburg Giants, Hilldale, Homestead Grays, and Pittsburgh Crawfords. He managed several of those clubs as well as, during the 1940s and 1950s, the Philadelphia Stars and Brooklyn Brown Dodgers. At his peak, Charleston was perhaps the most popular player in the game. While he was with Hilldale in 1928–29, "he was to Philadelphia what Smoky Joe Williams was to New Yorkers when the latter was with the Lincoln Giants—their hero," wrote Chester L. Washington in the *Pittsburgh Courier*. "Scores of school kids turned out regularly just to see Oscar perform. He was to them what Babe Ruth is to kids of a lighter hue."

Martin Dihigo

Placement of Martin Dihigo among the outfielders is an arbitrary decision. An excellent hitter and an outstanding pitcher, Dihigo was a star performer at *every* position. Cum Posey said that Dihigo's "gifts afield have not been approached by any one man, black or white," and Buck Leonard and others call Dihigo the greatest ball-player of all time. A Cuban, Dihigo first played in the United States in 1923 with Alex Pompez's Cuban Stars when he was about fifteen years old. He was used mostly at first base that year, but he also pitched and played second. In subsequent years, when he had attained his full size of 6 feet 1 inch and 190 pounds, Dihigo, a right-handed thrower and hitter, was used at every position by the Cubans, the Homestead Grays, and Hilldale. A measure of his versatility may be seen in the fact that in the 1935 East-West game, Dihigo started in centerfield and batted third for the East, and, in the late innings, was called upon to pitch in relief. He had an exceptionally strong arm, great speed, and the grace of a superlative athlete. In 1929 he was credited with a .386 batting average in the American Negro

Martin Dihigo—COURTESY OF ARTHUR M. CARTER

League. Dihigo played several seasons in Latin America in the late
Thirties and early Forties, returning to the Grays in 1945. After the
collapse of the Negro National League, he played in Mexico during
the 1950s.

Pete Hill

J. Preston (Pete) Hill, a lefthanded-hitting outfielder, was a contemporary of Rube Foster and served as Foster's field lieutenant
during the heyday of the Leland Giants and the early American Giants. Beginning in 1904, he was with the Philadelphia Giants, the
top club in the East, and he was one of those called to Chicago
when Foster decimated the Philadelphia club in 1909 to strengthen
the Leland Giants. He went with Foster when the American
Giants were formed in 1911 and played left field for that great
club until 1918. During much of this period he was captain and, in
effect, assistant manager. In 1919, when Foster established the Detroit Stars and stocked the new club with players, Hill became manager. He stayed three years. Later he managed the Madison Stars of
Philadelphia, the Milwaukee Bears, and the Baltimore Black Sox.
His last connection with baseball was in 1925, when he was Black
Sox business manager. Cum Posey called Hill "the most consistent
hitter of his time, and, while a lefthanded batter, he hit both left-
handers and righthanders equally well. He was the backbone, year
in and year out, of great ballclubs."

Christobel Torrienti

The certified power hitter on Foster's American Giants during
the early 1920s was Christobel Torrienti, a heavily muscled Cuban
who stood about 5 feet 10 inches and weighed 190 pounds. A lefthanded hitter, he had power to all fields but was especially strong
pulling the ball into right field, and even in the dead-ball era he
was capable of reaching deep fences. Jelly Gardner, Torrienti's
teammate on the American Giants, recalls: "The New York Giants
had a scout following us to Kansas City, St. Louis, and Indianapolis.
He was watching Torrienti. He hit a line drive in Indianapolis that
hit the top of the right-field wall and the rightfielder threw him out
at first base. That's how much power he had." Gardner said the
Giant scout liked Torrienti and would have signed him except for

the fact that the Cuban's hair was kinky. "He was a light brown, and he would have gone up to the major leagues, but he had real rough hair," Gardner explained. Torrienti was born about 1895 and came to the United States with the Cuban Stars in 1914. In 1918 he joined the American Giants and won the centerfield job, moving Oscar Charleston to left. He provided the big punch in Foster's lineup until 1926 when he went to the Kansas City Monarchs. The next year he was with the Detroit Stars. Torrienti also played with the traveling Gilkerson's Union Giants, the Atlanta Black Crackers, and semipro clubs in Chicago before retiring in the mid-Thirties. The Cuban outfielder, who had a strong, accurate arm, often pitched during his years with top clubs. C. I. Taylor, the astute manager of the Indianapolis ABCs, once commented, "If I should see Torrienti walking up the other side of this strcct, I would say, 'There walks a ballclub.' "

Christobel Torrienti

Also . . .

Chester Brooks

One of the few West Indians in top-level competition, Chester Brooks starred for the Brooklyn Royal Giants during the 1920s. He is remembered as a consistently strong righthanded hitter and a capable outfielder. Brooks played his whole career with the Royal Giants from 1918 to 1933, a period when the once strong club was on the decline.

Rap Dixon

Herbert (Rap) Dixon was a power hitter who, in 1930, in the first game ever played between Negro teams in Yankee Stadium, belted 3 home runs into the right-field seats. The year before he had gotten 14 straight hits against the best pitchers of the Homestead Grays. A native of Steelton, Pennsylvania, Dixon started in 1922 with the Harrisburg Giants. He played there six years before moving to the Baltimore Black Sox. He also was with the Chicago American Giants, Darby Daisies, Pittsburgh Crawfords, Philadelphia Stars, Brooklyn Eagles, and Homestead Grays until 1936. Dixon played part of one season, 1927, in Japan.

Jelly Gardner

Floyd (Jelly) Gardner was the lead-off man and an outfield fixture for the Chicago American Giants in the 1920s. A line-drive hitter and one of the fastest men in baseball, Gardner played in the bigtime from 1919 to 1933. He began with the Detroit Stars and moved to the American Giants in 1920. He left them to go with the Lincoln Giants in 1927 after a salary dispute with Rube Foster. Gardner, who threw righthanded but hit from the left side of the plate, also played for the Homestead Grays and the American Giants and Detroit Stars again before quitting baseball. Born in Russellville, Arkansas, in 1896, Gardner now lives in Chicago and is a retired railroader.

Vic Harris

As outfielder and manager, E. Victor (Vic) Harris was the steady keystone of the Homestead Grays for nearly a quarter of a century. A lefthanded hitter, Harris began his career as a seventeen-year-old with the Cleveland Tate Stars in 1923. He played with the Cleveland Browns and the American Giants before joining the Grays

Fats Jenkins—COURTESY OF BILL YANCEY

in 1925. From then until 1948 he was a fixture in the Grays' outfield, except 1934, which he spent with the Grays' arch-rivals, the Pittsburgh Crawfords. Harris was the Grays' manager from 1936 to 1948. He spent 1949 as coach of the Baltimore Elite Giants and was manager of the Birmingham Black Barons in 1950.

Fats Jenkins

A lefthanded hitter and thrower, Clarence (Fats) Jenkins starred in the outfield for several clubs from 1920 to 1938. Like Bill Yancey a member of the Renaissance basketball team during the winter, Jenkins spent most of his baseball career with the Harrisburg Giants and the New York Black Yankees. He also played for the Lincoln Giants, Bacharach Giants, Baltimore Black Sox, Brooklyn Eagles, and Philadelphia Stars. His last baseball position was as manager of the Brooklyn Royal Giants in 1940. Despite his nickname, Jenkins was not even chubby; he inherited the name Fats in childhood from a brother who merited it. Jenkins died in December, 1968.

Jimmie Lyons

A fleet baserunner and fielder whose career took him to several of the top clubs for a 15-year period beginning in 1911 was James (Jimmie) Lyons. In naming Lyons as one of the all-time greats, Dave Malarcher said that he was unsurpassed as an all-around ballplayer, combining excellent skills in fielding, speed on the bases, hitting, and especially drag bunting. Lyons began his career with the Lincoln Giants but reached his greatest fame in the outfield of the Chicago American Giants during the early Twenties. He also played for the St. Louis Giants, Chicago Giants, Brooklyn Royal Giants, Indianapolis ABCs, Detroit Stars, and Cleveland Browns through 1925. In 1932, his last year in baseball, he managed the Louisville Black Caps.

Spot Poles

Labeled "the Black Ty Cobb," Spottswood (Spot) Poles starred as the centerfielder of the great Lincoln Giant clubs before and after World War I. He started with the Philadelphia Giants in 1909 and played with them two seasons before joining the new Lincoln Giants in 1911. He was with the Giants until 1923, with occasional periods on the Lincoln Stars, Brooklyn Royal Giants, and Hilldale. A fleet outfielder, Poles was the sharp-hitting leadoff batter for the Lincolns. In 1911 he was credited with a .440 batting average and 41 stolen bases in 60 games.

Turkey Stearns

Chino Smith

A compact bundle of power built along the lines of Lloyd Waner of the Pittsburgh Pirates was Charles (Chino) Smith, whose career was cut short by death in the early 1930s. He was with the Philadelphia Giants and Brooklyn Royal Giants beginning in 1924 but reached the heights in the late Twenties with the Lincoln Giants and in the Cuban winter league of that period. In 1929 the left-handed hitting Smith led the American Negro League with a batting average of .464 and 23 home runs. In the first Negro game at Yankee Stadium, Smith blasted two homers into the right-field seats. A few older players consider Smith the greatest hitter Negro baseball produced.

Turkey Stearns

A long-ball hitting outfielder, Norman (Turkey) Stearns was good enough in his thirties to play in four of the first five East-West games, black baseball's biggest attraction. He started playing professionally with the Montgomery Grey Sox in 1921 and was the lefthanded power hitter for the Detroit Stars from 1923 through

1931. He also played with the Lincoln Giants, Chicago American Giants, Kansas City Monarchs, Detroit Stars, and Detroit Black Sox until 1942.

Clint Thomas

Clinton (Clint) Thomas was one of the offensive threats of the strong Hilldale Club of the Twenties and of the New York Black Yankees during the Thirties. A righthanded batter and thrower, Thomas was born in 1898 and started his career with the Brooklyn Royal Giants in 1920. After short stays with the Columbus Buckeyes and Detroit Stars, Thomas joined Hilldale in 1923 and batted .373. He stayed with Hilldale through 1928 and played with the Bacharach Giants, Lincoln Giants, and Darby Daisies before going to the Black Yankees in 1932. He also played with the Newark Eagles and Philadelphia Stars before quitting in 1937.

Chaney White

A threat both at the plate and on the basepaths for fifteen years, Chaney White was a fine outfielder whose only deficiency was a weak arm. A native of Dallas, White came North in 1920 for a trial with Foster's American Giants. He was rejected by Foster but caught on the next year with Hilldale. He was one of the stars of the strong Bacharach Giant teams of the late 1920s and also played with the Wilmington Potomacs, Quaker Giants, Homestead Grays, Darby Daisies, and Philadelphia Stars up to 1935. Judy Johnson calls White the best one-run-getter in baseball. He was very fast and came into a base with spikes high, often kicking the ball out of the infielder's glove. "He had little legs and a big body, but he could run like a deer," Johnson said. "And he knew how to take advantage of a pitcher." White was one of a rare breed—a lefthanded thrower who batted from the right side of the plate.

Managers

Most of the all-time greats of Negro baseball were managers as well as players, particularly as they grew older. Notably successful as managers were (besides Rube Foster) Dizzy Dismukes, Chappie

Johnson, Dave Malarcher, and Danny McClellan. Two of the managers usually considered outstanding, however, were only mediocre players. One was Cum Posey, whose career is sketched in Chapter 7. The other was Charles I. Taylor, who made the Indianapolis ABCs one of the nation's top clubs and who is regarded by some players as the finest manager in black baseball history. He was a patient, suave man, a shrewd psychologist and perhaps the first to have clubhouse meetings before and after games to discuss strategy and the strengths and weaknesses of the opposition.

Taylor, who was known by baseball men simply as C.I., was the oldest of the Taylor brothers, the youngest of whom was Ben. He was born in North Carolina in 1872, studied at Clark College in Atlanta, and served in the Army during the Spanish-American War. He began managing a club soon afterward in South Carolina and, beginning in 1904, for ten years Taylor ran the Birmingham Giants. In 1914 he moved the club to West Baden, Indiana, called it the West Baden Sprudels and, despite meager financial resources, challenged Foster for supremacy in the Chicago area. The following year, Taylor moved the club to Indianapolis with the backing of the American Brewing Company, whence the name ABCs. Able for the first time to pay his players guaranteed salaries, Taylor attracted such young stars as Oscar Charleston, Bingo DeMoss, Dave Malarcher, and his brothers Ben and Jim; in 1916 he was strong enough to play Foster's American Giants to a stalemate in a series for the "championship." Each team won four games and the ninth ended without decision in a protest.

C. I. was still playing sporadically when he was nearing his fiftieth birthday, usually using himself as a pinch-hitter. He was scrupulously fair and honest with his players and, according to one anecdote, carried his honesty to an unprecedented extreme on the field. He is supposed to have stolen third base one day in a game at West Baden, sliding in under a cloud of dust to the accompaniment of a safe ruling by the umpire. C. I. arose, brushed himself off, and raised his hand to the crowd and cried, "Ladies and gentlemen, I am an honest man. The umpire's decision is incorrect. I therefore declare myself out."

Taylor died on March 2, 1922. At his death his club was on firm financial ground and was among the top three black clubs in the Midwest. A year later, during the player war between the first Negro National League and Eastern Colored League, the ABCs were riddled and never regained their former glory.

While Rube Foster held sway over his players by stern discipline,

Taylor's methods were different. He was a careful handler of men who used persuasion rather than command. The result, according to Arthur W. Hardy, was that

> his players were tremendously loyal to him. The ABCs, in their dress and general decorum, more nearly approximated the modern professional athlete than any other group that I ever saw in those days. They were conservative in dress and quiet-spoken. I suppose some of them got liquored up and all that sort of thing, but if they did it was never ostentatiously.

EPILOGUE

At this point the writer intends to shed his mantle as an objective historian and assume the role of propagandist.

To make the point at once, I believe recognition should be accorded to the great stars of Negro baseball at the National Baseball Hall of Fame and Museum in Cooperstown, New York. And I do not mean in some obscure corner of the museum where Rube Foster and Satchel Paige and Josh Gibson and John Henry Lloyd can be segregated in a dusty pigeonhole as they were in life. I mean in the austere Hall of Fame where wide-eyed young fans now gape at the bronze likenesses of Honus Wagner and Ty Cobb and Babe Ruth and Walter Johnson and read summaries of their deeds.

In the face of the nation's wrenching debate over race, it seems a small injustice that black baseball players whose names appear in no record book are not represented at the game's holy of holies. But it is one wrong that can be righted easily by the committee that selects Hall of Fame members—merely by recognition that it *is* an injustice.*

It will be argued that the great stars of Negro baseball did not face teams of major-league quality day in and day out and thereby establish their greatness. As a boxing fan would put it, "Who did they ever lick?" This is a specious argument, for it can be demonstrated that more often than not they licked whomever they played and they played anybody who would play them, including major-league teams and big-league barnstormers. I have no supporting statistics, but after a careful study of contemporary accounts I have the distinct impression that the top black clubs won somewhat more than half of their games against big-leaguers. Well, a skeptic may say, the big-leaguers weren't really trying, because those games didn't mean anything to them. Perhaps. But there are very few professional baseball players who go to the plate without hoping for a base hit or pitch a game without trying to win, even when they are competing against sandlotters.

Critics may also point out that there are few certified records to support the nomination of a star of Negro baseball to the Hall of

---

* During 1969, while this book was in production, the Baseball Writers Association took the first steps toward election to the Hall of Fame of black stars who were barred from the big leagues by the color line. It goes without saying that the author applauds.—R.P.

Fame. This is quite true. There is, however, plenty of testimony to the talents of the greatest black stars, not only from other Negro players but from white major-leaguers, some of them with niches in the Hall. I am not speaking merely of a statement that this or that black player could have held his own in the major leagues. I am referring to statements by major-league stars that this or that black player was at least the equal of the best white players of his time.

It may be argued that making an exception for a few black men, permitting them to enter the Hall of Fame without supporting data, would represent a lowering of standards. On the contrary, it would *raise* the standards. No one who has read this far could fail to conclude that such men as Foster, Paige, Gibson, and Lloyd were among the most gifted baseball men of all time and of any color. To exclude them on grounds that, except for Paige, they never competed in the big leagues is to raise not just an unreasonable standard but an impossible one. And so long as the Hall of Fame is without a few of the great stars of Negro baseball, the notion that it represents the best in baseball is nonsense.

At first blush, it might appear impossible to determine how many Negro stars should be named and how they should be chosen. I don't believe either question is especially difficult, although it would be necessary to eliminate from consideration those men whose playing days ended before 1900 because no one now alive could remember them well.

There are now in the Hall of Fame sixty-eight players whose careers in the major leagues covered the period from 1900 to 1947, the year Jackie Robinson broke the major-league color line. (Some of them started before the turn of the century but played at least several seasons after 1900. All had retired by 1947.) During that 1900–1947 era, the Negro percentage of America's population remained fairly constant at ten percent. Arbitrarily, then, it could be assumed that ten percent of the Hall of Fame members for that era should be Negroes. (In view of the later success of black men in the major leagues, it could be argued that the proportion should be higher, but to avoid entanglements in statistical data and the laws of probability, leave it at ten percent.) This means that eight Negroes who played behind the color line should be added to the Hall of Fame.

How to select them? There are living today a number of knowledgeable Negro baseball men whose memories go back almost to the turn of the century. Choose two or three of them, add two or three others whose careers encompassed each decade up to 1950, and appoint them as a committee to select the players to be honored. Give each man on this committee of ten or twelve a piece of paper and ask him to write down the names of the sixteen greatest figures in Negro baseball. I will bet that eight names will appear on all lists. And there are the new Hall of Fame members.

Organized baseball's record since 1945 in offering equal opportunity to black men has been good. Not perfect, by any means, but far better than nearly any other segment of America's social and economic structure. It can enhance that record by recognizing, however belatedly, the players whose skin color alone kept them from earning a place in the Hall of Fame.

AUTHOR'S NOTE

The following appendixes, covering leagues, East-West games, and an all-time register of players and officials, are complete through the 1950 season.

Several teams and the Negro American League operated for ten more years, but because nearly all the first-rank players were in organized baseball, these teams and the NAL were no longer major operations. The 1950 cut-off date for the appendixes was an arbitrary choice; it could as well have been 1949 or 1952.

APPENDIX

LEAGUE STANDINGS YEAR-BY-YEAR

1920–1950

1920

Negro National League

Clubs were the Chicago American Giants, Chicago Giants, Cuban Stars, Dayton Marcos, Detroit Stars, Indianapolis ABCs, Kansas City Monarchs, and St. Louis Giants.

No final standings were published but the American Giants were awarded the pennant.

1921

Negro National League

	W	L	Pct.
Chicago American Giants	41	21	.661
Kansas City Monarchs	50	31	.617
St. Louis Giants	33	23	.589
Detroit Stars	30	27	.526
Indianapolis ABCs	30	29	.508
Columbus Buckeyes	24	38	.387
Cincinnati (Cuban Stars)	23	39	.371
Chicago Giants	10	32	.239

1922

Negro National League

	W	L	Pct.
Chicago American Giants	36	23	.610
Indianapolis ABCs	46	33	.582
Detroit Stars	43	32	.573
Kansas City Monarchs	44	33	.571
St. Louis Stars	23	23	.500
Pittsburgh Keystones	16	21	.432
Cuban Stars	19	30	.388
Cleveland Tate Stars	17	29	.370

1923

Negro National League

	W	L	Pct.
Kansas City Monarchs	57	33	.633
Detroit Stars	40	27	.597
Chicago American Giants	41	29	.586
Indianapolis ABCs	45	34	.570
Cuban Stars (West)	27	31	.466
St. Louis Stars	23	31	.426
*Toledo Tigers	11	15	.423
**Milwaukee Bears	14	32	.304

 * Disbanded July 15.
 ** Dropped in late season.

Eastern Colored League

	W	L	Pct.
Hilldale	32	17	.673
Cuban Stars (East)	23	17	.575
Brooklyn Royal Giants	18	18	.500
Bacharach Giants	19	23	.452
Lincoln Giants	16	22	.421
Baltimore Black Sox	19	30	.388

No World Series was held.

1924

Negro National League

	W	L	Pct.
Kansas City Monarchs	55	22	.714
Chicago American Giants	49	24	.671

Detroit Stars	37	27	.578
St. Louis Stars	40	36	.526
Birmingham Black Barons	32	37	.464
*Memphis Red Sox	29	37	.439
Cuban Stars (West)	16	33	.327
Cleveland Browns	15	34	.306

* Succeeded Indianapolis ABCs, who started season in league.

Eastern Colored League

	W	L	Pct.
Hilldale	47	22	.681
Baltimore Black Sox	30	19	.612
Lincoln Giants	31	25	.554
Bacharach Giants	30	29	.508
Harrisburg Giants	26	28	.481
Brooklyn Royal Giants	16	25	.390
Washington Potomacs	21	37	.362
Cuban Stars (East)	15	31	.326

World Series

1st game at Shibe Park, Philadelphia:

	R	H	E
Kansas City Monarchs	6	7	0
Hilldale	2	8	8

Winning pitcher, Bullet Rogan; loser, Phil Cockrell.

2nd game at Shibe Park, Philadelphia:

	R	H	E
Hilldale	11	15	2
Kansas City Monarchs	0	4	2

Winning pitcher, Nip Winters; loser, William Drake.

3rd game at Baltimore:

	R	H	E
Kansas City Monarchs	6	7	7
Hilldale	6	10	4

Game called for darkness after 13 innings.

4th game at Baltimore:

	R	H	E
Hilldale	4	4	1
Kansas City Monarchs	3	8	3

Winning pitcher, Rube Currie; loser, Cliff Bell.

5th game at Kansas City:

	R	H	E
Hilldale	5	9	1
Kansas City Monarchs	3	4	4

Winning pitcher, Nip Winters; loser, Bullet Rogan.

6th game at Kansas City:

	R	H	E
Kansas City Monarchs	6	12	1
Hilldale	5	10	1

Winning pitcher, William Bell; loser, Scrip Lee.

7th game at Kansas City (12 innings):

	R	H	E
Kansas City Monarchs	4	11	1
Hilldale	3	7	2

Winning pitcher, José Mendez; loser, Nip Winters.

8th game at Chicago:

	R	H	E
Kansas City Monarchs	3	9	0
Hilldale	2	8	1

Winning pitcher, Bullet Rogan; loser, Rube Currie.

9th game at Chicago:

	R	H	E
Hilldale	5	13	3
Kansas City Monarchs	3	9	4

Winning pitcher, Nip Winters; loser, William Drake.

10th game at Chicago:

	R	H	E
Kansas City Monarchs	5	6	0
Hilldale	0	3	0

Winning pitcher, José Mendez; loser, Scrip Lee.

Kansas City won Series, 5 games to 4.

1925

Negro National League

First Half

	W	L	Pct.
Kansas City Monarchs	31	9	.775
St. Louis Stars	31	14	.689

Detroit Stars	26	20	.565
Chicago American Giants	26	22	.542
Cuban Stars (West)	12	13	.480
Memphis Red Sox	18	24	.429
Indianapolis ABCs	13	24	.351
Birmingham Black Barons	14	33	.298

Second Half

	W	L	Pct.
St. Louis Stars	38	12	.760
Kansas City Monarchs	31	11	.738
Chicago American Giants	28	18	.609
Detroit Stars	27	20	.574
Cuban Stars (West)	10	12	.454
Birmingham Black Barons	10	16	.384
Memphis Red Sox	12	24	.333
Indianapolis ABCs	4	33	.108

Kansas City defeated St. Louis, 4 games to 3, in a playoff for the league pennant.

Eastern Colored League

	W	L	Pct.
Hilldale	45	13	.775
Harrisburg Giants	37	18	.673
Baltimore Black Sox	31	19	.620
Bacharach Giants	26	26	.500
Brooklyn Royal Giants	13	20	.394
Cuban Stars (East)	15	26	.366
Lincoln Giants	7	39	.152

World Series

1st game at Kansas City:

	R	H	E
Hilldale	5	11	1
Kansas City Monarchs	2	9	0

Winning pitcher, Rube Currie; loser, Cliff Bell.

2nd game at Kansas City:

	R	H	E
Kansas City Monarchs	5	10	2
Hilldale	3	10	2

Winning pitcher, Nelson Dean; loser, Phil Cockrell.

3rd game at Kansas City (10 innings):

	R	H	E
Hilldale	3	14	3
Kansas City Monarchs	1	4	0

Winning pitcher, Red Ryan; loser, José Mendez.

4th game at Kansas City:

	R	H	E
Hilldale	7	11	1
Kansas City Monarchs	3	8	1

Winning pitcher, Nip Winters; loser, William Drake.

5th game at Philadelphia:

	R	H	E
Hilldale	2	10	1
Kansas City Monarchs	1	6	0

Winning pitcher, Rube Currie; loser, Cliff Bell.

6th game at Philadelphia:

	R	H	E
Hilldale	5	9	3
Kansas City Monarchs	2	8	2

Winning pitcher, Phil Cockrell; loser, William Bell.

Hilldale won Series, 5 games to 1.

1926

Negro National League

First Half

	W	L	Pct.
Kansas City Monarchs	35	12	.745
Detroit Stars	33	17	.660
Chicago American Giants	28	16	.636
St. Louis Stars	29	18	.617
Indianapolis ABCs	28	18	.609
Cuban Stars (West)	6	27	.182
Dayton Marcos	7	32	.179
Cleveland Elites	5	32	.135

Second Half

	W	L	Pct.
Chicago American Giants	29	7	.806
Kansas City Monarchs	21	7	.750
St. Louis Stars	20	11	.645
Indianapolis ABCs	15	25	.375

| Detroit Stars | 13 | 23 | .361 |
| Cuban Stars (West) | 10 | 20 | .333 |

The American Giants defeated the Kansas City Monarchs, 5 games to 4, in a playoff for the pennant. On the final day of the playoff, Willie Foster won both games of a doubleheader for the American Giants. Bullet Rogan pitched both games for Kansas City.

Eastern Colored League

	W	L	Pct.
Bacharach Giants	34	20	.629
Harrisburg Giants	25	17	.595
Hilldale	34	24	.586
Cuban Stars (East)	28	21	.572
Lincoln Giants	19	22	.463
Baltimore Black Sox	18	29	.383
Brooklyn Royal Giants	7	20	.260
*Newark Stars	1	10	.091

* Disbanded in midseason.

World Series

1st game at Shibe Park, Philadelphia:

American Giants and Bacharach Giants were tied, 3–3, at the end of 9 innings, when the game was called for darkness.

2nd game at Atlantic City:

	R	H	E
American Giants	7	9	0
Bacharach Giants	6	7	1

Winning pitcher, George Harney; loser, Red Grier.

3rd game at Baltimore:

	R	H	E
American Giants	0	0	4
Bacharach Giants	10	14	2

Winning pitcher, Red Grier (a no-hitter); loser, Webster McDonald.

4th game at Shibe Park, Philadelphia:

The teams were tied, 4–4, at the end of 9 innings, when the game was called for darkness.

5th game at Philadelphia:

	R	H	E
American Giants	5	5	3
Bacharach Giants	7	13	3

Winning pitcher, Hooks Mitchell; loser, Rube Currie.

6th game at Chicago:

	R	H	E
Bacharach Giants	4	8	3
American Giants	5	10	0

Winning pitcher, Willie Foster; loser, Rats Henderson.

7th game at Chicago:

	R	H	E
Bacharach Giants	3	6	0
American Giants	0	3	2

Winning pitcher, Rats Henderson; loser, George Harney.

8th game at Chicago:

	R	H	E
Bacharach Giants	3	8	1
American Giants	6	7	1

Winning pitcher, Rube Currie; loser, Red Grier.

9th game at Chicago:

	R	H	E
Bacharach Giants	0	—	—
American Giants	13	12	0

Winning pitcher, Willie Powell; loser, Rats Henderson.

10th game at Chicago:

	R	H	E
Bacharach Giants	0	10	3
American Giants	1	4	0

Winning pitcher, Willie Foster; loser, Hubert Lockhart.

American Giants won Series, 5 games to 3.

1927

Negro National League

First Half

	W	L	Pct.
Chicago American Giants	32	14	.696
Kansas City Monarchs	36	18	.667
St. Louis Stars	32	19	.627
Detroit Stars	28	18	.609
Birmingham Black Barons	23	29	.442
Memphis Red Sox	19	25	.432
Cuban Stars (West)	15	23	.395
Cleveland Hornets	10	37	.213

Second Half

No final standings were published, but the Birmingham Black Barons were declared second-half winners.

The American Giants defeated the Black Barons in 4 straight playoff games to win the pennant.

Eastern Colored League

First Half

	W	L	Pct.
Bacharach Giants	29	17	.630
Baltimore Black Sox	23	17	.575
Cuban Stars (East)	24	19	.558
Harrisburg Giants	25	20	.556
Hilldale	17	28	.378
Brooklyn Royal Giants	10	21	.323

Second Half

	W	L	Pct.
Bacharach Giants	25	18	.581
Harrisburg Giants	16	12	.572
Hilldale	19	17	.528
Cuban Stars (East)	9	13	.409
Baltimore Black Sox	12	18	.400
Brooklyn Royal Giants	5	10	.333

World Series

1st game:

	R	H	E
Bacharach Giants	2	13	2
American Giants	6	8	1

Winning pitcher, Willie Foster; loser, Luther Farrell.

2nd game:

	R	H	E
Bacharach Giants	1	4	4
American Giants	11	14	1

Winning pitcher, Willie Powell; loser, Jesse Hubbard.

3rd game:

	R	H	E
Bacharach Giants	0	4	4
American Giants	7	10	0

Winning pitcher, George Harney; loser, Jesse Hubbard.

4th game:

	R	H	E
Bacharach Giants	1	16	6
American Giants	9	11	3

Winning pitcher, Webster McDonald; loser, Luther Farrell.

5th game (called for darkness after 6½ innings):

	R	H	E
American Giants	2	0	1
Bacharach Giants	3	4	4

Winning pitcher, Luther Farrell; loser, Willie Foster.

6th game:

The teams were tied, 1–1, in the tenth inning, when the game was called for darkness.

7th game:

	R	H	E
American Giants	1	7	2
Bacharach Giants	8	11	1

Winning pitcher, Luther Farrell; loser, George Harney.

8th game:

	R	H	E
American Giants	5	6	4
Bacharach Giants	6	10	1

Winning pitcher, Jesse Hubbard; loser, Willie Foster.

9th game:

	R	H	E
American Giants	11	15	1
Bacharach Giants	4	8	2

Winning pitcher, Willie Foster; loser, Hubert Lockhart.

American Giants won Series, 5 games to 3.

1928

Negro National League

No final standings were published for either the first or second half. The St. Louis Stars were awarded the first-half championship, the Chicago American Giants the second. Results of a playoff, if one was held, were not recorded.

Other clubs were the Birmingham Black Barons, Cuban Stars (West), and Detroit Stars.

Eastern Colored League

The league broke up in late spring. Clubs were the Bacharach Giants, Baltimore Black Sox, Cuban Stars (East), Lincoln Giants, and Philadelphia Tigers.

1929

Negro National League

First Half

	W	L	Pct.
Kansas City Monarchs	28	11	.718
St. Louis Stars	28	14	.667
Detroit Stars	24	16	.600
Birmingham Black Barons	20	24	.454
Chicago American Giants	22	29	.431
Memphis Red Sox	14	22	.389
Cuban Stars (West)	6	14	.300

Second Half

	W	L	Pct.
Kansas City Monarchs	34	6	.850
Chicago American Giants	26	9	.743
St. Louis Stars	28	16	.636
Cuban Stars (West)	12	12	.500
Detroit Stars	10	23	.303
Birmingham Black Barons	9	27	.250
Memphis Red Sox	5	22	.185

American Negro League

First Half

	W	L	Pct.
Baltimore Black Sox	24	11	.686
Lincoln Giants	22	11	.667
Homestead Grays	15	13	.536
Hilldale	15	20	.429
Bacharach Giants	11	20	.355
Cuban Stars (East)	6	16	.273

Second Half

	W	L	Pct.
Baltimore Black Sox	25	10	.714
Hilldale	24	15	.615
Lincoln Giants	18	15	.545
Homestead Grays	19	16	.543
Cuban Stars (East)	9	23	.281
Bacharach Giants	8	25	.242

No World Series was played.

1930

Negro National League

First Half

	W	L	Pct.
St. Louis Stars	41	15	.732
Kansas City Monarchs	31	14	.689
Memphis Red Sox	20	17	.541
Birmingham Black Barons	30	27	.526
Detroit Stars	26	26	.500
Cuban Stars (West)	17	23	.425
Chicago American Giants	24	39	.381
Nashville Elite Giants	13	35	.271

Second Half

	W	L	Pct.
Detroit Stars	24	7	.774
St. Louis Stars	22	7	.759
Chicago American Giants	19	12	.613
Kansas City Monarchs	8	12	.400
Nashville Elite Giants	7	12	.368

Cuban Stars (West)	6	12	.333
Memphis Red Sox	7	14	.333
Birmingham Black Barons	10	20	.333

The St. Louis Stars defeated the Detroit Stars in a playoff for the pennant.

1931

Negro National League

No final standings were published for either the first or second half, but the St. Louis Stars were declared winners of both. Other clubs were the Chicago American Giants, Cleveland Cubs, Detroit Stars, Indianapolis ABCs, and Louisville White Sox.

1932

Negro Southern League

First Half

	W	L	Pct.
Cole's American Giants (Chicago)	34	7	.829
Monroe Monarchs	33	7	.825
Nashville Elite Giants	24	13	.649
Montgomery Grey Sox	22	17	.564
Memphis Red Sox	22	22	.500
Louisville Black Caps	13	17	.433
Indianapolis ABCs	14	19	.424

Second Half

The Nashville Elite Giants, leading the league with a 12–0 record in early August, were declared second-half winners. During the second half, the Louisville Black Caps were replaced by the Columbus, Ohio, Turfs.

Cole's American Giants, first-half winners, defeated Nashville, 4 games to 3, in a playoff for the pennant.

East-West League

The league broke up in late June. Clubs were the Baltimore Black Sox, Cleveland Stars, Cuban Stars, Hilldale, Homestead Grays, and Newark Browns. The Baltimore Black Sox were in the lead.

1933

Negro National League

First Half

	W	L	Pct.
Cole's American Giants (Chicago)	21	7	.750
Pittsburgh Crawfords	20	8	.714
Baltimore Black Sox	10	9	.526
Nashville Elite Giants	12	13	.480
Detroit Stars	13	20	.394
Columbus Blue Birds	11	18	.379

Second Half

The second-half schedule was not completed. The Columbus Blue Birds dropped out in August and were replaced by the Cleveland Giants.

The American Giants claimed the pennant. Several months later, W. A. (Gus) Greenlee, league president, awarded the pennant to his club, the Pittsburgh Crawfords. This was, of course, disputed by the American Giants.

1934

Negro National League

First Half

	W	L	Pct.
Cole's American Giants (Chicago)	17	6	.739
Pittsburgh Crawfords	14	8	.636
Philadelphia Stars	12	9	.571
Newark Dodgers	6	5	.545
Nashville Elite Giants	9	11	.450
Cleveland Red Sox	2	22	.083

Second Half

	W	L	Pct.
Philadelphia Stars	11	4	.733
Nashville Elite Giants	6	3	.667
Pittsburgh Crawfords	15	9	.625
Cole's American Giants (Chicago)	11	9	.550

Cleveland Red Sox	2	3	.400
Newark Dodgers	5	9	.357
*Bacharach Giants	3	12	.200
*Baltimore Black Sox	1	6	.143

* Added for second half.

The Philadelphia Stars defeated Cole's American Giants, 4 games to 3, in a playoff for the pennant. (The American Giants protested one of their defeats because a Stars player was permitted to continue in a game after evidently being ordered to leave by an umpire. No action was taken on the protest.)

1935

Negro National League

First Half

	W	L	Pct.
Pittsburgh Crawfords	26	6	.785
Columbus Elite Giants	17	11	.607
Homestead Grays	14	13	.519
Brooklyn Eagles	15	15	.500
Cole's American Giants (Chicago)	14	16	.467
Philadelphia Stars	14	17	.452
New York Cubans	10	16	.385
Newark Dodgers	8	20	.286

Second Half

	W	L	Pct.
New York Cubans	20	7	.741
Pittsburgh Crawfords	13	9	.591
Philadelphia Stars	14	10	.583
Columbus Elite Giants	10	10	.500
Homestead Grays	9	10	.474
Brooklyn Eagles	13	16	.448
Cole's American Giants (Chicago)	7	13	.350
Newark Dodgers	9	21	.300

The Pittsburgh Crawfords defeated the New York Cubans, 4 games to 3, in a playoff for the pennant.

1936

Negro National League

First Half

	W	L	Pct.
Washington Elite Giants	14	10	.583
Philadelphia Stars	15	12	.556
Pittsburgh Crawfords	16	15	.516
Newark Eagles	15	18	.455
New York Cubans	9	11	.450
Homestead Grays	10	13	.435

Second Half

	W	L	Pct.
Pittsburgh Crawfords	20	9	.690
Newark Eagles	15	11	.577
New York Black Yankees	8	7	.533
New York Cubans	13	12	.520
Homestead Grays	12	14	.462
Philadelphia Stars	10	18	.357
Washington Elite Giants	7	14	.333

No playoff was held between the first- and second-half winners.

1937

Negro National League

First Half

	W	L	Pct.
Homestead Grays	21	9	.700
Newark Eagles	19	14	.576
Philadelphia Stars	12	11	.522
Washington Elite Giants	11	15	.423
Pittsburgh Crawfords	11	16	.407
New York Black Yankees	11	17	.393

Second Half

No final standings were published. The Homestead Grays were declared league champions.

Negro American League

First Half

	W	L	Pct.
Kansas City Monarchs	19	8	.704
Chicago American Giants	18	8	.692
Cincinnati Tigers	15	11	.577
Memphis Red Sox	13	13	.500
Detroit Stars	12	15	.444
Birmingham Black Barons	10	17	.370
Indianapolis Athletics	9	18	.333
St. Louis Stars	5	22	.185

Second Half

No final standings were published. However, the Kansas City Monarchs, first-half winners, defeated the Chicago American Giants in a series billed as a playoff, 4 games to 1.

No World Series was played, but the Homestead Grays, NNL champions, played a post-season series with a team made up of Kansas City and Chicago players.

1938

Negro National League

First Half

	W	L	Pct.
Homestead Grays	26	6	.813
Philadelphia Stars	20	11	.645
Newark Eagles	11	11	.500
Pittsburgh Crawfords	14	14	.500
Baltimore Elite Giants	12	14	.462
New York Black Yankees	4	17	.190
Washington Black Senators	1	20	.048

Second Half

No final standings were published, but the league office announced that the teams finished in this order: Homestead, Philadelphia, Pittsburgh, Baltimore, Newark, and New York. The Washington club folded during the second half.

Negro American League

First Half

	W	L	Pct.
Memphis Red Sox	21	4	.840
Kansas City Monarchs	19	5	.792
*Indianapolis ABCs	6	6	.500
*Atlanta Black Crackers	9	10	.474
*Jacksonville Red Caps	3	4	.429
*Chicago American Giants	8	13	.381
*Birmingham Black Barons	3	11	.214

* Not final; last published standings.

Second Half

	W	L	Pct.
Atlanta Black Crackers	12	4	.750
Chicago American Giants	17	7	.708
Kansas City Monarchs	13	10	.565
Indianapolis ABCs	8	13	.381
Memphis Red Sox	8	15	.348
Birmingham Black Barons	5	12	.294

A seven-game series between the first- and second-half champions was declared "no contest" by league commissioner Robert B. Jackson after two games had been played. His ruling followed several postponements caused by disagreements between the Memphis and Atlanta clubs over scheduling. Memphis won the two games that were played.

No World Series was played.

1939

Negro National League

	W	L	Pct.
Homestead Grays	33	14	.702
Newark Eagles	29	20	.592
Baltimore Elite Giants	25	21	.543
Philadelphia Stars	31	32	.492
New York Black Yankees	15	21	.417
New York Cubans	5	22	.185

The standings are for the whole season. To determine the champion, however, an elimination tourney was held among the top four teams. Baltimore which had compiled the best record for the second half of the season) defeated Newark in a series, and Homestead eliminated Philadelphia. Baltimore then beat Homestead, 2–0, and was declared the pennant-winner.

Negro American League

First Half

	W	L	Pct.
Kansas City Monarchs	17	7	.708
Chicago American Giants	17	11	.607
Memphis Red Sox	11	11	.500
Cleveland Bears	9	9	.500
St. Louis Stars	10	12	.455

The Indianapolis ABCs were entered but dropped out after a few games.

Second Half

No final standings were published. The Toledo Crawfords replaced the Indianapolis ABCs for the second half.

The Kansas City Monarchs were declared pennant-winners after defeating the St. Louis Stars, 3 games to 2, in a post-season series.

No World Series was played.

1940

Negro National League

	W	L	Pct.
Homestead Grays	28	13	.683
Baltimore Elite Giants	25	14	.641
Newark Eagles	25	17	.595
New York Cubans	12	19	.387
Philadelphia Stars	16	31	.340
New York Black Yankees	10	22	.313

Negro American League

First Half

	W	L	Pct.
Kansas City Monarchs	12	7	.632
Cleveland Bears	10	10	.500
Memphis Red Sox	12	12	.500
Birmingham Black Barons	9	9	.500
Chicago American Giants	9	15	.429
Indianapolis Crawfords	3	5	.375

Second Half

No final standings were published. The Kansas City Monarchs were declared pennant-winners.

No World Series was played.

1941

Negro National League

First Half

	W	L	Pct.
Homestead Grays	17	9	.654
Newark Eagles	11	6	.647
Baltimore Elite Giants	13	10	.565
New York Cubans	7	10	.412
Philadelphia Stars	10	18	.357
New York Black Yankees	7	13	.350

Second Half

	W	L	Pct.
New York Cubans	4	2	.667
Newark Eagles	8	5	.615
Baltimore Elite Giants	9	8	.529
Homestead Grays	8	8	.500
New York Black Yankees	5	5	.500
Philadelphia Stars	2	8	.200

The Homestead Grays defeated the New York Cubans, 3 games to 1, in a playoff for the pennant.

Negro American League

No final standings were published for either half of the split season. Clubs were Birmingham Black Barons, Chicago American Giants, Jacksonville Red Caps, Kansas City Monarchs, Memphis Red Sox, and New Orleans–St. Louis Stars.

In later years, the Monarchs were referred to as 1941 champions.

No World Series was played.

1942

Negro National League

	W	L	Pct.
Homestead Grays	21	11	.656
Baltimore Elite Giants	21	12	.636
Newark Eagles	18	16	.529
Philadelphia Stars	16	18	.471
New York Cubans	8	14	.364
New York Black Yankees	7	20	.259

Negro American League

No final standings were published for either half of the split season. The Kansas City Monarchs were declared winners of both halves. Other clubs were the Birmingham Black Barons, Chicago American Giants, Cincinnati Buckeyes, and Jacksonville Red Caps. The Red Caps dropped out in early July.

World Series

1st game at Griffith Stadium, Washington:

	R	H	E
Kansas City Monarchs	8	14	0
Homestead Grays	0	2	4

Winning pitcher, Satchel Paige; loser, Roy Welmaker.

2nd game at Forbes Field, Pittsburgh:

	R	H	E
Kansas City Monarchs	8	11	1
Homestead Grays	4	11	2

Winning pitcher, Hilton Smith; loser, Roy Partlow.

3rd game at Yankee Stadium, New York:

	R	H	E
Kansas City Monarchs	9	16	3
Homestead Grays	3	7	4

Winning pitcher, Satchel Paige; loser, Raymond Brown.

4th game at Kansas City:

	R	H	E
Homestead Grays	4	8	0
Kansas City Monarchs	1	5	2

Winning pitcher, Leon Day; loser, Satchel Paige.

The Monarchs protested this game on grounds that the Grays had used three players from the Newark Eagles, including Leon Day, the winning pitcher, plus one from the Philadelphia Stars. The Grays claimed the Monarchs had given permission to use them, but the Kansas City protest was upheld and the game was not counted.

5th game at Shibe Park, Philadelphia:

	R	H	E
Kansas City Monarchs	9	—	—
Homestead Grays	5	—	—

Winning pitcher Satchel Paige; loser, John Wright.

Kansas City won the Series in four straight games.

1943

Negro National League

First Half

	W	L	Pct.
Homestead Grays	17	4	.810
New York Cubans	13	6	.684
*Harrisburg–St. Louis Stars	5	4	.556
Newark Eagles	9	10	.474
Philadelphia Stars	11	16	.407
Baltimore Elite Giants	9	15	.375
New York Black Yankees	2	11	.154

* Suspended when they withdrew to go on a barnstorming tour with a team headed by Dizzy Dean.

Second Half

	W	L	Pct.
Homestead Grays	9	3	.750
Newark Eagles	9	4	.692
New York Cubans	4	3	.571
Baltimore Elite Giants	5	6	.455
Philadelphia Stars	7	9	.438
New York Black Yankees	0	10	.000

Negro American League

First Half

No final standings were published. The Birmingham Black Barons were declared winners.

Second Half

	W	L	Pct.
Chicago American Giants	13	5	.722
Birmingham Black Barons	5	3	.625
Cleveland Buckeyes	8	5	.615
Kansas City Monarchs	6	7	.462
Cincinnati Clowns	3	7	.300
Memphis Red Sox	4	11	.267

The Birmingham Black Barons defeated the Chicago American Giants, 3 games to 2, in a playoff for the pennant.

World Series

1st game at Griffith Stadium, Washington:

	R	H	E
Birmingham Black Barons	4	2	0
Homestead Grays	2	5	3

Winning pitcher, Alfred Saylor; loser, John Wright.

2nd game at Griffith Stadium, Washington:

	R	H	E
Birmingham Black Barons	3	5	4
Homestead Grays	4	9	2

Winning pitcher, Raymond Brown; loser, John Markham.

3rd game at Comiskey Park, Chicago:

	R	H	E
Homestead Grays	9	10	0
Birmingham Black Barons	0	5	3

Winning pitcher, John Wright; loser, Gready McKinnis.

4th game at Columbus:

	R	H	E
Homestead Grays	10	10	1
Birmingham Black Barons	11	16	1

Winning pitcher, Alfred Saylor; loser, Roy Partlow.

5th game at Indianapolis:

	R	H	E
Homestead Grays	8	8	1
Birmingham Black Barons	0	8	4

Winning pitcher, John Wright; loser, Gready McKinnis.

6th game at Birmingham:

	R	H	E
Homestead Grays	0	8	1
Birmingham Black Barons	1	10	0

Winning pitcher, John Markham; loser, Roy Partlow.

7th game at Montgomery:

	R	H	E
Homestead Grays	8	12	3
Birmingham Black Barons	4	8	2

Winning pitcher, Raymond Brown; loser, Alfred Saylor.

Homestead won the Series, 4 games to 3.

1944

Negro National League

First Half

	W	L	Pct.
Homestead Grays	15	8	.652
Newark Eagles	13	9	.591
New York Cubans	12	10	.545
Baltimore Elite Giants	12	11	.522
Philadelphia Stars	7	11	.389
New York Black Yankees	2	13	.133

Second Half

	W	L	Pct.
Homestead Grays	12	4	.750
Philadelphia Stars	12	7	.632
Baltimore Elite Giants	12	9	.571
New York Cubans	4	4	.500
Newark Eagles	6	13	.316
New York Black Yankees	2	11	.154

Negro American League

First Half

	W	L	Pct.
Birmingham Black Barons	24	9	.727
Indianapolis–Cincinnati Clowns	18	13	.581
Cleveland Buckeyes	20	20	.500
Memphis Red Sox	20	23	.465
Kansas City Monarchs	12	19	.387
Chicago American Giants	10	20	.333

Second Half

	W	L	Pct.
Birmingham Black Barons	24	13	.649
Indianapolis–Cincinnati Clowns	22	18	.550
Chicago American Giants	22	19	.537
Cleveland Buckeyes	20	21	.488
Memphis Red Sox	24	28	.462
Kansas City Monarchs	11	23	.324

World Series

1st game at Birmingham:
Homestead Grays, 8; Birmingham Black Barons, 3.

2nd game at New Orleans:
Homestead Grays, 6; Birmingham Black Barons, 1.

3rd game at Birmingham:
Homestead Grays, 9; Birmingham Black Barons, 0.

4th game at Pittsburgh:
Birmingham Black Barons, 6; Homestead Grays, 0.

5th game at Pittsburgh:
Homestead Grays, 4; Birmingham Black Barons, 2.

The Grays won the Series, 4 games to 1.

1945

Negro National League

First Half

	W	L	Pct.
Homestead Grays	18	7	.720
Philadelphia Stars	14	9	.609
Baltimore Elite Giants	13	9	.591
Newark Eagles	11	9	.550
New York Cubans	3	11	.214
New York Black Yankees	2	16	.111

Second Half

	W	L	Pct.
Homestead Grays	14	6	.700
Baltimore Elite Giants	12	8	.600
Newark Eagles	10	8	.556
Philadelphia Stars	7	10	.412
New York Black Yankees	5	10	.333
New York Cubans	3	9	.250

Negro American League

First Half

	W	L	Pct.
Cleveland Buckeyes	31	9	.775
Birmingham Black Barons	26	11	.703
Kansas City Monarchs	17	18	.486
Chicago American Giants	17	24	.415
Cincinnati Clowns	15	26	.366
Memphis Red Sox	13	31	.295

Second Half

	W	L	Pct.
Cleveland Buckeyes	22	7	.759
Chicago American Giants	22	11	.667
Kansas City Monarchs	15	12	.556
Cincinnati Clowns	15	13	.536
Birmingham Black Barons	13	19	.406
Memphis Red Sox	4	30	.118

World Series

1st game at Cleveland:

	R	H	E
Homestead Grays	1	6	1
Cleveland Buckeyes	2	6	0

Winning pitcher, Willie Jefferson; loser, Roy Welmaker.

2nd game at Pittsburgh:

	R	H	E
Cleveland Buckeyes	4	8	0
Homestead Grays	2	7	1

Winning pitcher, Gene Bremmer; loser, John Wright.

3rd game at Washington:

	R	H	E
Cleveland Buckeyes	4	7	0
Homestead Grays	0	4	0

Winning pitcher, George Jefferson; loser, Roy Welmaker.

4th game at Philadelphia:

	R	H	E
Cleveland Buckeyes	5	10	0
Homestead Grays	0	4	2

Winning pitcher, Frank Carswell; loser, Raymond Brown.

Cleveland won the Series in four straight games.

1946

Negro National League

First Half

	W	L	Pct.
Newark Eagles	25	9	.735
Philadelphia Stars	17	12	.586
Homestead Grays	18	15	.545
New York Cubans	13	13	.500
Baltimore Elite Giants	14	17	.451
New York Black Yankees	3	24	.111

Second Half

	W	L	Pct.
Newark Eagles	22	7	.759
New York Cubans	15	8	.652
Baltimore Elite Giants	14	14	.500
Homestead Grays	9	13	.409
Philadelphia Stars	10	17	.370
New York Black Yankees	5	16	.238

Negro American League

First Half

	W	L	Pct.
Kansas City Monarchs	27	8	.771
Birmingham Black Barons	22	15	.595
Indianapolis Clowns	15	19	.441
Cleveland Buckeyes	14	17	.452
Memphis Red Sox	16	21	.432
Chicago American Giants	14	28	.333

Second Half

No final standings were published. The Kansas City Monarchs were declared winners.

World Series

1st game at Polo Grounds, New York:
  Kansas City Monarchs, 2; Newark Eagles, 1.

2nd game at Newark:
  Newark Eagles, 7; Kansas City Monarchs, 4.

3rd game at Kansas City:
Kansas City Monarchs, 15; Newark Eagles, 5.

4th game at Kansas City:
Newark Eagles, 8; Kansas City Monarchs, 1.

5th game at Comiskey Park, Chicago:
Kansas City Monarchs, 5; Newark Eagles, 1.

6th game at Newark:
Newark Eagles, 9; Kansas City Monarchs, 7.

7th game at Newark:
Newark Eagles, 3; Kansas City Monarchs, 2.

Newark won the Series, 4 games to 3.

1947

Negro National League

First Half

	W	L	Pct.
Newark Eagles	27	15	.643
New York Cubans	20	12	.625
Baltimore Elite Giants	23	20	.535
Homestead Grays	19	20	.487
Philadelphia Stars	13	16	.448
New York Black Yankees	6	25	.193

Second Half

No final standings were published. There was no playoff and the New York Cubans were awarded the pennant because they were said to have the best record for the full season.

Negro American League

No final standings were published for either the first or second half. The Cleveland Buckeyes were declared pennant-winners. Other clubs were the Birmingham Black Barons, Chicago American Giants, Indianapolis Clowns, Kansas City Monarchs, and Memphis Red Sox.

World Series

1st game at New York:
Cleveland Buckeyes, 10; New York Cubans, 7.

2nd game at Cleveland:
New York Cubans, 6; Cleveland Buckeyes, 0.

3rd game at Philadelphia:
New York Cubans, 9; Cleveland Buckeyes, 4.

4th game at Chicago:
New York Cubans, 9; Cleveland Buckeyes, 2.

5th game at Cleveland:
New York Cubans, 6; Cleveland Buckeyes, 5.

New York won the Series, 4 games to 1.

1948

Negro National League

No final standings were published for either half of the split season. The Baltimore Elite Giants won the first-half championship and the Homestead Grays the second-half. The Grays won 3 straight in a playoff for the title. Other clubs were the Newark Eagles, New York Black Yankees, New York Cubans, and Philadelphia Stars.

Negro American League

First Half

No final standings were published. The Birmingham Black Barons were declared winners.

Second Half

	W	L	Pct.
Kansas City Monarchs	19	7	.731
Birmingham Black Barons	17	7	.708
Memphis Red Sox	20	15	.571
Indianapolis Clowns	7	13	.350
Cleveland Buckeyes	10	21	.323
Chicago American Giants	7	17	.292

The Birmingham Black Barons defeated the Kansas City Monarchs, 4 games to 3, in a playoff for the pennant.

World Series

1st game:
Homestead Grays, 3; Birmingham Black Barons, 2.

2nd game:
Homestead Grays won.

3rd game:
Birmingham Black Barons, 4; Homestead Grays, 3.

4th game:
Homestead Grays, 14; Birmingham Black Barons, 1.

5th game:
Homestead Grays, 10; Birmingham Black Barons, 6.

Homestead won the Series, 4 games to 1.

1949

Negro American League

Eastern Division

First Half

	W	L	Pct.
Baltimore Elite Giants	24	12	.667
New York Cubans	14	10	.583
Philadelphia Stars	13	20	.394
Indianapolis Clowns	14	23	.378
Louisville Buckeyes	8	29	.216

Second Half

No final standings were published. The Baltimore Elite Giants were declared winners.

Western Division

No final standings were published for either half of the split season. In the first half, the order of finish was: Kansas City Monarchs, Chicago American Giants, Birmingham Black Barons, Houston Eagles, and Memphis Red Sox. For the second half, the Chicago American Giants, with a record of 23–15, were declared winners.

Kansas City, first-half champion, declined to meet the American Giants in a divisional-championship series because several of the Monarchs' best players had gone into organized ball during the season. The American Giants were therefore named Western Division champions.

League Championship

The Baltimore Elite Giants defeated the Chicago American Giants in four straight games for the league title. The scores were 9–1, 5–4, 8–4, and 4–2.

1950

Negro American League

Eastern Division

First Half

	W	L	Pct.
Indianapolis Clowns	27	16	.628
Baltimore Elite Giants	10	9	.526
New York Cubans	12	13	.480
Philadelphia Stars	9	19	.321
*Cleveland Buckeyes	3	33	.083

* Disbanded at end of first half.

Second Half

	W	L	Pct.
New York Cubans	6	2	.750
Baltimore Elite Giants	14	11	.560
Indianapolis Clowns	18	21	.462
Philadelphia Stars	5	7	.417

Although finishing third, the Indianapolis Clowns were awarded the second-half championship because of a league ruling that the champion must play at least 30 games in a half.

Western Division

First Half

	W	L	Pct.
Kansas City Monarchs	30	11	.732
Birmingham Black Barons	38	14	.731
Houston Eagles	17	20	.459
Chicago American Giants	13	16	.448
Memphis Red Sox	11	19	.367

Second Half

	W	L	Pct.
Kansas City Monarchs	21	9	.700
Memphis Red Sox	18	8	.692
Birmingham Black Barons	13	10	.565
Houston Eagles	5	17	.227
Chicago American Giants	1	14	.067

No playoff was held between the divisional champions for the league title.

APPENDIX B

EAST-WEST ALL-STAR GAMES

1933–1950

1933

East

	AB	R	H	E
Cool Papa Bell (Pittsburgh Crawfords), cf	5	1	0	0
Rap Dixon (Philadelphia Stars), rf	4	2	1	0
Oscar Charleston (Pittsburgh Crawfords), 1b	3	2	0	0
Biz Mackey (Philadelphia Stars), c	3	0	1	0
Josh Gibson (Pittsburgh Crawfords), c	2	0	1	1
Jud Wison (Philadelphia Stars), 3b	3	1	2	0
Judy Johnson (Pittsburgh Crawfords), 3b	1	0	1	0
Dick Lundy (Philadelphia Stars), ss	3	0	0	1
Vic Harris (Homestead Grays), lf	2	0	0	1
Fats Jenkins (N.Y. Black Yankees), lf	2	0	0	0
John H. Russell (Pittsburgh Crawfords), 2b	3	0	0	0
Sam Streeter (Pittsburgh Crawfords), p	3	0	0	0
Bertrum Hunter (Pittsburgh Crawfords), p	0	0	0	0
George Britt (Homestead Grays), p	1	1	1	0
	35	7	7	3

West

	AB	R	H	E
Turkey Stearns (Chicago American Giants), cf	5	1	2	0
Willie Wells (Chicago American Giants), ss	4	2	2	0
W. Davis (Chicago American Giants), lf	3	2	2	0
Alex Radcliffe (Chicago American Giants), 3b	4	1	2	0

Mule Suttles (Chicago American Giants), 1b	4	2	2	0
Leroy Morney (Cleveland Giants), 2b	4	0	1	3
Sam Bankhead (Nashville Elite Giants), rf	4	2	1	0
Larry Brown (Chicago American Giants), c	4	0	2	0
Willie Foster (Chicago American Giants), p	4	1	1	0
	36	11	15	3

EAST 000 320 002—7
WEST 001 303 31x—11

2B—Stearns, Wells, Davis (2), Radcliffe. 3B—Brown. HR—Suttles. SB—Dixon, Charleston, Bankhead. SH—Dixon, Gibson, Russell. DP—Wells, Morney, and Suttles; Bankhead and Radcliffe. SO—by Foster, 4; Streeter, 4; Britt, 1. BB—off Foster, 3. Hits—off Streeter, 7 in 5⅓ innings; Hunter, 4 in ⅔; Britt, 4 in 2. HP*—by Foster, 2.
   Losing pitcher—Streeter.
   Attendance—20,000.

   * Hit by pitcher.

1934

East

	AB	R	H	E
Cool Papa Bell (Pittsburgh Crawfords), cf	3	1	0	0
Jimmie Crutchfield (Pittsburgh Crawfords), rf	3	0	0	0
W. G. Perkins (Pittsburgh Crawfords), c	1	0	0	0
Oscar Charleston (Pittsburgh Crawfords), 1b	4	0	0	1
Jud Wilson (Philadelphia Stars), 3b	3	0	1	0
Josh Gibson (Pittsburgh Crawfords), c-lf	4	0	2	0
Vic Harris (Pittsburgh Crawfords), lf	2	0	1	0
Dick Lundy (Newark Dodgers), ss	4	0	0	0
Chester Williams (Pittsburgh Crawfords), 2b	4	0	3	0
Slim Jones (Philadelphia Stars), p	1	0	0	0
Harry Kincannon (Pittsburgh Crawfords), p	1	0	1	0
Satchel Paige (Pittsburgh Crawfords), p	2	0	0	0
	32	1	8	1

West

	AB	R	H	E
Willie Wells (Chicago American Giants), ss	3	0	1	0
Alex Radcliffe (Chicago American Giants), 3b	4	0	0	0
Turkey Stearns (Chicago American Giants), cf	4	0	0	0
Mule Suttles (Chicago American Giants), 1b	4	0	3	1
Red Parnell (Nashville Elite Giants), lf	3	0	0	0
Sam Bankhead (Nashville Elite Giants), rf	3	0	1	0
Larry Brown (Chicago American Giants), c	3	0	1	0
Sammy T. Hughes (Nashville Elite Giants), 2b	2	0	0	0

J. Patterson (Cleveland Red Sox), 2b	1	0	0	0
Theodore Trent (Chicago American Giants), p	1	0	0	0
Chet Brewer (Kansas City Monarchs), p	1	0	0	0
Willie Foster (Chicago American Giants), p	1	0	1	0
	30	0	7	1

```
EAST   000   000   010—1
WEST   000   000   000—0
```

RBI—Wilson. 2B—Gibson, Williams, Wells. 3B—Suttles. SB—Bell. LOB—East, 8; West, 5. SO—by Jones, 4; Trent, 3; Brewer, 1; Paige, 5; Foster, 2. BB—off Brewer, 1; Jones, 1; Foster, 1.

Winning pitcher—Paige; loser—Foster.

Attendance—30,000.

1935

East

	AB	R	H	E
Paul Stevens (Philadelphia Stars), ss	6	1	2	1
George Giles (Brooklyn Eagles), 1b	5	1	0	0
Martin Dihigo (N.Y. Cubans), cf-p	5	1	1	2
Jud Wilson (Philadelphia Stars), 3b	5	1	2	0
Alejandro Oms (N.Y. Cubans), rf	4	1	2	0
Biz Mackey (Philadelphia Stars), c	5	1	0	0
Fats Jenkins (Brooklyn Eagles), lf	5	1	0	0
Dick Seay (Philadelphia Stars), 2b	3	0	1	2
Slim Jones (Philadelphia Stars), p	2	1	2	0
Leon Day (Brooklyn Eagles), p	1	0	0	0
*Ed Stone (Brooklyn Eagles)	1	0	0	0
Ray Dandridge (Newark Dodgers), 2b	1	0	1	U
Luis Tiant (N.Y. Cubans), p	2	0	0	0
Paul Arnold (Newark Dodgers), cf	0	0	0	0
	45	8	11	5

* Batted for Seay in 8th.

West

	AB	R	H	E
Cool Papa Bell (Pittsburgh Crawfords), cf	4	2	1	1
Sammy T. Hughes (Columbus Elite Giants), 2b	4	0	1	0
Willie Wells (Chicago American Giants), ss	3	0	0	1
Josh Gibson (Pittsburgh Crawfords), c	5	3	4	1
Mule Suttles (Chicago American Giants), lf	2	3	1	0
Oscar Charleston (Pittsburgh Crawfords), 1b	3	1	0	1
Alex Radcliffe (Chicago American Giants), 3b	5	1	2	0
Jimmie Crutchfield (Pittsburgh Crawfords), rf	2	0	0	0

Raymond Brown (Homestead Grays), p	1	0	0	0
Leroy Matlock (Pittsburgh Crawfords), p	2	0	0	0
*Turkey Stearns (Chicago American Giants)	3	0	1	0
†Buck Leonard (Homestead Grays), 1b	3	0	0	0
Theodore Trent (Chicago American Giants), p	0	0	0	0
Chester Williams (Pittsburgh Crawfords), ss	2	1	0	1
‡Bill Wright (Columbus Elite Giants)	1	0	0	0
Bob Griffith (Columbus Elite Giants), p	0	0	0	0
§Felton Snow (Columbus Elite Giants)	1	0	1	0
Willie Cornelius (Chicago American Giants), p	0	0	0	0
	41	11	11	5

* Batted for Matlock in 6th.
† Batted for Crutchfield in 6th.
‡ Batted for Trent in 8th.
§ Batted for Griffith in 10th.

EAST   200   110   000   40—8
WEST   000   003   100   43—11

There were two outs in the eleventh inning when Mule Suttles hit a home run with two men on base.

2B—Gibson (2). HR—Jones, Suttles. SB—Dihigo, Giles. SH—Hughes (2), Oms. DP—Wilson unassisted. SO—by Jones, 1; Brown, 1; Day, 3; Matlock, 1; Griffith, 3; Dihigo, 1. BB—off Jones, 2; Day, 2; Trent, 2; Griffith, 2; Tiant, 2; Dihigo, 1. PB—Gibson.

Winning pitcher—Cornelius; losing pitcher, Dihigo.
Attendance—25,000.

1936

East

	AB	R	H	E
Cool Papa Bell (Pittsburgh Crawfords), cf	3	1	3	0
Bill Wright (Washington Elite Giants), cf	2	0	0	0
Sammy T. Hughes (Washington Elite Giants), 2b	5	2	1	1
Sam Bankhead (Pittsburgh Crawfords), lf	4	1	2	0
Biz Mackey (Washington Elite Giants), c	2	0	2	0
Josh Gibson (Pittsburgh Crawfords), c	3	2	2	0
Jimmie Crutchfield (Pittsburgh Crawfords), rf	2	0	0	0
Zolley Wright (Washington Elite Giants), rf	1	2	1	0
Chester Williams (Pittsburgh Crawfords), ss	4	0	0	1
Jim West (Washington Elite Giants), 1b	3	1	1	1
John Washington (Pittsburgh Crawfords), 1b	1	0	0	1
Judy Johnson (Pittsburgh Crawfords), 3b	1	0	0	1
Felton Snow (Washington Elite Giants), 3b	2	1	1	0
Leroy Matlock (Pittsburgh Crawfords), p	1	0	0	0
Bill Byrd (Washington Elite Giants), p	3	0	0	0
Satchel Paige (Pittsburgh Crawfords), p	1	0	0	0
	38	10	13	5

West

	AB	R	H	E
Eddie Dwight (Kansas City Monarchs), cf	2	0	0	0
Henry Milton (Kansas City Monarchs), cf	2	0	0	0
Newt Allen (Kansas City Monarchs), 2b, ss	5	0	0	0
Wilson Redus (Chicago American Giants), rf	2	0	0	0
Odem Dials (Chicago American Giants), rf	2	0	0	1
Alex Radcliffe (Chicago American Giants), 3b	4	1	3	0
Bullet Rogan (Kansas City Monarchs), lf	1	0	0	0
Herman Dunlap (Chicago American Giants), lf	2	1	1	0
Harry Else (Kansas City Monarchs), c	0	0	0	0
Subby Byas (Chicago American Giants), c	3	0	1	0
Willard Brown (Kansas City Monarchs), ss	1	0	0	1
Pat Patterson (Kansas City Monarchs), 2b	2	0	2	0
Popsickle Harris (Kansas City Monarchs), 1b	4	0	1	0
Willie Cornelius (Chicago American Giants), p	1	0	0	0
Floyd Kranson (Kansas City Monarchs), p	0	0	0	0
Andy Cooper (Kansas City Monarchs), p	0	0	0	0
Theodore Trent (Chicago American Giants), p	0	0	0	0
	31	2	8	2

EAST   200   130   220—10
WEST   000   001   010—2

RBI—Mackey (2), Bell, Z. Wright (2), Johnson, Gibson, Williams, Patterson. 2B—Bell, Hughes, Bankhead, Patterson. SB—Bell, Gibson, Snow. SO—by Cornelius, 2; Kranson, 1; Byrd, 4; Trent, 1. BB—off Cornelius, 1; Matlock, 1; Kranson, 1; Byrd, 1; Trent, 2. DP—Cornelius, Allen, and Harris. Hits—off Matlock, 2 in 3 innings; Cornelius, 5 in 3; Kranson, 4 in 2; Cooper, 1 in 1; Byrd, 4 in 3; Trent, 3 in 3; Paige, 2 in 3. PB—Gibson. HP—by Kranson (West).

Winning pitcher—Matlock; loser—Cornelius.
Attendance—30,000.

1937

East

	AB	R	H	E
Jerry Benjamin (Homestead Grays), rf	5	0	1	0
Willie Wells (Newark Eagles), ss	5	2	1	0
B. Wright (Washington Elite Giants), cf	5	1	3	0

	AB	R	H	E
Buck Leonard (Homestead Grays), 1b	4	1	2	1
Mule Suttles (Newark Eagles), lf	3	0	1	0
Chester Williams (Pittsburgh Crawfords), 2b	3	0	0	0
Jake Dunn (Philadelphia Stars), 2b	1	0	0	0
Ray Dandridge (Newark Eagles), 3b	5	2	1	0
Pepper Bassett (Pittsburgh Crawfords), c	3	0	0	0
Barney Morris (Pittsburgh Crawfords), p	2	0	0	0
Barney Brown (N.Y. Black Yankees), p	1	0	1	0
Leon Day (Newark Eagles), p	1	1	1	0
	38	7	11	1

West

	AB	R	H	E
Newt Allen (Kansas City Monarchs), 2b-ss	4	0	0	0
Lloyd Davenport (Cincinnati Tigers), rf	4	1	1	0
Wilson Redus (Chicago American Giants), rf	0	0	0	0
Ted Strong (Indianapolis Athletics), 1b	4	1	2	2
Turkey Stearns (Detroit Stars), cf	4	0	0	0
Willard Brown (Kansas City Monarchs), lf	2	0	0	0
Alex Radcliffe (Chicago American Giants), 3b	3	0	1	0
Howard Easterling (Cincinnati Tigers), ss	2	0	0	0
Rainey Bibbs (Cincinnati Tigers), 2b	1	0	1	0
Ted Radcliffe (Cincinnati Tigers), c	3	0	0	1
Theodore Trent (Chicago American Giants), p	0	0	0	0
Hilton Smith (Kansas City Monarchs), p	0	0	0	1
Porter Moss (Cincinnati Tigers), p	2	0	0	0
*Henry Milton (Kansas City Monarchs)	1	0	0	0
†Subby Byas (Chicago American Giants)	1	0	0	0
‡Eldridge Mayweather (Kansas City Monarchs)	1	0	0	0
	32	2	5	4

* Batted for W. Brown in 9th.
† Batted for T. Radcliffe in 9th.
‡ Batted for Trent in 3rd.

EAST	010	200	130—7	
WEST	000	101	000—2	

2B—Allen, Wright, Bibbs, Day. HR—Leonard, Strong. SB—Dandridge, Wright, Suttles. DP—Moss, T. Radcliffe, and Strong; Wells, Dunn, and Leonard; Allen and Strong.
Winning pitcher—Morris; loser—Smith.
Attendance—20,000.

1938

East

	AB	R	H	E
Vic Harris (Homestead Grays), lf	5	1	1	0
Sammy T. Hughes (Baltimore Elite Giants), 2b	5	1	2	0
Willie Wells (Newark Eagles), ss	4	1	2	0
Buck Leonard (Homestead Grays), 1b	4	0	1	0
Rev Cannady (N.Y. Black Yankees), 3b	3	1	1	0
Sam Bankhead (Pittsburgh Crawfords), cf	4	0	2	0
Bill Wright (Baltimore Elite Giants), rf	4	0	0	0
Biz Mackey (Baltimore Elite Giants), c	4	0	0	0
Edsell Walker (Homestead Grays), p	0	0	0	0
Barney Brown (N.Y. Black Yankees), p	2	0	1	0
Johnny Taylor (Pittsburgh Crawfords), p	0	0	0	0
*—— Fisher (————)	1	0	1	0
	36	4	11	0

* Batted for Taylor in 9th.

West

	AB	R	H	E
Henry Milton (Kansas City Monarchs), rf	3	2	1	0
Newt Allen (Kansas City Monarchs), 2b	4	0	0	1
Alex Radcliffe (Chicago American Giants), 3b	4	1	2	0
Ted Strong (Indianapolis ABCs), 1b	3	1	0	0
Quincy Troupe (Indianapolis ABCs), lf	4	0	0	0
Neil Robinson (Memphis Red Sox), cf	4	1	3	0
Frank Duncan (Chicago American Giants), c	1	0	0	0
Larry Brown (Memphis Red Sox), c	0	0	0	0
Byron Johnson (Kansas City Monarchs), ss	4	0	1	0
Willie Cornelius (Chicago American Giants), p	0	0	0	0
Hilton Smith (Kansas City Monarchs), p	2	0	1	0
Ted Radcliffe (Memphis Red Sox), p	2	0	1	0
	31	5	9	1

```
EAST    300  010  000—4
WEST    104  000  00x—5
```

RBI—Wells, Cannady, Bankhead, A. Radcliffe (2), Robinson (3), Leonard. 2B—Harris, Cannady, Hughes. 3B—Wells. HR—Robinson. SH —Cannady. DP—Duncan and Radcliffe. LOB—East, 7; West, 8. Hits— off Cornelius, 5 in 1 inning; Walker, 4 in 3; Smith, 3 in 4; Brown, 2 in 3; Radcliffe, 3 in 4; Taylor, 3 in 2. SO—by Walker, 3; Smith, 3; Brown, 1; Taylor, 2. BB—off Smith, 1; Walker, 3; Taylor, 1. HP—by Smith. PB— Mackey.

Winning pitcher—Smith; loser—Walker.
Attendance—30,000.

1939

East

	AB	R	H	E
Bill Wright (Baltimore Elite Giants), cf	4	0	2	0
Willie Wells (Newark Eagles), ss	3	0	1	0
Josh Gibson (Homestead Grays), c	3	0	0	0
Mule Suttles (Newark Eagles), rf	4	0	0	0
Buck Leonard (Homestead Grays), 1b	3	1	0	0
Pat Patterson (Philadelphia Stars), 3b	4	1	1	0
Sammy T. Hughes (Baltimore Elite Giants), 2b	3	0	1	0
Roy Parnell (Philadelphia Stars), lf	3	0	0	0
Bill Byrd (Baltimore Elite Giants), p	1	0	0	0
Leon Day (Newark Eagles), p	1	0	0	0
Roy Partlow (Homestead Grays), p	1	0	0	0
Bill Holland (N.Y. Black Yankees), p	0	0	0	0
	30	2	5	0

West

	AB	R	H	E
Henry Milton (Kansas City Monarchs), rf	3	0	1	0
Parnell Woods (Cleveland Bears), 3b	0	0	0	0
Dan Wilson (St. Louis Stars), lf	3	1	1	0
Alex Radcliffe (Chicago American Giants), 3b-ss	5	1	1	0
Neil Robinson (Memphis Red Sox), cf	4	1	3	0
Ted Strong (Kansas City Monarchs), ss-1b	2	0	0	1
Jelly Taylor (Memphis Red Sox), 1b	1	0	0	0
Billy Horn (Chicago American Giants), 2b	2	0	1	0
Leroy Morney (Toledo Crawfords), 2b-ss	1	0	0	0
Jim Williams (Toledo Crawfords), rf	2	0	0	0
Pepper Bassett (Chicago American Giants), c	1	0	0	0
Larry Brown (Memphis Red Sox), c	2	0	0	0
Theolic Smith (St. Louis Stars), p	0	0	0	0
Hilton Smith (Kansas City Monarchs), p	1	0	0	0
Ted Radcliffe (Memphis Red Sox), p	1	1	1	0
	28	4	8	1

```
EAST    020    000    000—2
WEST    000    000    13x—4
```

RBI—Hughes (2), Wilson (2), Robinson, Horn. 2B—Wright, Robinson. HR—Wilson, Robinson. SB—Patterson. DP—T. Smith, Bassett, and Taylor. SO—by T. Smith, 1; T. Radcliffe, 1; H. Smith, 3; Byrd, 1; Day, 1. BB—off T. Smith, 1; T. Radcliffe, 2; Byrd, 1; Day, 2; Holland, 1. Hits—off T. Smith, 4 in 3 innings; H. Smith, 0 in 3; T. Radcliffe, 1 in 3; Byrd, 2 in 3; Day, 0 in 3; Partlow, 4 in 1⅓; Holland, 2 in ⅔.

Winning pitcher—T. Radcliffe; loser—Partlow.

Attendance—40,000.

1940

East

	AB	R	H	E
Gene Benson (Philadelphia Stars), cf	6	1	2	0
Rabbit Martinez (N.Y. Cubans), ss	3	1	1	0
Bus Clarkson (Newark Eagles), ss	2	1	0	0
Ed Stone (Newark Eagles), rf	3	0	0	0
Alejandro Crespo (N.Y. Cubans), lf	2	2	1	0
Buck Leonard (Homestead Grays), 1b	4	2	2	0
Howard Easterling (Homestead Grays), 3b	5	1	2	0
Marvin Barker (N.Y. Black Yankees), cf-rf	5	1	2	0
W. G. Perkins (Baltimore Elite Giants), c	5	0	2	0
Robert Clarke (N.Y. Black Yankees), c	0	0	0	0
Dick Seay (N.Y. Black Yankees), 2b	4	1	0	0
Henry McHenry (Philadelphia Stars), p	0	0	0	0
Poppa Ruiz (N.Y. Cubans), p	2	1	0	0
Raymond Brown (Homestead Grays), p	2	0	0	0
	43	11	12	0

West

	AB	R	H	E
Henry Milton (Kansas City Monarchs), rf	4	0	1	0
Parnell Woods (Birmingham Black Barons), 3b	4	0	1	0
Eldridge Mayweather (N.O.–St. L. Stars), 1b	3	0	1	0
Neil Robinson (Memphis Red Sox), cf	2	0	0	0
Leslie Green (N.O.–St. L. Stars), cf	2	0	1	0
Donald Reeves (Chicago American Giants), lf	4	0	0	0
James Green (Kansas City Monarchs), c	2	0	0	1
Larry Brown (Memphis Red Sox), c	1	0	1	0
Leroy Morney (Chicago American Giants), ss	2	0	0	4
Curt Henderson (Indianapolis Crawfords), ss	1	0	0	0
Tommy Sampson (Birmingham Black Barons), 2b	2	0	0	0
Marshall Riddle (N.O.–St. L. Stars), 2b	1	0	0	1
Gene Bremmer (Memphis Red Sox), p	0	0	0	0
Walt Calhoun (N.O.–St. L. Stars), p	1	0	0	0
Cliff Johnson (Indianapolis Crawfords), p	0	0	0	0
Hilton Smith (Kansas City Monarchs), p	1	0	0	0
*Jelly Taylor (Memphis Red Sox)	1	0	0	0
	31	0	5	6

* Batted for Henderson in 9th.

EAST	200	114	030—11
WEST	000	000	000—0

2B—Benson. 3B—Crespo. SB—Leonard. DP—Seay, Clarkson, and Leonard; Morney, Sampson, and Mayweather. SO—by Bremmer, 2; Calhoun, 1; Johnson, 1; Smith, 3; McHenry, 1. BB—off Bremmer, 5; Johnson, 1; Smith, 4; McHenry, 1; Ruiz, 2.

Winning pitcher—McHenry; loser—Bremmer.

Attendance—25,000.

1941

East

	AB	R	H	E
Henry Kimbro (N.Y. Black Yankees), cf	3	1	1	0
Lennie Pearson (Newark Eagles), cf	2	0	0	0
Al Coimbre (N.Y. Cubans), rf	5	2	0	1
Bill Hoskins (Baltimore Elite Giants), lf	5	1	1	0
Buck Leonard (Homestead Grays), 1b	5	1	2	0
Monte Irvin (Newark Eagles), 3b	5	0	2	0
Roy Campanella (Baltimore Elite Giants), c	5	0	1	1
Horacio Martinez (N.Y. Cubans), ss	4	1	2	1
Dick Seay (N.Y. Black Yankees), 2b	4	1	0	1
Terris McDuffie (Homestead Grays), p	0	0	0	0
Dave Barnhill (N.Y. Cubans), p	2	1	2	0
Henry McHenry (Philadelphia Stars), p	0	0	0	0
Jimmy Hill (Newark Eagles), p	0	0	0	0
Bill Byrd (Baltimore Elite Giants), p	0	0	0	0
	40	8	11	4

West

	AB	R	H	E
Dan Wilson (St. Louis Stars), lf	2	0	0	1
Jimmie Crutchfield (Chicago American Giants), lf	3	0	1	0
Newt Allen (Kansas City Monarchs), ss	2	0	0	2
Billy Horn (Chicago American Giants), ss	2	0	0	0
Neil Robinson (Memphis Red Sox), cf	2	1	1	0
Buddy Armour (St. Louis Stars), cf	2	1	1	0
Ted Strong (Kansas City Monarchs), rf	4	0	2	0
Jelly Taylor (Memphis Red Sox), 1b	2	0	1	0
Lyman Bostock (Birmingham Black Barons), 1b	2	1	1	0
Parnell Woods (Jacksonville Red Caps), 3b	4	0	0	0
Tommy Sampson (Birmingham Black Barons), 2b	0	0	0	1
Bill Ford (St. Louis Stars), 2b	3	0	0	0
Pepper Bassett (Chicago American Giants), c	1	0	0	0
Larry Brown (Memphis Red Sox), c	3	0	0	1
Hilton Smith (Kansas City Monarchs), p	1	0	0	0
Ted Radcliffe (Memphis Red Sox), p	0	0	0	0
Leo Henry (Jacksonville Red Caps), p	0	0	0	0

Dan Bankhead (Memphis Red Sox), p	0	0	0	0
Satchel Paige (Kansas City Monarchs), p	1	0	0	0
*Verdel Mathis (Memphis Red Sox)	0	0	0	0
†Howard Cleveland (Jacksonville Red Caps)	1	0	1	0
‡Henry Hudson (Chicago American Giants)	1	0	0	0
§George Mitchell (St. Louis Stars)	0	0	0	0
	36	3	8	5

* Ran for Bassett in 2nd.
† Batted for Henry in 5th.
‡ Batted for Bankhead in 7th.
§ Batted for Horn in 9th.

EAST   200   600   000—8
WEST   100   000   020—3

RBI—Kimbro, Coimbre, Hoskins, Leonard (3), Barnhill, Strong, Bostock, Woods. 2B—Strong, Irvin. 3B—Strong. HR—Leonard. SH—Leonard, Martinez, Barnhill. SB—Kimbro (2), Irvin, Martinez, Taylor. LOB—East, 10; West, 7. DP—Campanella and Martinez. SO—by Barnhill, 2; Hill 1; Smith, 1; Radcliffe, 1; Henry, 1; Paige, 2. BB—off Radcliffe, 1; Bankhead, 1; Paige, 1. Hits—off McDuffie, 3 in 2 innings; Barnhill, 2 in 3; McHenry, 2 in 2; Hill, 0 in 1; Byrd, 1 in 1; Smith, 2 in 3; Radcliffe, 4 in ⅔; Henry, 3 in 1⅓; Bankhead, 1 in 2; Paige, 1 in 2. PB—Bassett. Winning pitcher—McDuffie; loser—Smith. Attendance—50,256.

1942

East

	AB	R	H	E
Dan Wilson (N.Y. Black Yankees), lf	4	3	2	0
Sam Bankhead (Homestead Grays), 2b-cf	5	1	2	0
Willie Wells (Newark Eagles), ss	5	0	1	0
Josh Gibson (Homestead Grays), c	3	0	2	0
Bill Wright (Baltimore Elite Giants), rf	5	0	2	0
Jim West (Philadelphia Stars), 1b	4	0	0	0
Pat Patterson (Philadelphia Stars), 3b	3	0	0	2
Tetelo Vargas (N.Y. Cubans), cf	3	0	1	0
*Herberto Blanco (N.Y. Cubans), 2b	0	0	0	0
Jonas Gaines (Baltimore Elite Giants), p	1	0	0	0
†Vic Harris (Homestead Grays)	1	0	0	0
‡Lennie Pearson (Newark Eagles)	1	1	1	0

* Ran for Vargas in 8th.
† Batted for Gaines in 4th.
‡ Batted for Barnhill in 7th.

Dave Barnhill (N.Y. Cubans), p	0	0	0	0
Barney Brown (Philadelphia Stars), p	0	0	0	0
Leon Day (Newark Eagles), p	1	0	0	0
	36	5	11	2

West

	AB	R	H	E
Cool Papa Bell (Chicago American Giants), cf	4	0	1	0
Parnell Woods (Cincinnati Buckeyes), 3b	3	1	1	0
Marlin Carter (Memphis Red Sox), 3b	1	0	0	0
Ted Strong (Kansas City Monarchs), rf	3	0	1	0
Willard Brown (Kansas City Monarchs), lf	4	0	1	0
James Green (Kansas City Monarchs), c	4	0	0	0
John O'Neil (Kansas City Monarchs), 1b	4	0	0	1
Tommy Sampson (Birmingham Black Barons), 2b	3	0	0	1
*Art Pennington (Chicago American Giants)	1	0	0	0
T. J. Brown (Memphis Red Sox), ss	3	0	0	0
†Lloyd Davenport (Birmingham Black Barons)	1	0	0	0
Hilton Smith (Kansas City Monarchs), p	1	0	0	0
‡Fred Bankhead (Memphis Red Sox)	0	1	0	0
Porter Moss (Memphis Red Sox), p	0	0	0	0
Eugene Bremmer (Cincinnati Buckeyes), p	0	0	0	0
Satchel Paige (Kansas City Monarchs), p	1	0	1	0
§Sam Jethroe (Cincinnati Buckeyes)	1	0	0	0
	34	2	5	2

* Batted for Sampson in 9th.
† Batted for T. Brown in 9th.
‡ Ran for Smith in 3rd.
§ Batted for Moss in 5th.

EAST   001   010   102—5
WEST   001   001   000—2

RBI—Wright (2), Bankhead (2), Gibson, Green. 2B—Wilson, Bankhead, W. Brown, Pearson. 3B—Woods. SH—Wells. SB—Patterson, Wilson (2), Wells, Vargas. LOB—East, 8; West, 6. DP—Sampson, T. Brown, and O'Neil (2). SO—by H. Smith, 2; Moss, 1; Barnhill, 4; Bremmer, 1; Paige, 2; Day, 5. BB—off Moss, 2; Barnhill, 1; Paige, 1. Hits—off Smith, 4 in 3 innings; Moss, 2 in 2; Bremmer, 0 in 1; Paige, 5 in 3; Gaines, 1 in 3; Barnhill, 2 in 3; B. Brown, 2 in ⅔; Day, 0 in 2⅓.
   Winning pitcher—Day; loser—Paige.
   Attendance—48,400.

1943

East

	AB	R	H	E
Cool Papa Bell (Homestead Grays), lf	4	0	0	0
Henry Kimbro (Baltimore Elite Giants), cf	1	0	0	0
Juan Vargas (N.Y. Cubans), cf	2	0	0	0
Buck Leonard (Homestead Grays), 1b	4	1	1	0
Josh Gibson (Homestead Grays), c	3	0	1	0
Howard Easterling (Homestead Grays), 3b	4	0	1	0
Lennie Pearson (Newark Eagles), rf	3	0	0	0
Sam Bankhead (Homestead Grays), 2b	3	0	0	0
Horacio Martinez (N.Y. Cubans), ss	2	0	1	0
Dave Barnhill (N.Y. Cubans), p	1	0	0	0
John Wright (Homestead Grays), p	0	0	0	0
Bill Harvey (Baltimore Elite Giants), p	0	0	0	0
Leon Day (Newark Eagles), p	1	0	0	0
*George Scales (Baltimore Elite Giants)	1	0	0	0
†Jerry Benjamin (Homestead Grays)	1	0	0	0
‡Vic Harris (Homestead Grays)	1	0	0	0
	31	1	4	0

* Batted for Wright in 6th.
† Batted for Martinez in 9th.
‡ Batted for Pearson in 9th.

West

	AB	R	H	E
Jesse Williams (Kansas City Monarchs), ss	3	0	2	0
Lloyd Davenport (Chicago American Giants), rf	2	0	0	0
Alex Radcliffe (Chicago American Giants), 3b	4	0	1	0
Willard Brown (Kansas City Monarchs), cf	3	1	1	0
Neil Robinson (Memphis Red Sox), lf	2	1	0	0
Lester Lockett (Birmingham Black Barons), lf	0	0	0	0
John O'Neil (Kansas City Monarchs), 1b	2	0	0	0
Tommy Sampson (Birmingham Black Barons), 2b	3	0	1	0
Ted Radcliffe (Chicago American Giants), c	3	0	0	0
Satchel Paige (Kansas City Monarchs), p	1	0	1	0
Gread McKinnis (Birmingham Black Barons), p	1	0	0	0
Theolic Smith (Cleveland Buckeyes), p	1	0	0	0
Porter Moss (Memphis Red Sox), p	0	0	0	0
*Bubber Hyde (Memphis Red Sox)	0	0	0	0
†Fred Wilson (Cincinnati Clowns)	1	0	0	0
	26	2	6	0

* Ran for Paige in 3rd.
† Batted for Robinson in 8th.

EAST   000   000   001—1
WEST   010   100   00x—2

RBI—Leonard, Sampson. 2B—Paige. HR—Leonard. SB—Brown, Williams. LOB—East, 4; West, 6. DP—Bankhead and Leonard; Pearson, Gibson, and Easterling. SO—Paige, 4; McKinnis, 1; Wright, 2; Smith, 1. BB—off Paige, 1; Smith, 1; Barnhill, 1; Day, 1.
Winning pitcher—Paige; loser—Barnhill.
Attendance—51,723.

1944

East

	AB	R	H	E
Cool Papa Bell (Homestead Grays), lf	5	0	0	0
Ray Dandridge (Newark Eagles), 3b-2b	5	0	3	0
Al Coimbre (N.Y. Cubans), rf	5	0	0	0
Buck Leonard (Homestead Grays), 1b	3	1	1	1
Josh Gibson (Homestead Grays), c	3	1	2	0
John Davis (Newark Eagles), cf	3	0	2	0
Sam Bankhead (Homestead Grays), 2b-ss	3	1	1	1
Pee Wee Butts (Baltimore Elite Giants), ss	2	0	0	0
Horacio Martinez (N.Y. Cubans), ss	0	0	0	0
Terris McDuffie (Newark Eagles), p	1	0	1	0
Carranza Howard (N.Y. Cubans), p	1	0	0	0
Barney Morris (N.Y. Cubans), p	0	0	0	0
Bill Byrd (Baltimore Elite Giants), p	1	0	0	0
*Marvin Williams (Philadelphia Stars)	1	0	0	0
†Roy Campanella (Baltimore Elite Giants), 3b	1	1	1	0
‡Henry Kimbro (Baltimore Elite Giants), rf	1	0	0	0
	35	4	11	2

* Batted for Butts in 7th.
† Batted for Martinez in 8th.
‡ Batted for Morris in 7th.

West

	AB	R	H	E
Sam Jethroe (Cleveland Buckeyes), cf	3	0	0	0
Neil Robinson (Memphis Red Sox), cf	2	0	0	0
Art Wilson (Birmingham Black Barons), ss	5	1	2	0
Lloyd Davenport (Chicago American Giants), rf	4	1	1	0
Buddy Armour (Cleveland Buckeyes), lf	4	2	2	0
Alex Radcliffe (Cincinnati Clowns), 3b	4	0	1	0
Bonnie Serrell (Kansas City Monarchs), 2b	3	1	2	0
Archie Ware (Cleveland Buckeyes), 1b	4	1	1	0
Ted Radcliffe (Birmingham Black Barons), c	4	1	2	0
Verdel Mathis (Memphis Red Sox), p	1	0	1	0

Gentry Jessup (Chicago American Giants), p	2	0	0	0
Gread McKinnis (Chicago American Giants), p	0	0	0	0
Gene Bremmer (Cleveland Buckeyes), p	0	0	0	0
	36	7	12	0

EAST   010 100 200—4
WEST   101 050 00x—7

RBI—Bankhead, A. Radcliffe (2), Serrell, Ware, T. Radcliffe (2), Campanella, Dandridge, Davis. 2B—Gibson, Dandridge, Ware. 3B—Leonard, McDuffie, A. Radcliffe. HR—T. Radcliffe. SB—Armour. LOB—East, 8; West, 7. DP—Jethroe and T. Radcliffe; Wilson, Serrell, and Ware. SO—by McDuffie, 2; Morris, 1; McKinnis, 1; Bremmer, 2. BB—off Jessup, 2; McKinnis, 1; McDuffie, 1. Hits—off Mathis, 3 in 3 innings; McDuffie, 5 in 3; Howard, 4 in 1⅔; Morris, 1 in 1⅓; Jessup, 3 in 3; McKinnis, 4 in 1; Bremmer, 1 in 1⅔; Byrd, 2 in 2. PB—T. Radcliffe.
   Winning pitcher—Mathis; loser—Howard.
   Attendance—46,247.

1945

East

	AB	R	H	E
Jerry Benjamin (Homestead Grays), cf	5	1	1	0
Frank Austin (Philadelphia Stars), ss	2	0	0	1
Horacio Martinez (N.Y. Cubans), ss	2	0	2	0
John Davis (Newark Eagles), lf	2	0	0	0
Gene Benson (Philadelphia Stars), lf	2	1	0	0
Buck Leonard (Homestead Grays), 1b	3	1	1	0
Roy Campanella (Baltimore Elite Giants), c	5	1	2	0
Willie Wells (Newark Eagles), 2b	5	0	1	0
Bill Wright (Baltimore Elite Giants), rf	1	0	0	0
Rogelio Linares (N.Y. Cubans), rf	3	1	0	0
Marvin Barker (N.Y. Black Yankees), 3b	2	0	1	0
Murray Watkins (Newark Eagles), 3b	2	0	2	0
Tom Glover (Baltimore Elite Giants), p	0	0	0	0
Bill Ricks (Philadelphia Stars), p	0	0	0	0
Martin Dihigo (N.Y. Cubans), p	1	0	0	0
Roy Welmaker (Homestead Grays), p	0	0	0	0
*Lennie Pearson (Newark Eagles)	1	0	0	0
†Bill Byrd (Baltimore Elite Giants)	1	1	0	0
	37	6	10	1

   * Batted for Dihigo in 7th.
   † Batted for Welmaker in 9th.

West

	AB	R	H	E
Jesse Williams (Kansas City Monarchs), 2b	5	0	2	0
Jackie Robinson (Kansas City Monarchs), ss	5	0	0	0
Lloyd Davenport (Cleveland Buckeyes), rf	4	1	1	0
Neil Robinson (Memphis Red Sox), cf	2	2	2	0
Alex Radcliffe (Cincinnati–Ind. Clowns), 3b	4	2	2	1
Lester Lockett (Birmingham Black Barons), lf	4	0	0	0
Archie Ware (Cleveland Buckeyes), 1b	4	1	2	0
Quincy Troupe (Cleveland Buckeyes), c	1	2	1	0
Verdel Mathis (Memphis Red Sox), p	2	1	2	0
Gentry Jessup (Chicago American Giants), p	1	0	0	0
Booker McDaniels (Kansas City Monarchs), p	1	0	0	0
Gene Bremmer (Cleveland Buckeyes), p	0	0	0	0
	33	9	12	1

```
EAST    000    000    105—6
WEST    044    100    00x—9
```

RBI—Benjamin, Martinez (3), Wells (2), Williams (4), Radcliffe, Lockett, Ware (3). 2B—Wells, Davenport, Radcliffe. 3B—Williams. SH —N. Robinson. LOB—West, 5, East, 10. SO—by Mathis, 4; Jessup, 1; McDonald, 1. BB—off Mathis, 1; Jessup, 2; McDaniels, 2; Glover, 1; Ricks, 1; Welmaker, 1.

Winning pitcher—Mathis; loser—Glover.

Attendance—31,714.

1946

(At Griffith Stadium, Washington)

West

	AB	R	H	E
Art Wilson (Birmingham Black Barons), ss	3	1	1	0
Othello Renfroe (Kansas City Monarchs), ss	1	0	0	0
Archie Ware (Cleveland Buckeyes), 1b	4	0	0	0
Sam Jethroe (Cleveland Buckeyes), cf	4	1	0	0
Piper Davis (Birmingham Black Barons), 2b	4	1	2	0
Willie Grace (Cleveland Buckeyes), rf	4	0	1	0
Bubber Hyde (Memphis Red Sox), lf	3	0	1	0
John Scott (Kansas City Monarchs), lf	2	0	1	0
Alex Radcliffe (Memphis Red Sox), 3b	3	0	0	0
Quincy Troupe (Cleveland Buckeyes), c	1	0	0	0
Buster Haywood (Cincinnati–Ind. Clowns), c	1	0	0	0
*John Brown (Cleveland Buckeyes)	1	0	0	0
Dan Bankhead (Memphis Red Sox), p	1	0	0	0

	AB	R	H	E
Vibert Clarke (Cleveland Buckeyes), p	0	0	0	0
Gentry Jessup (Chicago American Giants), p	1	0	0	0
Clyde Nelson (Chicago American Giants), 3b	1	0	0	0
John Williams (Cincinnati–Ind. Clowns), p	0	0	0	0
	34	3	6	0

* Batted for Williams in 9th.

East

	AB	R	H	E
Henry Kimbro (Baltimore Elite Giants), cf	2	1	1	0
Larry Doby (Newark Eagles), 2b	4	2	2	0
Howard Easterling (Homestead Grays), 3b	4	2	3	0
Buck Leonard (Homestead Grays), 1b	3	0	0	0
Monte Irvin (Newark Eagles), lf	3	0	0	0
Josh Gibson (Homestead Grays), c	2	0	1	0
Leon Ruffin (Newark Eagles), c	1	0	0	0
Louis Louden (N.Y. Cubans), c	1	0	0	0
*Murray Watkins (Philadelphia Stars)	0	0	0	0
Gene Benson (Philadelphia Stars), rf	1	0	1	0
Lennie Pearson (Newark Eagles), rf	3	0	1	0
Sam Bankhead (Homestead Grays), ss	2	0	0	0
Silvio Garcia (N.Y. Cubans), ss	2	0	0	0
Barney Brown (Philadelphia Stars), p	1	0	0	0
†Frank Austin (Philadelphia Stars)	0	0	0	0
Pat Scantlebury (N.Y. Cubans), p	0	0	0	0
Bill Byrd (Baltimore Elite Giants), p	1	0	0	0
‡Pete Diaz (N.Y. Cubans)	1	0	0	0
Jonas Gaines (Baltimore Elite Giants), p	0	0	0	0
Leon Day (Newark Eagles), p	0	0	0	0
	31	5	9	0

* Ran for Gibson in 4th.
† Ran for Brown in 3rd.
‡ Batted for Byrd in 7th.

WEST	000	300	000—3
EAST	200	300	00x—5

RBI—Davis, Grace, Hyde, Easterling, Leonard, Irvin, Pearson. SB—Doby, Irvin. SH—Leonard. DP—Wilson, Ware, and Davis; Bankhead and Leonard. SO—by Bankhead, 2; Jessup, 1; Byrd, 4. BB—off Bankhead, 1; Jessup, 1; Byrd, 1. Hits—off Bankhead, 3 in 3 innings; Clark, 3 in ⅓; Jessup, 2 in 2⅔; Williams, 1 in 2; Brown, 0 in 2; Scantlebury, 3 in ⅓; Byrd, 1 in 2⅔; Gaines, 1 in 2; Day, 1 in 1. PB—Troupe, Haywood (2).
Winning pitcher—Byrd; loser—Clark.
Attendance—16,000.

(At Comiskey Park, Chicago)

East

	AB	R	H	E
Henry Kimbro (Baltimore Elite Giants), cf	4	0	0	0
Larry Doby (Newark Eagles), 2b	3	0	1	0
Howard Easterling (Homestead Grays), 3b	4	0	0	0
Buck Leonard (Homestead Grays), 1b	4	0	1	0
Monte Irvin (Newark Eagles), lf	4	0	1	0
Josh Gibson (Homestead Grays), c	3	0	0	0
Gene Benson (Philadelphia Stars), rf	3	0	0	1
Silvio Garcia (N.Y. Cubans), ss	1	0	0	2
*Pat Scantlebury (N.Y. Cubans)	1	0	1	0
†Pee Wee Butts (Baltimore Elite Giants), ss	0	0	0	0
Barney Brown (Philadelphia Stars), p	1	0	0	0
Bill Byrd (Baltimore Elite Giants), p	1	0	0	0
Jonas Gaines (Baltimore Elite Giants), p	0	0	0	0
‡Murray Watkins (Newark Eagles)	0	1	0	0
Leon Day (Newark Eagles), p	0	0	0	0
	29	1	4	3

* Batted for Gaines in 8th.
† Ran for Scantlebury in 8th.
‡ Batted for Garcia in 8th.

West

	AB	R	H	E
Art Wilson (Birmingham Black Barons), ss	4	1	1	0
Archie Ware (Cleveland Buckeyes), 1b	2	0	0	0
Sam Jethroe (Cleveland Buckeyes), cf	3	1	0	0
Piper Davis (Birmingham Black Barons), 2b	3	1	1	0
Willie Grace (Cleveland Buckeyes), rf	4	1	3	0
Alex Radcliffe (Cincinnati Clowns), 3b	3	0	0	0
Bubber Hyde (Memphis Red Sox), lf	3	0	2	1
Quincy Troupe (Cleveland Buckeyes), c	1	0	0	0
Felix Evans (Memphis Red Sox), p	1	0	0	0
Dan Bankhead (Memphis Red Sox), p	1	0	0	0
John Williams (Cincinnati–Ind. Clowns), p	1	0	0	0
	26	4	7	1

EAST   000   000   010—1
WEST   000   220   00x—4

RBI—Hyde, Davis, Doby. 2B—Hyde. SB—Wilson, Jethroe, Hyde. SH—Doby. DP—Davis, Wilson, and Ware. SO—by Brown, 3; Day, 1; Bankhead, 3; Gaines, 1; Evans, 1. BB—off Evans, 2; Brown, 1; Bankhead, 3; Byrd, 2. Hits—off Brown, 2 in 3 innings; Gaines, 0 in 2⅓; Byrd, 4 in 1⅓; Day, 1 in 1; Evans, 1 in 3; Williams, 2 in 3; Bankhead, 1 in 3. HP—by Bankhead (Garcia); Williams (Watkins); Brown (Jethroe).
Winning pitcher—Evans; loser—Byrd.
Attendance—45,474.

1947

East

	AB	R	H	E
Henry Kimbro (Baltimore Elite Giants), cf	4	0	0	0
Peewee Butts (Baltimore Elite Giants), ss	2	0	0	0
John Washington (Baltimore Elite Giants), 1b	4	0	0	0
Monte Irvin (Newark Eagles), lf	3	1	0	0
Silvio Garcia (N.Y. Cubans), 2b	3	0	0	0
Claro Duaney (N.Y. Cubans), rf	2	0	0	0
Orestes Minoso (N.Y. Cubans), 3b	3	0	0	0
John Hayes (N.Y. Black Yankees), c	1	0	0	0
Max Manning (Newark Eagles), p	2	0	1	0
Luis Tiant (N.Y. Cubans), p	1	0	0	0
Luis Marquez (Homestead Grays), rf	1	1	1	0
Louis Louden (N.Y. Cubans), c	1	0	1	0
Frank Austin (Philadelphia Stars), ss	2	0	0	0
Henry Miller (Philadelphia Stars), p	0	0	0	0
John Wright (Homestead Grays), p	0	0	0	0
*Bob Romby (Baltimore Elite Giants)	1	0	0	0
†Biz Mackey (Newark Eagles)	0	0	0	0
‡Vic Harris (Homestead Grays)	0	0	0	0
	30	2	3	0

* Flied out for Hayes in 6th.
† Walked for Miller in 8th.
‡ Ran for Mackey in 8th.

West

	AB	R	H	E
Art Wilson (Birmingham Black Barons), ss	4	0	0	0
Herb Souell (Kansas City Monarchs), 3b	5	1	1	0
Sam Jethroe (Cleveland Buckeyes), rf	3	1	1	0
Piper Davis (Birmingham Black Barons), 2b	3	1	2	0
Quincy Troupe (Cleveland Buckeyes), c	2	1	1	0
Jose Colas (Memphis Red Sox), lf	4	0	2	0
Goose Tatum (Indianapolis Clowns), 1b	4	0	2	0
Buddy Armour (Chicago American Giants), rf	4	1	2	0
Dan Bankhead (Memphis Red Sox), p	2	0	0	0
Gentry Jessup (Chicago American Giants), p	1	0	0	0
Chet Brewer (Cleveland Buckeyes), p	1	0	1	0
	33	5	12	0

```
EAST    010   000   010—2
WEST    211   000   01x—5
```

RBI—Davis, Colas (2), Duaney, Troupe, Louden, Brewer. 2B—Davis, Armour (2), Marquez. 3B—Souell, Troupe, Jethroe. SB—Jethroe, Davis. SH—Troupe. DP—Wilson, Davis, and Tatum. SO—by Bankhead, 2; Manning, 3; Jessup, 1; Brewer, 1; Miller, 1. BB—off Manning, 2; Miller, 1; Brewer, 1. Hits—off Manning, 5 in 2⅓ innings; Tiant, 2 in 2⅔; Miller, 2 in 2; Wright, 3 in 1; Bankhead, 1 in 3; Jessup, 0 in 3; Brewer, 2 in 3. HP—by Bankhead (Irvin); Manning (Jethroe). PB—Louden.

Winning pitcher—Bankhead; loser—Manning.

Attendance—48,112.

1948

East

	AB	R	H	E
Luis Marquez (Homestead Grays), cf	4	0	0	0
Orestes Minoso (N.Y. Cubans), 3b	4	0	1	0
Luke Easter (Homestead Grays), lf	0	0	0	1
Lester Lockett (Baltimore Elite Giants), lf	2	0	0	0
Buck Leonard (Homestead Grays), 1b	4	0	1	0
Bob Harvey (Newark Eagles), rf	1	0	0	0
Monte Irvin (Newark Eagles), rf	2	0	0	0
Jim Gilliam (Baltimore Elite Giants), 2b	3	0	1	0
Louis Louden (N.Y. Cubans), c	3	0	0	0
Bill Cash (Philadelphia Stars), c	0	0	0	0
Peewee Butts (Baltimore Elite Giants), ss	2	0	0	1
Frank Austin (Philadelphia Stars), ss	1	0	0	0
Rufus Lewis (Newark Eagles), p	1	0	0	0
Wilbur Fields (Homestead Grays), p	1	0	0	0
Robert Griffith (N.Y. Black Yankees), p	1	0	0	0
	29	0	3	2

West

	AB	R	H	E
Art Wilson (Birmingham Black Barons), ss	3	0	0	0
Herb Souell (Kansas City Monarchs), 3b	4	0	0	0
Piper Davis (Birmingham Black Barons), 2b	3	1	1	0
Willard Brown (Kansas City Monarchs), cf	4	1	2	0
Robert Boyd (Memphis Red Sox), 1b	4	1	2	1
Neil Robinson (Memphis Red Sox), lf	3	0	1	0
Quincy Troupe (Chicago American Giants), c	3	0	0	0
Sam Hill (Chicago American Giants), rf	3	0	0	0
Bill Powell (Birmingham Black Barons), p	1	0	0	0
Jim LaMarque (Kansas City Monarchs), p	1	0	0	0
Gentry Jessup (Chicago American Giants), p	1	0	1	0
	30	3	7	1

EAST   000   000   000—0
WEST   020   000   01x—3

RBI—Robinson, Hill, Boyd. 2B—Davis, Leonard. SB—Davis. DP—Gilliam, Louden, Minoso, Butts, and Minoso; Davis, Wilson, and Boyd. SO—by Powell, 2; Lewis, 4; LaMarque, 1; Fields, 2; Griffith, 2; Jessup, 1. BB—off Powell, 1; Lewis, 2; Fields, 1; Griffith, 1; Jessup, 1. Hits—off Powell, 1 in 3; Lewis, 3 in 3; LaMarque, 2 in 3; Fields, 1 in 3; Jessup, 0 in 3; Griffith, 3 in 2. WP—Powell.

Winning pitcher—Powell; loser—Lewis.

Attendance—42,000.

1949

East

	AB	R	H	E
Peewee Butts (Baltimore Elite Giants), ss	4	1	1	0
Pedro Diaz (N.Y. Cubans), cf	4	0	3	0
Lennie Pearson (Baltimore Elite Giants), 1b	5	0	0	0
Bus Clarkson (Philadelphia Stars), rf	2	0	1	0
Sherwood Brewer (Indianapolis Clowns), rf	2	1	1	0
Robert Davis (Baltimore Elite Giants), lf	4	1	1	1
Jim Gilliam (Baltimore Elite Giants), 2b	4	0	0	0
Howard Easterling (N.Y. Cubans), 3b	4	1	2	0
Bill Cash (Philadelphia Stars), c	4	0	1	0
Bob Griffith (Philadelphia Stars), p	1	0	1	0
*Dave Hoskins (Cleveland Buckeyes)	1	0	0	0
Andy Porter (Indianapolis Clowns), p	0	0	0	0
†Leon Kellman (Cleveland Buckeyes)	1	0	0	0
Pat Scantlebury (N.Y. Cubans), p	1	0	0	0
	37	4	11	1

* Struck out for Griffith in 4th.
† Struck out for Porter in 7th.

West

	AB	R	H	E
Jose Burgos (Birmingham Black Barons), ss	2	0	0	0
Orlando Verona (Memphis Red Sox), ss	1	0	0	1
*Herman Bell (Birmingham Black Barons)	1	0	0	0
Bob Boyd (Memphis Red Sox), 1b	4	0	0	0
Pedro Formenthal (Memphis Red Sox), cf	1	0	0	0
John Davis (Houston Eagles), cf	2	0	0	0
Piper Davis (Birmingham Black Barons), 2b	4	0	1	0
Willard Brown (Kansas City Monarchs), lf-3b	3	0	0	0

Lonnie Summers (Chicago American Giants), c	3	0	1	2
Robert Wilson (Houston Eagles), ss-3b	3	0	0	0
Gene Richardson (Kansas City Monarchs), p	1	0	0	0
Willie Greason (Birmingham Black Barons), p	0	0	0	0
†John O'Neil (Kansas City Monarchs)	1	0	0	0
Gread McKinnis (Chicago American Giants), p	0	0	0	0
Willie Hutchinson (Memphis Red Sox), p	1	0	0	0
Jim LaMarque (Kansas City Monarchs), p	1	0	0	0
	28	0	2	3

* Flied out for Verona in 6th.
† Struck out for Greason in 6th.

EAST   110   000   020—4
WEST   000   000   000—0

RBI—Clarkson, Griffith, Gilliam, Easterling. 2B—P. Davis, Butts, Cash. SB—Easterling, Diaz, R. Davis. DP—Boyd and P. Davis; Easterling, Gilliam, and Pearson. SO—by Griffith, 1; Scantlebury, 1; Richardson, 2; Greason, 1. BB—off Richardson, 2; Griffith, 1; Porter, 1. Hits—off Griffith, 0 in 3; Porter, 0 in 3; Scantlebury, 2 in 3; Richardson, 4 in 3; Greason, 2 in 3; McKinnis, 4 in 1⅔; Hutchinson, 0 in ⅓; LaMarque, 1 in 1. Winning pitcher—Griffith; loser—Richardson.
Attendance—26,697.

1950

East

	AB	R	H	E
Henry Merchant (Indianapolis Clowns), lf	5	0	0	0
Peewee Butts (Baltimore Elite Giants), ss	3	1	0	0
Rene Gonzalez (N.Y. Cubans), 1b	3	0	2	0
Pedro Diaz (N.Y. Cubans), cf	5	0	1	0
Louis Louden (N.Y. Cubans), c	5	1	1	0
Jim Gilliam (Baltimore Elite Giants), 2b	3	1	1	0
Ben Little (Philadelphia Stars), rf	3	0	2	0
Charles White (Philadelphia Stars), 3b	1	0	0	0
Sherwood Brewer (Indianapolis Clowns), 3b-rf	3	0	0	1
Joe Black (Baltimore Elite Giants), p	1	0	0	0
Raul Galata (N.Y. Cubans), p	2	0	0	0
Jonas Gaines (Philadelphia Stars), p	0	0	0	0
Pat Scantlebury (N.Y. Cubans), p	1	0	0	0
	35	3	7	1

West

	AB	R	H	E
Curley Williams (Houston Eagles), ss	1	1	0	0
Clyde McNeal (Chicago American Giants), ss	3	0	1	1
Herb Souell (Kansas City Monarchs), 3b	1	1	0	0
Leon Kellman (Memphis Red Sox), 3b	2	0	0	1
Jesse Douglas (Chicago American Giants), 3b	4	0	3	0
Alonzo Perry (Birmingham Black Barons), 1b	3	1	2	0
John Washington (Houston Eagles), 1b	2	0	0	1
Bob Harvey (Houston Eagles), rf	2	1	0	0
Pepper Bassett (Birmingham Black Barons), c	1	0	1	0
Art Pennington (Chicago American Giants), cf	3	1	1	0
Ed Steele (Birmingham Black Barons), lf	3	0	2	1
Casey Jones (Memphis Red Sox), c	2	0	0	0
Thomas Cooper (Kansas City Monarchs), c-rf	1	0	0	0
Vibert Clarke (Memphis Red Sox), p	1	0	0	0
Cliff Johnson (Kansas City Monarchs), p	2	0	1	0
Bill Powell (Birmingham Black Barons), p	1	0	0	0
	32	5	11	4

EAST   000   200   001—3
WEST   002   030   000—5

RBI—Diaz, Little, Douglas (2), Pennington (2), Steele. 2B—Little, Diaz, Washington. 3B—Johnson, Pennington. HR—Gilliam. SB—Douglas (2), Butts. SH—Souell, Gilliam. SO—Clark, 3; Johnson, 3; Powell, 4; Galata, 1; Gaines, 3; Scantlebury, 1. BB—off Clark, 2; Johnson, 2; Black, 1; Galata, 1. HP—by Galata (Steele).

Winning pitcher—Johnson; loser—Galata.

Attendance—24,614.

APPENDIX C

ALL-TIME REGISTER
OF PLAYERS AND OFFICIALS

1884–1950

This register of the top echelon of Negro baseball was compiled from a careful perusal of box scores and stories in the Negro press and old sporting papers. Considerable effort has gone into the work of making it as complete and accurate as possible. However, because until about 1930 first names were seldom used on sports pages, a certain amount of guesswork was inevitable. For example, if it was known that John Doe played for the Lincoln Giants in 1917 and a Doe appeared in the lineup in 1918 he was assumed to be the same man. Obviously there is a chance for error here. For the same reason, many players in this register are without first names. For some only nicknames are given; these are in parentheses. Such common nicknames as "Bill," "Joe," and "Ed" are in most cases treated as Christian names to avoid cluttering the record too much.

The author is indebted to the following men for valuable assistance in identifying many players by first names: Bobby Anderson, George Bennette, Jimmie Crutchfield, Jelly Gardner, Buck Leonard, Dave Malarcher, Armand Tyson (owner of Tyson's Chicago Monarchs), Gread McKinnis, and Bill Yancey.

Key

Position in boldface type—player's main position
Club in boldface type—club with which player was identified for a long period
Years following name—beginning and ending dates with top-flight clubs or leagues
ANL—American Negro League
ECL—Eastern Colored League
NAL—Negro American League
NNL—Negro National League (first NNL operated from 1920 to 1931, second from 1933 to 1948)
NSL—Negro Southern League

ABERNATHY, JAMES—1946—of, Boston Blues
ABREU, EUFEMIO—1920–30—**c, 1b, Cuban Stars (NNL),** Cuban Stars (ECL)
ACOSTA, JOSE—1915—p, Long Branch, N. J. Cubans
ADAMS, EMERY (ACE)—1932–45—p, Memphis Red Sox, **Baltimore Elite Giants,** New York Black Yankees
ADDISON, ——— —1910—ss, c, Philadelphia Giants
ADKINS, CLARENCE—1931—of, Nashville Elite Giants
ADKINS, STACY—1950—p, Chicago American Giants
ALBRITTON, ALEXANDER (ALEX)—1922–25—p, Baltimore Black Sox, Washington Potomacs, Hilldale
ALEXANDER, ——— —1918–21—**of,** 2b, Dayton Marcos, Columbus Buckeyes
ALEXANDER, (CHUFFY)—1928–32—3b, 1b, Birmingham Black Barons, Monroe Monarchs
ALEXANDER, (HUB)—1913—c, Chicago Giants
ALEXANDER, GROVER CLEVELAND (BUCK)—1923–26—p, Chicago Giants, Detroit Stars, Indianapolis ABCs, Cleveland Elites
ALEXANDER, FREYL—1912—president, Homestead Grays
ALEXANDER, TED—1940–49—p, Newark Eagles, Cleveland Bears, Chicago American Giants, **Kansas City Monarchs,** Birmingham Black Barons
ALFONSO, ANGEL—1924–30—ss, 3b, 2b, **Cuban Stars (NNL),** Cuban Stars (ECL)

ALLEN, (BUSTER)—1942–47—p, Jacksonville Red Caps, Cincinnati Clowns, Cincinnati–Indianapolis Clowns, Memphis Red Sox

ALLEN, CLIFFORD (CROOKS)—1932–38—p, Hilldale, Baltimore Black Sox, Homestead Grays, Memphis Red Sox

ALLEN, M. —— —1919—2b, Lincoln Giants

ALLEN, NEWTON (NEWT)—1922–44—**2b,** ss, of, mgr, All Nations, **Kansas City Monarchs,** St. Louis Stars

ALLEN, TODD—1915–25—3b, mgr, Indianapolis ABCs, Chicago American Giants, Lincoln Giants

ALLEN, TOUSSAINT (TOM)—1914–26—1b, Havana Red Sox, **Hilldale,** Wilmington Potomacs, Newark Stars

ALLEN, WILLIAM—1887—player, Cincinnati Browns

ALLISON, —— —1917—1b, Chicago Union Giants

ALLISON, —— —1921—c, Nashville Elite Giants

ALLISON, —— —1925—2b, Indianapolis ABCs

ALONSO, ROGELIO—1927–29—p, of, Cuban Stars (NNL)

ALVAREZ, RAUL—1924–33—p, Cuban Stars (NNL), Cuban Stars (East)

AMORO, EDMUNDO—1950—1b, N.Y. Cubans

ANDERSON, —— —1930—of, Nashville Elite Giants

ANDERSON, —— —1932—of, Indianapolis ABCs

ANDERSON, —— —1930–33—c, Chicago American Giants, Baltimore Black Sox

ANDERSON, ROBERT (BOBBY)—1915–25—ss, 2b, Peters' Union Giants, Chicago American Giants, Philadelphia Giants, Gilkerson's Union Giants, Chicago Giants

ANDERSON, THEODORE (BUBBLES)—1922–25—2b, Kansas City Monarchs, Birmingham Black Barons, Washington Potomacs, Indianapolis ABCs

ANDERSON, WILLIAM (BILL)—1940–47—p, Brooklyn Royal Giants, **Cuban Stars, New York Cubans**

ANDREWS, —— —1939—p, Cleveland Bears

ANDREWS, HERMAN (JABO)—1930–42—of, p, mgr, Birmingham Black Barons, Memphis Red Sox, Indianapolis ABCs, Detroit Wolves, Homestead Grays, Columbus Blue Birds, Pittsburgh Crawfords, Washington Black Senators, Chicago American Giants, Jacksonville Red Caps

ANDREWS, (POP)—1910–19—**p,** of, Brooklyn Royal Giants, Pittsburgh Stars of Buffalo

ANTHONY, PETE—1950—c, Houston Eagles, New York Cubans

ANTHONY, THAD—1950—c, Baltimore Elite Giants

ARANGO, LUIS—1925–39—**3b,** 1b, **Cuban Stars (NNL),** New York Cubans

ARCHER, —— —1920–22—p, Lincoln Giants, Baltimore Black Sox

ARENCIBIA, EDWARD—1948—of, New York Cubans

ARGUELLES, MARTINANO—1950—p, New York Cubans

ARIOSA, HOMERO—1947–49—of, New York Cubans

ARMOUR, ——— —1933—p, Detroit Stars
ARMOUR, ALFRED (BUDDY)—1936–47—**of,** ss, **St. Louis Stars,** Indianapolis ABCs, New Orleans–St. Louis Stars, Harrisburg–St. Louis Stars, Cleveland Buckeyes, Chicago American Giants
ARMSTEAD, ——— —1938–40—p, Indianapolis ABCs, St. Louis Stars
ARNET, ——— —1921—p, Bacharach Giants
ARNOLD, ——— —1927—of, Brooklyn Royal Giants
ARNOLD, PAUL —1934–35—of, Newark Dodgers
ARTHUR, ROBERT—1946—p, Pittsburgh Crawfords
ASCANIO, CARLOS—1946—1b, New York Black Yankees
ASH, ——— — 1926—p, Hilldale
ASHBY, EARL—1945–48—c, Cleveland Buckeyes, Birmingham Black Barons, Homestead Grays, Newark Eagles
ATKINS, ——— —1923—ss, Toledo Tigers
ATKINS, JOE—1946–47—3b, Pittsburgh Crawfords, Cleveland Buckeyes
AUGUSTINE, LEON—1923—umpire, NNL
AUSTIN, ——— —1930—p, Nashville Elite Giants
AUSTIN, FRANK—1944–48—ss, Philadelphia Stars
AUSTIN, JOHN—1887—player, Cincinnati Browns
AWKARD, RUSSELL—1940–41—of, Cuban Stars, Newark Eagles
AYLOR, JAMES—1887—player, Philadelphia Pythians

BAGLEY, ——— —1937—c, Cincinnati Tigers
BAILEY, D.—1916–19—**of,** 3b, Lincoln Stars, **Pennsylvania Red Caps of New York**
BAILEY, PERCY (BILL)—1927–34—p, Baltimore Black Sox, Nashville Elite Giants, Detroit Stars, Cole's American Giants, New York Black Yankees
BAILEY, WILLIAM—1950—c, Cleveland Buckeyes
BAIRD, THOMAS—1938–50—officer, Kansas City Monarchs; booking agent for NAL exhibition games
BAKER, EDGAR—1945—p, Memphis Red Sox
BAKER, EUGENE (GENE)—1948–50—ss, Kansas City Monarchs
BAKER, HENRY—1925–32—of, Indianapolis ABCs
BAKER, HOWARD (HOME RUN)—1910—player, Leland Giants
BAKER, NORMAN—1937—p, Newark Eagles
BAKER, RUFUS—1944–47—inf., of, New York Black Yankees
BAKER, W. B.—1937–38—bus. mgr., Atlanta Black Crackers
BALDWIN, ——— —1925–26—ss, 2b, Indianapolis ABCs, Cleveland Elites
BALL, GEORGE W. (GEORGIA RABBIT)—1904–05—p, Cuban X Giants, Augusta, Georgia
BALL, WALTER—1906–23—p, Philadelphia Giants, Leland Giants, **Chicago Giants,** Chicago American Giants, St. Louis Giants, Mohawk Giants, Brooklyn Royal Giants
BALLESTRO, MIGUEL—1948—ss, New York Cubans

BAMES, ———— —1937—c, Birmingham Black Barons

BANKHEAD, DANIEL ROBERT (DAN)—1940–47—p, Chicago American Giants, **Birmingham Black Barons,** Memphis Red Sox

BANKHEAD, FRED—1937–48—2b, 3b, 1b, Birmingham Black Barons, **Memphis Red Sox**

BANKHEAD, GARNETT—1948—p, Homestead Grays

BANKHEAD, JOE—1948—p, Birmingham Black Barons

BANKHEAD, SAMUEL (SAM)—1930–50—ss, of, 2b, p, mgr, Birmingham Black Barons, Nashville Elite Giants, Pittsburgh Crawfords, **Homestead Grays**

BANKS, ———— —1896—p, Cuban X Giants

BANKS, ———— —1930—2b, Hilldale

BANKS, ERNEST (ERNIE)—1950—ss, Kansas City Monarchs

BANKS, G. ——— —1915—p, Lincoln Giants

BANKS, S. ——— —1915—c, Lincoln Giants

BANTON, ———— —1914—p, Chicago American Giants

BARANDA, ———— —1915–16—3b, of, Long Branch, N.J. Cubans, Jersey City Cubans

BARBEE, (BUD)—1937–48—p, 1b, mgr, New York Black Yankees, Cincinnati Clowns, Cincinnati–Indianapolis Clowns, Philadelphia Stars, Baltimore Elite Giants, Raleigh Tigers

BARBEE, QUINCY—1949—of, Louisville Buckeyes

BARBER, ———— —1920—2b, Hilldale

BARBER, JOHN—1946—of, Pittsburgh Crawfords

BARBOUR, JESS—1910–1926—**of,** 1b, 3b, Philadelphia Giants, **Chicago American Giants,** Bacharach Giants, Detroit Stars, Pittsburgh Keystones, Harrisburg Giants

BARCELLO, ———— —1921—p, Cuban Stars (East)

BARKER, MARVIN—1936–48—**of,** 2b, 3b, mgr, **New York Black Yankees,** Philadelphia Stars

BARKINS, W. C.—1928—officer, Cleveland Stars

BARNES, ED—1937–38—p, Kansas City Monarchs

BARNES, (FAT)—1922–30—c, Cleveland Tate Stars, Cleveland Browns, Detroit Stars, St. Louis Stars, Cleveland Hornets, Cleveland Tigers, Memphis Red Sox

BARNES, FRANK—1947–50—p, Indianapolis ABCs, Kansas City Monarchs

BARNES, HARRY—1949—c, Memphis Red Sox

BARNES, JIMMY—1941–42—p, Baltimore Elite Giants

BARNES, O. ——— —1932—officer, New York Black Yankees

BARNES, (TUBBY)—1938—c, Birmingham Black Barons

BARNHILL, DAVID (DAVE, IMPO)—1941–49—p, New Orleans–St. Louis Stars, **New York Cubans**

BARNHILL, HERBERT (HERB)—1938–45—c, Jacksonville Red Caps, Kansas City Monarchs, Chicago American Giants

BARO, BERNARDO—1916–29—**of,** 1b, p, **Cuban Stars (East),** Cuban Stars (NNL)

BARR, ———— —1921—3b, ss, Kansas City Monarchs

BARROW, WESLEY—1945–47—mgr, New Orleans Black Pelicans, Nashville Cubs, Baltimore Elite Giants

BARTLETT, H. ——— —1913–25—p, **Indianapolis ABCs,** Kansas City Monarchs

BARTON, SHERMAN—1896–1911—of, Chicago Unions, Columbia Giants, Quaker Giants of New York, Cuban X Giants, St. Paul Gophers, Chicago Giants

BASHUM, ——— —1932—c, Indianapolis ABCs

BASS, (RED)—1940—c, Homestead Grays

BASSETT, LLOYD (PEPPER)—1934–50—c, New Orleans Crescent Stars, Philadelphia Stars, Chicago American Giants, Pittsburgh Crawfords, Cincinnati Clowns, Cincinnati–Indianapolis Clowns, **Birmingham Black Barons**

BATSON, ——— —1909—of, Philadelphia Giants

BATTLE, RAY—1944–45—3b, Homestead Grays

BATTLE, WILLIAM (BILL)—1947–49—p, Homestead Grays, Memphis Red Sox

BATUM, G. W.—1885—2b, Brooklyn Remsens

BAUCHMAN, HARRY—1915–23—**2b,** ss, 1b, Chicago American Giants, Chicago Union Giants, **Chicago Giants**

BAUZZ, ——— —1930—ss, Cuban Stars (NNL)

BAYLISS, HENRY—1948–50—inf., Chicago American Giants, Baltimore Elite Giants, Birmingham Black Barons

BAYNARD, ——— —1918–25—of, Pennsylvania Red Caps of New York

BAXTER, AL—1898—of, Celeron Acme Colored Giants (Iron and Oil League)

BEA, BILL—1940—player, New York Black Yankees, Philadelphia Stars

BEAL, (LEFTY)—1947—p, Newark Eagles

BEBLEY, ——— —1925—p, Birmingham Black Barons

BEBOP, RALPH (SPEC)—1950—player, Indianapolis Clowns

BECKER, ——— —1920—1b, Dayton Marcos

BECKWITH, JOHN—1919–34—ss, 3b, c, of, mgr, Chicago Giants, Chicago American Giants, Baltimore Black Sox, Homestead Grays, Harrisburg Giants, Lincoln Giants, Bacharach Giants, New York Black Yankees, Newark Dodgers

BEJERANO, AUGUSTIN—1928—of, Cuban Stars (ECL)

BELL, CHARLES (LEFTY)—1948—p, Homestead Grays

BELL, CLIFFORD (CLIFF)—1921–31—p, **Kansas City Monarchs,** Detroit Stars, **Memphis Red Sox,** Cleveland Cubs

BELL, FRANK—1888—player, New York Gorhams

BELL, FRED (LEFTY)—1922–26—p, St. Louis Stars

BELL, HERMAN—1945–49—c, Birmingham Black Barons

BELL, JAMES (COOL PAPA)—1922–46—**of, p, St. Louis Stars, Pittsburgh Crawfords,** Detroit Wolves, Kansas City Monarchs, Chicago American Giants, Memphis Red Sox, Homestead Grays

BELL, JAMES (STEEL ARM)—1933–40—c, Montgomery Grey Sox, Indianapolis Crawfords

BELL, JULIAN—1929—p, Birmingham Black Barons
BELL, WILLIAM—1902–04—**p,** of, Philadelphia Giants
BELL, WILLIAM—1923–48—**p,** mgr, **Kansas City Monarchs,** Detroit
Wolves, Homestead Grays, Pittsburgh Crawfords, Newark Dodgers,
Newark Eagles
BELL, WILLIAM (LEFTY)—1950—p, Kansas City Monarchs
BENJAMIN, JERRY—1932–48—of, Memphis Red Sox, Detroit Stars,
Birmingham Black Barons, **Homestead Grays,** Toledo Crawfords, New
York Cubans
BENNETT, ———— —1922—c, Pittsburgh Keystones
BENNETT, ———— —1932–34—2b, Cleveland Cubs, Memphis Red Sox
BENNETT, BRADFORD—1940–46—of, St. Louis Stars, New Orleans–
St. Louis Stars, New York Black Yankees, Boston Blues
BENNETT, FRANK—1918—mgr, Bacharach Giants
BENNETT, JIM—1945—p, Cincinnati–Indianapolis Clowns
BENNETT, SAM—1911–25—**of,** c, **St. Louis Giants,** St. Louis Stars
BENNETTE, GEORGE (JEW BABY)—1920–36—of, Columbus Buck-
eyes, Memphis Red Sox, Indianapolis ABCs, Detroit Stars, Chicago
Giants, Chicago Union Giants
BENSON, GENE—1934–48—of, Bacharach Giants, Pittsburgh Craw-
fords, **Philadelphia Stars,** Newark Eagles
BENTION, ———— —1933–34—of, Brooklyn Royal Giants, Bacharach
Giants
BENVENUTI, JULIUS—1939—vice-pres, Chicago American Giants
BERKLEY, ———— —1941—p, New Orleans–St. Louis Stars
BERNARD, ———— —1911–15—c, of, Pittsburgh Giants, Lincoln Stars
BERRY, ———— —1947—p, Kansas City Monarchs
BERRY, E.—1930—ss, 2b, Memphis Red Sox, Detroit Stars
BETTS, ———— —1938—of, Kansas City Monarchs
BEVERIE, ———— —1939—3b, Baltimore Elite Giants
BEVERLY, CHARLES—1924–36—p, Cleveland Browns, Birmingham
Black Barons, Kansas City Monarchs, Cleveland Stars, Pittsburgh Craw-
fords, New Orleans Crescent Stars, Newark Eagles
BEVERLY, (FIREBALL)—1950—p, Houston Eagles
BIBBS, RAINEY—1933–44—**2b,** ss, 3b, Detroit Stars, Cincinnati Tigers,
Chicago American Giants, Kansas City Monarchs, Indianapolis Craw-
fords, Chicago American Giants, Cleveland Buckeyes
BILLINGS, WILLIAM—1921—p, Nashville Elite Giants
BINDER, JAMES (JIMMY)—1930–36—**3b,** 2b, Memphis Red Sox,
Indianapolis ABCs, Detroit Stars, **Homestead Grays,** Washington Elite
Giants
BINGA, JESS E.—1887—player, Washington Capital Citys
BINGA, WILLIAM—1895–1909—3b, **Page Fence Giants,** Columbia
Giants, Philadelphia Giants, St. Paul Gophers
BINGHAM, (BINGO)—1917–21—of, Chicago Union Giants, Chicago
Giants
BIOT, CHARLIE—1939–41—of, Newark Eagles, New York Black
Yankees, Baltimore Elite Giants

BISSANT, JOHN—1934–47—**of,** p, Cole's American Giants, **Chicago American Giants,** Birmingham Black Barons, Chicago Brown Bombers

BIVINS, ———— —1948—p, Memphis Red Sox

BIX, ———— —1921—p, St. Louis Giants

BLACK, HOWARD—1928—inf, Brooklyn Cuban Giants

BLACK, JOSEPH (JOE)—1943–50—p, Baltimore Elite Giants

BLACKMAN, ———— —1937–38—p, Chicago American Giants, Birmingham Black Barons

BLACKMAN, HENRY—1922–24—3b, Indianapolis ABCs, Baltimore Black Sox

BLACKSTONE, WILLIAM—1887—player, Cincinnati Browns

BLACKWELL, CHARLES—1916–29—of, **St. Louis Giants,** St. Louis Stars, Birmingham Black Barons, Indianapolis ABCs, Nashville Elite Giants

BLAIR, GARNET—1945–46—p, Homestead Grays

BLAIR, LONNIE—1949–50—p, 2b, Homestead Grays

BLAKE, (BIG RED)—1932–35—p, Baltimore Black Sox, New York Black Yankees, New York Cubans

BLAKELY, ———— —1934—c, Cincinnati Tigers

BLANCHARD, CHESTER—1926—33, Dayton Marcos

BLANCO, C. ———— —1941—1b, Cuban Stars

BLANCO, HERBERTO—1941–42—2b, Cuban Stars, New York Cubans

BLATNER, ———— —1921—1b, of, Kansas City Monarchs

BLAVIS, FOX—1936—3b, Homestead Grays

BLEACH, ———— —1937—2b, Detroit Stars

BLEDSOE, ———— —1937—player, St. Louis Stars

BLOUNT, JOHN T. (TENNY)—1919–33—officer, Detroit Stars; vice-pres, NNL

BLUETT, ———— —1916–18—2b, Chicago Union Giants

BLUEITT, VIRGIL—1937–49—umpire, NAL

BLUKOI, FRANK—1920—2b, Kansas City Monarchs

BOADA, LUCAS—1921–24—p, Cuban Stars (NNL)

BOBO, J. ———— —1927—of, Cleveland Hornets

BOBO, WILLIE—1923–30—1b, All Nations, Kansas City Monarchs, **St. Louis Stars,** Nashville Elite Giants

BOGGS, G.—1923–34—**p,** of, Milwaukee Bears, Detroit Stars

BOLDEN, EDWARD (ED)—1910–50—officer, Hilldale, Darby Phantoms, Philadelphia Stars; officer, ECL, ANL, NNL

BOLDEN, L. W.—1885—player, Brooklyn Remsens

BOLDEN, OTTO—1910—c, Leland Giants

BOND, TIMOTHY—1935–40—ss, 3b, Pittsburgh Crawfords, Newark Dodgers, **Chicago American Giants**

BONNER, ROBERT—1922–26—1b, c, 2b, Cleveland Tate Stars, St. Louis Stars, Toledo Stars, Cleveland Elites

BOOKER, BILLY—1898—2b, Celeron Acme Colored Giants (Iron and Oil League)

BOOKER, JAMES (PETE)—1905–17—**c,** 1b, Philadelphia Giants, Leland Giants, Lincoln Giants, Chicago American Giants, Chicago Giants

BOONE, ALONZO—1931–50—p, mgr, Cleveland Cubs, Birmingham Black Barons, Chicago American Giants, Cincinnati Buckeyes, Cleveland Buckeyes, Louisville Buckeyes

BOONE, CHARLES (LEFTY)—1941–45—p, New Orleans–St. Louis Stars, Harrisburg–St. Louis Stars, Pittsburgh Crawfords

BOONE, OSCAR—1939–42—c, 1b, Indianapolis ABCs, **Chicago American Giants**

BOONE, ROBERT—1928—umpire, NNL

BOONE, STEVE (LEFTY)—1940—p, Memphis Red Sox

BORDEN, —————1933—ss, Birmingham Black Barons

BORDES, ED—1940—utility, Cleveland Bears

BORGES, —————1928—inf, Cuban Stars (NNL)

BOSTICK, —————1924—of, St. Louis Giants

BOSTOCK, LYMAN—1940–49—1b, of, Birmingham Black Barons, Chicago American Giants, New York Cubans

BOSTON, BOB—1948—3b, Homestead Grays

BOWE, RANDOLPH (BOB, LEFTY)—1939–40—p, Kansas City Monarchs, Chicago American Giants

BOWEN, (CHUCK)—1937–43—of, Indianapolis Athletics, Chicago Brown Bombers

BOWERS, —————1926—p, Baltimore Black Sox

BOWERS, JULIE—1947—c, New York Black Yankees

BOWMAN, EMMETT (SCOTTY)—1905–12—3b, p, c, ss, Philadelphia Giants, Leland Giants, Brooklyn Royal Giants

BOYD, —————1933—of, Kansas City Monarchs

BOYD, BEN—1885–87—2b, of, Argyle Hotel, Cuban Giants

BOYD, FRED—1922—of, Cleveland Tate Stars

BOYD, JAMES—1946—p, Newark Eagles

BOYD, LINCOLN—1949—of, Louisville Buckeyes

BOYD, ROBERT (BOB)—1947–50—1b, Memphis Red Sox

BRADFORD, CHARLES—1910–26—p, of, coach, Pittsburgh Giants, Lincoln Giants

BRADFORD, WILLIAM (BILL)—1938–42—of, Indianapolis ABCs, St. Louis Stars, Memphis Red Sox, Birmingham Black Barons

BRADLEY, FRANK—1937–43—p, Cincinnati Tigers, **Kansas City Monarchs**

BRADLEY, PHIL—1909–19—**c,** 1b, Brooklyn Royal Giants, Lincoln Giants, Smart Set, Pittsburgh Colored Stars, Pittsburgh Stars of Buffalo

BRADY, JOHN—1887—player, Pittsburgh Keystones

BRADY, (LEFTY)—1921—p, Cleveland Tate Stars

BRAGANA, —————1947—p, Cleveland Buckeyes

BRAGANA, RAMON—1928–37—**p,** of, Cuban Stars (ECL), Stars of Cuba, New York Cubans

BRAGG, —————1909–18—**3b,** ss, 2b, Cuban Giants, **Brooklyn Royal Giants,** Mohawk Giants, Lincoln Giants, Philadelphia Giants

BRAGG, EUGENE—1925—c, Chicago American Giants

BRAITHWAITE, ARCHIE—1944–47—of, Newark Eagles, Philadelphia Stars

BRANAHAN, J. ——— —1922–27—p, Cleveland Tate Stars, Harrisburg Giants, Detroit Stars, Cleveland Elites, Cleveland Hornets
BRANHAM, LUTHER—1949—inf, Birmingham Black Barons
BRANTLEY, OLLIE—1950—p, Memphis Red Sox
BRAY, JAMES—1922–30—c, of, Chicago Giants, Chicago American Giants
BRAZELTON, ——— —1916—c, Chicago American Giants
BREDA, BILL—1950—player, Kansas City Monarchs
BREMMER, EUGENE (GENE)—1932–48—p, New Orleans Crescent Stars, Cincinnati Tigers, Memphis Red Sox, Kansas City Monarchs, Cincinnati Buckeyes, **Cleveland Buckeyes**
BREWER, CHET—1925–48—p, **Kansas City Monarchs,** Washington Pilots, New York Cubans, Philadelphia Stars, Chicago American Giants, Cleveland Buckeyes
BREWER, LUTHER—1918–21—1b, of, Chicago Giants
BREWER, SHERWOOD—1949–50—of, ss, Indianapolis Clowns
BRIDGEFORT, R. ——— —1932—officer, Cleveland Cubs
BRIGGERY, ——— —1932—ss, Atlanta Black Crackers
BRIGGS, OTTO—1914–34—of, mgr, West Baden, Indiana, Sprudels, Dayton Marcos, **Hilldale,** Quaker Giants, Bacharach Giants
BRIGHT, JOHN M.—1888–1909—mgr, Cuban Giants
BRISKER, WILLIAM—1950—gen mgr, Cleveland Buckeyes
BRITT, CHARLES (CHARLIE)—1927–33—3b, Homestead Grays
BRITT, GEORGE (CHIPPY)—1920–42—**p, c,** inf, Dayton Marcos, Columbus Buckeyes, Baltimore Black Sox, Hilldale, Homestead Grays, Newark Dodgers, Columbus Elite Giants, Washington Black Senators, Jacksonville Red Caps, Brooklyn Royal Giants, Chicago American Giants
BRITTON, GEORGE—1943–44—c, Cleveland Buckeyes
BRITTON, JOHN (JACK)—1940–50—3b, St. Louis Stars, Cincinnati Clowns, **Birmingham Black Barons,** Indianapolis Clowns
BROADNAX, WILLIE—1929—p, of, Memphis Red Sox
BROILES, ——— —1925–27—p, St. Louis Stars
BROOKS, ——— —1895—of, Page Fence Giants
BROOKS, ——— —1926—3b, of, Dayton Marcos
BROOKS, ——— —1942—p, Memphis Red Sox
BROOKS, ALEX—1938–40—of, New York Black Yankees, Brooklyn Royal Giants
BROOKS, AMEAL—1929–45—c, Chicago American Giants, Cleveland Cubs, Cole's American Giants, Columbus Blue Birds, Cincinnati Clowns, New York Black Yankees, Cuban Stars, New York Cubans
BROOKS, BEATTIE—1918–21—inf, c, Lincoln Giants, **Brooklyn Royal Giants,** Philadelphia Giants
BROOKS, CHARLES—1919–24—**2b,** p, St. Louis Giants, St. Louis Stars
BROOKS, CHESTER—1918–33—of, Brooklyn Royal Giants
BROOKS, EDWARD (EDDIE)—1949–50—2b, Houston Eagles
BROOKS, IRVIN—1919–24—p, Brooklyn Royal Giants
BROOKS, JAMES—1887—player, Baltimore Lord Baltimores

BROOKS, JESSE—1934–37—**3b,** of, Cleveland Red Sox, Kansas City Monarchs

BROOM, ——— —1941–42—p, Jacksonville Red Caps

BROOME, J. B. ——— —1947—of, New York Black Yankees

BROWN, ——— —1887—player, Boston Resolutes

BROWN, ——— —1910–13—1b, Cuban Giants, Mohawk Giants

BROWN, ——— —1910–12—of, Brooklyn Royal Giants

BROWN, ——— —1921—of, Columbus Buckeyes

BROWN, B.—1918—of, Washington Red Caps

BROWN, BARNEY—1932–49—p, Cuban Stars (East-West), **Philadelphia Stars,** New York Black Yankees

BROWN, BEN—1900—p, of, Genuine Cuban Giants

BROWN, CHARLES—1887—player, Pittsburgh Keystones

BROWN, (COUNTRY)—1918–33—of, Bacharach Giants, Brooklyn Royal Giants

BROWN, CURTIS—1947—1b, New York Black Yankees

BROWN, DAVID (DAVE, LEFTY)—1918–24—p, Chicago American Giants, Lincoln Giants

BROWN, E. ——— —1918—3b, Chicago Union Giants

BROWN, EARL—1923–26—p, of, Lincoln Giants

BROWN, ELIAS—1922–25—**3b,** 2b, of, New York Bacharach Giants, Washington Potomacs, Wilmington Potomacs

BROWN, F.—1918—2b, Chicago Union Giants

BROWN, G. ——— —1942—of, Cincinnati Buckeyes

BROWN, G. ——— —1926–27—p, St. Louis Stars

BROWN, GEORGE—1916–28—of, mgr, Indianapolis ABCs, **Dayton Marcos,** Detroit Stars

BROWN, JAMES—1941–48—p, of, Newark Eagles

BROWN, JESSE—1939–41—p, New York Black Yankees, Newark Eagles, Baltimore Elite Giants

BROWN, JAMES (JIM)—1918–42—**c,** 1b, mgr, **Chicago American Giants,** Louisville Black Caps, Cole's American Giants, Minneapolis–St. Paul Gophers

BROWN, JEROME—1949—inf, Houston Eagles

BROWN, JIM—1934—ss, Monroe Monarchs

BROWN, JOHN W.—1942–49—p, St. Louis Giants, **Cleveland Buckeyes,** Houston Eagles

BROWN, L. A.—1926–27—officer, St. Louis Stars

BROWN, LARRY—1919–49—**c,** mgr, Birmingham Black Barons, Pittsburgh Keystones, Indianapolis ABCs, **Memphis Red Sox,** Detroit Stars, Chicago American Giants, Lincoln Giants, New York Black Yankees, Cole's American Giants, Philadelphia Stars

BROWN, (LEFTY)—1933–37—p, Memphis Red Sox

BROWN, MAYWOOD—1921–25—p, Indianapolis ABCs

BROWN, OLIVER—1932—bus mgr, Newark Browns

BROWN, OSCAR—1939—c, Indianapolis ABCs, Baltimore Elite Giants

BROWN, OSSIE—1935–39—p, of, Cole's American Giants, Indianapolis Athletics, Indianapolis ABCs, St. Louis Stars

BROWN, RAYMOND (RAY)—1930–48—p, Dayton Marcos, Indianapolis ABCs, Detroit Wolves, **Homestead Grays**

BROWN, (SCRAPPY)—1918–30—ss, Washington Red Caps, Lincoln Giants, **Baltimore Black Sox,** Brooklyn Royal Giants

BROWN, T. J. (TOM)—1939–50—**ss,** 3b, **Memphis Red Sox,** Cleveland Buckeyes

BROWN, THEO—1911—3b, Chicago Union Giants

BROWN, TOM—1919—p, Chicago American Giants

BROWN, (TUTE)—1918—3b, Washington Red Caps

BROWN, ULYSSES (BUSTER)—1937–42—**c,** of, Newark Eagles, Jacksonville Red Caps, Cincinnati Buckeyes

BROWN, WALTER—1887—pres, League of Colored Base Ball Clubs

BROWN, WILLARD JESSE—1936–50—**of,** ss, Kansas City Monarchs

BROWN, WILLIAM—1906—asst mgr, Leland Giants

BROWN, WILLIAM H.—1887—player, Pittsburgh Keystones

BROWN, WILLIAM M.—1931–32—officer, Montgomery Grey Sox

BROWNE, (HAP)—1924—p, Cleveland Browns

BRUCE, CLARENCE—1947–48—2b, Homestead Grays

BRUTON, JACK—1938–41—p, of, Philadelphia Stars, Cleveland Bears, New Orleans–St. Louis Stars

BRYANT, ———— —1928—player, Harrisburg Giants

BRYANT, JOHNNIE—1950—of, Cleveland Buckeyes

BRYANT, (LEFTY)—1938–46—p, All Nations, Kansas City Monarchs, Memphis Red Sox

BRYANT, R. B.—1937—ss, Memphis Red Sox

BUBBLES, ———— —1938—p, Atlanta Black Crackers

BUCHANAN, CHESTER (BUCK)—1941–42—p, Philadelphia Stars

BUCKNER, HARRY—1896–1918—**p,** of, Chicago Unions, Columbia Giants, Philadelphia Giants, Cuban X Giants, Brooklyn Royal Giants, Quaker Giants, Lincoln Giants, Smart Set, Chicago Giants

BUFORD, (BLACK BOTTOM)—1929–34—**3b,** ss, 2b, **Nashville Elite Giants,** Cleveland Cubs, Detroit Stars, Louisville Red Caps

BUMPUS, EARL—1944–48—**p,** of, Kansas City Monarchs, Birmingham Black Barons, Chicago American Giants

BURBAGE, BENJAMIN (BUDDY)—1930–40—of, Hilldale, Pittsburgh Crawfords, Baltimore Black Sox, Bacharach Giants, Newark Dodgers, Homestead Grays, Washington Black Senators, Brooklyn Royal Giants

BURCH, WALTER—1931–44—**c,** 2b, ss, mgr, Bacharach Giants, Baltimore Black Sox, Cleveland Bears, St. Louis Stars, New Orleans–St. Louis Stars, Cincinnati Buckeyes, Cleveland Buckeyes

BURDINE, J.—1927–32—**p,** of, Birmingham Black Barons

BURGESS, ———— —1942—p, Chicago American Giants

BURGIN, RALPH—1917–1940—**2b,** ss, 3b, of, Hilldale, New York Black Yankees, Philadelphia Stars, Brooklyn Royal Giants

BURGOS, JOSE—1949–50—ss, Birmingham Black Barons
BURKE, ———— —1937—ss, Indianapolis Athletics
BURKE, ERNEST—1947–48—p, Baltimore Elite Giants
BURNETT, FRED (TEX)—1922–45—c, 1b, of, coach, mgr, Pittsburgh
   Keystones, Indianapolis ABCs, Lincoln Giants, Harrisburg Giants,
   Brooklyn Royal Giants, New York Black Yankees, Baltimore Black Sox,
   Homestead Grays, Brooklyn Eagles, Newark Eagles, Pittsburgh Craw-
   fords
BURNHAM, WILLIE (BEE)—1930–34—p, Monroe Monarchs
BURNS, ———— —1895–99—c, of, Page Fence Giants, Columbia Giants
BURNS, WILLIE—1943–44—p, Memphis Red Sox, Cincinnati–Indian-
   apolis Clowns
BURRELL, GEORGE—1884–85—p, c, Baltimore Atlantics
BURRIS, SAMUEL—1939–40—p, Memphis Red Sox, Birmingham Black
   Barons
BURTON, ———— —1928–40—p, of, inf, Birmingham Black Barons
BUSBY, ———— —1933—of, Detroit Stars
BUSBY, MAURICE (LEFTY)—1920–21—p, Bacharach Giants, All
   Cubans
BUSH, ———— —1946—p, Cleveland Buckeyes
BUSTAMENTE, LUIS—1905–11—ss, 2b, **Cuban Stars,** All Cubans
BUSTER, HERBERT—1943—inf, Chicago American Giants
BUTLER, J. ———— —1884—Philadelphia Mutual B.B.C.
BUTTS, HARRY—1950—p, Indianapolis Clowns
BUTTS, THOMAS (TOMMY, PEEWEE)—1938–50—ss, Atlanta Black
   Crackers, Indianapolis ABCs, **Baltimore Elite Giants**
BYAS, RICHARD T. (SUBBY)—1931–41—c, 1b, of, Kansas City Mon-
   archs, Cole's American Giants, **Chicago American Giants,** Newark
   Dodgers, Memphis Red Sox
BYATT, ———— —1940—1b, Philadelphia Stars
BYRD, JAMES F.—1927–30—officer, Hilldale
BYRD, WILLIAM (BILL)—1932–49—p, of, Columbus Turfs, Colum-
   bus Blue Birds, Columbus Elite Giants, Washington Elite Giants, **Balti-
   more Elite Giants**
BYRD, PRENTICE—1934—officer, Cleveland Red Sox

CABALLERO, LUIS—1950—3b, New York Cubans
CABRERA, LORENZO—1947–50—1b, New York Cubans
CABRERA, LUIS—1948—p, Indianapolis Clowns
CABRERA, RAFAEL—1944—player, Indianapolis Clowns
CABRERA, VILLA—1948—of, Indianapolis Clowns
CADE, ———— —1929—p, Bacharach Giants
CAIN, MARLON (SUGAR)—1938–49—p, Pittsburgh Crawfords,
   Brooklyn Royal Giants, Indianapolis Clowns
CALDERIN, ———— —1917–18—p, of, Havana Stars, Cuban Stars
CALDERON, ———— —1927–28—c, Cuban Stars (NNL), Homestead
   Grays
CALDWELL, ———— —1933—of, Birmingham Black Barons

CALHOUN, ———— —1923—2b, Toledo Tigers
CALHOUN, WALTER (LEFTY)—1931–46—p, Birmingham Black
Barons, Montgomery Grey Sox, Washington Black Senators, Pittsburgh
Crawfords, Indianapolis ABCs, St. Louis Stars, New Orleans–St. Louis
Stars, New York Black Yankees, Harrisburg–St. Louis Stars, Cleveland
Buckeyes
CALHOUN, WESLEY—1950—inf, Cleveland Buckeyes
CALL, F. ———— —1884–85—inf, Baltimore Atlantics
CALVO, JACINTO—1915—of, Long Branch, N.J. Cubans
CALVO, T. ———— —1915–16—of, Long Branch, N.J. Cubans, Jersey City
Cubans
CAMBRIA, JOE—1933—officer, Baltimore Black Sox
CAMPANELLA, ROY—1937–45—c, Baltimore Elite Giants
CAMPBELL, ———— —1922—of, Pittsburgh Keystones
CAMPBELL, (BUDDY)—1932—c, Cole's American Giants
CAMPBELL, DAVID (DAVE)—1938–41—2b, New York Black
Yankees, Philadelphia Stars
CAMPBELL, HUNTER—1942—officer, Cincinnati Clowns
CAMPBELL, WILLIAM (ZIP)—1923–29—p, Washington Potomacs,
Philadelphia Giants, **Hilldale,** Lincoln Giants
CAMPOS, ———— —1916–23—**p,** of, 1b, 2b, 3b, Cuban Stars (East),
Cuban Stars (NNL)
CAMPOS, MANUEL—1905—mgr, Cuban Stars of Santiago
CANADA, JAMES—1937–45—1b, Birmingham Black Barons, Memphis
Red Sox, Baltimore Elite Giants, Jacksonville Red Caps
CANNADY, WALTER (REV)—1921–45—**2b,** ss, of, 3b, 1b, p, mgr,
Columbus Buckeyes, Dayton Marcos, Cleveland Tate Stars, Homestead
Grays, Harrisburg Giants, Hilldale, Lincoln Giants, Darby Daisies, Pitts-
burgh Crawfords, **New York Black Yankees,** Philadelphia Stars, Brook-
lyn Royal Giants, Chicago American Giants, Cincinnati–Indianapolis
Clowns, New York Cubans
CANNON, RICHARD (SPEED BALL)—1928–34—p, St. Louis Stars,
Nashville Elite Giants, Birmingham Black Barons, Louisville Red Caps
CANOZERIS, AVELINO—1945—ss, Cleveland Buckeyes
CAPERS, (LEFTY)—1931—p, Louisville White Sox
CARABELLO, ESTERIO—1939—of, Cuban Stars
CARD, AL—1887—player, Pittsburgh Keystones
CARDENAS, P. ———— —1924–27—**c,** of, Cuban Stars (ECL), Cuban
Stars (NNL)
CARRERA, (SUNGO)—1940–41—2b, of, Cuban Stars
CAREY, ———— —1921—3b, Dayton Marcos
CARLISLE, MATTHEW—1931–46—**2b,** ss, Birmingham Black Barons,
Montgomery Grey Sox, Memphis Red Sox, **Homestead Grays**
CARMICHAEL, LUTHER—1948—sec, NSL
CARPENTER, CLAY—1926—p, Baltimore Black Sox
CARR, GEORGE (TANK)—1912–1934—**1b,** 3b, of, c, **Los Angeles
White Sox,** Kansas City Monarchs, Hilldale, **Bacharach Giants**
CARR, WAYNE—1921–28—p, St. Louis Giants, Indianapolis ABCs,

Baltimore Black Sox, Washington Potomacs, Bacharach Giants, Wilmington Potomacs, Newark Stars, Brooklyn Royal Giants, Lincoln Giants

CARROLL, HAL—1887—player, Cincinnati Browns

CARRY, ——— —1917—2b, St. Louis Giants

CARSWELL, FRANK—1944–46—p, Cleveland Buckeyes

CARTER, ——— —1918—2b, Chicago Giants

CARTER, ——— —1920—c, Detroit Stars

CARTER, ——— —1932—c, Birmingham Black Barons

CARTER, ——— —1943—3b, Harrisburg–St. Louis Stars

CARTER, DR. A. B.—1933—vice-pres, NSL

CARTER, BILL—1948—p, Newark Eagles

CARTER, (BO)—1931—president, Chattanooga Black Lookouts

CARTER, CHARLES (KID)—1902–06—p, **Philadelphia Giants,** Wilmington Giants, Brooklyn Royal Giants

CARTER, CLIFFORD—1923–34—p, Baltimore Black Sox, Bacharach Giants, Harrisburg Giants, Philadelphia Tigers, Hilldale, Philadelphia Stars

CARTER, ERNEST (SPOON)—1932–49—p, Pittsburgh Crawfords, Memphis Red Sox, Cleveland Red Sox, Toledo Crawfords, Indianapolis Crawfords, Newark Eagles, Philadelphia Stars, Homestead Grays, Birmingham Black Barons

CARTER, IKE—1884—2b, St. Louis Black Stockings

CARTER, JIMMY—1938–39—p, Philadelphia Stars

CARTER, KENNETH—1950—c, Cleveland Buckeyes

CARTER, MARLIN (MEL)—1937–48—**3b,** 2b, Cincinnati Tigers, Atlanta Black Crackers, **Memphis Red Sox,** Chicago American Giants

CARTER, PAUL—1929–36—p, Hilldale, Darby Daisies, Philadelphia Stars, New York Black Yankees

CARTER, ROBERT—1947—p, Homestead Grays

CASEY, WILLIAM (MICKEY)—1931–43—**c,** mgr, Baltimore Black Sox, Bacharach Giants, **Philadelphia Stars,** Washington Black Senators, New York Cubans, Cuban Stars, Baltimore Grays, New York Black Yankees

CASH, WILLIAM (BILL, READY)—1943–50—**c,** of, 3b, Philadelphia Stars

CASON, JOHN—1918–32—**c,** of, 2b, ss, **Brooklyn Royal Giants,** Norfolk Stars, Hilldale, Lincoln Giants, Bacharach Giants, Baltimore Black Sox

CASTILLO, ——— —1911–12—1b, All Cubans, Cuban Stars

CASTRO, ——— —1929—c, Cuban Stars (East)

CATES, JOE—1931–34—ss, Louisville White Sox, Louisville Red Caps

CATHEY, WILLIS (JIM)—1948–50—p, Indianapolis Clowns

CATO, HARRY—1893–96—2b, p, of, Cuban X Giants, Cuban Giants

CAULFIELD, FRED—1926—mgr, New Orleans Ads

CELADA, ——— —1928—ss, Cuban Stars (NNL)

CEPHAS, ——— —1938—ss, Birmingham Black Barons

CEPHUS, GOLDIE—1926–31—of, Philadelphia Giants, Bacharach Giants

CHACON, PELAYO—1910–30—ss, mgr, Stars of Cuba, Cuban Stars, Havana Stars, **Cuban Stars (ECL)**

CHAMBERS, (RUBE)—1925–27—p, Lincoln Giants

CHAPMAN, ——— —1931—p, Chicago Columbia Giants

CHAPMAN, J. W.—1887—player, Cincinnati Browns

CHAPMAN, JOHN—1887—player, Cincinnati Browns

CHARLESTON, ——— —1942—c, Cincinnati Buckeyes

CHARLESTON, BENNY—1930—of, Homestead Grays

CHARLESTON, OSCAR—1915–50—**of, 1b,** mgr, **Indianapolis ABCs,** Lincoln Stars, **Chicago American Giants,** St. Louis Giants, **Harrisburg Giants,** Hilldale, Homestead Grays, **Pittsburgh Crawfords,** Toledo Crawfords, Indianapolis Crawfords, Philadelphia Stars, Brooklyn Brown Dodgers

CHARLESTON, PORTER—1927–35—p, Hilldale, Darby Daisies, Philadelphia Stars

CHARLESTON, (RED)—1929–32—c, Nashville Elite Giants

CHARTER, W. M. (BILL)—1943–46—1b, c, Chicago American Giants

CHARTER, WILLIAM—1934—of, Louisville Red Caps

CHASE, ——— —1923—of, Toledo Tigers

CHATMAN, EDGAR—1944–45—p, Memphis Red Sox

CHAVOUS, ——— —1896—p, Page Fence Giants

CHEATHAM, ——— —1934—p, Pittsburgh Crawfords, Homestead Grays

CHERRY, HUGH—1949—officer, Houston Eagles

CHESTNUT, JOE—1950—p, Indianapolis Clowns, Philadelphia Stars

CHILDS, ANDY—1937–45—2b, p, Indianapolis Athletics, Memphis Red Sox

CHIRBAN, LOUIS—1950—p, Chicago American Giants

CHISM, ELI—1947—player, Birmingham Black Barons

CHRETIAN, ERNEST—1950—of, inf, Kansas City Monarchs

CHRISTOPHER, THADDEUS (THAD)—1936–45—**of,** 1b, Newark Eagles, Pittsburgh Crawfords, New York Black Yankees, Cincinnati Buckeyes, Cincinnati Clowns, Cleveland Buckeyes

CISCO, J. ——— —1884—player, Philadelphia Mutual B.B.C.

CLARK, ——— —1919–23—p, Cleveland Tate Stars, Pittsburgh Keystones, Indianapolis ABCs

CLARK, ——— —1923—p, Brooklyn Royal Giants

CLARK, ——— —1923–24—1b, p, Washington Potomacs

CLARK, ——— —1931—p, Kansas City Monarchs

CLARK, ALBERT—1920—player, Dayton Marcos

CLARK, CLEVELAND—1945–50—of, New York Cubans

CLARK, DELL—1914–23—ss, Brooklyn Royal Giants, Indianapolis ABCs, Lincoln Giants, Washington Potomacs

CLARK, (EGGIE)—1928—of, Memphis Red Sox

CLARK, JOHN L.—1932–46—bus. mgr, Pittsburgh Crawfords; public relations man, Homestead Grays; sec, NNL

CLARK, MILTON J., JR.—1937—sec, Chicago American Giants

CLARK, MORTEN—1915–23—ss, **Indianapolis ABCs,** Baltimore Black Sox

CLARK, ROY—1934–35—p, Newark Dodgers

CLARKE, ———— —1938—2b, Washington Black Senators

CLARKE, ROBERT—1922–48—c, mgr, Richmond Giants, **Baltimore Black Sox, New York Black Yankees,** Philadelphia Stars, **Baltimore Elite Giants**

CLARKE, VIBERT—1946–50—p, **Cleveland Buckeyes,** Louisville Buckeyes, Memphis Red Sox

CLARKSON, ———— —1915—c, Chicago Giants

CLARKSON, JAMES (BUS)—1937–50—ss, of, 2b, Pittsburgh Crawfords, Toledo Crawfords, Indianapolis Crawfords, Newark Eagles, **Philadelphia Stars,** Baltimore Elite Giants

CLAY, ———— —1932—p, Kansas City Monarchs

CLAYTON, LEROY—1943—c, Chicago Brown Bombers

CLAYTON, ZACK—1934–44—1b, Bacharach Giants, Cole's American Giants, Chicago American Giants, New York Black Yankees

CLAXTON, JAMES E.—1932—p, Cuban Stars

CLEAGE, PETE—1936—umpire, NNL

CLEAGE, RALPH—1924—of, St. Louis Stars

CLEVELAND, HOWARD (DUKE)—1938–43—of, Jacksonville Red Caps, Cleveland Bears, Cleveland Buckeyes

CLIFFORD, LUTHER—1949–50—c, of, Homestead Grays

COBB, L. S. N.—1920–34—officer, St. Louis Giants, Birmingham Black Barons, Memphis Red Sox; sec, NSL

COBB, W.—— —1915–20—c, **St. Louis Giants,** Lincoln Giants

COCKRELL, PHILIP (PHIL)—1913–46—p, Havana Red Sox, Lincoln Giants, **Hilldale,** Darby Daisies, Bacharach Giants, Philadelphia Stars; umpire, NNL

COFFIE, CLIFFORD—1950—of, Cleveland Buckeyes

COHEN, JIM—1948–50—p, Indianapolis Clowns

COIMBRE, AL—1940–44—of, Cuban Stars

COLAS, ———— —1941—c, Cuban Stars

COLAS, JOSE—1947–50—of, mgr, Memphis Red Sox

COLE, ———— —1923—p, Toledo Tigers

COLE, CECIL—1946—p, Newark Eagles

COLE, RALPH (PUNJAB)—1939–43—of, Jacksonville Red Caps, Cleveland Bears, Cincinnati Clowns

COLE, ROBERT A.—1932–35—officer, Chicago American Giants; tres, NNL; vice-pres, NSL

COLE, WILLIAM—1896—c, Cuban Giants

COLEMAN ———— —1919—2b, St. Louis Giants

COLEMAN, ———— —1921—of, 1b, Columbus Buckeyes, Dayton Marcos

COLEMAN, ———— —1926—p, Lincoln Giants

COLEMAN, ———— —1937—ss, Birmingham Black Barons

COLEMAN, CLARENCE—1913–19—p, c, Chicago Giants, Chicago Union Giants, Indianapolis ABCs, Cleveland Tate Stars
COLEMAN, GILBERT—1928—inf, Brooklyn Cuban Giants
COLEMAN, JOHN—1885—of, Brooklyn Remsens
COLEMAN, JOHN—1950—p, Baltimore Elite Giants
COLLIER, ———— —1928—c, Bacharach Giants
COLLINS, ———— —1910–18—c, New York Black Sox, Brooklyn Royal Giants, Pennsylvania Red Caps of New York, Lincoln Giants
COLLINS, ———— —1923—p, Toledo Tigers
COLLINS, ———— —1925—ss, Indianapolis ABCs
COLLINS, ———— —1928—p, Baltimore Black Sox
COLLINS, EUGENE (GENE)—1947–50—p, of, Kansas City Monarchs
COLLINS, GEORGE—1922–33—of, 2b, New Orleans Crescent Stars, Milwaukee Bears
COLLINS, NAT—1888—player, New York Gorhams
COLLINS, WALTER—1947—p, Chicago American Giants
COLZIE, JIM—1946–47—p, Cincinnati–Indianapolis Clowns, Indianapolis Clowns
COMBS, A. (JACK)—1922–25—p, Detroit Stars
CONDON, LAFAYETTE—1887—player, Louisville Falls Citys
CONNORS, JOHN W.—1905–1922—officer, Brooklyn Royal Giants, Bacharach Giants
COOK, ———— —1937—p, Indianapolis Athletics
COOK, WALTER—1886–87—officer, Cuban Giants
COOKE, JAMES—1932–33—p, Baltimore Black Sox, Bacharach Giants
COOLEY, ———— —1931—c, Birmingham Black Barons
COOPER, ———— —1946—p, New York Black Yankees
COOPER, A.—1941—ss, of, 2b, New York Black Yankees
COOPER, ALEX—1928—of, Philadelphia Tigers, Harrisburg Giants
COOPER, ALFRED (ARMY)—1928–32—Kansas City Monarchs, Cleveland Stars
COOPER, ANDY (LEFTY)—1920–41—p, mgr, **Detroit Stars,** Chicago American Giants, St. Louis Stars, **Kansas City Monarchs**
COOPER, ANTHONY—1929–34—ss, Birmingham Black Barons, Cleveland Stars, Baltimore Black Sox, Cleveland Red Sox
COOPER, C. ———— —1884—player, Philadelphia Mutual B.B.C.
COOPER, (CHIEF)—1928—umpire, NNL
COOPER, DALTIE—1921–40—p, Nashville Elite Giants, Indianapolis ABCs, Harrisburg Giants, Lincoln Giants, Hilldale, Bacharach Giants, Homestead Grays, Baltimore Black Sox, Newark Eagles
COOPER, E. ———— —1921—1b, Cleveland Tate Stars
COOPER, THOMAS (TOM)—1948–50—c, of, 1b, Kansas City Monarchs
COOPER, W. (BILL)—1938–42—c, Atlanta Black Crackers, Philadelphia Stars
CORBETT, CHARLES—1922–28—p, Pittsburgh Keystones, Indianapolis ABCs, **Harrisburg Giants**
CORCORAN, TOM—1942—p, Homestead Grays

CORDOVA, ———— —1921–23—3b, ss, Kansas City Monarchs, Cleveland Tate Stars

CORNELIUS, WILLIE—1929–46—p, Nashville Elite Giants, Memphis Red Sox, **Chicago American Giants,** Cole's American Giants

CORNETT, HARRY—1913—c, Indianapolis ABCs

CORREA, (CHO-CHO)—1926–35—ss, Cuban Stars (NNL), Cuban Stars (East), New York Cubans

CORTEZ, ———— —1928–30—c, Cuban Stars (NNL)

COSA, ———— —1932—of, Memphis Red Sox

COTTON, ———— —1948—p, Newark Eagles

COTTON, JAMES—1945—officer, Chattanooga Choo Choos

COWAN, EDDIE—1919—player, Cleveland Tate Stars

COWAN, JOHN—1934–50—3b, 2b, Birmingham Black Barons, Cleveland Buckeyes, Memphis Red Sox

COWANS, RUSS—1942—sec, Negro Baseball League of America

COX, ———— —1943—p, Memphis Red Sox

COX, HANNIBAL—1931—of, Nashville Elite Giants

COX, ROOSEVELT—1937–43—3b, 2b, ss, Detroit Stars, Kansas City Monarchs, New York Cubans, Cuban Stars

COZART, HARRY—1939–43—p, Newark Eagles

CRAIG, CHARLES—1926–28—p, Lincoln Giants, Brooklyn Cuban Giants

CRAIG, DICK—1940—1b, Indianapolis Crawfords

CRAIG, JOHN—1935–46—umpire, NNL

CRAIN, A. C.—1887—player, Baltimore Lord Baltimores

CRAWFORD, JOHN—1943—umpire, NNL

CRAWFORD, SAM—1910–37—p, mgr, coach, New York Black Sox, Chicago Giants, Chicago American Giants, Chicago Union Giants, Detroit Stars, Kansas City Monarchs, Brooklyn Royal Giants, Birmingham Black Barons, Chicago Columbia Giants, Cole's American Giants, Indianapolis Athletics

CRAWFORD, WILLIE W.—1934—of, Birmingham Black Barons

CREACY, A. D. (DEWEY)—1924–40—3b, Kansas City Monarchs, **St. Louis Stars,** Detroit Wolves, Washington Pilots, Columbus Blue Birds, Cleveland Giants, Philadelphia Stars, Brooklyn Royal Giants

CREEK, WILLIE—1930—c, Brooklyn Royal Giants

CRESPO, ALEX (HOME RUN)—1940–46—of, Cuban Stars, New York Cubans

CRESPO, ALEJANDRO—1918–33—**2b,** 3b, **Cuban Stars (East),** Cuban Stars of Havana

CROCKETT, ———— —1916–23—of, Bacharach Giants

CROMATIE, LEROY—1945—player, Cincinnati–Indianapolis Clowns

CROSS, NORMAN—1932—p, Cole's American Giants

CROWE, GEORGE—1948–49—inf, New York Cubans

CROXTON, ———— —1909—p, Cuban Giants

CRUE, MARTIN (MATTY)—1942–47—p, New York Cubans

CRUMBIE, RALPH—1946—c, Pittsburgh Crawfords

CRUMBLEY, ALEX—1938—of, New York Black Yankees

CRUMP, JAMES—1921–38—2b, Norfolk Giants, Hilldale, Philadelphia Giants; umpire, NNL

CRUMP, WILLIS—1916–23—of, 2b, Bacharach Giants

CRUTCHFIELD, JOHN W. (JIMMIE)—1930–45—of, Birmingham Black Barons, Indianapolis ABCs, **Pittsburgh Crawfords,** Newark Eagles, Toledo Crawfords, Indianapolis Crawfords, Chicago American Giants, Cleveland Buckeyes

CUERIRA, ———— —1921–22—p, All Cubans, Cuban Stars (NNL)

CULCRA, ———— —1922—3b, Cuban Stars (NNL)

CUMMING, HUGH S.—1887—player, Baltimore Lord Baltimores

CUMMINGS, ———— —1932—c, Louisville Black Caps

CUMMINGS, NAPOLEON (CHANCE)—1916–29—**1b,** 2b, **Bacharach Giants,** Hilldale

CUNNINGHAM, ———— —1917–20—ss, St. Louis Giants, Dayton Marcos

CUNNINGHAM, ———— —1934—of, Baltimore Black Sox

CUNNINGHAM, HARRY (BABY)—1930–37—p, Memphis Red Sox

CUNNINGHAM, MARION (DADDY)—1924–26—1b, mgr, Memphis Red Sox, Montgomery Grey Sox

CUNNINGHAM, (ROUNDER)—1918–31—ss, Montgomery Grey Sox

CURRIE, REUBEN (RUBE)—1919–32—p, Chicago Unions, Kansas City Monarchs, Hilldale, Chicago American Giants, Detroit Stars

CURRY, HOMER (GOOSE)—1930–50—**of,** p, mgr, **Memphis Red Sox,** Washington Elite Giants, New York Black Yankees, Newark Eagles, Baltimore Elite Giants, **Philadelphia Stars**

CURTIS, ———— —1923—p, Harrisburg Giants

CURTIS, ———— —1932—c, Louisville Black Caps

CURTIS, HARRY—1898—mgr, Celeron Acme Colored Giants (Iron and Oil League)

CYRUS, HERB—1940–43—3b, Kansas City Monarchs

DABNEY, MILTON—1885–96—of, p, Argyle Hotel, Cuban X Giants

DALLARD, WILLIAM (EGGIE)—1925–33—**1b, of,** c, 2b, Wilmington Potomacs, Baltimore Black Sox, Bacharach Giants, Hilldale, Quaker Giants, Darby Daisies, Philadelphia Stars

DALLAS, (BIG BOY)—1929–32—3b, Birmingham Black Barons, Monroe Monarchs

DALTON, ROSSIE—1940—utility, Chicago American Giants

DANDRIDGE, JOHN—1949—p, Houston Eagles

DANDRIDGE, (PING)—1919–20—ss, Lincoln Giants, St. Louis Giants

DANDRIDGE, RAYMOND (HOOKS)—1933–49—**3b,** 2b, ss, Detroit Stars, Newark Dodgers, **Newark Eagles,** New York Cubans

DANDRIDGE, TROY—1929—3b, Chicago Giants

DANDY, ———— —1917—p, Lincoln Giants

DANIELS, EDDIE—1947—p, New York Cubans

DANIELS, FRED—1919–27—p, St. Louis Giants, Hilldale, Birmingham Black Barons

DANIELS, HAMMOND—1924–26—officer, Bacharach Giants

DANIELS, LEON (PEPPER)—1921–35—**c,** 1b, **Detroit Stars,** Harrisburg Giants, Cuban Stars, Brooklyn Eagles

DANIELS, (SCHOOLBOY)—1943—p, Birmingham Black Barons

DARDEN, FLOYD—1950—2b, Baltimore Elite Giants

DAVENPORT, LLOYD (BEAR MAN)—1934–49—of, mgr, Monroe Monarchs, Philadelphia Stars, Cincinnati Tigers, Memphis Red Sox, Birmingham Black Barons, Chicago American Giants, Cleveland Buckeyes, Pittsburgh Crawfords, Louisville Buckeyes

DAVIDSON, CHARLES—1939–40—p, New York Black Yankees, Brooklyn Royal Giants

DAVIS ———— —1922–23—3b, Bacharach Giants

DAVIS, A. ——— —1887–91—player, mgr, Boston Resolutes, New York Gorhams

DAVIS, ALBERT—1928–37—p, **Detroit Stars,** Baltimore Black Sox

DAVIS, (BIG BOY)—1932—p, Indianapolis ABCs

DAVIS, DWIGHT—1930—p, Detroit Stars

DAVIS, EDWARD A. (EDDIE, PEANUTS)—1942–50—p, Cincinnati Clowns, Cincinnati–Indianapolis Clowns, Indianapolis Clowns

DAVIS, HY—1934—1b, Hilldale, Newark Dodgers

DAVIS, JAMES—1920—p, Chicago Giants

DAVIS, JOHN—1943–50—of, Newark Eagles, Houston Eagles

DAVIS, JOHN—1905–10—p, Leland Giants, Cuban Giants, Philadelphia Giants

DAVIS, LEE—1945—p, Kansas City Monarchs

DAVIS, LORENZO (PIPER)—1943–50—**1b, 2b,** ss, mgr, Birmingham Black Barons

DAVIS, NATHANIEL—1947–50—1b, New York Black Yankees, Philadelphia Stars

DAVIS, (QUACK)—1913—player, Indianapolis ABCs

DAVIS, (RED)—1925—of, Indianapolis ABCs

DAVIS, ROBERT (BUTCH)—1947–50—of, Baltimore Elite Giants

DAVIS, ROOSEVELT—1924–45—p, **St. Louis Stars,** Columbus Blue Birds, Pittsburgh Crawfords, New York Black Yankees, Philadelphia Stars, Memphis Red Sox, Brooklyn Royal Giants, Baltimore Elite Giants, Chicago Brown Bombers, Cincinnati Clowns, Cincinnati–Indianapolis Clowns, Cleveland Buckeyes

DAVIS, ROSS—1947—p, Cleveland Buckeyes

DAVIS, S.—1938–39—of, 3b, Atlanta Black Crackers, Indianapolis ABCs

DAVIS, SAUL—1925–31—3b, 2b, ss, Birmingham Black Barons, Cleveland Tigers, Memphis Red Sox, Chicago American Giants, Detroit Stars

DAVIS, SPENCER (BABE)—1941–48—ss, mgr, New York Black Yankees, Winston-Salem Giants

DAVIS, W. ——— —1939—of, Indianapolis ABCs

DAVIS, WALTER (STEEL ARM)—1923–34—of, 1b, p, Detroit Stars, **Chicago American Giants,** Chicago Columbia Giants, Cole's American Giants, Nashville Elite Giants

DAVIS, WILLIAM—1937—3b, of, St. Louis Stars

DAVIS, WILLIE—1945—officer, Mobile Black Shippers

DAWSON, JOHNNY—1940–42—c, Memphis Red Sox, Kansas City Monarchs

DAY, EDDIE—1898—ss, Celeron Acme Colored Giants (Iron and Oil League)

DAY, GUY—1885—c, Argyle Hotel

DAY, LEON—1934–50—p, Bacharach Giants, Brooklyn Eagles, **Newark Eagles,** Baltimore Elite Giants

DAY, WILSON C. (CONNIE)—1920–32—**2b,** 3b, ss, Indianapolis ABCs, Baltimore Black Sox, Harrisburg Giants, Bacharach Giants

DEAN, ———— —1925–30—3b, 2b, Lincoln Giants, Pennsylvania Red Caps of New York

DEAN, BOB—1939–40—p, St. Louis Stars

DEAN, CHARLIE—1947—p, New York Black Yankees

DEAN, NELSON—1925–32—p, Kansas City Monarchs, Cleveland Hornets, Cleveland Tigers, Detroit Stars, Cleveland Stars

DEANE, ALPHEUS—1947—p, New York Black Yankees

DEAS, JAMES (YANK)—1916–23—c, **Bacharach Giants,** Pennsylvania Giants, Lincoln Giants, Hilldale

DEBERRY, C. I.—1948—mgr, Greensboro Red Wings; vice-pres, Negro American Association

DEBRAN, ROY—1940—of, New York Black Yankees

DECUIR, LIONEL—1939–40—c, Kansas City Monarchs

DELGARDO, ———— —1941—of, 1b, Cuban Stars

DeLUGO, ———— —1935—p, New York Cubans

DeMOSS, ELWOOD (BINGO)—1905–43—**2b,** ss, **mgr,** Topeka Giants, Kansas City, Kansas, Giants, Oklahoma Giants, Indianapolis ABCs, **Chicago American Giants,** Detroit Stars, Cleveland Giants, Chicago Brown Bombers

DENNIS, WESLEY—1944–48—1b, of, Baltimore Elite Giants, Philadelphia Stars

DESPERT, ———— —1915–16—of, Lincoln Giants, Brooklyn Royal Giants

DEVOE, ———— —1918—c, Chicago Giants

DEVOE, J. R.—1922—bus. mgr, Cleveland Tate Stars

DeWITT, ———— —1917–27—3b, Dayton Giants, Dayton Marcos, Indianapolis ABCs, Columbus Buckeyes, Toledo Tigers, Kansas City Monarchs, Cleveland Tigers

DIAL, KERMIT—1933—2b, Columbus Blue Birds

DIALS, ALONZO—1931—1b, Detroit Stars

DIALS, ODEM—1927–36—of, Chicago American Giants, Memphis Red Sox, Hilldale, Cleveland Giants

DIAMOND, (BLACK)—1929—p, Birmingham Black Barons

DIAZ, E. (YOYO)—1926–35—p, Cuban Stars (NNL), New York Cubans

DIAZ, FERNANDO—1950—of, New York Cubans

DIAZ, PABLO—1930–32—c, 1b, Cuban Stars (NNL), Cuban Stars (East)

DIAZ, PEDRO (MANNY)—1945–50—2b, ss, New York Cubans

DICKERSON, ———— —1950—p, Homestead Grays

DICKERSON, LOU—1921—p, Hilldale

DICKEY, (STEEL ARM)—1921—p, Montgomery Grey Sox

DIHIGO, MARTIN—1923–1945—**2b, p, of, ss, 3b, 1b, c,** mgr, **Cuban Stars (East), New York Cubans,** Homestead Grays, Hilldale, Darby Daisies

DILWORTH, ARTHUR—1916–18—p, of, c, Bacharach Giants, Hilldale, Lincoln Giants

DIREAUX, JIMMY—1937–39—p, Washington Elite Giants, Baltimore Elite Giants

DISMUKES, WILLIAM (DIZZY)—1913–50—**p, mgr,** NNL sec, club sec, Philadelphia Giants, Brooklyn Royal Giants, Mohawk Giants, **Indianapolis ABCs,** Chicago American Giants, Dayton Marcos, Pittsburgh Keystones, Memphis Red Sox, St. Louis Stars, Cincinnati Dismukes, Detroit Wolves, Homestead Grays, Columbus Blue Birds, Birmingham Black Barons, Kansas City Monarchs

DIXON, ———— —1915–16—p, Chicago Giants, Chicago American Giants

DIXON, ED—1938–39—p, Atlanta Black Crackers, Indianapolis ABCs, Baltimore Elite Giants

DIXON, GEORGE—1917–28—c, **Chicago American Giants,** Indianapolis ABCs, Birmingham Black Barons, Cleveland Hornets, Cleveland Tigers

DIXON, HERBERT (RAP)—1922–37—of, **Harrisburg Giants,** Baltimore Black Sox, Chicago American Giants, Darby Daisies, Pittsburgh Crawfords, Philadelphia Stars, Brooklyn Eagles, Homestead Grays

DIXON, JOHN—1928–34—**p,** ss, Cleveland Tigers, Detroit Stars, Cuban Stars, Cleveland Giants, Cleveland Red Sox

DIXON, P.—1934—of, Baltimore Black Sox

DIXON, T. ———— —1934—c, Baltimore Black Sox

DOBBINS, ———— —1921—p, ss, Hilldale

DOBY, LAWRENCE EUGENE (LARRY)—1943–47—2b, Newark Eagles

DOMINGUEZ, ———— —1925—p, Cuban Stars (NNL)

DONALDSON, JOHN—1916–32—**p,** of, All Nations, Los Angeles White Sox, Chicago Giants, Indianapolis ABCs, **Kansas City Monarchs,** Detroit Stars, Brooklyn Royal Giants, Donaldson All-Stars

DONALDSON, W. W. (BILLY)—1923–37—umpire, NNL

DONOSO, LINO—1947–49—p, New York Cubans

DORSEY, F. T.—1884–85—inf, Baltimore Atlantics

DOUGHERTY, CHARLES (PAT)—1909–15—p, Leland Giants, Chicago American Giants, Chicago Giants

DOUGLAS, GEORGE—1885—of, Brooklyn Remsens

DOUGLAS, JESSE—1937–50—inf, of, Kansas City Monarchs, Birmingham Black Barons, **Chicago American Giants,** Memphis Red Sox

DOUGLASS, EDWARD (EDDIE)—1918–29—1b, mgr, **Brooklyn Royal Giants,** Lincoln Giants

DOWNS, ELLSWORTH—1887—player, Cincinnati Browns
DOWNS, McKINLEY (BUNNY)—1916–43—**2b,** ss, 3b, mgr, St. Louis Giants, Bacharach Giants, Hilldale, Brooklyn Royal Giants, Brooklyn Cuban Giants, Philadelphia Tigers, Cincinnati Clowns
DRAKE, ANDREW—1932—c, Birmingham Black Barons
DRAKE, VERDES—1945–50—of, Cincinnati–Indianapolis Clowns, Indianapolis Clowns
DRAKE, WILLIAM (PLUNK)—1916–27—p, St. Louis Giants, St. Louis Stars, Kansas City Monarchs, Indianapolis ABCs, Detroit Stars
DREKE, VALENTIN—1919–28—of, Cuban Stars of Havana, **Cuban Stars (NNL)**
DREW, JOHN M.—1931–32—officer, Darby Daisies, Hilldale
DRUMMER, ———— —1948—p, Newark Eagles
DUANY, CLARO—1944–47—of, New York Cubans
DUBISSON, D. J.—1932—officer, Little Rock Grays
DUCEY, ———— —1924–26—inf, of, St. Louis Giants, Dayton Marcos
DUCKETT, MAHLON—1940–48—3b, 2b, ss, Philadelphia Stars
DUCY, EDDIE—1947—2b, Homestead Grays
DUDLEY, C. A.—1920–22—of, St. Louis Giants, St. Louis Stars
DUDLEY, EDWARD—1926–28—p, Lincoln Giants, Brooklyn Royal Giants
DUFF, E.—1925–32—of, Indianapolis ABCs, Cleveland Elites, Cleveland Hornets, Cleveland Tigers, Cuban Stars
DUKES, ———— —1939–41—of, Cleveland Bears, Jacksonville Red Caps
DUKES, TOMMY—1928–45—**c,** 3b, Chicago American Giants, Memphis Red Sox, Nashville Elite Giants, Columbus Elite Giants, Homestead Grays, Toledo Crawfords, Indianapolis Crawfords
DULA, LOUIS—1934–37—p, Homestead Grays
DUMAS, JIM—1940–41—p, Memphis Red Sox
DUMPSON, BILL—1950—p, Indianapolis Clowns, Philadelphia Stars
DUNBAR, ASHBY—1909–19—of, Brooklyn Royal Giants, Lincoln Stars, Indianapolis ABCs, Pennsylvania Red Caps of New York, Lincoln Giants
DUNBAR, (VET)—1937—inf, c, Memphis Red Sox, Indianapolis Athletics
DUNCAN, CHARLIE—1938–40—p, Atlanta Black Crackers, Indianapolis ABCs, St. Louis Stars
DUNCAN, FRANK—1909–28—of, mgr, Philadelphia Giants, Leland Giants, **Chicago American Giants,** Detroit Stars, Chicago Giants, Toledo Tigers, Cleveland Elites, Cleveland Hornets, Cleveland Tigers
DUNCAN, FRANK—1920–48—**c,** of, mgr, Chicago Giants, **Kansas City Monarchs,** New York Black Yankees, Pittsburgh Crawfords, Homestead Grays, New York Cubans, Chicago American Giants
DUNCAN, FRANK, JR.—1945—p, Baltimore Elite Giants
DUNCAN, MELVIN—1949–50—p, Kansas City Monarchs
DUNCAN, WARREN—1922–1927—c, of, Bacharach Giants
DUNLAP, HERMAN—1937–39—of, Chicago American Giants

DUNN, ———— —1942—p, Jacksonville Red Caps
DUNN, ALPHONSE (BLUE)—1937–43—1b, of, Detroit Stars, New York Cubans, Birmingham Black Barons
DUNN, JAKE—1930–41—ss, of, 2b, mgr, Detroit Stars, Washington Pilots, Nashville Elite Giants, Baltimore Black Sox, **Philadelphia Stars**
DURANT, ———— —1932—of, Washington Pilots
DURVANT, ———— —1923—p, Cuban Stars (NNL)
DWIGHT, EDDIE—1925–37—of, Indianapolis ABCs, **Kansas City Monarchs**
DYKES, JOHN—1932—officer, Washington Pilots
DYLL, FRANK—1950—ss, Chicago American Giants

EARLE, ———— —1906–19—**of,** p, Wilmington Giants, Cuban Giants, Philadelphia Giants, **Brooklyn Royal Giants,** Lincoln Giants, Bacharach Giants
EASTER, LUSCIOUS LUKE (LUKE)—1946–48—of, 1b, Cincinnati Crescents, Homestead Grays
EASTERLING, HOWARD—1936–49—**3b,** ss, 2b, Cincinnati Tigers, Chicago American Giants, **Homestead Grays,** New York Cubans
EATON, ———— —1937–38—p, Birmingham Black Barons
EDSALL, GEORGE—1898—of, Celeron Acme Colored Giants (Iron and Oil League)
EDWARDS, ———— —1916–17—p, of, Lincoln Stars, Pennsylvania Red Caps of New York
EDWARDS, ———— —1919—c, Bacharach Giants
EDWARDS, ———— 1937—2b, c, St. Louis Stars
EDWARDS, CHANCELLOR (JACK)—1928—c, Cleveland Tigers
EDWARDS, JESSE—1929–30—2b, of, Nashville Elite Giants
EGGLESTON, MACK—1917–34—c, of, 3b, Dayton Giants, Dayton Marcos, Detroit Stars, Indianapolis ABCs, Washington Potomacs, Columbus Buckeyes, Wilmington Potomacs, Harrisburg Giants, Baltimore Black Sox, Bacharach Giants, New York Black Yankees, Washington Pilots, Homestead Grays
EGGLESTON, WILLIAM—1885—ss, Argyle Hotel
EKELSON, ———— —1925—p, Cuban Stars (NNL)
ELLIS, ———— —1921—1b, Dayton Marcos, Nashville Elite Giants
ELLIS, ———— —1925—3b, Cleveland Browns
ELLIS, ALBERT—1950—p, Cleveland Buckeyes
ELLIS, (ROCKY)—1934–42—p, Hilldale, Philadelphia Stars, Homestead Grays, Jacksonville Red Caps, Baltimore Grays
ELSE, HARRY—1932–38—c, Monroe Monarchs, Kansas City Monarchs
EMBRY, WILLIAM—1923—umpire, NNL
EMERY, JACK—1909–16—p, of, Philadelphia Giants, Smart Set, Pittsburgh Colored Stars
ENGLISH, ———— —1931–34—**c,** of, Louisville White Sox, Louisville Black Caps, Louisville Red Caps
ENGLISH, H. D.—1932—officer, Monroe Monarchs

ERYE, JOHN—1887—player, New York Gorhams
ESPENOSIA, ———— —1947—p, Indianapolis Clowns
ESTENZA, ———— —1927–28—p, of, Cuban Stars (NNL)
ESTRADA, OSCAR—1924–25—p, of, Cuban Stars (ECL)
ETCHEGOYEN, ———— —1930–32—of, 3b, Cuban Stars (East)
EVANS, ———— —1926–27—of, Dayton Marcos, Cleveland Hornets
EVANS, ———— —1934—ss, of, 3b, Cincinnati Tigers
EVANS, BILL (HAPPY)—1930–34—of, ss, Brooklyn Royal Giants,
Homestead Grays, Washington Pilots, Detroit Wolves
EVANS, (COWBOY)—1943—p, Cincinnati Clowns
EVANS, FELIX (CHIN)—1937–49—p, of, Atlanta Black Crackers, In-
dianapolis ABCs, **Memphis Red Sox,** Birmingham Black Barons
EVANS, FRANK—1950—of, Cleveland Buckeyes
EVANS, GEORGE—1887—player, New York Gorhams
EVANS, JOHN—1887—player, New York Gorhams
EVANS, ROBERT (BOB)—1934–43—p, Newark Dodgers, Newark
Eagles, Jacksonville Red Caps, New York Black Yankees
EVANS, ULYSSES—1943—p, Cincinnati Clowns, Chicago Brown
Bombers
EVANS, W. P.—1924—of, Chicago American Giants
EVANS, WILLIAM—1903—player, Philadelphia Giants
EVANS, WILLIAM—1925—p, Lincoln Giants
EVERETT, ———— —1927—ss, Kansas City Monarchs
EVERETT, CURTIS—1950—c, Kansas City Monarchs
EVERETT, DEAN—1929—p, Lincoln Giants
EVERETT, JIMMY—1931–43—p, of, Pennsylvania Red Caps of New
York, Cincinnati Clowns
EWELL, ———— —1926–34—c, Indianapolis ABCs, Cincinnati Tigers
EWING, ———— —1920–25—c, Chicago American Giants, Columbus
Buckeyes, Indianapolis ABCs
EWING, (BUCK)—1929–30—c, Homestead Grays
EYERS, HENRY—1887—player, Pittsburgh Keystones

FABELO, ———— —1916–23—inf, of, Cuban Stars (East), Havana
Stars
FABRE, ISIDRO—1918–39—p, of, **Cuban Stars (ECL),** Cuban Stars
(NNL)
FAGAN, ———— —1921–23—2b, Kansas City Monarchs, St. Louis Stars
FAGAN, ———— —1942–43—inf, Memphis Red Sox, Jacksonville Red
Caps, Philadelphia Stars
FALLINGS, JOHN—1947—p, New York Black Yankees
FARMER, GREENE—1942–47—of, Cincinnati Clowns, New York Cu-
bans, New York Black Yankees
FARRELL, ———— —1937—p, Birmingham Black Barons
FARRELL, LUTHER—1926–34—p, **Bacharach Giants,** Lincoln Giants,
New York Black Yankees
FELDER, JAMES—1948—ss, Indianapolis Clowns

FELDER, KENDALL—1944–45—player, Memphis Red Sox, Chicago American Giants, Birmingham Black Barons
FELDER, WILLIAM (BENNY)—1946–47—ss, Newark Eagles
FELLOWS, ———— —1937—p, c, Birmingham Black Barons
FERNANDEZ, JOSE M.—1917–50—c, 1b, **mgr,** Havana Stars, **Cuban Stars (East), New York Cubans**
FERNANDEZ, RONALDO—1950—of, New York Cubans
FERNANDEZ, RUDOLFO—1935–39—p, New York Cubans, Cuban Stars
FERNANDEZ, T.—1941—p, Cuban Stars
FERRELL, LEROY—1949–50—p, Baltimore Elite Giants
FERRELL, TRUEHART—1941–43—p, of, Chicago American Giants
FERRELL, W. E.—1918—1b, Pennsylvania Giants
FERRELL, WILLIE (RED)—1940–43—p, Homestead Grays, Chicago American Giants, Cincinnati Clowns
FERRER, ———— —1925—2b, Cuban Stars (ECL)
FERRER, EFIGENIO—1948—2b, ss, Indianapolis Clowns
FIALL, GEORGE—1920–26—ss, 3b, Lincoln Giants, Harrisburg Giants, Baltimore Black Sox
FIALL, TOM—1918–25—**of,** c, **Brooklyn Royal Giants,** Lincoln Giants
FIELDS, ———— —1918–25—p, Chicago American Giants, Cleveland Browns
FIELDS, BENNY—1930–32—2b, of, Memphis Red Sox, Cleveland Cubs
FIELDS, WILBUR (RED)—1941–49—p, 3b, of, Homestead Grays
FIGAROLA, JOSE—1910–15—c, Stars of Cuba, Cuban Stars
FIGUEROA, ———— —1946—p, Baltimore Elite Giants
FILLMORE, JOE—1941–46—p, Philadelphia Stars, Baltimore Grays
FINCH, RAYFORD—1950—p, Cleveland Buckeyes
FINDELL, THOMAS—1887—player, Washington Capital Citys
FINLEY, THOMAS (TOM)—1925–33—**3b,** c, Bacharach Giants, Lincoln Giants, Brooklyn Royal Giants, Pennsylvania Red Caps of New York, Darby Daisies, New York Black Yankees, Baltimore Black Sox, Philadelphia Stars
FINNER, JOHN—1919–25—p, St. Louis Giants, St. Louis Stars, Milwaukee Bears, Birmingham Black Barons
FINNEY, ED—1948–50—3b, Baltimore Elite Giants
FISHER, ———— —1909—p, Philadelphia Giants
FISHER, ———— —1932—p, Columbus Turfs
FISHER, A. ———— —1884—player, Philadelphia Mutual B.B.C.
FISHER, F. ———— —1884—player, Philadelphia Mutual B.B.C.
FISHER, GEORGE—1922–23—of, Richmond Giants, Harrisburg Giants
FISHER, W ———— —1884—player, Philadelphia Mutual B.B.C.
FLEMING, BUDDY—1950—inf, Baltimore Elite Giants
FLOOD, JESS—1919—c, Cleveland Tate Stars
FLOURNOY, FRED—1928—c, Brooklyn Cuban Giants
FLOURNOY, (PUD)—1919–33—p, Hilldale, Brooklyn Royal Giants, Baltimore Black Sox, Bacharach Giants

FLOWERS, JAKE—1941–42—inf, New York Black Yankees
FLOYD, ———— —1937—p, Indianapolis Athletics
FLOYD, J. J.—1932—officer, Little Rock Greys
FOOTS, ROBERT—1899–1909—c, Chicago Unions, Philadelphia Giants, Brooklyn Royal Giants
FORBES, FRANK—1929–43—umpire; bus mgr, New York Cubans; NNL promoter
FORBES, JOE—1915–19—ss, 3b, Lincoln Giants, Pennsylvania Red Caps of New York, Bacharach Giants
FORCE, WILLIAM—1921–29—p, Detroit Stars, **Baltimore Black Sox**
FORD, ———— —1921–23—2b, Baltimore Black Sox, Harrisburg Giants
FORD, (BUBBER)—1947—officer, Jacksonville Eagles
FORD, C. ———— —1918—p, Pennsylvania Giants
FORD, CARL—1947—officer, Shreveport Tigers
FORD, F. ———— —1918—c, Pennsylvania Giants
FORD, JAMES (JIMMY)—1931–45—**3b,** 2b, **Memphis Red Sox,** St. Louis Stars, New Orleans–St. Louis Stars, New York Black Yankees, Cincinnati Clowns, Philadelphia Stars
FOREMAN, F. (HOOKS)—1921–32—c, Kansas City Monarchs, Indianapolis ABCs, Washington Pilots
FOREST, CHARLES—1920—player, St. Louis Giants
FORKINS, MARTY—1931—officer, New York Black Yankees
FORMENTHAL, PEDRO—1947–49—of, Memphis Red Sox
FORREST, ———— —1921–25—of, Lincoln Giants
FORREST, PERCY—1939–49—p, Chicago American Giants, Newark Eagles, New York Black Yankees, Indianapolis Clowns
FOSTER, ALBERT (RED)—1910—1b, Kansas City, Kansas, Giants
FOSTER, ANDREW (RUBE)—1902–26—**p, mgr,** Chicago Union Giants, Cuban X Giants, Philadelphia Giants, Leland Giants, **Chicago American Giants;** founder and pres, tres, NNL
FOSTER, JIM—1945—officer, Chicago Brown Bombers
FOSTER, LELAND—1934—p, Monroe Monarchs
FOSTER, WILLIE H. (BILL)—1923–37—p, mgr, Memphis Red Sox, **Chicago American Giants,** Homestead Grays, Kansas City Monarchs, Cole's American Giants
FOWIKES, ERWIN—1947–48—ss, Chicago American Giants, Homestead Grays
FOWIKES, SAMUEL—1950—p, Kansas City Monarchs
FOWLER, J. W. (BUD)—(real name John Jackson)—1872–1899—**2b,** p, of, 3b, c, ss, mgr, New Castle, Pa.; Stillwater (Northwestern League); Keokuk and Topeka (Western League); Binghamton (International League); Crawfordsville, Terre Haute, and Galesburg (Central Interstate League); Lafayette, Indiana; Greenville (Michigan League); Sterling and Davenport (Illinois–Iowa League); Evansville, New York Gorhams, All-American Black Tourists
FRANCIS, DEL—1917—2b, Indianapolis ABCs
FRANCIS, WILLIAM (BILLY)—1906–25—**3b,** ss, Wilmington Giants,

Cuban Giants, Philadelphia Giants, Lincoln Giants, **Chicago American Giants,** Hilldale, Bacharach Giants, Cleveland Browns, Chicago Giants

FRAZIER, O. —— —1932–40—2b, 3b, Montgomery Grey Sox, Jacksonville Red Caps, Cleveland Bears

FREEMAN, BILL—1933—p, Cuban Stars

FREEMAN, CHARLIE—1927–30—officer, Hilldale

FREIHOFER, WILLIAM—1906—pres, International League of Independent Professional Base Ball Clubs

FRIELY, —— —1922—2b, Bacharach Giants

FRYE, JACK—1886–96—1b, Cuban Giants

FULCUR, ROBERT—1940—p, Chicago American Giants

FULLER, (CHICK)—1918—2b, Hilldale

FULLER, JIMMY—1917–20—c, Cuban Giants, Bacharach Giants

FULLER, W. W.—1916–19—ss, 2b, Bacharach Giants, Cuban Giants, Pennsylvania Giants, Cleveland Tate Stars

FUMES, —— —1925–30—of, Cuban Stars (NNL), Cuban Stars (East)

GADSDEN, GUS—1932—of, Hilldale

GAICHEY, —— —1948—p, Memphis Red Sox

GAIDERIA, —— —1918—p, Cuban Stars

GAINES, JONAS—1937–50—p, Newark Eagles, **Baltimore Elite Giants,** Philadelphia Stars

GAINES, WILLIE—1950—p, Philadelphia Stars

GALATA, DOMINGO—1949—p, New York Cubans

GALATA, RAUL—1949–50—p, Indianapolis Clowns

GALVEZ, CUNEO—1929–32—p, Cuban Stars (NNL), Cuban Stars (East)

GANS, ROBERT EDWARD (JUDE)—1910–38—**of,** p, mgr, Cuban Giants, Smart Set, **Lincoln Giants,** Chicago American Giants, Chicago Giants, Lincoln Stars; umpire, East-West League, NNL

GANTZ, —— —1926—c, Harrisburg Giants

GARAY, JOSE—1950—p, New York Cubans

GARCIA, —— —1926—2b, Bacharach Giants

GARCIA, A. —— —1909–12—c, 1b, Cuban Stars, All Cubans

GARCIA, ATIRES—1945–46—p, Cincinnati–Indianapolis Clowns

GARCIA, JOHN—1904—c, Cuban Giants

GARCIA, MANUEL—1926–35—**p,** of, Cuban Stars (NNL), New York Cubans

GARCIA, SILVIO—1940–47—inf, Cuban Stars, New York Cubans

GARDNER, FLOYD (JELLY)—1919–1933—**of,** 1b, Detroit Stars, **Chicago American Giants,** Lincoln Giants, Homestead Grays

GARDNER, JAMES—1908–17—player, Brooklyn Royal Giants, Havana Red Sox, Cuban Giants

GARDNER, (PING)—1918–30—p, Washington Red Caps, Brooklyn Royal Giants, Hilldale, Philadelphia Royal Stars, Lincoln Giants, Harrisburg Giants, Bacharach Giants, Cleveland Tigers

GARNER, HORACE—1949—player, Indianapolis Clowns
GARRIDO, GIL—1945—inf, New York Cubans
GARRETT, FRANK—1887—player, Louisville Falls Citys
GARRETT, WILLIAM—1943—officer, New York Black Yankees
GARRISON, ROBERT—1909—player, St. Paul Gophers
GARY, CHARLES—1948–49—3b, Homestead Grays
GASTON, ROBERT (RAB ROY)—1933–48—c, Homestead Grays
GATEWOOD, BILL—1905–28—p, mgr, Cuban X Giants, Philadelphia
    Giants, Brooklyn Royal Giants, Leland Giants, Chicago Giants, Chicago
    American Giants, St. Louis Giants, Detroit Stars, St. Louis Stars, To-
    ledo Tigers, Albany, Georgia, Giants, Birmingham Black Barons
GATEWOOD, ERNEST—1915–27—**c,** 1b, Lincoln Giants, **Brooklyn**
    Royal Giants, Bacharach Giants, Harrisburg Giants
GAVIN, ———— —1935—p, Brooklyn Eagles
GAY, H. ———— —1929—p, of, Chicago American Giants
GEE, RICHARD (RICH)—1923–29—**c,** of, Lincoln Giants
GEE, TOM—1925–26—c, Lincoln Giants
GEORGE, JOHN—1921–24—ss, New Orleans Crescent Stars, Chicago
    Giants, Harrisburg Giants
GERRARD, ALPHONSO—1945–49—of, New York Black Yankees,
    Chicago American Giants, Indianapolis Clowns
GHOLSTON, BERT E.—1923–43—umpire, NNL, East-West League
GIBBONS, ———— —1923—3b, Harrisburg Giants
GIBSON, JERRY—1943—player, Cincinnati Tigers
GIBSON, JOSHUA (JOSH)—1930–46—**c,** of, Homestead Grays, Pitts-
    burgh Crawfords
GIBSON, JOSHUA, JR.—1949–50—inf, Homestead Grays
GIBSON, TED—1940—inf, Columbus Buckeyes
GIBSON, WELDA—1950—p, Houston Eagles
GILBITEE, JUAN—1947—p, Indianapolis Clowns
GILCREST, DENNIS—1931–35—**c,** 2b, Indianapolis ABCs, Columbus
    Blue Birds, Cleveland Red Sox, Brooklyn Eagles
GILES, GEORGE—1927–38—1b, Kansas City Monarchs, St. Louis Stars,
    Brooklyn Eagles, New York Black Yankees, Philadelphia Stars
GILL, ———— —1933–37—1b, 3b, of, Detroit Stars, Louisville Red Caps,
    Indianapolis Athletics
GILLARD, (HAMP)—1911–12—p, St. Louis Giants
GILLARD, LUTHER—1934–40—of, 1b, Memphis Red Sox, Chicago
    American Giants, Indianapolis Crawfords
GILLESPIE, H. ———— —1887—player, Louisville Falls Citys
GILLESPIE, HENRY—1918–34—**p,** of, Pennsylvania Giants, Hill-
    dale, Lincoln Giants, Bacharach Giants, Philadelphia Tigers, Quaker
    Giants
GILLESPIE, MURRAY (LEFTY)—1930–32—p, Memphis Red Sox,
    Nashville Elite Giants
GILLIAM, JAMES (JUNIOR)—1945–50—2b, Nashville Black Vols,
    Baltimore Elite Giants

GILMORE, ———— —1926–28—p, Lincoln Giants

GILMORE, QUINCY J.—1922–37—bus mgr, Kansas City Monarchs; sec, tres, NNL; pres, Texas–Oklahoma–Louisiana League

GILYARD, LUTHER—1937–42—1b, Chicago American Giants, St. Louis Stars, Birmingham Black Barons

GIPSON, ALVIN (BUBBER)—1941–49—p, Chicago American Giants, **Birmingham Black Barons,** Houston Eagles

GISENTANER, WILLIE (LEFTY)—1921–35—p, Columbus Buckeyes, Washington Potomacs, Kansas City Monarchs, Harrisburg Giants, Newark Stars, Lincoln Giants, Cuban Stars (East), Louisville White Sox, Pittsburgh Crawfords, Nashville Elite Giants, Louisville Red Caps, Homestead Grays

GIVENS, OSCAR—1946–48—ss, Newark Eagles

GLADNEY, ———— —1932—ss, Indianapolis ABCs

GLADSTONE, GRANVILLE—1950—of, Indianapolis Clowns

GLASS, CARL—1924–36—p, mgr, **Memphis Red Sox,** Cincinnati Tigers

GLENN, ———— —1937–38—3b, Atlanta Black Crackers

GLENN, HUBERT (COUNTRY)—1945–49—p, New York Black Yankees, Brooklyn Brown Dodgers, Indianapolis Clowns

GLENN, STANLEY—1944–50—c, Philadelphia Stars

GLOVER, THOMAS (LEFTY)—1934–45—p, Birmingham Black Barons, Cleveland Red Sox, New Orleans Black Pelicans, Washington Elite Giants, Memphis Red Sox, **Baltimore Elite Giants**

GODINEZ, MANUEL—1946–49—p, Cincinnati–Indianapolis Clowns, Indianapolis Clowns

GOINS, ———— —1932—p, Montgomery Grey Sox

GOLDEN, CLYDE—1948–50—p, Newark Eagles, Houston Eagles

GOLDIE, ———— —1927–28—1b, Indianapolis ABCs, Cleveland Tigers

GOLIATH, FRED—1920—of, Chicago Giants

GOMEZ, ———— —1926–28—c, Harrisburg Giants, Phildelphia Tigers

GOMEZ, D. ———— —1925–28—p, Cuban Stars (NNL)

GOMEZ, JOE—1933—p, Bacharach Giants

GONZALES, A.—1910—p, Cuban Stars

GONZALES, G. ———— —1910–17—1b, c, Cuban Stars

GONZALES, RENE—1950—of, New York Cubans

GOOD, CLEVELAND—1937—p, Newark Eagles

GOODEN, ERNEST (PUD)—1922–23—2b, 3b, Pittsburgh Keystones, Toledo Tigers, Chicago American Giants

GOODGAME, JOHN—1917—p, Chicago Giants

GOODMAN, ———— —1928—of, Harrisburg Giants

GOODRICH, JOE—1923–26—2b, ss, 3b, Washington Potomacs, Philadelphia Giants

GOODSON, M. E.—1932—officer, New York Black Yankees

GORDON, ———— —1915—of, Indianapolis ABCs

GORDON, ———— —1950—p, Chicago American Giants

GORDON, ———— —1906–10—ss, Genuine Cuban Giants

GORDON, HERMAN—1923–24—p, of, Toledo Tigers, Birmingham Black Barons

GOSHAY, SAMUEL—1949—of, Kansas City Monarchs

GOTTLIEB, EDDIE—1936–48—officer, Philadelphia Stars; sec, NNL; promoter and booking agent

GOVANTES, MANUEL—1909–10—2b, of, Cuban Stars, Stars of Cuba

GOVERN, S. K.—1896—mgr, Cuban Giants

GRACE, WILLIE—1942–50—of, Cincinnati Buckeyes, **Cleveland Buckeyes,** Louisville Buckeyes, Houston Eagles

GRAHAM, ———— —1895–96—c, of, Lansing, Michigan, Colored Capital All-Americans, Page Fence Giants

GRAHAM, ———— —1918–21—of, Washington Red Caps, Bacharach Giants

GRAHAM, DENNIS—1925–30—of, Homestead Grays

GRANSBERRY, BILL—1929—of, 1b, Chicago American Giants, Chicago Giants

GRANT, ART—1920—player, Baltimore Black Sox

GRANT, CHARLES—1896–1910—2b, Page Fence Giants, Columbia Giants, Cuban X Giants, Philadelphia Giants, New York Black Sox

GRANT, FRANK—1886–1903—**2b,** ss, Meriden (Eastern League); Buffalo (International League); **Cuban Giants,** Harrisburg (Eastern Interstate League); Lansing, Michigan, Colored Capital All-Americans

GRANT, LEROY—1911–25—1b, **Chicago American Giants,** Lincoln Giants

GRAVES, BOB—1932–37—p, Indianapolis ABCs, Indianapolis Athletics

GRAVES, LAWRENCE —1923—p, Harrisburg Giants

GRAVES, WHITT—1950—p, Indianapolis Clowns

GRAY, ———— —1923—1b, Cleveland Tate Stars

GRAY, ———— —1940–45—c, St. Louis Stars, New York Black Yankees, Harrisburg–St. Louis Stars, Kansas City Monarchs

GRAY, G. E.—1922—of, Pittsburgh Keystones

GRAY, WILLIAM—1884–87—of, Baltimore Atlantics, Baltimore Lord Baltimores

GRAY, WILLIE (DOLLY)—1923–31—of, Cleveland Tate Stars, Homestead Grays, Lincoln Giants, Pennsylvania Red Caps of New York

GREASON, WILLIAM (WILLIE)—1948–50—p, Birmingham Black Barons

GREEN, ———— —1916—of, Lincoln Stars

GREEN, ———— —1919—of, Brooklyn Royal Giants

GREEN, ALVIN—1950—inf, Baltimore Elite Giants

GREEN, CHARLES (JOE)—1909–31—**mgr,** of, Leland Giants, Chicago Giants, Chicago American Giants

GREEN, CURTIS—1925–26—1b, of, Birmingham Black Barons, Brooklyn Cuban Giants

GREEN, DAVE—1950—of, Baltimore Elite Giants

GREEN, (FAT)—1921—c, Nashville Elite Giants

GREEN, JAMES—1932–43—c, 1b, Atlanta Black Crackers, Kansas City Monarchs

GREEN, JULIUS—1929–30—of, Memphis Red Sox, Detroit Stars

GREEN, LESLIE (CHIN)—1939–42—of, St. Louis Stars, New York Black Yankees

GREEN, P. —— —1910—of, Pittsburgh Giants

GREEN, VERNON—1942–48—officer, Baltimore Elite Giants

GREEN, W. —— —1910—c, Pittsburgh Giants

GREEN, WILLIAM—1915–23—**3b,** of, **Chicago Giants,** Chicago Union Giants

GREEN, WILLIE—1912—c, St. Louis Giants

GREENE, —— —1928—1b, Bacharach Giants

GREENE, JOSEPH (JOE)—1946–48—c, Kansas City Monarchs, Cleveland Buckeyes

GREENE, WALTER—1928—of, Brooklyn Cuban Giants

GREENEGE, VICTOR (SLICKER)—1941–45—p, Cuban Stars, New York Cubans

GREENLEE, W. A. (GUS)—1931–45—officer, Pittsburgh Crawfords; founder and pres, second NNL; founder, United States Baseball League

GREER, J. B.—1939–41—officer, Cleveland Bears, Knoxville Red Caps, Jacksonville Red Caps

GREGORY, —— —1940—p, Birmingham Black Barons

GREY, WILLIAM —1920—p, Dayton Marcos

GREYER, —— —1921—1b, Baltimore Black Sox

GRIER, CLAUDE (RED)—1925–28—p, Wilmington Potomacs, Bacharach Giants

GRIFFIN, C. B.—1933–35—of, Columbus Blue Birds, Cleveland Red Sox, Brooklyn Eagles

GRIFFIN, (HORSE) —1921—2b, Nashville Elite Giants

GRIFFIN, ROBERT—1931–37—p, Chicago Columbia Giants, St. Louis Stars

GRIFFITH, ROBERT (BOB)—1934–49—p, Nashville Elite Giants, Columbus Elite Giants, Washington Elite Giants, **Baltimore Elite Giants,** New York Black Yankees

GRIGGS, ROBERT—1948—player, Birmingham Black Barons

GRIGGS, WILLIE—1950—3b, Houston Eagles, Cleveland Buckeyes

GRIMES, —— —1943—of, Cleveland Buckeyes

GROSS, BEN, JR.—1887—player, Pittsburgh Keystones

GUILBE, —— —1940–47—p, Cuban Stars, Baltimore Elite Giants

GUITERREZ, LUIS —1926—of, Cuban Stars (NNL)

GUERRA, JUAN—1910–24—of, 1b, c, Stars of Cuba, Cuban Stars (NNL)

GULLEY, NAPOLEON—1945—p, Cleveland Buckeyes

GURLEY, JAMES —1923–32—of, p, 1b, St. Louis Stars Memphis Red Sox, Chicago American Giants, Montgomery Grey Sox

GUY, WESLEY—1927–29—p, Chicago Giants

HACKETT, ——— —1932—p, Washington Pilots
HACKLEY, AL—1895—player, Chicago Unions
HADLEY, ——— —1937–38—c, of, Atlanta Black Crackers
HAIRSTON, HAROLD—1946–47—p, Homestead Grays
HAIRSTON, NAPOLEON—1938–40—of, Pittsburgh Crawfords, Indianapolis Crawfords
HAIRSTON, (RAP)—1934—player, Newark Dodgers
HAIRSTON, SAMUEL (SAM)—1945–50—c, 3b, Cincinati–Indianapolis Clowns, Indianapolis Clowns
HALE, ——— —1937—ss, Detroit Stars
HALEY, (RED)—1928—2b, Chicago American Giants
HALL, ——— —1915–25—of, Lincoln Giants, Philadelphia Giants, Baltimore Black Sox
HALL, ——— —1921—p, St. Louis Giants
HALL, (BAD NEWS)—1937–40—3b, Indianapolis Athletics, Indianapolis Crawfords
HALL, HORACE G.—1933–42—officer, Chicago American Giants; vice pres, NAL
HALL, JOSEPH W.—1945—officer, Hilldale Club of Philadelphia
HALL, PERRY—1927–47—3b, of, Memphis Red Sox, Cleveland Tigers, Chicago Giants, Indianapolis Athletics
HALL, SELLERS McKEE (SELL)—1916–20—p, Pittsburgh Colored Giants, **Homestead Grays,** Chicago American Giants
HAMILTON, ——— —1921—p, Kansas City Monarchs
HAMILTON, GEORGE—1924—c, Memphis Red Sox
HAMILTON, J. C. (ED)—1940–42—p, Homestead Grays
HAMILTON, J. H.—1924–27—3b, Washington Potomacs, Birmingham Black Barons
HAMILTON, THERON B.—1934—vice pres, Homestead Grays
HAMMOND, ——— —1923–24—3b, ss, Cleveland Tate Stars, Cleveland Browns
HAMPTON, EPPIE—1927–37—c, p, **Memphis Red Sox,** Washington Pilots, New Orleans Crescent Stars
HAMPTON, LEWIS—1921–27—p, Columbus Buckeyes, Indianapolis ABCs, Bacharach Giants, Washington Potomacs, Lincoln Giants, Detroit Stars
HAMPTON, WADE—1918–23—p, Pennsylvania Giants, Hilldale
HANCOCK, ——— —1921—c, St. Louis Giants
HANCOCK, W. ——— —1885—player, Brooklyn Remsens
HANDY, BILL—1910–21—**2b,** ss, 3b, New York Black Sox, **Brooklyn Royal Giants,** St. Louis Giants, Lincoln Giants, Bacharach Giants, Philadelphia Royal Giants
HANDY, GEORGE—1947–49—inf, Memphis Red Sox, Houston Eagles
HANNIBAL, ——— —1916–17—of, Indianapolis ABCs
HANNIBAL, ——— —1937—p, Indianapolis Athletics
HANNON, ——— —1909—of, Philadelphia Giants

HANSON, HARRY—1926—vice pres, NSL

HARDEN, JAMES—1947—p, Homestead Grays

HARDEN, JOHN—1939–48—officer, Atlanta Black Crackers, Indianapolis ABCs, New York Black Yankees; tres, NSL

HARDEN, LOVELL—1943–45—p, Cleveland Buckeyes

HARDING, HALLIE—1926–31—ss, 2b, 3b, Indianapolis ABCs, Detroit Stars, Kansas City Monarchs, Chicago Columbia Giants, Bacharach Giants

HARDING, TOM—1940—of, Indianapolis Crawfords

HARDY, ARTHUR W.—1906–12—p, Topeka Giants, Kansas City, Kansas, Giants

HARDY, PAUL—1931–43—c, Montgomery Grey Sox, Detroit Stars, **Birmingham Black Barons,** Baltimore Elite Giants, Columbus Elite Giants, Chicago American Giants, Kansas City Monarchs, Memphis Red Sox

HARDY, WALTER—1945–50—ss, 2b, New York Black Yankees, New York Cubans

HARGETT, YOOK—1887—player, Philadelphia Pythians

HARLAND, BILL—1929—p, Lincoln Giants

HARNEY, GEORGE—1923–30—p, **Chicago American Giants,** Chicago Giants

HARPER, ———— —1920—ss, Hilldale, Norfolk Stars

HARPER, ———— —1920—of, Kansas City Monarchs

HARPER, (CHICK)—1922—p, Detroit Stars

HARPER, DAVID (DAVE)—1944–45—player, Kansas City Monarchs

HARPER, JOHN—1923–26—p, Bacharach Giants, Lincoln Giants

HARPER, WALTER—1929–31—1b, c, Chicago American Giants

HARPS, FRED—1928—inf, Brooklyn Cuban Giants

HARRIS, ———— —1887—player, Boston Resolutes

HARRIS, ———— —1919—of, Lincoln Giants

HARRIS, ———— —1921–23—p, Brooklyn Royal Giants, Hilldale, Harrisburg Giants

HARRIS, ———— —1927—1b, Lincoln Giants

HARRIS, ANDY—1917–26—3b, Hilldale, Pennsylvania Giants, Pennsylvania Red Caps of New York, Newark Stars

HARRIS, BILL—1930–32—c, Memphis Red Sox, Indianapolis ABCs, Monroe Monarchs

HARRIS, CHARLIE—1943—inf, Cincinnati Clowns, Chicago Brown Bombers

HARRIS, CURTIS—1934–40—2b, ss, 1b, c, Pittsburgh Crawfords, **Philadelphia Stars**

HARRIS, DIXON—1932—player, Homestead Grays

HARRIS, E.—1884—player, Philadelphia Mutual B.B.C.

HARRIS, E. VICTOR (VIC)—1923–50—of, mgr, coach, Cleveland Tate Stars, Cleveland Browns, Chicago American Giants, **Homestead Grays,** Pittsburgh Crawfords, Baltimore Elite Giants, Birmingham Black Barons

HARRIS, FRANK—1885—p, Argyle Hotel

HARRIS, G.—1932—2b, Louisville Black Caps
HARRIS, H. B.—1919—bus mgr, Brooklyn Royal Giants
HARRIS, HENRY—1929–34—ss, Memphis Red Sox, Louisville Black Caps, Baltimore Black Sox
HARRIS, ISAIAH—1949–50—p, Memphis Red Sox
HARRIS, JAMES—1884–87—of, Baltimore Atlantics, Baltimore Lord Baltimores
HARRIS, (LEFTY)—1941—p, Cuban Stars
HARRIS, M. (MO)—1916–43—2b, of, Homestead Grays; umpire, East-West League, NNL
HARRIS, (MOOCHA)—1932–34—of, Detroit Wolves, Kansas City Monarchs, New Orleans Crescent Stars
HARRIS, NATHAN (NATE)—1906–11—2b, of, Philadelphia Giants, Leland Giants, Chicago Giants
HARRIS, (POPSICKLE)—1931–36—1b, Kansas City Monarchs, Cleveland Stars
HARRIS, SAMUEL—1940—p, Chicago American Giants
HARRIS, SONNY—1942—of, Cincinnati Buckeyes
HARRIS, TOMMY—1947–49—c, Cleveland Buckeyes, Louisville Buckeyes
HARRIS, V—1936–37—p, of, 2b, Cincinnati Tigers
HARRIS, WILMER—1945–50—p, Philadelphia Stars
HARRISON, ABE—1885–93—ss, Philadelphia Orions, Argyle Hotel, Cuban Giants
HARRISON, TOMLINI—1927—p, St. Louis Stars
HARRISTON, CLYDE—1944—player, Birmingham Black Barons, Cincinnati–Indianapolis Clowns
HART, FRANK—1884—ss, St. Louis Black Stockings
HARTLEY, (HOP)—1925—p, Kansas City Monarchs
HARVEY, ———— —1912–21—p, St. Louis Giants, Brooklyn Royal Giants, Lincoln Stars, Lincoln Giants, Bacharach Giants
HARVEY, ———— —1937—ss, Philadelphia Stars
HARVEY, B. T.—1950—sec, NSL
HARVEY, ROBERT (BOB)—1944–50—of, Newark Eagles, Houston Eagles
HARVEY, WILLIAM (BILL)—1932–45—p, Memphis Red Sox, Pittsburgh Crawfords, **Baltimore Elite Giants**
HARVEY, WILLIE—1939–40—p, Pittsburgh Crawfords, Indianapolis Crawfords
HASLETT, CLAUDE—1937—p, Memphis Red Sox, Indianapolis Athletics
HAVIS, CHESTER—1947—p, Memphis Red Sox
HAWKINS, LEMUEL (HAWK)—1919–27—**1b,** of, Los Angeles White Sox, **Kansas City Monarchs**
HAWLEY, ———— —1932—c, Memphis Red Sox
HAYES, ———— 1940—ss, 2b, Philadelphia Stars, St. Louis Stars
HAYES, BUDDY—1916–24—c, Chicago American Giants, Indianapolis ABCs, Pittsburgh Keystones, Cleveland Browns

HAYES, (BUN)—1930–33—p, Baltimore Black Sox, Washington Pilots
HAYES, JOHN—1934–50—c, Newark Dodgers, Newark Eagles, New York Black Yankees, Boston Blues, Baltimore Elite Giants
HAYES, THOMAS H.—1939–50—officer, Birmingham Black Barons; vice pres, NAL
HAYES, WILBUR—1942–50—officer, Cincinnati Buckeyes, Cleveland Buckeyes; sergeant-at-arms, NAL
HAYMAN, CHARLES (BUGS)—1909–16—p, 1b, Philadelphia Giants
HAYNES, SAM—1943–45—c, Kansas City Monarchs
HAYNES, WILLIE—1921–22—p, Dallas Giants, Hilldale
HAYWOOD, ALBERT (BUSTER)—1940–50—c, mgr, Chicago American Giants, Birmingham Black Barons, New York Cubans, Cincinnati–Indianapolis Clowns, Indianapolis Clowns
HEARD, JEHOSIE—1948–50—p, Birmingham Black Barons, Memphis Red Sox, Houston Eagles
HEAT, —————1941—p, Cuban Stars
HEFNER, ARTHUR—1948—of, New York Black Yankees
HENDERSON, —————1922–23—of, 3b, Cleveland Tate Stars
HENDERSON, —————1925—c, Birmingham Black Barons
HENDERSON, ARMOUR—1915—p, Mohawk Giants
HENDERSON, ARTHUR (RATS)—1922–31—p, Richmond Giants, **Bacharach Giants,** Detroit Stars
HENDERSON, CURTIS (CURT)—1936–41—ss, 3b, Philadelphia Stars, New York Black Yankees, Washington Black Senators, Indianapolis Crawfords, Chicago American Giants
HENDERSON, H. (LONG)—1932—1b, Nashville Elite Giants
HENDERSON, L.—1932–33—3b, ss, Nashville Elite Giants, Birmingham Black Barons, Montgomery Grey Sox
HENDRICKS, —————1918—p, of, Lincoln Giants
HENDRIX, —————1934—p, Nashville Elite Giants
HENRY, —————1937—of, Indianapolis Athletics
HENRY, ALFRED—1950—of, Baltimore Elite Giants
HENRY, CHARLES (CHARLIE)—1922–42—p, mgr, Hilldale, Harrisburg Giants, Detroit Stars, Bacharach Giants, Detroit Black Sox
HENRY, JOE—1950—player, Memphis Red Sox
HENRY, OTIS—1931–34—2b, 3b, Memphis Red Sox, Monroe Monarchs
HENRY, LEO (PREACHER)—1938–47—p, Jacksonville Red Caps, Cleveland Bears, Cincinnati Clowns, Indianapolis Clowns
HENSLEY, (SLAP)—1923–39—p, **St. Louis Stars,** Toledo Tigers, Indianapolis ABCs, Detroit Stars, Cleveland Giants, Chicago American Giants
HEREDIA, RAMON—1939–44—3b, ss, Cuban Stars, New York Cubans
HERMAN, —————1932—of, Memphis Red Sox
HERNANDEZ, —————1920–22—p, Cuban Stars (NNL)
HERNANDEZ, RAMON—1929–30—3b, Cuban Stars (NNL)
HERNANDEZ, RICARDO (CHICO)—1909–14—2b, 3b, Cuban Stars, All Cubans

HERRERA, RAMON—1916-28—**2b,** 3b, Jersey City Cubans, Cuban Stars (NNL), Cuban Stars (ECL)

HERRON, ROBERT LEE—1950—of, Houston Eagles

HEWITT, JOE—1910-31—**ss,** of, 2b, mgr, **St. Louis Giants,** Brooklyn Royal Giants, Lincoln Giants, Philadelphia Giants, Detroit Stars, Chicago American Giants, St. Louis Stars, Cleveland Cubs

HEYWOOD, DOBIE—1926—p, Lincoln Giants

HICKS, EUGENE—1940—p, Homestead Grays

HICKS, WESLEY—1927-31—of, Chicago American Giants, Memphis Red Sox, Kansas City Monarchs

HIDALGO, HEIODORO—1910-12—of, 3b, Stars of Cuba, Cuban Stars

HIGDON, BARNEY—1943—p, Cincinnati Clowns

HIGGINS, ROBERT (BOB)—1887-88—p, Syracuse (International League)

HILL, ———— —1923-27—3b, Brooklyn Royal Giants

HILL, ———— —1937—of, Atlanta Black Crackers

HILL, BEN—1946—p, Pittsburgh Crawfords

HILL, C.—1915-24—**of,** p, Chicago Union Giants, Dayton Marcos, Detroit Stars, St. Louis Giants

HILL, FRED—1920-23—2b, 3b, of, St. Louis Giants, Detroit Stars, Milwaukee Bears

HILL, J. PRESTON (PETE)—1904-25—**of,** 2b, mgr, bus mgr, Philadelphia Giants, Leland Giants, **Chicago American Giants,** Detroit Stars, Milwaukee Bears, Baltimore Black Sox

HILL, JIMMY (LEFTY)—1939-45—p, Newark Eagles

HILL, JOHN—1900-04—**3b,** ss, Genuine Cuban Giants, Philadelphia Giants, Cuban X Giants

HILL, (LEFTY)—1918-20—of, Dayton Marcos, Detroit Stars

HILL, SAMUEL (SAM)—1947-48—of, Chicago American Giants

HILL, W. R.—1885—ss, Brooklyn Remsens

HINES, JOHN—1925-34—**c,** of, Chicago American Giants, Cole's American Giants

HINSON, FRANK—1896—p, Cuban Giants

HINTON, ARCHIE—1945—p, inf, Baltimore Elite Giants

HOAGLAND, F. B.—1885—sec, Brooklyn Remsens

HOBGOOD, FREDDIE (LEFTY)—1941-43—p, Newark Eagles

HODGES, ———— —1925—p, Lincoln Giants

HOLCOMB, ———— —1923—p, Detroit Stars

HOLIDAY, ———— —1938—of, Atlanta Black Crackers

HOLLAND, BILL—1920-41—p, mgr, Detroit Stars, Chicago American Giants, Lincoln Giants, Brooklyn Royal Giants, **New York Black Yankees,** Philadelphia Stars

HOLLAND, WILLIAM (BILLY)—1896-1905—p, Page Fence Giants, Chicago Unions, Brooklyn Royal Giants

HOLLINGSWORTH, CURTIS—1947—p, Birmingham Black Barons

HOLLOWAY, O. (CRUSH)—1921-34—of, Indianapolis ABCs, **Baltimore Black Sox,** Hilldale, Detroit Stars, Bacharach Giants

HOLMES, BEN—1885–87—3b, Argyle Hotel, Cuban Giants
HOLMES, FRANK—1931–34—p, Bacharach Giants, Philadelphia Stars
HOLMES, LEROY (PHILLIE)—1938–45—ss, Jacksonville Red Caps, Cleveland Bears, Atlanta Black Crackers, Kansas City Monarchs, Cincinnati–Indianapolis Clowns, New York Black Yankees
HOLSEY, (FROG)—1929–32—p, Chicago American Giants, Chicago Columbia Giants, Cleveland Cubs, Nashville Elite Giants
HOLT, JOHNNY —1922–23—of, Pittsburgh Keystones, Toledo Tigers
HOLT, JOSEPH—1928—of, Brooklyn Cuban Giants
HOLTZ, EDDIE—1920–24—**2b**, ss, St. Louis Giants, Chicago American Giants, St. Louis Stars
HOODS, WILLIAM—1887—player, Philadelphia Pythians
HOOKER, ——— —1916—of, Lincoln Stars
HOOKER, LEN—1940–48—p, Newark Eagles
HOPKINS, ——— —1896–99—p, Chicago Unions
HOPWOOD, ——— —1928—of, Kansas City Monarchs
HORDY, J. H.—1887—player, Baltimore Lord Baltimores
HORN, WILL—1896–1904—p, Chicago Unions, Philadelphia Giants
HORNE, WILLIAM (BILLY)—1938–46—ss, 2b, Monroe Monarchs, Chicago American Giants, Cincinnati Buckeyes, Cleveland Buckeyes
HOSKINS, DAVID (DAVE)—1942–49—of, p, Cincinnati Clowns, Chicago American Giants, Homestead Grays, Louisville Buckeyes
HOSKINS, WILLIAM (BILL)—1937–46—of, Detroit Stars, Memphis Red Sox, **Baltimore Elite Giants,** New York Black Yankees
HOUSE, (RED)—1937—3b, Detroit Stars
HOUSTON, ——— —1920—p, Indianapolis ABCs
HOUSTON, BILL—1941–42—p, Homestead Grays
HOUSTON, JESS—1930–39—p, inf, Memphis Red Sox, Cincinnati Tigers, Chicago American Giants
HOWARD, ——— —1899—player, Cuban X Giants
HOWARD, ——— —1921–22—p, 3b, Detroit Stars, Indianapolis ABCs
HOWARD, ——— —1921–22—ss, Norfolk Giants, Harrisburg Giants
HOWARD, ——— —1922—p, Baltimore Black Sox
HOWARD, CARRANZA—1941–47—p, Cuban Stars, New York Cubans, Indianapolis Clowns
HOWARD, ELSTON—1948–50—of, c, Kansas City Monarchs
HOWARD, HERMAN (RED)—1932–46—p, Atlanta Black Crackers, Memphis Red Sox, Washington Elite Giants, Indianapolis Athletics, Jacksonville Red Caps, Indianapolis ABCs, Chicago American Giants, Birmingham Black Barons
HOWARD, W. —— —1931–33—1b, 3b, Birmingham Black Barons
HOWELL, HENRY—1918–21—p, Pennsylvania Giants, Bacharach Giants, Pennsylvania Red Caps of New York, Brooklyn Royal Giants
HUBBARD, DeHART—1942—sec, Cleveland–Cincinnati Buckeyes
HUBBARD, JESSE (MOUNTAIN)—1919–34—**p,** of, Bacharach Giants, **Brooklyn Royal Giants,** Baltimore Black Sox, Hilldale, Homestead Grays
HUBER, ——— —1930–31—c, of, Memphis Red Sox, Nashville Elite Giants

HUBER, JOHN—1942–50—p, c, Chicago American Giants, Birmingham Black Barons, Cincinnati Clowns, Memphis Red Sox

HUBERT, WILLIE (BUBBER)—1939–46—p, Newark Eagles, Baltimore Elite Giants, Cincinnati Buckeyes, Baltimore Grays, Homestead Grays, Pittsburgh Crawfords, Brooklyn Brown Dodgers

HUDSON, WILLIAM—1940–42—p, Chicago American Giants

HUDSPETH, ROBERT (HIGHPOCKETS)—1921–32—1b, Indianapolis ABCs, Columbus Buckeyes, Bacharach Giants, Lincoln Giants, Brooklyn Royal Giants, Hilldale, New York Black Yankees

HUESTON, WILLIAM C.—1927–31—pres, NNL

HUFF, EDDIE—1923–32—c, of, mgr, Bacharach Giants, Dayton Marcos

HUGHES, C. —— —1934—2b, Cleveland Red Sox

HUGHES, ROBERT—1931—p, Louisville White Sox

HUGHES, SAMMY T.—1931–46—2b, Louisville White Sox, Nashville Elite Giants, Homestead Grays, Columbus Elite Giants, Washington Elite Giants, **Baltimore Elite Giants**

HUMBER, —— —1945—2b, Newark Eagles

HUMES, JOHN—1937—p, Newark Eagles

HUMPHRIES, —— —1937—of, Atlanta Black Crackers

HUNDLEY, JOHNNY LEE—1943—c, of, Cleveland Buckeyes

HUNT, GROVER—1946—c, Chicago American Giants

HUNT, LEONARD (LEN)—1949–50—of, Kansas City Monarchs

HUNTER, —— —1924—p, Memphis Red Sox

HUNTER, BERTRUM—1931–35—p, St. Louis Stars, Detroit Wolves, Pittsburgh Crawfords

HUTCHINSON, FRED (HUTCH)—1910–25—ss, 3b, Leland Giants, Chicago American Giants, Indianapolis ABCs, Bacharach Giants

HUTCHINSON, WILLIE (ACE)—1939–49—p, Kansas City Monarchs, **Memphis Red Sox**

HUTT, —— —1921–24—1b, Dayton Marcos, Toledo Tigers, St. Louis Giants

HYDE, COWAN (BUBBER)—1937–49—**of,** 2b, Cincinnati Tigers, **Memphis Red Sox**

HYDE, HARRY—1896–99—player, Chicago Unions

INGRAM, —— —1942—p, Jacksonville Red Caps

IPENA, —— —1929—c, Cuban Stars (NNL)

IRVIN, BILL—1919—mgr, Cleveland Tate Stars

IRVIN, MONFORD MERRILL (MONTE)—1938–48—of, ss, 3b, Newark Eagles

ISRAEL, CLARENCE—1940–47—**3b,** 2b, Newark Eagles, Homestead Grays

JACKMAN, BILL—1925–42—p, Lincoln Giants, Philadelphia Giants, Quaker Giants, Brooklyn Eagles, Boston Royal Giants

JACKSON, —— —1915—ss, Chicago Giants

JACKSON, ———— —1917–25—c, of, Pennsylvania Red Caps of New York, Lincoln Giants

JACKSON, ———— —1928—of, Bacharach Giants

JACKSON, ———— —1934—1b, Cincinnati Tigers

JACKSON, A.—1932–34—3b, ss, Montgomery Grey Sox, Birmingham Black Barons

JACKSON, ANDREW—1888–96—3b, New York Gorhams, Cuban Giants, Lansing, Mich. Colored Capital All-Americans, Cuban X Giants

JACKSON, B. ———— —1945—3b, Homestead Grays

JACKSON, (BIG TRAIN)—1938–40—p, Kansas City Monarchs, Memphis Red Sox

JACKSON, BOB—1887–96—c, 1b, New York Gorhams, Cuban X Giants

JACKSON, C. ———— —1929—3b, Homestead Grays

JACKSON, CARLTON—1928—officer, Harrisburg Giants

JACKSON, DALLAS—1950—inf, Cleveland Buckeyes

JACKSON, DAN—1949—of, Homestead Grays

JACKSON, F. ———— —1885—officer, Brooklyn Remsens

JACKSON, (GEN)—1947—of, Baltimore Elite Giants

JACKSON, GEORGE—1887—player, Philadelphia Pythians

JACKSON, (LEFTY)—1926—p, Philadelphia Giants

JACKSON, NORMAN (JELLY)—1934–45—**ss,** 2b, Cleveland Red Sox, **Homestead Grays**

JACKSON, OSCAR—1887–96—of, 1b, New York Gorhams, Cuban Giants, Cuban X Giants

JACKSON, R. B.—1931–50—pres, vice pres, NSL; officer, Nashville Black Vols

JACKSON, R. T.—1928–31—officer, Birmingham Black Barons; pres, NSL

JACKSON, RICHARD—1921–31—**2b,** ss, 3b, Bacharach Giants, Harrisburg Giants, Baltimore Black Sox, Hilldale

JACKSON, ROBERT—1899—c, Chicago Unions

JACKSON, ROBERT R.—1939–42—commissioner, NAL

JACKSON, RUFUS (SONNYMAN)—1934–49—pres, tres, Homestead Grays

JACKSON, S.—1937—c, Memphis Red Sox

JACKSON, SAM—1887—player, Pittsburgh Keystones

JACKSON, SAMUEL—1944—player, Chicago American Giants

JACKSON, STANFORD—1924–31—**of,** ss, 3b, 2b, Memphis Red Sox, **Chicago American Giants**

JACKSON, (STONY)—1950—p, Houston Eagles

JACKSON, THOMAS—1916–28—officer, Bacharach Giants

JACKSON, TOM—1924–29—p, St. Louis Stars, Cleveland Tigers, Nashville Elite Giants

JACKSON, WILLIAM—1893–1903—of, c, Cuban Giants, Cuban X Giants

JACKSON, WILLIAM (ASHES)—1910—3b, Kansas City, Kansas, Giants

JAMES, ———— —1896—p, Cuban X Giants

JAMES, (GUS)—1909–11—c, of, Brooklyn Royal Giants
JAMES, J. —— —1912—1b, Smart Set
JAMES, W. (NUX)—1909–17—2b, Philadelphia Giants, Smart Set, Mohawk Giants, Lincoln Giants, Bacharach Giants
JAMES, TICE—1942—player, Cincinnati Clowns
JAMES, WILLIAM—1887—player, Philadelphia Pythians
JAMES, (WINKY)—1942—ss, Cincinnati Buckeyes
JAMISON, CAESAR—1923–32—umpire, NNL, East-West League
JAMISON, EDDIE—1950—c, Cleveland Buckeyes
JASPER, —— —1932—p, Birmingham Black Barons
JEFFERSON, EDDIE—1946—p, Philadelphia Stars
JEFFERSON, GEORGE LEO—1942–50—p, Jacksonville Red Caps, Cleveland Buckeyes
JEFFERSON, RALPH—1920–26—of, Indianapolis ABCs, Bacharach Giants, Philadelphia Royal Stars, Washington Potomacs, Philadelphia Giants
JEFFERSON, WILLIE—1937–50—p, Cincinnati Tigers, Memphis Red Sox, Cincinnati Buckeyes, Cleveland Buckeyes
JEFFREYS, FRANK—1919–20—of, Chicago Giants
JEFFRIES, E. —— —1922—c, Chicago Giants
JEFFRIES, HARRY—1920–48—**3b,** c, ss, 1b, mgr, Chicago Giants, Chicago American Giants, Detroit Stars, Cleveland Tigers, Chicago Columbia Giants, Bacharach Giants, Knoxville Giants
JEFFRIES, JAMES C.—1916–31—**p,** of, **Indianapolis ABCs,** Baltimore Black Sox, Birmingham Black Barons
JEFFRIES, JEFF—1940—p, Brooklyn Royal Giants
JEFFRIES, M. —— —1925—3b, Baltimore Black Sox
JENKINS, CLARENCE—1926—c, Philadelphia Giants
JENKINS, CLARENCE (FATS)—1920–40—of, mgr, Lincoln Giants, Harrisburg Giants, Bacharach Giants, Baltimore Black Sox, **New York Black Yankees,** Philadelphia Stars, Brooklyn Eagles, Brooklyn Royal Giants
JENKINS, HORACE—1914–25—**of,** p, Chicago American Giants, **Chicago Giants,** Chicago Union Giants
JENKINS, JAMES (PEEWEE)—1946–50—p, New York Cubans
JENKINS, TOM—1928—sec, Hilldale
JENNINGS, THURMAN—1915–27—2b, ss, of, Chicago Giants
JESSIE, W. —— —1887—player, Louisville Falls Citys
JESSUP, GENTRY—1940–49—p, **Chicago American Giants,** Birmingham Black Barons
JETHROE, SAMUEL (SAM)—1942–48—of, Cincinnati Buckeyes, **Cleveland Buckeyes**
JEWELL, WARNER—1917–25—owner, Jewell's ABCs, Indianapolis ABCs
JIMENEZ, B. (HOOKS)—1916–29—2b, Cuban Stars (NNL), Cuban Stars (ECL)
JIMENEZ, E. —— —1921—of, Cuban Stars (NNL)
JOHNSON, —— —1916–19—of, ss, Brooklyn Royal Giants

JOHNSON, —— —1922—of, Detroit Stars
JOHNSON, A. —— —1916–22—c, Bacharach Giants, Pennsylvania Giants, Homestead Grays
JOHNSON, ALLEN—1942–46—officer, St. Louis Stars, New York Black Yankees, Harrisburg–St. Louis Stars, Boston Blues
JOHNSON, B. —— —1917–25—1b, 2b, p, of, **Pennsylvania Red Caps of New York,** Lincoln Giants
JOHNSON, B. —— —1940—ss, Brooklyn Royal Giants
JOHNSON, BEN—1916–23—p, Bacharach Giants
JOHNSON, BERT—1934–35—of, Newark Dodgers
JOHNSON, BILL—1939—c, New York Black Yankees
JOHNSON, BYRON—1938–39—ss, Kansas City Monarchs
JOHNSON, C. —— —1922–26—2b, ss, Cleveland Tate Stars, Baltimore Black Sox, Harrisburg Giants
JOHNSON, C. (SESS)—1928—1b, Philadelphia Tigers
JOHNSON, CHARLES—1950—3b, Cleveland Buckeyes
JOHNSON, CLAUDE (HOOKS)—1929–30—3b, p, Detroit Stars, Memphis Red Sox
JOHNSON, CLIFFORD (CLIFF)—1940–50—p, Indianapolis Crawfords, **Kansas City Monarchs**
JOHNSON, DAN (SHANG)—1916–18—p, Bacharach Giants, Brooklyn Royal Giants
JOHNSON, ERNEST—1949—p, Kansas City Monarchs
JOHNSON, FRANK—1934–37—mgr, Monroe Monarchs, Memphis Red Sox
JOHNSON, FRED—1946—p, Pittsburgh Crawfords
JOHNSON, G. —— —1927–30—3b, 2b, Detroit Stars, Birmingham Black Barons
JOHNSON, GEORGE (CHAPPIE)—1899–1921—c, 1b, mgr, Columbia Giants, Chicago Union Giants, Brooklyn Royal Giants, Leland Giants, Chicago Giants, St. Louis Giants, Dayton Chappies, Custer's Baseball Club of Columbus, Philadelphia Royal Stars, Norfolk Stars
JOHNSON, GEORGE (DIBO)—1909–28—of, Fort Worth Wonders, Kansas City, Kansas, Giants, Brooklyn Royal Giants, **Hilldale,** Lincoln Giants, Philadelphia Tigers
JOHNSON, GRANT (HOME RUN)—1895–1921—**ss,** 2b, mgr, Page Fence Giants, Columbia Giants, Brooklyn Royal Giants, Cuban X Giants, Philadelphia Giants, Lincoln Giants, Lincoln Stars, Pittsburgh Colored Stars, Pittsburgh Stars of Buffalo
JOHNSON, H. —— —1933–34—of, Birmingham Black Barons
JOHNSON, HARRY—1886–88—utility, Cuban Giants
JOHNSON, J. —— —1922–26—p, Cleveland Tate Stars, Cleveland Elites
JOHNSON, J. —— —1931–32—1b, Memphis Red Sox
JOHNSON, JACK—1903–04—1b, Philadelphia Giants
JOHNSON, JACK—1938–39—3b, Homestead Grays, Toledo Crawfords
JOHNSON, JIM—1932–33—ss, Hilldale, Bacharach Giants

JOHNSON, JIMMY (SLIM)—1939–40—p, Toledo Crawfords, Indian-
apolis Crawfords
JOHNSON, JIMMY (JEEP)—1946—ss, Pittsburgh Crawfords
JOHNSON, JOE—1884–85—p, c, Baltimore Atlantics
JOHNSON, JOHN (JOHNNY)—1942–45—p, Birmingham Black Bar-
ons, Homestead Grays, New York Black Yankees
JOHNSON, JOHN B.—1925–28—pres, mgr, Brooklyn Cuban Giants
JOHNSON, REV. JOHN H.—1947–48—pres, NNL
JOHNSON, JOSEPH—1937—officer, Indianapolis Athletics
JOHNSON, JOSH—1936–39—c, p, Cincinnati Tigers, Homestead Grays,
New York Black Yankees
JOHNSON, JUDY—see Johnson, William J.
JOHNSON, JUNIOR—1899–1906—1b, c, Columbia Giants, Philadel-
phia Giants, Quaker Giants, Brooklyn Royal Giants
JOHNSON, L. ———1948—p, Kansas City Monarchs
JOHNSON, LEAMAN—1945—ss, Memphis Red Sox
JOHNSON, LEE—1941—c, Birmingham Black Barons
JOHNSON, (LEFTY)—1930—p, Memphis Red Sox
JOHNSON, LEONARD—1947–48—p, Chicago American Giants
JOHNSON, LOUIS (DICTA)—1911–25—p, mgr, coach, Twin City
Gophers, Chicago American Giants, Indianapolis ABCs, Detroit Stars,
Toledo Tigers, Pittsburgh Keystones, Milwaukee Bears
JOHNSON, M. ———1920—of, Lincoln Giants
JOHNSON (MONK)—1925—player, Lincoln Giants
JOHNSON, NAT—1922–24—p, Bacharach Giants, Cleveland Browns
JOHNSON, O. ———1919—p, Bacharach Giants
JOHNSON, OSCAR (HEAVY)—1922–33—of, c, 2b, Kansas City Mon-
archs, Baltimore Black Sox, Harrisburg Giants, Cleveland Tigers, Mem-
phis Red Sox
JOHNSON, P. ———1926—p, Baltimore Black Sox
JOHNSON, (PEE WEE)—1939—2b, Newark Eagles
JOHNSON, R. ———1932—of, Washington Pilots
JOHNSON, RALPH—1950—ss, Indianapolis Clowns
JOHNSON, (RAT)—1909—player, St. Paul Gophers
JOHNSON, RAY—1923—of, St. Louis Stars
JOHNSON, RICHARD—1887–90—c, of, Zanesville (Ohio State League,
Tri-State League), Springfield and Peoria (Central Interstate League)
JOHNSON, ROBERT—1928—inf, Brooklyn Cuban Giants
JOHNSON, ROBERT—1944—player, Kansas City Monarchs
JOHNSON, ROBERT—1939—of, New York Black Yankees
JOHNSON, RUDOLPH—1950—of, Cleveland Buckeyes
JOHNSON, S. ———1922—3b, Philadelphia Royal Stars
JOHNSON, THOMAS (TOMMY)—1915–25—p, Indianapolis ABCs,
Chicago American Giants, Pittsburgh Keystones
JOHNSON, TOM—1937—p, St. Louis Stars
JOHNSON, TOMMY—1938–40—p, Chicago American Giants

JOHNSON, W. —— —1945—p, Memphis Red Sox
JOHNSON, W. —— —1925—player, Wilmington Potomacs
JOHNSON, W. —— —1928—of, Detroit Stars
JOHNSON, WILLIAM (BILL)—1927–31—c, of, mgr, Hilldale, Philadelphia Tigers, Pennsylvania Red Caps of New York
JOHNSON, WILLIAM J. (JUDY)—1921–38—**3b,** ss, mgr, **Hilldale,** Homestead Grays, Darby Daisies, **Pittsburgh Crawfords**
JOHNSTON, —— —1916—2b, Lincoln Stars
JOHNSTON, TOM—1923—umpire, NNL
JOHNSTON, WADE—1922–33—of, Cleveland Tate Stars, Kansas City Monarchs, Baltimore Black Sox, Detroit Stars
JONES, —— —1919—3b, St. Louis Giants
JONES, —— —1938–41—1b, Jacksonville Red Caps, Cleveland Bears
JONES, —— —1950—of, Philadelphia Stars
JONES, A. —— —1934—p, Birmingham Black Barons
JONES, ALONZO—1944–45—p, Chicago American Giants, Memphis Red Sox
JONES, ALVIN—1928—officer, Harrisburg Giants
JONES, B. —— —1934—of, Cleveland Red Sox
JONES, BERT—1899—player, Chicago Unions
JONES, CLINTON (CASEY)—1944–50—c, Memphis Red Sox
JONES, COLLIS—1944—utility, Birmingham Black Barons
JONES, (COUNTRY)—1933—2b, Brooklyn Royal Giants
JONES, D. —— —1884—player, Philadelphia Mutual B.B.C.
JONES, EDWARD—1915–29—c, Chicago American Giants, Chicago Giants, **Bacharach Giants**
JONES, J. —— —1932–34—of, Memphis Red Sox
JONES, JOHN—1922–29—**of,** 1b, Detroit Stars
JONES, LEE—1912–22—of, Brooklyn Royal Giants, Dallas Giants
JONES, PAUL—1950—p, Cleveland Buckeyes
JONES, REUBEN—1918–49—of, mgr, Dallas Giants, Birmingham Black Barons, Indianapolis ABCs, Chicago American Giants, Little Rock, Memphis Red Sox, Houston Eagles
JONES, SAM (RED)—1946–48—p, Homestead Grays, Cleveland Buckeyes
JONES, STUART (SLIM)—1933–38—p, Baltimore Black Sox, **Philadelphia Stars**
JONES, W. —— —1934—of, Birmingham Black Barons
JONES, W. —— —1934—of, Memphis Red Sox
JONES, WILL—1896–1911—ss, Chicago Unions, Leland Giants
JONES, WILLIAM (FOX)—1915–30—**c,** p, Chicago American Giants, Chicago Giants, Bacharach Giants, Hilldale
JORDAN, —— —1933—p, Chicago American Giants
JORDAN, —— —1940–42—ss, Philadelphia Stars, New York Black Yankees
JORDAN, H. (HEN)—1922–25—c, of, Harrisburg Giants
JORDAN, ROBERT—1896–1904—c, 1b, Cuban Giants, Cuban X Giants

JORDAN, WILLIAM F.—1899—mgr, Baltimore Giants
JOSEPH, NEWTON (NEWT)—1922–39—**3b,** 2b, mgr, **Kansas City Monarchs,** Birmingham Black Barons, Satchel Paige's All-Stars
JUANELO, ———— —1923–28—p, Cuban Stars (ECL)
JUILLO, ———— —1940—p, Cuban Stars
JUNCO, ———— —1912–21—p, Cuban Stars (East)
JURAN, E. ———— —1926—p, Newark Stars
JUSTICE, CHARLEY—1937—p, Detroit Stars

KAISER, CECIL—1947–49—p, Homestead Grays
KEATON, ———— —1921–26—p, Dayton Marcos, Cleveland Tate Stars
KECK, D. J.—1948—tres, Negro American Association
KEENAN, JAMES J.—1919–30—bus mgr, Lincoln Giants; sec-tres, ECL
KELLMAN, LEON—1947–50—3b, Cleveland Buckeyes, Louisville Buckeyes, Memphis Red Sox
KELLY, ———— —1900—ss, Genuine Cuban Giants
KELLY, ———— —1916–18—p, Chicago Giants, Chicago Union Giants
KELLY, ———— —1945—player, New York Black Yankees
KELLY, ———— —1941—p, Jacksonville Red Caps
KELLY, (LEFTY)—1950—p, Baltimore Elite Giants
KELLY, R. A.—1889–91—**1b,** 2b, ss, Danville (Illinois–Indiana League); Jamestown (Pennsylvania–New York League)
KELLY, WILLIAM—1898—3b, Celeron Acme Colored Giants (Iron and Oil League)
KELLY, WILLIAM—1947—c, Homestead Grays
KEMP, JAMES—1937–39—2b, Atlanta Black Crackers, Jacksonville Red Caps, Indianapolis ABCs
KEMP, JOHN—1921–25—of, Norfolk Giants, Philadelphia Royal Stars, Baltimore Black Sox, Lincoln Giants, Memphis Red Sox
KENNARD, DAN—1916–25—c, Indianapolis ABCs, Chicago American Giants, St. Louis Giants, Lincoln Giants, St. Louis Stars, Detroit Stars
KENT, RICHARD—1922–31—officer, St. Louis Stars
KENYON, HARRY C.—1920–29—p, 2b, of, mgr, Brooklyn Royal Giants, Hilldale, Indianapolis ABCs, Chicago American Giants, Lincoln Giants, Detroit Stars, Kansas City Monarchs, Memphis Red Sox
KERNER, ———— —1933—of, Columbus Blue Birds
KEYES, ROBERT—1944–45—p, Memphis Red Sox
KEYES, STEVE (YOUNGIE)—1941–48—p, **Memphis Red Sox,** Philadelphia Stars
KEY, LUDIE—1934—pres, Birmingham Black Barons
KEYS, DR. GEORGE B.—1922–32—officer, St. Louis Stars; officer, NNL
KIMBRO, ARTHUR—1915–17—3b, 2b, St. Louis Giants, Lincoln Giants
KIMBRO, HENRY—1937–50—of, mgr, Washington Elite Giants, **Baltimore Elite Giants,** New York Black Yankees
KIMBROUGH, LARRY—1945–46—p, Philadelphia Stars
KINARD, ———— —1932—3b, Washington Pilots

KINCAIDE, C. J.—1945–47—officer, NSL

KINCANNON, HARRY—1932–38—p, **Pittsburgh Crawfords,** Philadelphia Stars, New York Black Yankees, Washington Black Senators

KINDLE, WILLIAM (BILL)—1911–20—ss, 2b, of, Brooklyn Royal Giants, Indianapolis ABCs, Chicago American Giants, Lincoln Stars, Lincoln Giants

KING, ———— —1921—of, Kansas City Monarchs

KING, BRENDAN—1943—p, Cincinnati Clowns

KING, (PIJO)—1950—of, Birmingham Black Barons

KING, WILBUR—1944–45—ss, Memphis Red Sox, Cleveland Buckeyes, Chicago American Giants

KINKEIDE, JOHN—1887—player, Louisville Falls Citys

KIRKSEY, ———— —1926—c, Dayton Marcos

KLEPP, EDDIE—1946—p, Cleveland Buckeyes

KNIGHT, ———— —1921—of, Detroit Stars

KNIGHT, ———— —1922—1b, Baltimore Black Sox

KNOX, ELWOOD C.—1920—co-drafter of constitution, NNL

KRANSON, FLOYD—1936–41—p, **Kansas City Monarchs,** Memphis Red Sox

KRIDER, J. MONROE—1890—mgr, Cuban Giants (Colored Monarchs of York, Pa., Eastern Interstate League)

KYLE, ———— —1922—of, Baltimore Black Sox

LACKEY, OBIE—1930–34—ss, 2b, p, Hilldale, Bacharach Giants, Pittsburgh Crawfords

LAIN, WILLIAM—1911—3b, Chicago Giants

LAIR, ———— —1925—of, Pennsylvania Red Caps of New York

LAMAR, CLARENCE—1937–42—ss, St. Louis Stars, Cleveland Bears, Jacksonville Red Caps

LAMAR, E. B., JR.—1895–1926—mgr, club officer, booker, Cuban X Giants, Cuban Stars, Bacharach Giants, Harrisburg Giants, Brooklyn Cuban Giants

LaMARQUE, JAMES (JIM)—1942–50—p, Kansas City Monarchs

LAND, ———— —1909–12—of, Cuban Giants, Smart Set

LANE, ALTO—1929–34—p, Memphis Red Sox, Indianapolis ABCs, Cincinnati Tigers

LANE, I. S.—1917–22—of, 3b, p, Dayton Giants, Dayton Marcos, Columbus Buckeyes, Detroit Stars

LANG, JOHN F.—1885—mgr, Argyle Hotel

LANGFORD, (AD)—1912–19—**p,** of, St. Louis Giants, Lincoln Stars, Brooklyn Royal Giants, Pennsylvania Red Caps of New York

LANGRUM, DR. E. L.—1934—officer, Cleveland Red Sox

LANIER, A. S.—1921—officer, Cuban Stars (NNL)

LANSING, WILBUR—1949—p, Houston Eagles

LANTIQUA, ———— —1935—c, New York Cubans

LANUZA, PEDRO—1932—c, Cuban Stars

LATIMER, ———— —1921—p, Indianapolis ABCs

LATTIMORE, ——— —1929–33—c, Baltimore Black Sox, Brooklyn Royal Giants, Columbus Blue Birds

LAURENT, MILTON—1929–35—3b, 1b, of, 2b, c, Memphis Red Sox, Cleveland Cubs, Birmingham Black Barons, Nashville Elite Giants, New Orleans Crescent Stars

LAVERA, ——— —1919—c, Cuban Stars

LAWSON, ——— —1940—p, Philadelphia Stars

LAZAGA, ——— —1916–22—of, Cuban Stars (NNL)

LEAK, CURTIS A.—1944–48—officer, New York Black Yankees; sec, NNL

LEARY, ——— —1920—3b, Dayton Marcos

LeBEAUX, ——— —1936—ss, Chicago American Giants

LeBLANC, ——— —1915—ss, Lincoln Giants

LeBLANC, ——— —1919–21—p, Cuban Stars (NNL)

LEE, DICK—1917–18—of, Chicago Union Giants

LEE, HOLSEY S. (SCRIP)—1920–43—**p,** of, 1b, Norfolk Stars, Philadelphia Stars, Hilldale, Norfolk Giants, Richmond Giants, Baltimore Black Sox, Bacharach Giants, Cleveland Red Sox; umpire, NNL

LEFTWICH, JOHN—1945—p, Homestead Grays

LELAND, FRANK C.—1887–1912—player, mgr, Washington Capital Citys, Chicago Unions, Chicago Union Giants, Leland Giants, Chicago Giants

LEMON, ——— —1939—2b, Indianapolis ABCs

LEON, ——— —1918—of, Cuban Stars

LEONARD, (BOBO)—1923–31—of, Chicago American Giants, Bacharach Giants, Lincoln Giants, Baltimore Black Sox, Homestead Grays, Pennsylvania Red Caps of New York

LEONARD, JAMES—1919–25—p, of, Cleveland Tate Stars, Cleveland Browns

LEONARD, WALTER F. (BUCK)—1933–50—**1b,** of, Brooklyn Royal Giants, **Homestead Grays**

LeRUE, ——— —1921—c, Detroit Stars

LETT, ROGER—1943—player, Cincinnati Clowns

LETTLERS, GEORGE—1887—player, Washington Capital Citys

LEUSCHNER, W. A. (BILL)—1940–43—booking agent; officer, New York Black Yankees

LEVIS, OSCAR (OSCAL)—1923–31—p, Cuban Stars (East), Hilldale, Darby Daisies, Baltimore Black Sox

LEWIS, ——— —1887—player, Boston Resolutes

LEWIS, ——— —1917—p, Lincoln Giants

LEWIS, CARY B.—1920—co-drafter, constitution of NNL; sec, NNL

LEWIS, CHARLES—1926—ss, Lincoln Giants

LEWIS, CLARENCE (FOOTS)—1931–37—ss, Memphis Red Sox

LEWIS, F. ——— —1932—of, Montgomery Grey Sox

LEWIS, GROVER—1928—3b, Homestead Grays

LEWIS, HENRY N.—1945—officer, Knoxville Black Smokies

LEWIS, HENRY N.—1943—mgr, Atlanta Black Crackers

LEWIS, IRA F.—1922—sec, Pittsburgh Keystones

LEWIS, JIM—1943—p, Chicago Brown Bombers

LEWIS, JOSEPH (SLEEPY)—1919–34—**c,** 3b, Baltimore Black Sox, Washington Potomacs, Homestead Grays, Hilldale, Lincoln Giants, Quaker Giants, Darby Daisies, Bacharach Giants, Norfolk–Newport News Royals

LEWIS, MILTON—1925–28—2b, 1b, Wilmington Potomacs, Bacharach Giants

LEWIS, R. S. (BUBBLES)—1923–28—officer, Memphis Red Sox; vice pres, NNL

LEWIS, RUFUS—1937–50—p, Pittsburgh Crawfords, **Newark Eagles,** Houston Eagles

LIGGONS. JAMES—1934—p, of, Monroe Monarchs, Memphis Red Sox

LIGHTNER, ———— —1932—p, Cole's American Giants

LIGON, RUFUS—1944–45—p, Memphis Red Sox

LILLARD, JOE—1932–37—**p,** of, c, Cole's American Giants, Chicago American Giants, Cincinnati Tigers

LILLIE, ———— —1925—utility, Birmingham Black Barons

LINARES, ROGELIO—1940–46—**1b,** of, Cuban Stars, New York Cubans

LINDER, ———— —1922—p, Kansas City Monarchs

LINDSAY, BILL—1910–14—p, Kansas City, Kansas, Giants, Leland Giants, Chicago American Giants

LINDSAY, CLARENCE—1922–31—ss, Richmond Giants, Bacharach Giants, Baltimore Black Sox, Wilmington Potomacs, Pennsylvania Red Caps of New York

LINDSAY, LEONARD—1942–43—1b, p, Cincinnati Clowns, Birmingham Black Barons

LINDSAY, ROBERT (FROG)—1910—ss, Kansas City, Kansas, Giants

LINDSEY, ———— —1912—of, Lincoln Giants

LINDSEY, ———— —1931—p, Indianapolis ABCs

LINDSEY, BEN—1929—ss, Bacharach Giants

LINDSEY, BILL—1924–26—ss, 2b, of, Washington Potomacs, Lincoln Giants, Dayton Marcos

LINDSEY, JAMES—1887—player, Pittsburgh Keystones

LINTON, BENJAMIN—1945—officer, Detroit Giants

LISBY, ———— —1934—p, Newark Dodgers, Bacharach Giants

LISTACH, ———— —1941—of, Birmingham Black Barons

LITTLE, BEN—1947–50—of, Homestead Grays, New York Black Yankees, Philadelphia Stars

LITTLE, WILLIAM—1937–50—officer, Chicago American Giants

LIVINGSTON, CURTIS—1950—of, Cleveland Buckeyes

LIVINGSTON, L. D. (GOO GOO)—1928–32—of, Kansas City Monarchs, New York Black Yankees, Pittsburgh Crawfords

LLOYD, JOHN HENRY—1905–31—**ss,** 1b, 2b, c, mgr, Macon Acmes, Cuban X Giants, Philadelphia Giants, Leland Giants, Lincoln Giants, Chicago American Giants, Brooklyn Royal Giants, Columbus Buckeyes, Bacharach Giants, Hilldale, New York Black Yankees

LOCKE, CLARENCE—1945–48—p, 1b, Chicago American Giants

LOCKE, EDDIE—1943–45—p, Cincinnati Clowns, Kansas City Monarchs

LOCKETT, LESTER—1939–50—2b, 3b, Chicago American Giants, Birmingham Black Barons, Cincinnati–Indianapolis Clowns, Baltimore Elite Giants, Memphis Red Sox

LOCKHART, HUBERT—1923–28—p, Bacharach Giants

LOFTIN, LOUIS SANTOP—see Santop, Louis

LOGAN, ——— —1921–23—p, Baltimore Black Sox

LONDO, JULIUS—1909—player, St. Paul Gophers

LONG, ——— —1920–25—of, Detroit Stars, Indianapolis ABCs

LONG, (BANG)—1932–40—3b, Atlanta Black Crackers, Chicago American Giants, Indianapolis Athletics, Philadelphia Stars

LONG, ERNEST—1948–49—p, Cleveland Buckeyes, Louisville Buckeyes

LONGEST, BERNELL—1942–47—2b, Chicago Brown Bombers, Chicago American Giants

LONGEST, JIMMY—1942—1b, Chicago Brown Bombers

LONGLEY, WYMAN (RED)—1934–49—2b, of, ss, c, 1b, 3b, Memphis Red Sox

LONGWARE, ——— —1920—2b, Detroit Stars

LOPEZ, CANDO—1920–35—**of,** 3b, Cuban Stars (NNL), New York Cubans

LOPEZ, JUSTO—1939—1b, Cuban Stars

LOPEZ, PEDRO—1939—of, Cuban Stars

LOPEZ, RAUL—1949—p, New York Cubans

LOPEZ, V. ——— —1923–39—p, Cuban Stars (ECL), Cuban Stars (NNL)

LORENZO, ——— —1929–30—p, Cuban Stars (NNL)

LOTT, (HONEY)—1950—player, Indianapolis Clowns

LOUDEN, LOUIS—1942–50—c, New York Cubans, Cuban Stars

LOVE. WILLIAM—1930–31—c, of, Detroit Stars

LOVING, J. G.—1887—player, Washington Capital Citys

LOWE, WILLIAM M.—1921–31—3b, ss, 2b, of, mgr, Indianapolis ABCs, Detroit Stars, **Memphis Red Sox,** Chattanooga Black Lookouts

LUCAS, ——— —1919–20—p, of, Cuban Stars of Havana, Cuban Stars (East)

LUCAS, (SCOTTY)—1928—officer, Philadelphia Tigers

LUGO, LEO—1944—player, Cincinnati–Indianapolis Clowns

LUNDY, RICHARD (DICK)—1916–48—**ss,** 3b, 2b, mgr, **Bacharach Giants,** Lincoln Giants, Hilldale, Baltimore Black Sox, Philadelphia Stars, Newark Dodgers, New York Cubans, Newark Eagles, Jacksonville Eagles

LUTHER, ——— —1920–25—p, Chicago Giants, Chicago American Giants, Lincoln Giants, Hilldale

LYLES, ——— —1932—c, Indianapolis Clowns

LYLES, JOHN—1934–43—of, ss, 2b, 3b, Homestead Grays, Indianapolis ABCs, Cleveland Bears, St. Louis Stars, Chicago American Giants, Cincinnati Buckeyes, Cleveland Buckeyes

LYNCH, THOMAS—1917—of, Indianapolis ABCs

LYONS, BENNIE—1917—1b, Jewell's ABCs of Indianapolis

LYONS, CHASE—1899—p, Genuine Cuban Giants

LYONS, GRANVILLE—1931–37—1b, p, Nashville Elite Giants, Louisville Black Caps, Detroit Stars, Louisville Red Caps, Philadelphia Stars, Memphis Red Sox

LYONS, JAMES (JIMMIE)—1911–32—of, mgr, Lincoln Giants, St. Louis Giants, Chicago Giants, Brooklyn Royal Giants, Indianapolis ABCs, Chicago American Giants, Detroit Stars, Cleveland Browns, Louisville Black Caps

MACK, —————1945—p, New York Black Yankees

MACK, PAUL—1916–17—of, 3b, Bacharach Giants, Jersey City Colored Giants

MACKEY, RALEIGH (BIZ)—1918–47—**c**, ss, mgr, San Antonio Giants, Indianapolis ABCs, **Hilldale,** Darby Daisies, Philadelphia Stars, Washington Elite Giants, Baltimore Elite Giants, **Newark Eagles**

MACKLIN, —————1924–29—3b, of, Chicago Giants

MADDIX, RAYDELL—1950—p, Indianapolis Clowns

MADERT, —————1917—2b, Chicago Giants

MADISON, —————1936–38—p, of, 3b, Kansas City Monarchs, Memphis Red Sox

MAGRINAT, HECTOR—1909–16—of, Cuban Stars, All Cubans

MAINOR, HANK—1950—p, Baltimore Elite Giants

MAHONEY, —————1921–23—p, Norfolk Giants, Indianapolis ABCs, Baltimore Black Sox

MAHONEY, ULYSSES—1944—p, Philadelphia Stars

MAISON, J. —————1887—player, Pittsburgh Keystones

MAKELL, FRANK—1944–49—c, Newark Eagles, Baltimore Elite Giants

MALARCHER, DAVID J. (GENTLEMAN DAVE)—1916–34—**3b**, of, 2b, mgr, Indianapolis ABCs, Detroit Stars, **Chicago American Giants,** Cole's American Giants

MALLOY, —————1918–21—of, Pennsylvania Red Caps of New York, Nashville Elite Giants

MALONE, WILLIAM H.—1887–95—p, Cuban Giants, Pittsburgh Keystones, New York Gorhams, Page Fence Giants

MANELLA, —————1921—p, Cuban Stars (NNL)

MANESE, E.—1923–26—2b, Detroit Stars, Kansas City Monarchs, Indianapolis ABCs

MANGRUM, —————1948—of, New York Cubans

MANLEY, ABRAHAM—1935–46—officer, Brooklyn Eagles, Newark Eagles; vice pres, tres, NNL

MANLEY, EFFA (MRS. ABRAHAM)—1935–48—officer, Brooklyn Eagles, Newark Eagles

MANN, —————1918—1b, Chicago Union Giants

MANNING, JOHN—1902—of, Philadelphia Giants

MANNING, MAXWELL (MAX)—1939–49—p, Newark Eagles, Houston Eagles

MANNO, ———— —1918—1b, Cuban Stars
MANUEL, ———— —1940—of, Cleveland Bears
MARA, CANDIDO—1948—3b, Memphis Red Sox
MARAVALE, ———— —1923—p, Cuban Stars (ECL)
MARCELL, EVERETT—1942–48—c, Chicago American Giants, Newark Eagles
MARCELLE (also Marcel, Marcell), OLIVER H. (GHOST)—1918–30 —**3b,** ss, Brooklyn Royal Giants, **Bacharach Giants,** Lincoln Giants, Detroit Stars, Baltimore Black Sox
MARCELLO, ———— —1921—p, Cuban Stars (NNL)
MARKHAM, JOHN—1930–45—p, Kansas City Monarchs, Monroe Monarchs, Birmingham Black Barons
MARQUEZ, LUIS ANGEL—1945–48—ss, 2b, 3b, New York Black Yankees, Homestead Grays, Baltimore Elite Giants
MARSANS, ARMANDO—1923—player, Cuban Stars
MARSELLAS, DAVID, JR.—1941—c, New York Black Yankees
MARSH, LORENZO—1950—c, Cleveland Buckeyes
MARSHALL, BOBBY—1909–11—1b, mgr, St. Paul Gophers, Leland Giants, Twin City Gophers
MARSHALL, JACK—1920–29—p, Chicago American Giants, Detroit Stars, Kansas City Monarchs
MARSHALL, WILLIAM (JACK, BOISY)—1926–44—**2b,** 3b, 1b, Dayton Marcos, Gilkerson's Union Giants, Chicago Columbia Giants, Cole's American Giants, Chicago American Giants, Philadelphia Stars, Cincinnati–Indianapolis Clowns
MARTIN, ———— —1927—1b, Detroit Stars
MARTIN, ALEXANDER—1932—officer, Cleveland Cubs
MARTIN, DR. B. B.—1933–50—officer, Memphis Red Sox; officer, NSL
MARTIN, DR. J. B.—1929–50—officer, Memphis Red Sox, Chicago American Giants; pres, Negro Dixie League, NSL, NAL
MARTIN, R. ———— —1885—p, Argyle Hotel
MARTIN, (STACK)—1925–26—of, Indianapolis ABCs
MARTIN, DR. W. S.—1929–50—officer, Memphis Red Sox; pres, NSL, officer, NAL
MARTINEZ, FRANCISCO—1939—p, Cuban Stars
MARTINEZ, HORACIO (RABBIT)—1935–47—**ss,** 3b, New York Cubans, Cuban Stars
MARTINEZ, PASQUEL—1924—p, Cuban Stars (NNL)
MARVRAY, CHARLES—1950—of, Cleveland Buckeyes
MASON, CHARLES—1922–29—**of,** p, Richmond Giants, Bacharach Giants, Lincoln Giants, Newark Stars, Homestead Grays
MASON, JIM—1932–34—1b, of, Washington Pilots, Memphis Red Sox
MASSIP, ———— —1925–30—1b, Cuban Stars (ECL)
MATCHETT, JACK—1940–45—p, Kansas City Monarchs
MATHIS, VERDEL—1940–49—**p,** of, 1b, Memphis Red Sox
MATLOCK, LEROY—1929–42—p, St. Louis Stars, Detroit Wolves, Washington Pilots, Homestead Grays, Pittsburgh Crawfords, New York Cubans
MATTHEWS, ———— —1923—3b, Toledo Tigers

MATTHEWS, ———— —1932–33—p, Monroe Monarchs, New Orleans Crescent Stars

MATTHEWS, CLIFFORD—1945—officer, New Orleans Black Pelicans

MATTHEWS, FRANCIS—1940–45—1b, **Newark Eagles,** Boston Royal Giants

MATTHEWS, JOHN—1919–33—officer, Dayton Marcos

MATTHEWS, WILLIAM CLARENCE—1905–10—ss, 2b, Burlington (Vermont League); New York Black Sox

MAXWELL, ZEARLEE (JIGGS)—1934–38—3b, 2b, Monroe Monarchs, Memphis Red Sox

MAYARI, ———— —1923—1b, Cuban Stars (ECL)

MAYERS, GEORGE—1923—p, St. Louis Stars

MAYFIELD, FRED—1887—player, Louisville Falls Citys

MAYO, ———— —1911–17—1b, of, Pittsburgh Giants, Pittsburgh Colored Stars, Hilldale

MAYO, GEORGE—1928—officer, Hilldale

MAYS, ———— —1937—p, St. Louis Stars

MAYS, DAVE—1937—of, Kansas City Monarchs

MAYS, WILLIE—1948–50—of, Birmingham Black Barons

MAYWEATHER, ELDRIDGE—1934–46—1b, Monroe Monarchs, Kansas City Monarchs, St. Louis Stars, New Orleans–St. Louis Stars, New York Black Yankees, Boston Blues

MAYWOOD, ———— —1917–19—p, Lincoln Giants

MAZAAR, ROBERT—1945—officer, Hilldale Club of Philadelphia

McADOO, (TULLY)—1907–24—1b, Topeka Giants, Kansas City, Kansas, Giants, **St. Louis Giants,** St. Louis Stars, Cleveland Browns

McALLISTER, ———— —1921—of, Kansas City Monarchs

McALLISTER, FRANK (CHIP)—1938–46—p, Indianapolis ABCs, St. Louis Stars, New Orleans–St. Louis Stars, New York Black Yankees, Harrisburg–St. Louis Stars, Brooklyn Brown Dodgers

McALLISTER, GEORGE—1924–34—1b, **Birmingham Black Barons,** Chicago American Giants, Indianapolis ABCs, Memphis Red Sox, Homestead Grays, Cleveland Red Sox

McBRIDE, FRED—1931–40—1b, of, Indianapolis ABCs, Chicago American Giants

McCALL, (BUTCH)—1937–38—1b, Chicago American Giants, Birmingham Black Barons

McCALL, HENRY—1945—player, Chicago American Giants

McCALL, WILLIAM (BILL)—1922–26—p, Pittsburgh Keystones, Birmingham Black Barons, Kansas City Monarchs, Chicago American Giants, Indianapolis ABCs

McCARTHY, C. H.—1921—pres, Southeastern Negro League

McCAULEY, ———— —1930—p, Nashville Elite Giants

McCLAIN, BILL—1933—p, Columbus Blue Birds

McCLAIN, EDWARD (BOOTS)—1921–26—ss, p, Dayton Marcos, Cleveland Tate Stars, Toledo Tigers, Cleveland Browns, Detroit Stars

McCLINIC, NAT—1948—of, Cleveland Buckeyes

McCLELLAN, DAN—1903–30—p, mgr, Cuban X Giants, **Philadelphia Giants,** Smart Set, Lincoln Giants, Quaker Giants

McCLELLAND, DR. J. W.—1922—officer, St. Louis Stars

McCLURE, ROBERT (BOB)—1921–30—p, Indianapolis ABCs, Cleveland Tate Stars, Baltimore Black Sox, Bacharach Giants, Brooklyn Royal Giants

McCLURE, WILL—1947—officer, Chattanooga Choo Choos

McCORD, (BUTCH)—1949–50—inf, Baltimore Elite Giants, Chicago American Giants

McCOY, (CHINK)—1934–43—c, Newark Dodgers, Harrisburg–St. Louis Stars

McCOY, ROY—1932—officer, Washington Pilots

McCOY, WALTER—1945–48—p, Chicago American Giants

McCREARY, FRED—1938–49—umpire, NNL

McCURRINE, JAMES—1946–48—of, Chicago American Giants

McDANIELS, BOOKER—1940–49—**p,** of, **Kansas City Monarchs,** Memphis Red Sox

McDANIELS, FRED—1943–45—of, Memphis Red Sox

McDEVITT, JOHN J.—1922—officer, Baltimore Black Sox

McDONALD, EARL—1938—officer, Washington Black Senators

McDONALD, LUTHER (VET)—1927–32—p, St. Louis Stars, Chicago American Giants, Chicago Columbia Giants, Cole's American Giants

McDONALD, WEBSTER—1918–45—p, mgr, Philadelphia Giants, Richmond Giants, Chicago American Giants, Hilldale, Darby Daisies, Washington Pilots, **Philadelphia Stars**

McDOUGAL, LEMUEL (LEM)—1917–20—p, Chicago American Giants, Indianapolis ABCs, Chicago Giants

McDUFFIE, TERRIS—1930–45—p, Birmingham Black Barons, Baltimore Black Sox, New York Black Yankees, Newark Eagles, Homestead Grays, Philadelphia Stars

McFARLAND, JOHN—1944–47—p, New York Black Yankees

McGOWAN, CURTIS—1950—p, Memphis Red Sox

McHASKELL, J. C.—1927–29—1b, Memphis Red Sox

McHENRY, HENRY—1930–50—p, Kansas City Monarchs, New York Black Yankees, Philadelphia Stars, Indianapolis Clowns

McINTOSH, ———— —1937—player, Detroit Stars

McKELLAM, ———— —1942—p, Cincinnati Buckeyes

McKINNIS, GREAD (LEFTY)—1941–49—p, Birmingham Black Barons, Chicago American Giants, Pittsburgh Crawfords

McLAIN, ———— —1920–21—3b, 2b, Indianapolis ABCs, Columbus Buckeyes

McLAUGHLIN, ———— —1917–1919—p, Lincoln Giants

McLAURIN, FELIX—1942–49—of, Jacksonville Red Caps, Birmingham Black Barons, New York Black Yankees, Chicago American Giants

McMAHON, JESS—1911–14—officer, Lincoln Giants

McMAHON, ROD—1911–14—officer, Lincoln Giants

McMEANS, WILLIE—1945—p, Chicago American Giants

McMILLAN, EARL—1923—of, Toledo Tigers

McMULLIN, CLARENCE—1945–49—of, Kansas City Monarchs, Houston Eagles

McMURRAY, WILLIAM—1909–11—c, St. Paul Gophers, St. Louis Giants

McNAIR, HURLEY—1912–42—of, Chicago Giants, Gilkerson's Union Giants, Chicago American Giants, Detroit Stars, Chicago Union Giants, **Kansas City Monarchs,** Cincinnati Tigers; umpire, NAL

McNEAL, CLYDE—1945–50—ss, Chicago American Giants

McNEIL, ———— —1918–20—1b, c, Dayton Marcos

McNEIL, ———— —1931–33—of, Louisville White Sox, Louisville Black Caps, Nashville Elite Giants

McQUEEN, PETE—1937–45—of, Memphis Red Sox, New York Black Yankees

McREYNOLDS, ———— —1916—of, Indianapolis ABCs

MEADE, (CHICK)—1916–22—**3b,** ss, Pittsburgh Colored Stars, Hilldale, Pittsburgh Stars of Buffalo, Bacharach Giants, Baltimore Black Sox, Harrisburg Giants

MEADOWS, ———— —1934—of, Cincinnati Tigers

MEANS, ———— —1924—c, Birmingham Black Barons

MEANS, LEWIS—1920–27—**2b,** 1b, Bacharach Giants

MEDERO, FRANK—1911–20—p, All Cubans, Bacharach Giants

MEDINA, LAZARUS—1944–45—p, Cincinnati–Indianapolis Clowns

MEDINA, PEDRO—1905—c, Cuban Stars of Santiago

MELLITO,———— —1928—ss, Cuban Stars (East)

MELLIX, GEORGE—1946—mgr, Brooklyn Brown Dodgers

MELTON, ———— —1916—p, St. Louis Giants

MELTON, ELBERT—1928–29—of, Brooklyn Cuban Giants, Lincoln Giants

MENDEZ, JOSE (JOE)—1908–26—**p,** ss, 3b, 2b, mgr, Cuban Stars, Stars of Cuba, All Nations, Los Angeles White Sox, Chicago American Giants, Detroit Stars, Kansas City Monarchs

MEREDITH, BUFORD (GEETCHIE)—1924–30—ss, 2b, **Birmingham Black Barons,** Nashville Elite Giants

MERCHANT, HENRY L.—1940–50—p, of, Chicago American Giants, Cincinnati–Indianapolis Clowns, Indianapolis Clowns

MERRITT, ———— —1905–17—Brooklyn Royal Giants, Lincoln Giants

MERRITT, SCHUTE—1934–35—utility, Newark Dodgers

MESA, ANDRES—1948—of, Indianapolis Clowns

MESA, PABLO—1921–27—of, Cuban Stars (ECL)

MEYERS, GEORGE—1924–26—p, St. Louis Stars, Dayton Marcos

MICKEY, JAMES—1940—ss, 3b, Chicago American Giants, Birmingham Black Barons

MICKEY, JOHN—1898—p, Celeron Acme Colored Giants (Iron and Oil League)

MILES, JOHN (MULE)—1937–38—of, Chicago American Giants

MILES, W. —— —1923–27—of, 1b, 3b, Toledo Tigers, Cleveland Tate Stars, Cleveland Browns, Cleveland Elites, Cleveland Hornets

MILLER, —— —1895–99—p, Page Fence Giants, Columbia Giants

MILLER, —— —1912–21—3b, 2b, Smart Set, Lincoln Giants, Lincoln Stars, **Brooklyn Royal Giants**

MILLER, —— —1911–20—c, Pittsburgh Giants, Dayton Marcos

MILLER, —— —1934—2b, Cincinnati Tigers

MILLER, —— —1937—1b, Indianapolis Athletics

MILLER, A. —— —1927—of, Memphis Red Sox

MILLER, BOB—1924–28—2b, 3b, Memphis Red Sox

MILLER, (BUCK)—1929–31—ss, 3b, Homestead Grays, Chicago American Giants, Chicago Columbia Giants

MILLER, DEMPSEY (DIMP)—1927–45—p, mgr, Cleveland Hornets, Cleveland Tigers, Nashville Elite Giants, Detroit Stars, Detroit Giants

MILLER, EDDIE (BUCK)—1925–29—p, Chicago American Giants, Indianapolis ABCs

MILLER, EUGENE—1909—of, St. Paul Gophers

MILLER, FRANK—1887–97—p, Pittsburgh Keystones, Cuban Giants, Cuban X Giants

MILLER, HENRY—1940–48—p, Philadelphia Stars

MILLER, L.—1917—3b, Bacharach Giants

MILLER, LEROY (FLASH)—1935–40—ss, 2b, Newark Dodgers, New York Black Yankees

MILLER, PERCY—1923–33—p, St. Louis Stars, St. Louis Giants, Nashville Elite Giants

MILLER, PLEAS (HUB)—1913—p, West Baden, Indiana, Sprudels, St. Louis Giants

MILLON, HERALD—1946—utility, Chicago American Giants

MILLS, CHARLES A.—1911–24—officer, St. Louis Giants, St. Louis Black Sox

MILTON, C. —— —1934—inf, Cleveland Red Sox

MILTON, HENRY—1934–41—of, Chicago Giants, Indianapolis ABCs, Chicago American Giants, Brooklyn Royal Giants, **Kansas City Monarchs**

MIMMS, —— —1932—p, Columbus Turfs

MINOR, GEORGE—1944–49—of, Chicago American Giants, Cleveland Buckeyes, Louisville Buckeyes

MINOSO, SATURNINO ORESTES ARRIETA ARMAS (MINNIE)— 1946–48—3b, New York Cubans

MIRABLE, AUTORIO—1939–40—c, Cuban Stars

MIRAKA, STANLEY—1950—2b, Chicago American Giants

MIRO, PEDRO—1945–47—2b, New York Cubans

MISSOURI, JIM—1938–41—p, Philadelphia Stars

MITCHELL, A. —— —1884—player, Philadelphia Mutual B.B.C.

MITCHELL, ALONZO—1938–41—mgr, 1b, p, club officer, Jacksonville Red Caps, Cleveland Bears

MITCHELL, ARTHUR—1939—inf, New York Black Yankees

MITCHELL, (BUD)—1929–34—of, p, c, Hilldale, Darby Daisies, Bacharach Giants

MITCHELL, (FLUKE)—1938–39—p, Atlanta Black Crackers, Jacksonville Red Caps, Indianapolis ABCs

MITCHELL, GEORGE—1925–49—p, mgr, bus mgr, Chicago American Giants, Indianapolis ABCs, Montgomery Grey Sox, Cleveland Cubs, Mounds City, Illinois, Blues (became Indianapolis ABCs), St. Louis Stars, New Orleans–St. Louis Stars, New York Black Yankees, Harrisburg–St. Louis Stars, Houston Eagles

MITCHELL, (HOOKS)—1923–28—p, Baltimore Black Sox, Bacharach Giants, Harrisburg Giants

MITCHELL, OTTO—1930—2b, Birmingham Black Barons

MITCHELL, ROBERT—1924—player, St. Louis Stars

MOLES, (LEFTY)—1935—p, Philadelphia Stars

MOLINA, ———— —1929–30—p, Cuban Stars (NNL)

MOLINA, AUGUSTIN—1921–31—officer, Cuban Stars (NNL)

MONGIN, SAM—1909–21—3b, 2b, Brooklyn Royal Giants, Lincoln Stars, Lincoln Giants, Bacharach Giants, St. Louis Giants

MONROE, AL—1937—sec, NAL

MONROE, BILL—1927—3b, Baltimore Black Sox

MONROE, WILLIAM (BILL)—1896–1914—2b, Chicago Unions, Philadelphia Giants, Brooklyn Royal Giants, Chicago American Giants

MONTALVO, ESTABAN—1923–28—1b, of, Cuban Stars (NNL), Lincoln Giants

MONTGOMERY, A. G.—1926—sec, NSL

MONTGOMERY, LOU—1942—p, of, inf, Cincinnati Clowns

MOODY, ———— —1931—ss, Memphis Red Sox

MOODY, ———— —1940—p, Birmingham Black Barons

MOODY, LEE—1944–45—1b, Kansas City Monarchs

MOODY, WILLIS—1922–29—of, Homestead Grays

MOORE, ———— —1911–20—of, St. Louis Giants

MOORE, C. L.—1945–48—officer, Asheville Blues; pres. Negro American Association

MOORE, CHARLES—1943—umpire, NNL

MOORE, HARRY (MIKE)—1896–1911—of, 1b, Chicago Unions, Algona Brownies, Cuban X Giants, Philadelphia Giants, Leland Giants, Chicago Giants, Lincoln Giants

MOORE, HENRY L.—1937–38—officer, St. Louis Stars, Birmingham Black Barons

MOORE, JAMES (RED)—1937–40—1b, Newark Eagles, Atlanta Black Crackers, Baltimore Elite Giants

MOORE, N. ———— —1920–24—of, Detroit Stars

MOORE, RALPH—1921—p, Cleveland Tate Stars

MOORE, ROY—1921—1b, Cleveland Tate Stars

MOORE, SQUIRE (SQUARE)—1924–28—p, Memphis Red Sox, Kansas City Monarchs, Cleveland Hornets, Cleveland Tigers

MOORE, WALTER (DOBIE)—1921–26—ss, of, Kansas City Monarchs
MOORHEAD, ALBERT —1925–29—c, Chicago Giants
MORAN, FRANCISCO—1911—of, Cuban Stars
MOREFIELD, FRED—1946—of, Pittsburgh Crawfords
MOREHEAD, ALBERT—1943—c, Birmingham Black Barons, Chicago Brown Bombers
MORELAND, NATE—1940–45—p, Baltimore Elite Giants, Kansas City Monarchs
MORGAN, J. L.—1937—of, Memphis Red Sox, Indianapolis Athletics
MORGAN, WILLIAM (WILD BILL)—1948—p, Memphis Red Sox
MORIN, EUGENIO—1910–22—2b, 3b, c, Cuban Stars (NNL)
MORNEY, LEROY—1932–44—ss, 3b, 2b, Monroe Monarchs, Columbus Blue Birds, Cleveland Giants, Pittsburgh Crawfords, Columbus Elite Giants, Washington Elite Giants, New York Black Yankees, Philadelphia Stars, Chicago American Giants, Birmingham Black Barons, Cincinnati Clowns
MORRIS, BARNEY—1932–47—p, Monroe Monarchs, Pittsburgh Crawfords, Cuban Stars, **New York Cubans**
MORRIS, F. B.—1948—sec, Negro American Association
MORRIS, HAROLD (YELLOWHORSE)—1924–32—p, Kansas City Monarchs, Detroit Stars, Chicago American Giants, Monroe Monarchs
MORRISON, JIMMY—1930—utility, Memphis Red Sox
MORRISON, W. —— —1925—1b, Cleveland Browns
MORTON, CY—1940–47—ss, 2b, Philadelphia Stars, Pittsburgh Crawfords, Chicago American Giants
MORTON, FERDINAND Q.—1935–38—commissioner, NNL
MOSELEY, BEAUREGARD F.—1910–11—officer, Leland Giants
MOSES, —— —1938–40—p, Kansas City Monarchs
MOSLEY, WILLIAM—1928–33—officer, Detroit Stars
MOSS, PORTER—1934–44—p, Cincinnati Tigers, **Memphis Red Sox**
MOTHEL, CARROL (DINK)—1920–34—of, 2b, 1b, ss, c, All Nations, **Kansas City Monarchs,** Cleveland Stars
MOTT, —— —1931—3b, Birmingham Black Barons
MUNGIN, —— —1925–26—p, Baltimore Black Sox
MUNOZ, JOSE (JOE)—1909–16—p, of, Cuban Stars, Stars of Cuba, Jersey City Cubans
MURRAY, CHARLES—1949–50—player, Cleveland Buckeyes
MURRAY, MITCHELL—1920–32—c, Indianapolis ABCs, Dayton Marcos, Cleveland Tate Stars, Toledo Tigers, **St. Louis Stars,** Chicago American Giants
MUSE, B. —— —1922–34—p, Hilldale, Monroe Monarchs
MYERS, —— —1910—ss, Brooklyn Royal Giants

NAPIER, EUTHUMN (EUDIE)—1935–50—c, **Homestead Grays,** Pittsburgh Crawfords
NARANJO, PEDRO—1950—p, Indianapolis Clowns
NASH, WILLIAM—1933–34—p, of, Birmingham Black Barons

NAVARRO, RAUL—1945—of, Cincinnati–Indianapolis Clowns

NEAL, GEORGE—1911—2b, Chicago Giants

NEARS, (RED)—1940—c, of, Memphis Red Sox

NEELY, ———— —1932–33—p, Louisville Black Caps, Cuban Stars

NEIL, RAY—1942–50—2b, Cincinnati Clowns, **Indianapolis Clowns**

NELSON, ———— —1931–33—p, Montgomery Grey Sox

NELSON, CLYDE—1943–49—3b, 2b, 1b, of, Chicago Brown Bombers, **Chicago American Giants,** Cleveland Buckeyes, Indianapolis Clowns

NELSON, JOHN—1887–1903—p, New York Gorhams, Cuban Giants, **Cuban X Giants,** Philadelphia Giants

NESBIT, DR. E. E.—1929—officer, Memphis Red Sox

NESTOR, S. ———— —1926—of, Lincoln Giants

NEWBERRY, HENRY—1947—p, Chicago American Giants

NEWBERRY, JAMES (JIMMY)—1943–50—p, Birmingham Black Barons

NEWBERRY, RICHARD—1947—ss, Chicago American Giants

NEWCOMBE, DONALD (DON)—1944–45—p, Newark Eagles

NEWKIRK, ALEXANDER (ALEX)—1946–49—p, New York Black Yankees, New York Cubans

NEWMAN, ———— —1940—p, Memphis Red Sox

NEWSOME, OMER—1923–24—p, Indianapolis ABCs, Washington Potomacs

NEWSON, ———— —1940—of, Newark Eagles

NICHOLAS, ———— —1936—p, Newark Eagles

NICHOLS, CHARLES—1885—of, Argyle Hotel

NIRSA, ———— —1923—of, Cuban Stars

NIXON, ———— —1940–41—of, Birmingham Black Barons

NOBLE, CARLOS—1950—p, New York Cubans

NOBLE, JUAN—1949–50—p, New York Cubans

NOBLE, RAFAEL MIGUEL (RAY)—1947–50—c, New York Cubans

NOBLE, SAM—1945—c, New York Cubans

NOLAN, ———— —1916—c, St. Louis Giants

NOEL, ———— —1921—p, Nashville Elite Giants

NORMAN, ———— —1920–26—ss, Lincoln Giants, Cleveland Elites

NORMAN, JIM—1909—inf, Kansas City, Kansas, Giants

NORMAN, WILLIAM (SHIN)—1909–10—p, Leland Giants

NORWOOD, C. H.—1887—player, Philadelphia Pythians

NORWOOD, WALTER—1933—officer, Detroit Stars

NUNLEY, ———— —1934—1b, Memphis Red Sox

NUTTALL, H. ———— —1925–26—p, Lincoln Giants

NUTTER, ISAAC H.—1927–28—officer, Bacharach Giants; pres., Eastern League

O'BRIEN, ———— —1932—ss, Washington Pilots

O'DELL, JOHN—1950—p, Houston Eagles

ODEN, J. ——— —1928–32—ss, of, Birmingham Black Barons, Knoxville Giants, Louisville Black Caps

O'FARRELL, ORLANDO—1949—ss, Indianapolis Clowns

OFFERT, ——— —1925–26—p, Indianapolis ABCs

OLDHAM, JIMMY—1921–22—p, St. Louis Giants, St. Louis Stars

OLIVER, ——— —1932–34—c, of, Birmingham Black Barons

OLIVER, JOHN—1885—3b, Brooklyn Remsens

OLIVER, JOHN—1945–46—ss, Memphis Red Sox, Cleveland Buckeyes

OMS, ALEJANDRO—1921–35—of, **Cuban Stars (ECL),** New York Cubans

O'NEIL, JOHN (BUCK)—1938–50—1b, mgr, Kansas City Monarchs

O'NEILL, CHARLES —1921–22—c, Columbus Buckeyes, New York Bacharach Giants

ORANGE, GRADY—1925–31—ss, 2b, 3b, Birmingham Black Barons, Kansas City Monarchs, Detroit Stars

ORMES, A. W.—1911—player, Leland Giants

ORTIZ, ORTIE—1945—player, Cincinnati–Indianapolis Clowns

ORTIZ, RAFAELITO—1948—p, Chicago American Giants

OSLEY, ——— —1938—p, Birmingham Black Barons

OSORIO, ALBERTO—1949—p, Louisville Buckeyes

OTIS, AMOS—1921—of, Nashville Elite Giants

OUSLEY, GUY—1931–32—**ss,** 2b, 3b, Chicago Columbia Giants, Cleveland Cubs, Memphis Red Sox

OVERTON, JOHN—1925—officer, Indianapolis ABCs

OWENS, ——— —1931—p, Nashville Elite Giants

OWENS, ——— —1937–39—of, Birmingham Black Barons, Indianapolis ABCs

OWENS, AUBREY—1920–25—p, Indianapolis ABCs, **Chicago American Giants,** New Orleans Caulfield Ads, Chicago Giants

OWENS, RAYMOND (SMOKY)—1939–42—**p,** of, Cleveland Bears, New Orleans–St. Louis Stars, Cincinnati Clowns, Jacksonville Red Caps

OWENS, W. E.—1887—player, Cincinnati Browns

OWENS, W. OSCAR—1913–30—**p,** 1b, of, **Homestead Grays,** Indianapolis ABCs

OWENS, WILLIAM (WILLIE)—1923–33—**ss,** 2b, p, Washington Potomacs, Chicago American Giants, Indianapolis ABCs, Dayton Marcos, Birmingham Black Barons, Memphis Red Sox, Detroit Stars

PACE, ——— —1922—c, Pittsburgh Keystones

PADRONE, J. ——— —1909–26—**p,** 2b, of, Cuban Stars (ECL), Smart Set, Long Branch Cubans, Chicago American Giants, Lincoln Giants, Cuban Stars (NNL), Indianapolis ABCs

PAGE, ——— —1930—1b, of, Quaker Giants, Brooklyn Royal Giants

PAGE, ALLEN—1945–50—vice-pres, tres, NSL; officer, New Orleans Creoles; promoter

PAGE, PEDRO—1947—of, New York Cubans

PAGE, R.—1925—officer, Indianapolis ABCs

PAGE, THEODORE (TED)—1931–37—of, Homestead Grays, Pittsburgh Crawfords, New York Black Yankees, Newark Eagles, Philadelphia Stars

PAIGE, LeROY (SATCHEL)—1926–50—p, Chattanooga Black Lookouts, Birmingham Black Barons, Cleveland Cubs, **Pittsburgh Crawfords, Kansas City Monarchs,** New York Black Yankees, Satchel Paige's All-Stars, Philadelphia Stars

PAINE, HENRY—1884—of, Brooklyn Remsons

PAINE, JOHN—1887—player, Philadelphia Pythians

PAIZE, PEDRO—1939—utility, Cuban Stars

PALM, CLARENCE (SPOONY)—1927–46—c, Birmingham Black Barons, St. Louis Stars, Detroit Stars, Cleveland Giants, Homestead Grays, Brooklyn Eagles, New York Black Yankees, Philadelphia Stars

PALMER, EARL—1918–19—of, Chicago Union Giants, Lincoln Giants

PALMER, JAMES—1887—player, New York Gorhams

PANIER, ——— —1917—p, Cuban Giants

PAREDA, (MONK)—1910–21—p, 1b, Stars of Cuba, Cuban Stars

PAREGO, GEORGE—1885–88—p, Argyle Hotel, Cuban Giants

PARKER, ——— —1900—of, Genuine Cuban Giants

PARKER, ——— —1919—p, Lincoln Giants

PARKER, ——— —1943—p, Kansas City Monarchs

PARKER, JACK—1938—inf, Pittsburgh Crawfords

PARKER, THOMAS (TOM, BIG TRAIN)—1929–46—**p,** of, mgr, Memphis Red Sox, Indianapolis ABCs, Monroe Monarchs, Homestead Grays, New Orleans–St. Louis Stars, New York Black Yankees, Harrisburg–St. Louis Stars, New York Cubans, Boston Blues

PARKINSON (PARKY)—1950—p, Houston Eagles

PARKS, CHARLES (CHARLIE)—1946–47—c, Newark Eagles

PARKS, JOHN—1939–47—c, of, New York Black Yankees, Newark Eagles

PARKS, JOSEPH B.—1909–19—of, **c,** ss, Cuban Giants, Philadelphia Giants, Brooklyn Royal Giants, Pennsylvania Red Caps of New York

PARKS, SAM—1945—officer, Memphis Grey Sox

PARKS, WILLIAM—1911–19—ss, 2b, of, Chicago Giants, Lincoln Giants, Lincoln Stars, American Giants, Pennsylvania Red Caps of New York

PARNELL, ROY (RED)—1926–50—**of,** 1b, mgr, Birmingham Black Barons, Monroe Monarchs, New Orleans Crescent Stars, Columbus Elite Giants, **Philadelphia Stars,** Pittsburgh Crawfords, Houston Eagles

PARPETTI, AUGUSTIN—1915–23—**1b,** of, **Cuban Stars,** Kansas City Monarchs, Bacharach Giants

PARRIS, CLYDE—1946–49—2b, 3b, of, New York Black Yankees, Louisville Buckeyes

PARSONS, A. S.—1897—mgr, Page Fence Giants

PARTLOW, ROY—1934–50—p, Cincinnati Tigers, Memphis Red Sox, **Homestead Grays,** Philadelphia Stars

PASSON, HARRY—1934—officer, Bacharach Giants
PATE, ARCHIE—1909—player, St. Paul Gophers
PATTERSON, ———— —1941—of, New York Black Yankees
PATTERSON, GABRIEL—1946–48—of, Pittsburgh Crawfords, Homestead Grays, New York Black Yankees, Philadelphia Stars
PATTERSON, JOHN W. (PAT)—1890–1906—2b, mgr, Lincoln (Nebraska) Giants, Page Fence Giants, Columbia Giants of Chicago, Philadelphia Giants, Cuban X Giants, Cuban Giants, Quaker Giants of New York, Brooklyn Royal Giants
PATTERSON, PAT—1934–49—2b, **3b,** of, Cleveland Red Sox, Pittsburgh Crawfords, Kansas City Monarchs, **Philadelphia Stars,** Newark Eagles, Houston Eagles
PATTERSON, WILLIAM B.—1914–25—mgr, Houston Black Buffaloes, Austin, Texas, Senators, Birmingham Black Barons
PATTERSON, WILLIE—1950—c, New York Cubans
PATTON, ———— —1909—of, p, Philadelphia Giants
PAYNE, ———— —1933—of, Homestead Grays
PAYNE, ———— - 1927—2b, Brooklyn Royal Giants
PAYNE, ANDREW H. (JAP)—1902–22—of, Philadelphia Giants, Cuban X Giants, Leland Giants, Chicago American Giants, Chicago Union Giants, New York Central Red Caps
PAYNE, JAMES—1887—player, Baltimore Lord Baltimores
PAYNE, RUSTY—1940—of, Indianapolis Crawfords
PAYNE, WILLIAM (DOC)—1898—of, Celeron Acme Colored Giants (Iron and Oil League)
PEACE, WARREN—1945–48—p, Newark Eagles
PEACOCK, ———— —1933—3b, Homestead Grays
PEAK, RUFUS—1931—officer, Detroit Stars
PEARSON, FRANK—1945–49—p, Memphis Red Sox
PEARSON, JIMMY—1949—p, New York Cubans
PEARSON, LEONARD (LENNIE)—1937–50—of, 3b, ss, 1b, mgr, **Newark Eagles,** Baltimore Elite Giants
PEATROSS, MAURICE—1947—1b, Homestead Grays
PEDROSO, EUSTAQUIO—1910–30—p, of, 1b, c, **Cuban Stars (NNL),** All Cubans, Cuban Stars (ECL)
PEDROSO, FERNANDO—1949—inf, New York Cubans
PEEBLES, A. J.—1933—officer, Columbus Blue Birds
PEEKS, A. J.—1932—officer, Atlanta Black Crackers
PEEPLES, NATHANIEL—1950—c, Kansas City Monarchs, Indianapolis Clowns
PELHAM, WILLIAM—1933–38—ss, Bacharach Giants, Atlanta Black Crackers
PENA, ———— —1929—player, Cuban Stars (NNL)
PENDLETON, JAMES (JIM)—1948—ss, Chicago American Giants
PENNINGTON, ———— —1929—p, Nashville Elite Giants
PENNINGTON, ARTHUR (ART)—1940–50—**of,** 1b, 2b, **Chicago American Giants,** Pittsburgh Crawfords

PENNO, DAN—1893—p, of, Cuban Giants

PERDUE, FRANK M.—1920–34—pres, NSL; officer, Birmingham Black Barons

PEREIRA, JOSE—1947—p, Baltimore Elite Giants

PEREZ, JAVIER—1942–45—3b, New York Cubans, Cuban Stars

PEREZ, JOSE—1911–37—p, 1b, c, 2b, ss, 3b, Cuban Stars (ECL), Cuban Stars (NNL), Harrisburg Giants, Bacharach Giants, Hilldale, New York Cubans, Homestead Grays

PEREZ, LUIS—1948—3b, Indianapolis Clowns

PERKINS, W. G. (BILL)—1928–47—c, of, mgr, Birmingham Black Barons, Cleveland Cubs, Pittsburgh Crawfords, Cleveland Stars, Philadelphia Stars, Baltimore Elite Giants, New York Black Yankees

PERRY, ———— —1921–25—2b, 3b, ss, Detroit Stars, Bacharach Giants, Washington Potomacs, Lincoln Giants, Cleveland Browns

PERRY, ALONZO—1940–50—p, 1b, Homestead Grays, Birmingham Black Barons

PERRY, ED—1887—player, Washington Capital Citys

PETERS, FRANK—1916–23—ss, Chicago Union Giants, Peters Union Giants

PETERS, W. S.—1896–1923—owner, mgr, Chicago Unions, Peters Union Giants

PETERSON, HARVEY—1931–36—of, p, Montgomery Grey Sox, Birmingham Black Barons, Memphis Red Sox, Cincinnati Tigers

PETERSON, L. ———— —1885—1b, Brooklyn Remsens

PETTUS, WILLIAM T. (ZACK)—1909–23—c, 1b, 2b, mgr, Kansas City Giants, Leland Giants, Chicago Giants, Lincoln Stars, Lincoln Giants, St. Louis Giants, Hilldale, Bacharach Giants, Richmond Giants, Harrisburg Giants

PETWAY, ———— —1931–32—ss, 2b, Nashville Elite Giants, Birmingham Black Barons

PETWAY, BRUCE—1906–25—c, of, mgr, Leland Giants, Brooklyn Royal Giants, Philadelphia Giants, **Chicago American Giants,** Detroit Stars

PETWAY, SHIRLEY—1937—c, Detroit Stars

PFIFFER, ———— —1937—3b, St. Louis Stars

PHILLIPS, ———— —1921–23—ss, 2b, Nashville Elite Giants, Detroit Stars

PHILLIPS, JOHN—1939—p, Baltimore Elite Giants

PHILLIPS, NORRIS—1942–43—p, Kansas City Monarchs

PIERCE, HERBERT—1925–26—c, Homestead Grays

PIERCE, STEVE—1925–28—officer, Detroit Stars

PIERCE, WILLIAM H. (BILL)—1910–32—1b, c, of, Philadelphia Giants, Chicago American Giants, Lincoln Stars, Lincoln Giants, Pennsylvania Red Caps of New York, Bacharach Giants, Norfolk Giants, Detroit Stars; umpire, East-West League

PIERSON, ———— —1937—of, St. Louis Stars

PIERSON, ———— —1933—3b, Homestead Grays

PIGG, LEONARD—1947–50—c, Indianapolis Clowns, Cleveland Buckeyes

PILLOTT, GUIDO—1943—p, Cincinnati Clowns

PINDER, ———— —1917—ss, Hilldale

PIPKIN, (BLACK DIAMOND)—1942—p, Birmingham Black Barons

PIPKIN, ROBERT (LEFTY)—1929–33—p, Birmingham Black Barons, Cleveland Cubs, New Orleans Crescent Stars

PITTS, ———— —1950—c, Chicago American Giants, Cleveland Buckeyes

PLA, ———— —1933—p, Cuban Stars

POINDEXTER, ROBERT—1924–29—**p,** lb, **Birmingham Black Barons,** Chicago American Giants, Memphis Red Sox

POINSETTE, ROBERT—1939—of, New York Black Yankees

POLES, E. (POSSUM)—1922–28—**ss,** 3b, Baltimore Black Sox, Harrisburg Giants

POLES, SPOTTSWOOD (SPOT)—1909–23—of, Philadelphia Giants, **Lincoln Giants,** Brooklyn Royal Giants, Lincoln Stars, Hilldale

POLLARD, NAT— 1946–50—p, Birmingham Black Barons

POLLOCK, SYD—1926–50—officer, Havana Red Sox, Cuban House of David, Cuban Stars, Ethiopian Clowns, Cincinnati Clowns, Indianapolis Clowns

POMPEZ, ALLESANDRO (ALEX)—1922–50—officer, Cuban Stars (ECL), New York Cubans; vice-pres, NNL

POOLE, CLAUDE—1945–46—p, New York Black Yankees

POPE, ———— —1938—of, Atlanta Black Crackers

POPE, ———— —1931–32—p, Louisville White Sox, Montgomery Grey Sox

POPE, A. ———— —1948—of, Homestead Grays

POPE, DAVE—1946—utility, Homestead Grays

POPE, WILLIE (BILL)—1947–48—p, Homestcad Grays

PORTER, ANDREW (ANDY)—1932–50—p, Cleveland Cubs, Nashville Elite Giants, Washington Elite Giants, **Baltimore Elite Giants,** Indianapolis Clowns

PORTUANDO, BARTOLO—1918–27—**3b,** 1b, Cuban Stars, Kansas City Monarchs, Cuban Stars (ECL)

POSEY, CUMBERLAND WILLIS (CUM)—1911–46—of, officer, **Homestead Grays,** Detroit Wolves; founder, East-West League; sec, tres, NNL

POSEY, SEWARD H.—1911–48—officer, bus mgr, Homestead Grays

POSTELL, ———— —1934—2b, Cincinnati Tigers

POTTER, ———— —1921—c, Kansas City Monarchs

POWELL, ———— —1931—2b, Memphis Red Sox

POWELL, EDDIE—1937–38—c, New York Black Yankees

POWELL, J. J.—1931—officer, Little Rock Black Travelers

POWELL, MELVIN (PUT)—1932–43—**p,** of, Cole's American Giants, **Chicago American Giants,** Chicago Brown Bombers

POWELL, RUSSELL—1915–20—**c,** 2b, Indianapolis ABCs

POWELL, WILLIAM (BILL)—1947–50—p, Birmingham Black Barons
POWELL, WILLIE (WEE WILLIE)—1927–35—p, **Chicago American Giants,** Detroit Stars, Cole's American Giants, Cleveland Red Sox
PRESSWOOD, HENRY—1948–50—ss, Cleveland Buckeyes
PRESTON, ALBERT—1947—p, New York Black Yankees
PRESTON, ROBERT—1950—p, Baltimore Elite Giants
PRITCHETT, WILBUR—1926–30—p, Harrisburg Giants, Baltimore Black Sox, Brooklyn Cuban Giants, Hilldale
PROCTOR, JAMES (CUB)—1884–87—p, c, Baltimore Atlantics, Baltimore Lord Baltimores
PRYOR, ———— —1916—p, Indianapolis ABCs, St. Louis Giants
PRYOR, ANDERSON—1923–33—2b, ss, Milwaukee Bears, Detroit Stars, Memphis Red Sox
PRYOR, BILL —1927–28—p, Memphis Red Sox
PRYOR, EDWARD—1925—2b, Lincoln Giants
PRYOR, WES—1910–12—3b, Leland Giants, American Giants, St. Louis Giants, Chicago Giants
PUGH, JOHNNY—1916–22—3b, 2b, **of, Brooklyn Royal Giants,** Philadelphia Giants, Bacharach Giants, Harrisburg Giants
PULLEN, C. NEIL—1920–24—c, Brooklyn Royal Giants, Kansas City Monarchs, Baltimore Black Sox
PURCELL, ———— —1947—p, Memphis Red Sox

QUINONES, THOMAS—1947—p, Indianapolis Clowns
QUINTANA, BUSTA—1928–33—inf, Cuban Stars (NNL)

RADCLIFFE, ALEX—1927–46—ss, **3b,** Chicago Giants, Cole's American Giants, **Chicago American Giants,** New York Cubans, Kansas City Monarchs, Cincinnati–Indianapolis Clowns, Memphis Red Sox
RADCLIFFE, THEODORE (DOUBLE DUTY)—1928–50—**c, p,** mgr, Detroit Stars, St. Louis Stars, Pittsburgh Crawfords, Homestead Grays, Columbus Blue Birds, New York Black Yankees, Brooklyn Eagles, Cincinnati Tigers, Memphis Red Sox, Birmingham Black Barons, Chicago American Giants, Louisville Buckeyes
RAGLAN, ———— —1920–21—p, Indianapolis ABCs, Kansas City Monarchs, Columbus Buckeyes
RAGGS, HARRY—1921–23—of, Norfolk Giants, Harrisburg Giants, Baltimore Black Sox
RAINE, J. ———— —1884–85—of, Baltimore Atlantics
RAMIREZ, RAMIRO—1916–48—of, mgr, Cuban Stars, Havana Stars, Cuban Stars (East), All Cubans, Bacharach Giants, Baltimore Black Sox, Havana Red Sox, Cuban House of David, Indianapolis Clowns
RAMOS, JOSE—1921–29—of, All Cubans, Cuban Stars (ECL)
RANDOLPH, A. ———— —1885—1b, Argyle Hotel
RANKIN, GEORGE—1887—player, Cincinnati Browns
RAY, ———— —1921–24—p, c, Kansas City Monarchs, Chicago Giants, St. Louis Stars, Cleveland Tate Stars, Cleveland Browns

RAY, JOHN—1932–45—of, Montgomery Grey Sox, Birmingham Black Barons, Cleveland Bears, Jacksonville Red Caps, Cincinnati–Indianapolis Clowns, Kansas City Monarchs

RAY, RICHARD—1943—inf, of, Chicago Brown Bombers

RAY, THOMAS—1887—player, New York Gorhams

REAVIS, ——— —1920–30—p, Lincoln Giants, Pennsylvania Red Caps of New York

RECTOR, CORNELIUS (CONNIE)—1921–44—p, Hilldale, **Brooklyn Royal Giants,** Lincoln Giants, **New York Black Yankees,** New York Cubans

REDD, ULYSSES A.—1940–41—ss, Chicago American Giants, Birmingham Black Barons

REDDING, RICHARD (DICK) (CANNONBALL)—1911–38—**p,** of, mgr, **Lincoln Giants,** Lincoln Stars, Indianapolis ABCs, Chicago American Giants, **Brooklyn Royal Giants,** Bacharach Giants

REDDON, BOB—1919—p, Cleveland Tate Stars

REDMON, TOM—1911—player, Leland Giants

REDUS, WILSON— 1924–40—of, mgr, coach, **St. Louis Stars,** Cleveland Stars, Columbus Blue Birds, Cleveland Giants, Kansas City Monarchs, Cleveland Red Sox, Chicago American Giants

REED, ——— —1937—of, St. Louis Stars

REED, ——— —1918–19—3b, Chicago Union Giants, Detroit Stars

REED, AMBROSE—1922–32—**of,** 2b, 1b, 3b, **Bacharach Giants,** Hilldale, Pittsburgh Crawfords, Atlanta Black Crackers

REED, FLEMING—1950—player, Baltimore Elite Giants

REED, JOHN—1934–42—p, Cole's American Giants, Indianapolis ABCs, **Chicago American Giants,** Chicago Brown Bombers

REEL, ——— —1923—of, Toledo Tigers

REESE, ——— —1910—p, Cuban Giants

REESE, JAMES—1934–35—p, Cleveland Red Sox, Brooklyn Eagles

REESE, JOHN E.—1918–26—of, Bacharach Giants, Hilldale, Chicago American Giants, Detroit Stars, Toledo Tigers, St. Louis Stars

REEVES, DONALD—1937–41—1b, of, Atlanta Black Crackers, Indianapolis ABCs, Chicago American Giants

RENA, ——— —1929—c, Cuban Stars (NNL)

RENFROE, OTHELLO—1945–50—of, c, ss, Kansas City Monarchs, Cleveland Buckeyes, Indianapolis Clowns

REVERIA, CHARLIE—1939—3b, Baltimore Elite Giants

REYNOLDS, ——— —1899—of, Chicago Columbia Giants

REYNOLDS, ERNEST—1948—2b, ss, Cleveland Buckeyes

REYNOLDS, JIMMY—1940—3b, Indianapolis Crawfords

REYNOLDS, JOE—1935—p, Philadelphia Stars

RHODES, ——— —1917—c, Hilldale

RHODES, (DUSTY)—1932—p, Louisville Black Caps

RHODES, HARRY—1942–50—p, 1b, Chicago American Giants

RICE, ——— —1934—of, Cincinnati Tigers

RICH, ——— —1924—3b, St. Louis Giants

RICHARDSON, ———— —1943—ss, Newark Eagles
RICHARDSON, BOB—1949—ss, Homestead Grays
RICHARDSON, DEWEY—1922—c, Hilldale
RICHARDSON, EUGENE (GENE)—1948–50—p, Kansas City Monarchs
RICHARDSON, GEORGE—1925—officer, Detroit Stars
RICHARDSON, GLEMBY—1947—2b, New York Black Yankees
RICHARDSON, HENRY—1922–38—**p**, of, **Baltimore Black Sox,** Washington Pilots, Bacharach Giants, Washington Black Senators, Pittsburgh Crawfords
RICHARDSON, JIM—1939—p, New York Black Yankees
RICHARDSON, JOHN—1925—player, Birmingham Black Barons
RICKS, ———— —1921–22—of, p, Dayton Marcos, Cleveland Tate Stars
RICKS, NAPOLEON—1887—player, Louisville Falls Citys
RICKS, WILLIAM (BILL)—1944–50—p, Philadelphia Stars
RIDDICK, VERNON—1941—ss, Newark Eagles
RIDDLE, MARSHALL—1938–43—2b, Indianapolis ABCs, St. Louis Stars, New Orleans–St. Louis Stars, Cleveland Buckeyes
RIDGELY, ———— —1920—ss, Lincoln Giants
RIDLEY, JACK—1929–34—of, Nashville Elite Giants, Cleveland Cubs, Louisville Red Caps
RIGAL, ———— —1923–27—ss, 3b, Cuban Stars (NNL)
RIGGINS, ORVILLE—1920–33—ss, 3b, 2b, mgr, Detroit Stars, Cleveland Hornets, Homestead Grays, Lincoln Giants, New York Black Yankees, Brooklyn Royal Giants
RIGNEY, H. G. (HANK)—1939–45—officer, Toledo Crawfords, Indianapolis Crawfords, Toledo Rays
RILE, EDWARD (ED)—1920–33—**p**, 1b, Indianapolis ABCs, Chicago American Giants, Lincoln Giants, Columbus Buckeyes, Detroit Stars, Cole's American Giants, Brooklyn Royal Giants
RIOS, HERMAN—1915–24—3b, ss, Cuban Stars (NNL), Havana Stars
RISLEY, ———— —1922–23—3b, Baltimore Black Sox, Washington Potomacs
RITCHEY, JOHN—1947—c, Chicago American Giants
RIVERA, NENENE—1933—p, inf, Cuban Stars
RIVERO, CARLOS—1943–44—ss, 3b, Cuban Stars, New York Black Yankees
ROBERTS, ———— —1931—c, Chicago Columbia Giants
ROBERTS, CHARLEY—1938—p, Washington Black Senators
ROBERTS, CURTIS—1947–50—2b, Kansas City Monarchs
ROBERTS, ELIHU—1916–20—of, Bacharach Giants, Hilldale
ROBERTS, HARRY—1923—of, Baltimore Black Sox
ROBERTS, J. D.—1918–19—ss, 3b, 2b, Pennsylvania Giants, Hilldale
ROBERTS, LEROY (ROY)—1916–29—p, **Bacharach Giants,** Columbus Buckeyes
ROBERTS, R.—1933–34—p, Cleveland Giants, Cleveland Red Sox
ROBERTS, (RAGS)—1926–28—c, Homestead Grays

ROBERTS, SARAH MUTT—1939—player, Baltimore Elite Giants
ROBERTS, (SPECK)—1939-45—p, Homestead Grays, New York Black Yankees, Newark Eagles
ROBERTSON, BOBBIE—1929—ss, Detroit Stars
ROBINSON, ———— —1925—p, Birmingham Black Barons
ROBINSON, AL—1909-12—1b, Brooklyn Royal Giants
ROBINSON, BILL (BOJANGLES)—1931—officer, New York Stars (Black Yankees)
ROBINSON, BOBBY—1940—utility, St. Louis Stars
ROBINSON, CHARLES—1939—of, Chicago American Giants
ROBINSON, FRAZIER—1942-50—c, Baltimore Grays, **Baltimore Elite Giants**
ROBINSON, GEORGE—1924—officer, Washington Potomacs
ROBINSON, GEORGE (SIS)—1918—p, Bacharach Giants
ROBINSON, J. ———— —1938-39—3b, Indianapolis ABCs, St. Louis Stars
ROBINSON, JACK ROOSEVELT (JACKIE)—1945—ss, Kansas City Monarchs
ROBINSON, JACOB—1947—3b, Chicago American Giants
ROBINSON, JAMES (BLACK RUSIE)—1895-1904—p, Lansing, Michigan, Colored Capital All-Americans, Cuban Giants, Cuban X Giants
ROBINSON, JOSHUA—1939—of, New York Black Yankees
ROBINSON, NEIL—1936-50—**of,** ss, Cincinnati Tigers, Homestead Grays, **Memphis Red Sox**
ROBINSON, NEWT—1925-27—ss, Hilldale, Lincoln Giants
ROBINSON, NORMAN—1939-50—**of,** ss, Baltimore Elite Giants, Birmingham Black Barons
ROBINSON, RAY—1941-47—p, Newark Eagles, Cincinnati Buckeyes, Philadelphia Stars
ROBINSON, WALTER (SKINDOWN)—1940-42—2b, Cleveland Bears, Jacksonville Red Caps
ROBINSON, WILLIAM—1925-34—3b, ss, Indianapolis ABCs, Cleveland Elites, Memphis Red Sox, Detroit Stars, Cleveland Stars, Cleveland Red Sox
RODDY, B. M.—1926—pres, NSL
RODGERS, SYLVESTER—1950—p, Baltimore Elite Giants
RODRIGUEZ, ANTONIO—1939—p, Cuban Stars
RODRIGUEZ, B. ———— —1922—p, of, Cuban Stars (NNL)
RODRIGUEZ, BENVIENIDO—1948—of, Chicago American Giants
RODRIGUEZ, HERRADO—1944—3b, New York Cubans
RODRIGUEZ, J. ———— —1915-29—c, Cuban Stars (East), Detroit Stars, Kansas City Monarchs, Cuban Stars (NNL)
ROESINK, JOHN—1925-30—officer, Detroit Stars
ROGAN, WILBUR (BULLET)—1917-46—**p,** of, 1b, 2b, 3b, ss, mgr, Los Angeles White Sox, **Kansas City Monarchs;** umpire, NAL
ROGERS, ———— —1900—p, Genuine Cuban Giants
ROGERS, ———— —1934—p, Cincinnati Tigers

ROGERS, ———— —1939—p, Chicago American Giants
ROGERS, NAT—1927–45—of, **Memphis Red Sox,** Chicago Columbia Giants, Cole's American Giants, Chicago American Giants
ROGERS, SID—1887—player, Cincinnati Browns
ROGERS, WILLIAM—1928–30—of, Chicago American Giants, Memphis Red Sox
ROJO, JULIO—1916–30—c, Cuban Stars, Havana Stars, Bacharach Giants, Baltimore Black Sox, Cuban Stars of Havana, Lincoln Giants
ROLLS, CHARLES—1911—player, Leland Giants
ROMBY, BOB—1947–50—p, Baltimore Elite Giants
RONSELL, ———— —1929—of, Birmingham Black Barons
ROQUE, ———— —1928—of, Cuban Stars (NNL)
ROSE, ———— —1924—p, St. Louis Stars
ROSELLO, ———— —1921—of, Detroit Stars
ROSS, H. ———— —1922–25—p, Indianapolis ABCs, Washington Potomacs, Chicago American Giants
ROSS, WILLIAM—1925–30—p, St. Louis Stars, Cleveland Hornets, Homestead Grays
ROSSELLE, B. ———— —1926–28—p, Cuban Stars (NNL)
ROSSITER, GEORGE—1922–32—officer, Baltimore Black Sox
ROTH, HERMAN (BOBBY)—1921–25—c, New Orleans Crescent Stars, Chicago American Giants, Milwaukee Bears, Detroit Stars, Birmingham Black Barons
ROVIRA, JAIME—1911—3b, All Cubans
ROWE, (SCHOOLBOY)—1943–45—p, Chicago Brown Bombers, Pittsburgh Crawfords
ROYALL, JOHN—1937–42—p, Indianapolis Athletics, Jacksonville Red Caps, New York Black Yankees
RUFFIN, LEON—1936–50—c, mgr, **Newark Eagles,** Pittsburgh Crawfords, Philadelphia Stars, Houston Eagles
RUIZ, ANTONIO—1944—p, Cincinnati–Indianapolis Clowns
RUIZ, SILVINO (POPPA)—1928–42—p, Cuban Stars (ECL), New York Cubans
RUSH, JOE—1923–26—officer, Birmingham Black Barons; sec, NNL; pres, NSL
RUSS, PYTHIAS—1926–29—c, ss, Chicago American Giants
RUSSELL, ———— —1929–31—of, Nashville Elite Giants, Memphis Red Sox
RUSSELL, ———— —1933—p, Brooklyn Royal Giants
RUSSELL, ———— —1940—of, Cuban Stars
RUSSELL, AARON A.—1913–20—3b, Homestead Grays
RUSSELL, BRANCH—1922–32—3b, of, Kansas City Monarchs, **St. Louis Stars,** Cleveland Stars, Cleveland Cubs
RUSSELL, E. ———— —1926—3b, Harrisburg Giants
RUSSELL, FRANK (JUNIOR)—1943–49—2b, of, Baltimore Elite Giants
RUSSELL, JOHN HENRY—1924–33—2b, 3b, Memphis Red Sox, **St. Louis Stars,** Indianapolis ABCs, Pittsburgh Crawfords, Detroit Wolves

RUTLEDGE, —— —1921—p, Dayton Marcos
RYAN, MERVEN J. (RED)—1915–30—p, Pittsburgh Stars of Buffalo, Brooklyn Royal Giants, **Hilldale,** Harrisburg Giants, Bacharach Giants, Baltimore Black Sox, Lincoln Stars, Newark Browns, Lincoln Giants

ST. THOMAS, LARRY—1947—c, New York Black Yankees
SALAZAR, LAZARO—1924–35—**of,** p, 1b, Cuban Stars (NNL), New York Cubans
SALAZAR, SANTIAGO—1945—utility, New York Cubans
SALMON, HARRY—1924–35—p, Birmingham Black Barons, Homestead Grays
SALTERS, EDWARD—1937—of, Detroit Stars
SAMA, PABLO—1950—3b, Indianapolis Clowns
SAMPSON, —— —1905—p, Genuine Cuban Giants
SAMPSON, —— —1932–33—ss, Atlanta Black Crackers, Brooklyn Royal Giants
SAMPSON, EDDIE—1941—of, Birmingham Black Barons
SAMPSON, JOHN—1942—of, New York Cubans
SAMPSON, SAM—1940–41—2b, of, Cleveland Bears, Jacksonville Red Caps
SAMPSON, THOMAS (TOMMY)—1940–48—**2b,** 1b, mgr, Chicago American Giants, **Birmingham Black Barons,** New York Cubans
SAMUELS, —— —1940—p, Philadelphia Stars
SAN, —— —1928—player, Cuban Stars (ECL)
SANCHEZ, AMANDO—1948—p, Memphis Red Sox
SANDS, SAM (PIGGY)—1950—ss, Indianapolis Clowns
SANTA CRUZ, (SANTA)—1909–10—of, Cuban Stars
SANTELLA, —— —1935—2b, New York Cubans
SANTIAGO, JOSE—1947–48—p, New York Cubans
SANTOP, LOUIS (TOP)—(real name Louis Santop Loftin)—1909–26 —c, of, mgr, Fort Worth Wonders, Oklahoma Monarchs, Philadelphia Giants, **Lincoln Giants,** Chicago American Giants, Lincoln Stars, Brooklyn Royal Giants, **Hilldale**
SAPERSTEIN, A. M. (ABE)—1932–50—booking agent; officer, Cleveland Cubs, Cincinnati Clowns, Chicago American Giants; pres, Negro Midwestern League, West Coast Negro Baseball Association
SARVIS, ANDREW (SMOKY)—1940–42—p, Cleveland Bears, Jacksonville Red Caps
SAUNDERS, —— —1925—c, Pennsylvania Red Caps of New York
SAUNDERS, —— —1931–37—**2b,** ss, Detroit Stars, Bacharach Giants, Monroe Monarchs, Louisville Red Caps
SAUNDERS, BOB—1926—p, Kansas City Monarchs
SAUNDERS, LEO—1940—p, ss, Chicago American Giants, Birmingham Black Barons
SAUNDERS, WILLIAM—1950—c, Baltimore Elite Giants
SAVAGE, —— —1925—p, Bacharach Giants
SAVAGE, ARTIE—1932—officer, Cleveland Stars
SAVAGE, JUNIOR—1940—p, Memphis Red Sox

SAXON, THOMAS (LEFTY)—1942—p, New York Cubans
SAYLOR, ALFRED—1941–45—p, Birmingham Black Barons
SCALES, GEORGE—1921–48—**2b,** 3b, of, ss, mgr, St. Louis Giants, St. Louis Stars, **Lincoln Giants,** Newark Stars, Homestead Grays, New York Black Yankees, Philadelphia Stars, **Baltimore Elite Giants**
SCANTLEBURY, PATRICIO ATHELSTAN (PAT)—1944–50—p, New York Cubans
SCHLICHTER, H. WALTER—1902–10—officer, Philadelphia Giants; pres, National Association of Colored Base Ball Clubs of the United States and Cuba
SCHORLING, JOHN M.—1911–27—officer, Chicago American Giants
SCOTLAND, ———— —1916–17—of, Chicago Union Giants, Indianapolis ABCs
SCOTT, ———— —1916—p, Chicago Giants
SCOTT, BILL—1950—player, Philadelphia Stars
SCOTT, C. L.—1915—player, Mohawk Giants
SCOTT, CHARLES—1919–20—of, St. Louis Giants
SCOTT, ELISHA—1920—co-drafter, constitution of NNL
SCOTT, JIMMY—1950—p, Memphis Red Sox
SCOTT, JOE—1933—1b, Columbus Blue Birds
SCOTT, JOHN—1944–49—of, Birmingham Black Barons, **Kansas City Monarchs,** Louisville Buckeyes
SCOTT, JOSEPH (JOE)—1948–49—1b, Birmingham Black Barons
SCOTT, JOSEPH (JOE)—1947–49—of, Memphis Red Sox
SCOTT, ROBERT—1920–26—of, **Brooklyn Royal Giants,** Lincoln Giants
SCOTT, WILLIAM—1932—officer, Louisville Black Caps
SCOTT, WILLIE LEE—1927–32—1b, Memphis Red Sox, Louisville White Sox, Indianapolis ABCs
SCRUGGS, WILLIE—1950—p, Cleveland Buckeyes
SEAGRAVES, ———— —1937—of, Indianapolis Athletics
SEAGRAVES, SAMUEL—1946—c, Chicago American Giants
SEAY, RICHARD (DICK)—1925–47—**2b,** ss, Pennsylvania Red Caps of New York, Newark Stars, Baltimore Black Sox, Brooklyn Royal Giants, Philadelphia Stars, Pittsburgh Crawfords, Newark Eagles, New York Black Yankees
SELDEN, WILLIAM—1887–95—p, Boston Resolutes, Cuban Giants, New York Gorhams, Lansing, Michigan, Colored Capital All-Americans, Cuban X Giants
SELLER, ———— —1921–24—c, of, Bacharach Giants, Birmingham Black Barons
SEMLER, JAMES—1932–48—officer, New York Black Yankees
SERRELL, WILLIAM (BONNIE)—1942–50—2b, 3b, Kansas City Monarchs
SHACKLEFORD, JOHN G.—1924–45—3b, 2b, Cleveland Browns, Chicago American Giants, Birmingham Black Barons; pres, United States League

SHARPE, ROBERT (PEPPER)—1943–49—p, of, **Memphis Red Sox,** Chicago American Giants
SHAW, ——— —1897—player, Page Fence Giants
SHAW, THEODORE (TED)—1927–31—p, Chicago American Giants, Detroit Stars, Memphis Red Sox
SHELTON, ——— —1920—c, Dayton Marcos
SHEPARD, FRED—1945—player, Birmingham Black Barons
SHEPPARD, RAY—1929–32—ss, Birmingham Black Barons, Detroit Wolves, Homestead Grays
SHEPPARD, SAMUEL (SAM)—1887–1922—player, New York Gorhams; officer, St. Louis Stars
SHIELDS, CHARLIE (LEFTY)—1941–45—p, Chicago American Giants, Homestead Grays
SHIPP, JESSE—1911–12—p, Brooklyn Royal Giants
SHIVELY, GEORGE—1915–24—of, **Indianapolis ABCs,** Bacharach Giants, Washington Potomacs
SHROPSHINE, ——— —1937—c, St. Louis Stars
SIBLEY, ——— —1913—p, Indianapolis ABCs
SIEBERT, ——— —1937—of, St. Louis Stars
SIERRA, FELIPE—1921–30—ss, 2b, 3b, of, All Cubans, Cuban Stars (NNL)
SIGENERO, ——— —1940—p, Cuban Stars
SIJO, ——— —1929—c, Cuban Stars (East)
SIKI, ROQUE—1932—of, Cuban Stars
SILVA, PEDRO—1921–22—p, All Cubans, Cuban Stars (NNL)
SIMMONS, ——— —1926—p, Lincoln Giants
SIMMONS, J. R.—1887—player, Baltimore Lord Baltimores
SIMMONS, R. S.—1943–49—officer, Chicago American Giants; sec, NAL
SIMMS, WILLIAM (BILL)—1934–43—of, Monroe Monarchs, Cincinnati Tigers, Kansas City Monarchs, Chicago American Giants
SIMPSON, ——— —1933—player, Cleveland Giants
SIMPSON, HARRY (SUITCASE)—1946–48—of, Philadelphia Stars
SIMPSON, JAMES—1887—player, Philadelphia Pythians
SIMPSON, LAWRENCE—1916–20—p, Chicago Union Giants, Chicago Giants
SINCLAIR, HARRY—1931—sec, NNL
SINGER, ORVILLE—1923–32—of, inf, Lincoln Giants, Cleveland Browns, Cleveland Tigers, Cleveland Cubs, Cleveland Stars
SINGLETON, ——— —1896—c, Cuban X Giants
SINGLONG, ——— —1929—2b, Nashville Elite Giants
SKINNER, ——— —1910—c, Leland Giants
SLAUGHTER, C.—1884–85—inf, Baltimore Atlantics
SLOAN, ROBERT—1919–21—of, Brooklyn Royal Giants
SMALLWOOD, LOUIS—1923–29—2b, Milwaukee Bears, Chicago Giants
SMART, ——— —1932—p, Indianapolis ABCs

SMITH, ———— —1887—player, Boston Resolutes
SMITH, ———— —1912–15—p, of, Lincoln Giants
SMITH, ———— —1924—p, Washington Potomacs
SMITH, ———— —1925—c, St. Louis Stars
SMITH, ALPHONSE—1947–48—of, ss, Cleveland Buckeyes
SMITH, B. ———— —1887—player, New York Gorhams
SMITH, B. ———— —1932–33—p, 1b, Birmingham Black Barons
SMITH, C. ———— —1931—1b, Chicago Columbia Giants
SMITH, C. ———— —1933–38—c, Birmingham Black Barons
SMITH, CHARLES (CHINO)—1924–30—of, 2b, Philadelphia Giants,
   Brooklyn Royal Giants, Lincoln Giants
SMITH, CHARLIE—1938—inf, Washington Black Senators
SMITH, CLARENCE—1921–31—of, mgr, Columbus Buckeyes, Detroit
   Stars, Birmingham Black Barons, Baltimore Black Sox, Cleveland Cubs
SMITH, CLEVELAND (CLEO)—1923–28—2b, 3b, ss, Baltimore Black
   Sox, Lincoln Giants, Homestead Grays, Philadelphia Tigers, Harrisburg
   Giants
SMITH, CLYDE—1938—3b, Pittsburgh Crawfords
SMITH, DOUGLAS—1943—officer, Baltimore Elite Giants
SMITH, E. ———— —1942—3b, Jacksonville Red Caps, Cincinnati Buck-
   eyes
SMITH, ERNEST—1934–40—c, Monroe Monarchs, **Chicago American
   Giants**
SMITH, EUGENE (GENE)—1940–49—p, St. Louis Stars, New Or-
   leans–St. Louis Stars, New York Black Yankees, Homestead Grays,
   Cleveland Buckeyes, Louisville Buckeyes
SMITH, FORD—1946–48—p, Kansas City Monarchs
SMITH, G. ———— —1941—p, Kansas City Monarchs
SMITH, HARRY—1902—1b, Philadelphia Giants
SMITH, HENRY—1942–45—2b, ss, Jacksonville Red Caps, Chicago
   American Giants, Cincinnati Clowns, Cincinnati–Indianapolis Clowns
SMITH, HILTON—1933–48—p, Monroe Monarchs, **Kansas City Mon-
   archs**
SMITH, HY—1885—of, Brooklyn Remsens
SMITH, J. ———— —1904—3b, Cuban X Giants
SMITH, J. ———— —1925–27—2b, ss, Brooklyn Royal Giants
SMITH, JOHN—1940–48—of, p, Indianapolis Crawfords, Chicago Amer-
   ican Giants, New York Black Yankees
SMITH, L. ———— —1922–23—of, Baltimore Black Sox
SMITH, L. ———— —1942—c, Jacksonville Red Caps
SMITH, (LEFTY)—1921—p, Kansas City Monarchs
SMITH, (LEFTY)—1940–43—1b, of, Indianapolis Crawfords, Chicago
   American Giants
SMITH, MANCE—1944—player, Kansas City Monarchs
SMITH, MILT—1950—player, Philadelphia Stars
SMITH, O. H.—1885—p, Brooklyn Remsens
SMITH, OLLIE—1945—p, Cincinnati–Indianapolis Clowns
SMITH, P. ———— —1939—p, St. Louis Stars

SMITH, QUINCY—1943–45—of, Cleveland Buckeyes, Birmingham Black Barons

SMITH, ROBERT (BOB)—1930–44—c, 3b, Birmingham Black Barons, Memphis Red Sox, Cincinnati Tigers, St. Louis Stars, New Orleans–St. Louis Stars, Chicago American Giants, Pittsburgh Crawfords

SMITH, THEOLIC (FIREBALL)—1936–49—p, Pittsburgh Crawfords, St. Louis Stars, New Orleans–St. Louis Stars, Cleveland Buckeyes, Kansas City Monarchs

SMITH, W. —— —1921—ss, Hilldale

SMITH, WARDELL—1946—p, Chicago American Giants

SMITH, WILLIAM T.—1900–11—c, of, Genuine Cuban Giants, Cuban X Giants, Philadelphia Giants, Brooklyn Royal Giants

SMITH, WILLIE D.—1948—p, Homestead Grays

SMITH, WYMAN—1921–24—of, Baltimore Black Sox

SNAER, LUCIAN—1923—umpire, NNL

SNEAD, SYLVESTER—1941–46—of, 2b, Kansas City Monarchs, Cincinnati Clowns, New York Black Yankees

SNEED, EDDIE (LEFTY)—1940–42—p, Birmingham Black Barons

SNOW, FELTON—1931–47—3b, 2b, mgr, Louisville White Sox, Louisville Black Caps, Nashville Elite Giants, Columbus Elite Giants, Washington Elite Giants, **Baltimore Elite Giants,** Nashville Cubs

SNOWDEN, —— —1933—p, Detroit Stars

SOCKARD, —— —1927—3b, Cleveland Hornets

SOLIS, L. —— —1928–33—2b, 3b, Cuban Stars (East)

SOSS, RAMON—1948—c, Homestead Grays

SOSTRO, FRANCISCO—1947—p, New York Cubans

SOUELL, HERBERT (HERB)—1944–50—inf, Kansas City Monarchs

SOUTHALL, JOHN—1898—c, Celeron Acme Colored Giants (Iron and Oil League)

SOUTHY, —— —1921—ss, Lincoln Giants

SPARKS, JOE—1937–40—2b, St. Louis Stars, Chicago American Giants

SPARROW, ROY—1938—officer, Washington Black Senators

SPEARMAN, CHARLES—1919–31—c, 2b, 3b, ss, **Brooklyn Royal Giants,** Cleveland Elites, Homestead Grays, Lincoln Giants, Pennsylvania Red Caps of New York

SPEARMAN, CLYDE (SPLO)—1932–46—of, Pittsburgh Crawfords, New York Black Yankees, New York Cubans, Newark Eagles, Philadelphia Stars, Chicago American Giants, Birmingham Black Barons

SPEARMAN, HENRY (SPLO)—1936–46—3b, 1b, Homestead Grays, Pittsburgh Crawfords, Washington Black Senators, New York Black Yankees, Baltimore Elite Giants, Philadelphia Stars

SPEARMAN, WILLIAM—1924–27—p, Memphis Red Sox, Cleveland Elites, Cleveland Hornets

SPEDDEN, CHARLES P.—1922–23—officer, Baltimore Black Sox

SPENCER, —— —1922—of, Pittsburgh Keystones

SPENCER, J. C.—1945—2b, Birmingham Black Barons

SPENCER, JOSEPH B.—1942–46—2b, ss, Birmingham Black Barons, Homestead Grays, Pittsburgh Crawfords, New York Cubans

SPENCER, (PEE WEE)—1933–40—c, 3b, Chicago American Giants, Toledo Crawfords, Indianapolis Crawfords
SPENCER, WILLIE—1941—of, Birmingham Black Barons
SPENCER, ZACK—1931—p, Chicago Columbia Giants
SPIKE, ———— —1923—p, Washington Potomacs
SPOTTSVILLE, BILL—1950—p, Houston Eagles
STAMPS, HULAN (LEFTY)—1925–27—p, Memphis Red Sox
STANLEY, JOHN (NECK)—1928–48—p, Bacharach Giants, Lincoln Giants, Quaker Giants, Brooklyn Royal Giants, Baltimore Black Sox, **New York Black Yankees,** New York Cubans, Philadelphia Stars
STAPLES, JOHN—1921—mgr, Montgomery Grey Sox
STARK, L. ———— —1887—player, Cincinnati Browns
STARKS, JAMES—1938–46—1b, **New York Black Yankees,** Harrisburg–St. Louis Stars
STARKS, LESLIE—1934—of, Newark Dodgers
STARKS, OTIS (LEFTY)—1919–24—p, Hilldale, Chicago American Giants, Brooklyn Royal Giants, Lincoln Giants
STEARNS, NORMAN (TURKEY)—1921–42—of, Montgomery Grey Sox, **Detroit Stars,** Lincoln Giants, Cole's American Giants, Chicago American Giants, Philadelphia Stars, Kansas City Monarchs, Detroit Black Sox
STEELE, EDWARD (ED)—1941–50—of, Birmingham Black Barons
STEPHENS, ———— —1927—of, 1b, Cleveland Hornets
STEVENS, ———— —1929—p, Bacharach Giants
STEVENS, FRANK—1925–26—p, Chicago American Giants, Indianapolis ABCs
STEVENS, JIM—1933—2b, Philadelphia Stars
STEVENS, L. ———— —1923—p, 1b, Toledo Tigers
STEVENS, PAUL (JAKE)—1921–37—ss, **Hilldale,** Philadelphia Giants, Homestead Grays, Pittsburgh Crawfords, Philadelphia Stars, New York Black Yankees
STEVENSON, ———— —1928—p, Cleveland Tigers
STEVENSON, WILLIE—1943—p, Homestead Grays
STEWART, RILEY—1947–50—p, Chicago American Giants, New York Cubans
STILL, BOBBY—1887—player, Philadelphia Pythians
STILL, JOE—1887—player, Philadelphia Pythians
STINSON, C. P.—1887—player, Philadelphia Pythians
STITLER, ———— —1922—p, Bacharach Giants
STOCKARD, T. ———— —1928—ss, Cleveland Tigers
STONE, ED—1931–45—of, Bacharach Giants, Brooklyn Eagles, **Newark Eagles,** Philadelphia Stars
STOVALL, ———— —1924—p, Cleveland Browns
STOVALL, FRED—1930–35—officer, Monroe Monarchs
STOVEY, GEORGE W.—1886–96—p, Jersey City (Eastern League); Newark (International League); Cuban Giants, New York Gorhams, Cuban X Giants

STRATTON, ——— —1930—c, Hilldale
STRATTON, LEROY—1921–33—ss, 3b, 2b, mgr, **Nashville Elite Giants,** Milwaukee Bears, Birmingham Black Barons
STREETER, SAMUEL (SAM)—1920–35—Montgomery Grey Sox, Atlanta Black Crackers, Chicago American Giants, Bacharach Giants, Lincoln Giants, Birmingham Black Barons, Homestead Grays, Cleveland Cubs, Pittsburgh Crawfords
STREETS, ALBERT—1925—inf, Chicago American Giants
STRONG, ——— —1922–23—p, New Orleans Crescent Stars, Milwaukee Bears
STRONG, F. ——— —1922–23—p, Cleveland Tate Stars, Chicago American Giants
STRONG, JOSEPH C. (JOE)—1928–35—p, Hilldale, St. Louis Stars, Homestead Grays
STRONG, J. T.—1925–28—p, Baltimore Black Sox
STRONG, NAT C.—1908–34—booking agent; officer, Brooklyn Royal Giants, New York Black Yankees
STRONG, OTHELLO—1950—p, Chicago American Giants
STRONG, T. R. (TED)—1937–48—of, inf, mgr, Indianapolis Athletics, Indianapolis ABCs, Kansas City Monarchs, Indianapolis Clowns
STROTHERS, C. W.—1924–27—officer, Harrisburg Giants
STROTHERS, TIM SAMUEL (SAM)—1909–18—c, 1b, 2b, Leland Giants, Chicago American Giants, Chicago Giants, Chicago Union Giants
STUART, JOE—1884–85—p, c, Brooklyn Atlantics
STURDEVEN, MARK—1928—tres, Hilldale
SUAREZ, ——— —1916–21—p, Cuban Stars, Havana Stars, Cuban Stars of Havana, Cuban Stars (NNL)
SULLIVAN, ——— —1918—of, Chicago Union Giants
SUMMERALL, (BIG)—1940—p, Memphis Red Sox
SUMMERS, LONNIE—1938–49—of, c, Baltimore Elite Giants, Chicago American Giants
SUMMERS, S. ——— —1923–29—of, Toledo Tigers, Cleveland Browns, Cleveland Elites, Cleveland Hornets, Cleveland Tigers, Chicago American Giants
SUSINI, ——— —1921—2b, All Cubans
SUNKETT, ——— —1945—p, Philadelphia Stars
SUTTLES, EARL—1950—1b, Cleveland Buckeyes
SUTTLES, GEORGE (MULE)—1918–48—1b, of, **Birmingham Black Barons, St. Louis Stars,** Detroit Wolves, Washington Pilots, Chicago American Giants, Cole's American Giants, **Newark Eagles,** New York Black Yankees; umpire
SUTTON, LEROY—1941–45—p, New Orleans–St. Louis Stars, Chicago American Giants, Cincinnati–Indianapolis Clowns
SWEATT, GEORGE—1921–27—3b, 2b, of, Chicago Giants, Kansas City Monarchs, Chicago American Giants
SYKES, JOE—1942—player, Cincinnati Clowns

SYKES, MELVIN (DOC)—1915–26—p, Lincoln Stars, **Hilldale,** Baltimore Black Sox

TABORN, EARL—1946–50—c, Kansas City Monarchs
TALBERT, DANGER—1909–11—3b, Leland Giants, Chicago Giants
TALBERT, JAMES—1947–48—c, Chicago American Giants
TATE, GEORGE—1918–22—officer, Cleveland Tate Stars; vice pres, NNL
TATE, ROOSEVELT (SPEED)—1932–37—of, Birmingham Black Barons, Nashville Elite Giants, Memphis Red Sox, Cincinnati Tigers
TATUM, REECE (GOOSE)—1941–42—of, 1b, Birmingham Black Barons, Minneapolis–St. Paul Gophers, Cincinnati Clowns, Cincinnati–Indianapolis Clowns, Indianapolis Clowns
TAYLOR, B.—1912—p, St. Louis Giants
TAYLOR, BENJAMIN—1947—p, New York Black Yankees
TAYLOR, BENJAMIN H. (BEN)—1913–40—1b, mgr, Chicago American Giants, Indianapolis ABCs, St. Louis Giants, Bacharach Giants, Washington Potomacs, Harrisburg Giants, Baltimore Black Sox, Baltimore Stars, Brooklyn Eagles, Washington Black Senators, New York Cubans
TAYLOR, (BIG)—1920–22—p, Chicago Giants, Kansas City Monarchs
TAYLOR, CHARLES I. (C. I.)—1904–22—**mgr,** Birmingham Giants, West Baden, Indiana, Sprudels, **Indianapolis ABCs;** vice pres, NNL
TAYLOR, MRS. C. I.—1922–24—officer, Indianapolis ABCs
TAYLOR, G. —— —1925—of, Lincoln Giants
TAYLOR, GEORGE—1895–97—1b, Page Fence Giants
TAYLOR, JAMES (CANDY JIM)—1904–48—**3b,** 2b, **mgr,** Birmingham Giants, St. Paul Gophers, Leland Giants, Indianapolis ABCs, St. Louis Giants, Chicago American Giants, Dayton Marcos, Cleveland Tate Stars, St. Louis Stars, Cleveland Elites, Memphis Red Sox, Detroit Stars, Nashville Elite Giants, Columbus Elite Giants, Homestead Grays, Baltimore Elite Giants; vice chairman, NNL
TAYLOR, JIM—1896—of, Cuban Giants
TAYLOR, JOHN (STEEL ARM JOHNNY)—1909–12—p, St. Paul Gophers, Leland Giants, Chicago Giants, St. Louis Giants, Lincoln Giants
TAYLOR, JOHN—1920–25—p, Chicago Giants, Lincoln Giants
TAYLOR, JOHN—1935–45—p, New York Cubans, Cuban Stars
TAYLOR, LEROY R.—1925–36—of, Chicago American Giants, Indianapolis ABCs, **Kansas City Monarchs,** Detroit Wolves, Homestead Grays, Cleveland Red Sox
TAYLOR, OLAN (JELLY)—1934–46—**1b,** c, mgr, Cincinnati Tigers, **Memphis Red Sox,** Birmingham Black Barons
TAYLOR, RAYMOND—1931–44—c, **Memphis Red Sox,** Cincinnati Buckeyes, Cleveland Buckeyes, Kansas City Monarchs
TAYLOR, ROBERT—1938–42—c, Indianapolis ABCs, St. Louis Stars, New Orleans–St. Louis Stars, New York Black Yankees

TAYLOR, S. —— —1912–31—p, mgr, St. Louis Giants, Little Rock Black Travelers
TAYLOR, (SHINE)—1939—of, Toledo Crawfords
TENNEY, WILLIAM—1910—c, Kansas City, Kansas, Giants
TERAN, —— —1916–21—**2b,** 3b, Cuban Stars (East), Cuban Stars of Havana
TERRELL, —— —1924–25—p, Detroit Stars
TERRELL, S. M.—1928—officer, Cleveland Stars
TERRILL, —— —1887–96—ss, Boston Resolutes, Cuban X Giants
TERRY, —— —1931–34—2b, 3b, Indianapolis ABCs, Homestead Grays, Cincinnati Tigers
TEVERA, —— —1924—2b, Cuban Stars (NNL)
THOMAS, —— —1909–11—p, of, Brooklyn Royal Giants
THOMAS, —— —1921–22—c, Baltimore Black Sox
THOMAS, ARTHUR—1886–91—**c,** 1b, Cuban Giants, New York Gorhams
THOMAS, (BOY)—1929—p, Lincoln Giants
THOMAS, CLINTON (CLINT)—1920–37—**of,** 2b, Brooklyn Royal Giants, Columbus Buckeyes, Detroit Stars, **Hilldale,** Bacharach Giants, Lincoln Giants, Darby Daisies, New York Black Yankees, Newark Eagles, Philadelphia Stars
THOMAS, D.—1921–23—2b, Indianapolis ABCs, St. Louis Stars
THOMAS, D.—1936–37—p, Cincinnati Tigers
THOMAS, DAN—1938–40—of, Jacksonville Red Caps, Chicago American Giants, Birmingham Black Barons
THOMAS, DAVID (SHOWBOAT)—1923–46—**1b,** of, mgr, Montgomery Grey Sox, Birmingham Black Barons, Baltimore Black Sox, New York Black Yankees, **New York Cubans,** Washington Black Senators, Brooklyn Royal Giants
THOMAS, HENRY—1931—of, New York Black Yankees
THOMAS, J.—1887—player, Louisville Falls Citys
THOMAS, JEROME—1887—player, Washington Capital Citys
THOMAS, JOHN—1950—p, Cleveland Buckeyes
THOMAS, JULES—1914–25—of, Brooklyn Royal Giants, **Lincoln Giants**
THOMAS, L. —— —1929–30—c, of, 1b, Birmingham Black Barons
THOMAS, NELSON—1947—p, Newark Eagles
THOMAS, WALTER—1937–45—p, of, Detroit Stars, Kansas City Monarchs
THOMAS, WILLIAM—1943—of, Chicago Brown Bombers
THOMPSON, —— —1916–19—p, Lincoln Stars, Pittsburgh Stars of Buffalo
THOMPSON, —— —1923—p, Harrisburg Giants
THOMPSON, —— —1933—p, Cuban Stars
THOMPSON, (COPPERKNEE)—1942—inf, Cincinnati Clowns, Minneapolis–St. Paul Gophers
THOMPSON, FRANK—1885—organizer, Argyle Hotel

THOMPSON, FRANK (GROUNDHOG)—1945–50—p, Birmingham Black Barons, Homestead Grays, Memphis Red Sox

THOMPSON, HAROLD—1949—p, Kansas City Monarchs

THOMPSON, HENRY CURTIS—1943–48—**of,** 2b, ss, Kansas City Monarchs

THOMPSON, JAMES—1920–25—of, c, Dayton Marcos, Milwaukee Bears, Birmingham Black Barons

THOMPSON, JIMMY—1945—umpire, NAL

THOMPSON, LLOYD P.—1922–30—officer, Hilldale

THOMPSON, SAMUEL (SAD SAM)—1931–42—p, Kansas City Monarchs, Indianapolis ABCs, Detroit Stars, Columbus Elite Giants, **Philadelphia Stars,** Chicago American Giants

THOMPSON, SAMMY (RUNT)—1931—2b, Memphis Red Sox, Little Rock Black Travelers

THOMPSON, SANDY—1926–32—of, Chicago American Giants, Birmingham Black Barons, Chicago Columbia Giants, Cole's American Giants

THOMPSON, W. —— —1949–50—p, Philadelphia Stars

THOMPSON, WILLIAM—1887–1900—c, Louisville Falls Citys, Genuine Cuban Giants

THORNTON, CHARLES—1887—player, Pittsburgh Keystones

THORNTON, H. —— —1931—of, Memphis Red Sox

THORNTON, JACK—1932–37—p, 2b, 1b, Atlanta Black Crackers

THORNTON, JESSE—1937—officer, Indianapolis Athletics

THORPE, JIM—1928—p, Hilldale

THRILKILL, —— —1929–31—ss, of, Nashville Elite Giants

THURMAN, —— —1932—p, of, Louisville Black Caps

THURMAN, ROBERT—1946–49—p, Homestead Grays, Kansas City Monarchs

THURSTON, —— —1938—p, Birmingham Black Barons

THURSTON, BOBBY—1911—of, Chicago Giants

TIANT, LUIS (LEFTY)—1930–47—p, Cuban Stars (NNL), New York Cubans

TINDLE, LEVY—1933—officer, Detroit Stars

TITUS, JAMES—1937—officer, Detroit Stars

TOLES, (LEFTY)—1946—p, Pittsburgh Crawfords

TOMM, —— —1918—of, Brooklyn Royal Giants, Philadelphia Giants

TONEY, ALBERT—1908–16—**ss,** 2b, Chicago Union Giants, Leland Giants, Chicago American Giants, Chicago Giants

TORRES, ARMANDO—1939—p, Cuban Stars

TORRIENTI, CHRISTOBEL—1914–32—**of,** p, Cuban Stars, **Chicago American Giants,** Kansas City Monarchs, Detroit Stars, Gilkerson's Union Giants, Atlanta Black Crackers, Cleveland Cubs

TOWN, —— —1917—of, Bacharach Giants

TRAMMEL, —— —1930—1b, Birmingham Black Barons

TREADWELL, HAROLD—1919–26—p, **Brooklyn Royal Giants,** Bacharach Giants, Harrisburg Giants, Chicago American Giants, Indianapolis ABCs, Dayton Marcos

TREADWAY, ———— —1939—p, Kansas City Monarchs
TRENT, THEODORE (TED)—1927–39—p, St. Louis Stars, Detroit Wolves, Homestead Grays, Cole's American Giants, Chicago American Giants
TRICE, BILL—1949–50—p, of, Homestead Grays
TRIMBLE, WILLIAM E.—1927–32—officer, Chicago American Giants
TROUPE, QUINCY THOMAS—1930–49—c, of, p, mgr, St. Louis Stars, Detroit Wolves, Homestead Grays, Kansas City Monarchs, Chicago American Giants, Indianapolis ABCs, Cleveland Buckeyes, New York Cubans
TROY, DONALD—1944–45—p, Baltimore Elite Giants
TRUSTY, JOB—1896—3b, Cuban Giants
TRUSTY, SHEP—1885–86—p, Philadelphia Orions, Cuban Giants
TUCKER, HENRY—1916–22—officer, Bacharach Giants
TURNER, ———— —1916—1b, Chicago Union Giants
TURNER, ———— —1923—of, Toledo Tigers
TURNER, ———— —1928—p, St. Louis Stars
TURNER, ———— —1930—1b, Kansas City Monarchs
TURNER, BOB—1950—c, Houston Eagles
TURNER, E. C. (POP)—1929–37—3b, ss, Homestead Grays, Birmingham Black Barons, Cleveland Cubs, Cole's American Giants; umpire, NNL
TURNER, (FLASH)—1938–42—c, 2b, 1b, of, Jacksonville Red Caps, Cleveland Bears
TURNER, J. O.—1887—player, Philadelphia Pythians
TURNER, (LITTLE LEFTY)—1940–42—1b, Indianapolis Crawfords, Baltimore Elite Giants
TURNER, OLIVER—1943—p, Chicago Brown Bombers
TURNER, THOMAS—1947—1b, Chicago American Giants
TURNER, (TUCK)—1919—p, Chicago American Giants
TURNSTALL, WILLIE—1950—p, Cleveland Buckeyes
TUT, RICHARD (KING)—1943–50—1b, Cincinnati Clowns, Indianapolis Clowns
TYE, DAN—1930–36—3b, ss, p, Memphis Red Sox, Cincinnati Tigers
TYLER, CHARLES H.—1934–35—officer, Newark Dodgers
TYLER, EDWARD—1928—p, Brooklyn Cuban Giants
TYLER, EUGENE—1943—c, inf, Chicago Brown Bombers
TYLER, ROY—1925–26—p, of, Chicago American Giants
TYLER, WILLIAM (STEEL ARM)—1925–32—p, Memphis Red Sox, Detroit Stars, Kansas City Monarchs, Cole's American Giants
TYREE, RUBY—1916–24—p, All Nations, Chicago American Giants, Cleveland Browns
TYSON, ———— —1938—c, Birmingham Black Barons

UNDERWOOD, ELY—1937—of, Detroit Stars

VACTOR, JOHN—1887–88—player, Philadelphia Pythians, New York Gorhams

VALDES, FERMIN—1944—player, Cincinnati–Indianapolis Clowns
VALDEZ, R. —— —1911—of, All Cubans
VALDEZ, STRICO (SWAT)—1932–39—2b, Cuban Stars, Atlanta Black Crackers
VALDEZ, TONY—1910–20—of, Stars of Cuba, Cuban Stars (NNL)
VAN BUREN, —— —1931—of, Memphis Red Sox
VANCE, COLUMBUS—1930–34—p, Birmingham Black Barons, Homestead Grays, Detroit Wolves, Detroit Stars
VANDYKE, —— —1895–97—of, Page Fence Giants
VARGAS, GUILLERMO—1949—of, New York Cubans
VARGAS, JOSE (TETELO)—1939–44—of, Cuban Stars, New York Cubans
VARGAS, ROBERT—1948—p, Chicago American Giants
VASQUEZ, ARMANDO—1944–46—utility, Cincinnati–Indianapolis Clowns, Indianapolis Clowns
VAUGHN, —— —1934—p, Newark Dodgers
VAUGHN, JOE—1931—sec, NSL
VEAL, —— —1931—p, of, Birmingham Black Barons
VENEY, JEROME—1908–17—of, mgr, Homestead Grays
VENTURA, —— —1929—p, Cuban Stars (NNL)
VERNAL, (SLEEPY)—1941—p, Cuban Stars
VERONA, ORLANDO—1948–50—ss, Memphis Red Sox
VICTORY, GEORGE M.—1919–20—officer, Pennsylvania Giants
VILLA, ROBERTO (BOBBY)—1910–22—of, 2b, Stars of Cuba, Cuban Stars, All Cubans
VILLODOS, —— —1946–47—c, Baltimore Elite Giants
VINCENT, IRVING (LEFTY)—1934—p, Pittsburgh Crawfords
VINES, EDDIE—1940—p, 3b, Chicago American Giants, Birmingham Black Barons

WADDY, (LEFTY)—1932–33—p, Indianapolis ABCs, Detroit Stars
WADE, LEE—1909–16—**p,** of, 1b, Cuban Giants, Philadelphia Giants, St. Louis Giants, Lincoln Giants, Chicago American Giants
WAGNER, BILL—1921–27—**ss,** 2b, mgr, Lincoln Giants, **Brooklyn Royal Giants**
WAITE, ARNOLD—1936–37—p, Homestead Grays
WALDON, (ALLIE)—1944—player, Chicago American Giants
WALKER, —— —1887—player, Boston Resolutes
WALKER, —— —1923—p, Milwaukee Bears
WALKER, —— —1937—c, Indianapolis Athletics
WALKER, A. M.—1937—mgr, Birmingham Black Barons
WALKER, CHARLIE—1930–34—officer, Homestead Grays
WALKER, EDSELL (BIG)—1937–45—p, **Homestead Grays,** Philadelphia Stars
WALKER, GEORGE (LITTLE)—1937–50—p, Homestead Grays, **Kansas City Monarchs**
WALKER, H. —— —1932—c, Monroe Monarchs

WALKER, JESSE (HOSS)—1929–50—ss, 3b, mgr, club officer, Bacharach Giants, Cleveland Cubs, Nashville Elite Giants, Washington Elite Giants, Baltimore Elite Giants, New York Black Yankees, Birmingham Black Barons, Cincinnati Clowns, Cincinnati–Indianapolis Clowns, Nashville Cubs

WALKER, LARRY—1942—3b, Newark Eagles

WALKER, MOSES FLEETWOOD (FLEET)—1883–89—c, of, Toledo (Northwestern League and American Association); Cleveland (Western League); Waterbury (Southern New England and Eastern Leagues); Newark and Syracuse (International League)

WALKER, MOSES L.—1928–31—officer, Detroit Stars

WALKER, ROBERT T.—1945–49—p, Homestead Grays

WALKER, W. —— —1932—of, Monroe Monarchs

WALKER, WELDY WILBERFORCE—1884–87—of, c, Toledo (American Association); Akron (Ohio State League); Pittsburgh Keystones

WALLACE, —— —1931—3b, Cleveland Cubs

WALLACE, FELIX—1909–21—ss, 2b, 3b, mgr, St. Paul Gophers, Leland Giants, Chicago Giants, St. Louis Giants, Bacharach Giants, Lincoln Giants

WALLACE, JAMES—1949—c, Houston Eagles

WALLER, GEORGE—1943—inf, Chicago Brown Bombers

WALLS, (GREENIE)—1941–42—umpire

WALTERS, —— —1924—p, Cleveland Browns

WALTON, (FUZZY)—1938—of, Pittsburgh Crawfords

WARD, C. —— —1925–34—of, Memphis Red Sox, Chicago Columbia Giants, Louisville Black Caps, Cincinnati Tigers

WARD, IRA —1922–27—ss, 1b, Chicago Giants

WARE, —— —1921—of, Nashville Elite Giants

WARE, —— —1932—of, Cleveland Stars

WARE, ARCHIE V.—1940–50—1b, Chicago American Giants, Kansas City Monarchs, Cleveland Buckeyes, Louisville Buckeyes, Indianapolis Clowns

WARE, WILLIAM—1926—1b, Chicago American Giants

WARFIELD, FRANK—1916–32—2b, ss, 3b, mgr, St. Louis Giants, Indianapolis ABCs, Kansas City Monarchs, Detroit Stars, Hilldale, Baltimore Black Sox, Washington Pilots

WARMACK, SAM—1929–33—of, Hilldale, Bacharach Giants

WARREN, CICERO—1946–47—p, Homestead Grays

WARREN, JESSE—1940–47—2b, 3b, p, Memphis Red Sox, New Orleans–St. Louis Stars, Birmingham Black Barons, Chicago American Giants

WASHINGTON, —— —1929—c, Nashville Elite Giants

WASHINGTON, (BLUE)—1920—1b, Kansas City Monarchs

WASHINGTON, ED—1915—p, Chicago American Giants

WASHINGTON, FAY—1940–41—p, St. Louis Stars, New Orleans–St. Louis Stars

WASHINGTON, ISAAC—1928—officer, Bacharach Giants

WASHINGTON, (JAP)—1922-37—3b, 1b, of, Pittsburgh Keystones, **Homestead Grays,** Pittsburgh Crawfords; umpire, NNL

WASHINGTON, JOHN—1933-50—1b, Montgomery Grey Sox, Birmingham Black Barons, Pittsburgh Crawfords, New York Black Yankees, Baltimore Elite Giants, Houston Eagles

WASHINGTON, L. —— —1884-85—ss, Baltimore Atlantics

WASHINGTON, LAFAYETTE—1943-45—p, Chicago American Giants, Birmingham Black Barons, Cincinnati–Indianapolis Clowns, Kansas City Monarchs

WASHINGTON, NAMON—1921-30—of, ss, Indianapolis ABCs, Hilldale, Brooklyn Cuban Giants, Philadelphia Tigers, Lincoln Giants, Brooklyn Royal Giants

WASHINGTON, PETER (PETE)—1923-35—of, Washington Potomacs, Wilmington Potomacs, **Baltimore Black Sox,** Philadelphia Stars

WASHINGTON, TOM—1905-10—c, Philadelphia Giants, Chicago Giants, Pittsburgh Giants

WATERS, DICK—1916—mgr, St. Louis Giants

WATKINS, G. C.—1937—officer, Indianapolis Athletics

WATKINS, MURRAY—1944-48—3b, Newark Eagles, Philadelphia Stars

WATKINS, (POP)—1900-19—1b, c, mgr, Genuine Cuban Giants, Havana Red Sox

WATKINS, RICHARD—1950—inf, Memphis Red Sox

WATSON, AMOS—1945-47—p, Cincinnati–Indianapolis Clowns, Baltimore Elite Giants

WATSON, EVERETT—1931—officer, Detroit Stars

WATSON, J. —— —1922-31—of, Detroit Stars, Brooklyn Royal Giants, Bacharach Giants

WATSON, JIMMY—1950—p, New York Cubans

WATTS, ANDREW—1950—inf, Birmingham Black Barons

WATTS, DICK—1949—p, Birmingham Black Barons

WATTS, EDDIE—1924-26—2b, 1b, St. Louis Stars, Cleveland Hornets, Cleveland Elites

WATTS, HERMAN (LEFTY)—1941-42—p, Jacksonville Red Caps, Cleveland Buckeyes

WATTS, JACK—1913-19—c, Louisville Cubs, Chicago American Giants, Indianapolis ABCs, Dayton Marcos

WEBB, JAMES (BABY)—1910—c, Leland Giants

WEBSTER, JIM—1933-37—c, p, Detroit Stars

WEBSTER, WILLIAM (SPECK)—1912-26—**c,** 1b, St. Louis Giants, Chicago Giants, Brooklyn Royal Giants, Mohawk Giants, Lincoln Giants, Hilldale, Detroit Stars, Dayton Marcos, Brooklyn Cuban Giants

WEEKS, —— —1918-23—2b, 3b, Pennsylvania Giants, Harrisburg Giants

WEEKS, WILLIAM—1922—officer, Bacharach Giants

WELCH, WINFIELD SCOTT—1926-49—**mgr,** player, New Orleans Black Pelicans, Monroe Monarchs, Shreveport Giants, Cincinnati Buckeyes, Birmingham Black Barons, Cincinnati Crescents, New York Cubans, Chicago American Giants

WELLS, ——— —1918—2b, c, Lincoln Giants, Pennsylvania Giants

WELLS, I. ——— —1948—p, Memphis Red Sox

WELLS, WILLIE—1925–49—ss, 3b, mgr, **St. Louis Stars,** Detroit Wolves, Kansas City Monarchs, Chicago American Giants, Cole's American Giants, **Newark Eagles,** Memphis Red Sox, New York Black Yankees, Baltimore Elite Giants, Indianapolis Clowns

WELLS, WILLIE, JR.—1945–50—ss, Memphis Red Sox

WELMAKER, ROY—1932–45—p, Atlanta Black Crackers, **Homestead Grays,** Philadelphia Stars

WESLEY, CHARLES—1924–29—2b, mgr, Birmingham Black Barons

WESLEY, (CONNIE)—1921–27—of, Columbus Buckeyes, Pittsburgh Keystones, Indianapolis ABCs, Memphis Red Sox

WESLEY, EDGAR—1919–31—1b, **Detroit Stars,** Cleveland Hornets, Bacharach Giants

WEST, C. ——— —1930—2b, Birmingham Black Barons, Memphis Red Sox

WEST, JAMES (JIM)—1930–47—1b, Birmingham Black Barons, Cleveland Cubs, Memphis Red Sox, Nashville Elite Giants, Columbus Elite Giants, Washington Elite Giants, Baltimore Elite Giants, **Philadelphia Stars,** New York Black Yankees

WEST, OLLIE—1942–46—p, Chicago American Giants, Pittsburgh Crawfords, Birmingham Black Barons

WESTON, ——— —1930—p, Hilldale

WESTON, (DEACON)—1949—p, Louisville Buckeyes

WEYMAN, J. B.—1887—player, Baltimore Lord Baltimores

WHATLEY, DAVID (SPEED)—1937–46—of, Birmingham Black Barons, Homestead Grays, Pittsburgh Crawfords

WHEELER, JOE—1923–28—p, Baltimore Black Sox, Brooklyn Cuban Giants

WHITE, ——— —1923—3b, Toledo Tigers

WHITE, ——— —1922—2b, Pittsburgh Keystones

WHITE, ARTHUR—1934—p, Newark Dodgers

WHITE, BURLIN—1915–42—c, mgr, West Baden, Indiana, Sprudels, Bacharach Giants, Lincoln Giants, Philadelphia Royal Stars, Harrisburg Giants, Philadelphia Giants, Quaker Giants, Cuban Stars, Boston Royal Giants

WHITE, BUTLER—1920–23—1b, Chicago Giants

WHITE, CHANEY—1921–35—of, Hilldale, **Bacharach Giants,** Wilmington Potomacs, Quaker Giants, Homestead Grays, Darby Daisies, Philadelphia Stars

WHITE, CHARLES—1950—3b, Philadelphia Stars

WHITE, EDWARD—1944—p, Homestead Grays

WHITE, EUGENE—1935—3b, Brooklyn Eagles

WHITE, EUGENE—1950—inf, Chicago American Giants

WHITE, LADD—1947–48—p, Memphis Red Sox

WHITE, (LEFTY)—1940—p, Cleveland Bears
WHITE, M. ——— —1887—player, New York Gorhams
WHITE, R. W.—1887—player, Washington Capital Citys
WHITE, (RED)—1929—p, Nashville Elite Giants
WHITE, SOL—1887-1926—**2b,** 3b, of, 1b, **mgr,** coach, bus mgr, Pitts-
    burgh Keystones, Washington Capital Citys, Wheeling (Ohio State
    League); New York Gorhams, York Monarchs (Eastern Interstate
    League); Cuban Giants, Genuine Cuban Giants, Fort Wayne (Western
    Interstate League); Page Fence Giants, Cuban X Giants, Columbia
    Giants, **Philadelphia Giants,** Lincoln Giants, Quaker Giants, Cleveland
    Browns, Newark Stars
WHITE, ZARLIE—1934—player, Monroe Monarchs
WHITFIELD, (LEFTY)—1950—p, Baltimore Elite Giants
WHITLOCK, ——— —1926—1b, Dayton Marcos
WHITWORTH, RICHARD—1915-24—p, **Chicago American Giants,**
    Chicago Giants, Hilldale
WHYTE, WILLIAM (BILLY)—1893—p, of, Cuban Giants
WICKWARE, FRANK—1910-25—p, Leland Giants, St. Louis Giants,
    Philadelphia Giants, Mohawk Giants, Lincoln Stars, Chicago American
    Giants, Chicago Giants, Brooklyn Royal Giants, Detroit Stars, Norfolk
    Stars, Lincoln Giants
WIGGINS, JOE—1931-34—3b, Nashville Elite Giants, Bacharach Giants
WILBERT, ART—1942—of, Cincinnati Clowns, Minneapolis–St. Paul
    Gophers
WILEY, F.—1923-25—2b, p, of, Lincoln Giants, Pennsylvania Red Caps
    of New York
WILEY, JOE—1947—3b, Baltimore Elite Giants
WILEY, WASHEBA (DOC)—1911–23—**c,** 1b, Brooklyn Royal Giants,
    Lincoln Giants, Philadelphia Giants
WILKES, BARRON—1919—officer, New York Bacharach Giants
WILKES, JAMES (JIMMY)—1945-50—of, Newark Eagles, Houston
    Eagles
WILKINS, WESLEY—1910—of, Kansas City, Kansas, Giants
WILKINSON, J. L.—1909-48—officer, All Nations, **Kansas City Mon-
    archs;** sec, NNL; tres, NAL
WILLAS, S. ——— —1887—player, New York Gorhams
WILLBURN, ——— —1926—p, Baltimore Black Sox
WILLETT, ——— —1923-28—ss, of, Lincoln Giants, Cleveland Browns,
    Cleveland Tigers
WILLIAMS, ——— —1887—player, Boston Resolutes
WILLIAMS, ——— —1939—c, Indianapolis ABCs
WILLIAMS, A. ——— —1916-18—p, of, 2b, Brooklyn Royal Giants
WILLIAMS, A. D.—1925—officer, Indianapolis ABCs
WILLIAMS, A. N.—1922—officer, Pittsburgh Keystones
WILLIAMS, ANDREW (STRINGBEAN)—1915-25—p, mgr, St. Louis
    Giants, Lincoln Giants, Pennsylvania Red Caps of New York, Indian-
    apolis ABCs, Chicago American Giants, Dayton Marcos, Bacharach
    Giants, Brooklyn Royal Giants, Washington Potomacs

WILLIAMS, B. —— —1931–32—of, Montgomery Grey Sox, Indianapolis ABCs
WILLIAMS, BERT—1923—officer, Philadelphia Giants
WILLIAMS, BILL—1900—p, Genuine Cuban Giants
WILLIAMS, C.—1885—mgr, Brooklyn Remsens
WILLIAMS, CHARLES ARTHUR—1924–31—ss, 2b, Lincoln Giants, Memphis Red Sox, Chicago American Giants, Indianapolis ABCs, Chicago Columbia Giants
WILLIAMS, CHARLES (LEFTY)—1915–34—p, Homestead Grays
WILLIAMS, CHESTER—1930–43—**ss,** 2b, Memphis Red Sox, **Pittsburgh Crawfords,** Homestead Grays, Philadelphia Stars
WILLIAMS, CLARENCE—1886–1912—c, Cuban Giants, New York Gorhams, Cuban X Giants, Philadelphia Giants, Lansing, Michigan, Colored Capital All-Americans, Smart Set
WILLIAMS, CLARENCE—1939–40—p, of, Baltimore Elite Giants
WILLIAMS, CLYDE—1947—p, Cleveland Buckeyes
WILLIAMS, (COTTON)—1950—p, Houston Eagles
WILLIAMS, CRAIG (STRINGBEAN)—1928—p, Brooklyn Cuban Giants
WILLIAMS, (CURLEY)—1945–50—3b, ss, Newark Eagles, Houston Eagles
WILLIAMS, E. —— —1943—of, Harrisburg–St. Louis Stars
WILLIAMS, E. J.—1887—player, Washington Capital Citys
WILLIAMS, EDDIE—1945—of, Kansas City Monarchs
WILLIAMS, ELBERT—1931–34—p, Louisville White Sox, Monroe Monarchs
WILLIAMS, F. —— —1924—player, Washington Potomacs
WILLIAMS, FRANK—1942–46—of, Homestead Grays
WILLIAMS, GEORGE—1885–1902—2b, 1b, Philadelphia Orions, Argyle Hotel, Cuban Giants, New York Gorhams, Cuban X Giants
WILLIAMS, GERARD—1921–25—ss, Indianapolis ABCs, Homestead Grays
WILLIAMS, H. —— —1929–33—p, Homestead Grays, Monroe Monarchs, New Orleans Crescent Stars
WILLIAMS, HARRY—1931–47—**3b,** 2b, ss, mgr, Pittsburgh Crawfords, Baltimore Black Sox, Homestead Grays, Brooklyn Eagles, Newark Eagles, New York Black Yankees, Harrisburg–St. Louis Stars, Baltimore Elite Giants, New York Cubans, New Orleans Creoles
WILLIAMS, HENRY—1922–29—c, Kansas City Monarchs, St. Louis Stars
WILLIAMS, J. —— —1928–34—**of,** p, St. Louis Stars, Indianapolis ABCs, Detroit Stars, Homestead Grays
WILLIAMS, JAMES—1885—c, Brooklyn Remsens
WILLIAMS, JAMES (JIM)—1937–48—of, mgr, Homestead Grays, Toledo Crawfords, Cleveland Bears, New York Black Yankees, New York Cubans, Birmingham Black Barons, Durham Eagles
WILLIAMS, JEFF—1950—2b, Houston Eagles
WILLIAMS, JESSE—1944–45—player, Cleveland Buckeyes

WILLIAMS, JESSE—1940–49—ss, 3b, **Kansas City Monarchs,** Indianapolis Clowns

WILLIAMS, JIM—1934–37—of, 1b, Newark Dodgers, New York Black Yankees, Philadelphia Stars

WILLIAMS, JIM (BULLET)—1929–32—p, Nashville Elite Giants, Cleveland Cubs, Detroit Wolves

WILLIAMS, JOE (CYCLONE, SMOKY)—1897–1932—p, mgr, San Antonio Bronchos, Leland Giants, Chicago Giants, **Lincoln Giants,** Chicago American Giants, Bacharach Giants, Brooklyn Royal Giants, **Homestead Grays**

WILLIAMS, JOHN—1948—1b, Chicago American Giants

WILLIAMS, JOHNNY—1943–48—p, Chicago Brown Bombers, Cincinnati–Indianapolis Clowns, Indianapolis Clowns

WILLIAMS, L. —— —1909—of, Cuban Giants

WILLIAMS, L. C.—1942—of, New York Cubans

WILLIAMS, L. R.—1931—officer, Cleveland Stars

WILLIAMS, (LEFTY)—1950—p, Cleveland Buckeyes

WILLIAMS, LEM—1923—umpire, NNL

WILLIAMS, LEN—1950—inf, of, Indianapolis Clowns

WILIAMS, LEROY—1947–48—ss, 2b, Newark Eagles

WILLIAMS, MARVIN—1944–49—2b, Philadelphia Stars

WILLIAMS, MATT—1922—ss, 3b, Pittsburgh Keystones

WILLIAMS, MORRIS—1921—p, Indianapolis ABCs

WILLIAMS, NISH—1929–38—**c,** of, 3b, 1b, **Nashville Elite Giants,** Cleveland Cubs, Columbus Elite Giants, Washington Elite Giants, Birmingham Black Barons

WILLIAMS, P. —— —1931–39—2b, Baltimore Black Sox, Toledo Crawfords

WILLIAMS, POINDEXTER—1921–33—c, mgr, Chicago American Giants, Detroit Stars, Kansas City Monarchs, **Birmingham Black Barons,** Louisville White Sox, Nashville Elite Giants, Homestead Grays

WILLIAMS, RAY—1933–39—p, New York Black Yankees

WILLIAMS, ROBERT—1948–49—p, Newark Eagles, Houston Eagles

WILLIAMS, ROBERT L. (BOBBY)—1918–45—ss, 2b, 3b, mgr, **Chicago American Giants,** Indianapolis ABCs, Homestead Grays, Pittsburgh Crawfords, Cleveland Red Sox

WILLIAMS, ROY—1932–41—p, Pittsburgh Crawfords, Columbus Blue Birds, Baltimore Black Sox, Brooklyn Royal Giants, Brooklyn Eagles, Philadelphia Stars, New York Black Yankees, Baltimore Elite Giants

WILLIAMS, S. —— —1916–18—p, Brooklyn Royal Giants, Philadelphia Giants

WILLIAMS, S. —— —1945—p, Newark Eagles

WILLIAMS, SAM—1947–50—p, Birmingham Black Barons

WILLIAMS, SOL—1884–85—of, Baltimore Atlantics

WILLIAMS, STUART—1950—2b, Cleveland Buckeyes

WILLIAMS, T. —— —1896—c, of, Cuban X Giants

WILLIAMS, THOMAS (TOM)—1916–25—p, Bacharach Giants, **Chi-**

cago **American Giants,** Lincoln Giants, Brooklyn Royal Giants, Hilldale, Chicago Giants

WILLIAMS, W.—1929–33—ss, 2b, Bacharach Giants, Brooklyn Royal Giants

WILLIAMS, WALTER—1898—p, Celeron Acme Colored Giants (Iron and Oil League)

WILLIAMS, (ZEKE)—1930–31—c, Birmingham Black Barons, Cleveland Cubs

WILLIS, JIM—1928–39—p, Birmingham Black Barons, Nashville Elite Giants, Cleveland Cubs, Philadelphia Stars, Columbus Elite Giants, Washington Elite Giants, Baltimore Elite Giants

WILMORE, ALFRED (APPLE)—1947–50—p, Philadelphia Stars, Baltimore Elite Giants

WILSON, —— ——1917—ss, Bacharach Giants

WILSON, —— ——1917–20—p, of, Dayton Giants, Dayton Marcos

WILSON, ALEC—1939—of, New York Black Yankees

WILSON, ANDREW—1922–27—of, New Orleans Crescent Stars, Milwaukee Bears, Chicago Giants

WILSON, ARTHUR LEE (ARTIE)—1944–48—ss, Birmingham Black Barons

WILSON, BENJAMIN (BENNY)—1923–25—of, Lincoln Giants, Pennsylvania Red Caps of New York

WILSON, BILL—1948—3b, Newark Eagles

WILSON, CARTER—1920–23—of, Gilkerson's Union Giants, Peters' Union Giants

WILSON, CHARLES—1948–49—of, Indianapolis Clowns

WILSON, CHARLES—1921–22—p, Columbus Buckeyes, Detroit Stars

WILSON, (CHUBBY)—1929—of, Bacharach Giants

WILSON, DAN—1937–47—**of,** 3b, 2b, ss, Pittsburgh Crawfords, St. Louis Stars, New Orleans–St. Louis Stars, New York Black Yankees, Harrisburg–St. Louis Stars, Homestead Grays, Philadelphia Stars

WILSON, E. —— ——1921–25—2b, 3b, Dayton Marcos, Detroit Stars

WILSON, ED—1896–1903—1b, Cuban X Giants, Lansing, Michigan, Colored Capital All-Americans

WILSON, EDWARD—1898—p, Celeron Acme Colored Giants (Iron and Oil League)

WILSON, EMMETT—1937–46—of, Pittsburgh Crawfords, Cincinnati Buckeyes, Cincinnati Clowns, Boston Blues

WILSON, FELTON—1937—c, Detroit Stars

WILSON, FRED—1938–45—**of,** p, mgr, New York Black Yankees, Newark Eagles, Cincinnati Clowns, Cincinnati–Indianapolis Clowns

WILSON, GEORGE—1896–1905—p, of, Page Fence Giants, Columbia Giants, Chicago Union Giants

WILSON, J. —— ——1922–24—1b, 2b, Baltimore Black Sox

WILSON, J. H.—1887—player, Baltimore Lord Baltimores

WILSON, JAMES—1947—p, Memphis Red Sox

WILSON, JAMES—1940—of, 2b, Indianapolis Crawfords

WILSON, JOSEPH—1887—player, Washington Capital Citys

WILSON, JUDSON (JUD, BOJUNG)—1924–45—**3b,** 1b, mgr, Baltimore Black Sox, Homestead Grays, Philadelphia Stars

WILSON, (LEFTY)—1936–40—p, Kansas City Monarchs, Memphis Red Sox

WILSON, PERCY—1922–33—1b, New Orleans Crescent Stars, Milwaukee Bears

WILSON, RAY—1902–09—1b, Cuban X Giants, Philadelphia Giants

WILSON, ROBERT (BOB)—1947–50—3b, Newark Eagles, Houston Eagles

WILSON,THOMAS T. (TOM)—1918–47—officer, Nashville Standard Giants, Nashville Elite Giants, Cleveland Cubs, Baltimore Elite Giants; vice-chairman, tres, pres, NNL; sec, pres, NSL

WILSON, W. ROLLO—1929–34—sec, ANL; commissioner, NNL

WILSON, WILLIAM H.—1887—player, Pittsburgh Keystones

WINFIELD, ———— —1931—ss, Memphis Red Sox

WINGFIELD, ———— —1923—p, Toledo Tigers

WINGFIELD, ———— —1920—2b, Dayton Marcos

WINGO, (DOC)—1944—player, Kansas City Monarchs

WINSTON, ———— —1929–32—p, of, Chicago Giants, Chicago Columbia Giants, Atlanta Black Crackers

WINSTON, CLARENCE (BOBBY)—1906–23—of, Philadelphia Giants, Leland Giants, **Chicago Giants**

WINTERS, JESSE (NIP)—1919–33—p, Norfolk Stars, Bacharach Giants, Norfolk Giants, **Hilldale,** Philadelphia Stars, Harrisburg Giants, Lincoln Giants, Darby Daisies

WISE, RUSSELL—1940—1b, Indianapolis Crawfords

WISHER, ———— —1923—of, Harrisburg Giants

WITHERSPOON, LESTER—1949—p, of, Indianapolis Clowns

WOLFOLK, LEWIS—1923–24—p, Chicago American Giants

WOMACK, ———— —1928–33—1b, Cleveland Tigers, Indianapolis ABCs, Cuban Stars, Columbus Turfs, Columbus Blue Birds, Baltimore Black Sox

WOODS, ———— —1919–26—of, Brooklyn Royal Giants, Indianapolis ABCs, Columbus Buckeyes, St. Louis Stars, Washington Potomacs, Bacharach Giants

WOODS, PARNELL—1933–49—3b, mgr, Birmingham Black Barons, Cleveland Bears, Jacksonville Red Caps, Cincinnati Buckeyes, Cleveland Buckeyes, Louisville Buckeyes

WOODS, SAM—1946–50—p, Cleveland Buckeyes, Memphis Red Sox

WRIGHT, ———— —1946—3b, New York Cubans

WRIGHT, BURNIS (BILL)—1932–45—of, Nashville Elite Giants, Columbus Elite Giants, Washington Elite Giants, **Baltimore Elite Giants,** Philadelphia Stars

WRIGHT, CLARENCE (BUGGY)—1898—1b, Celeron Acme Colored Giants (Iron and Oil League)

WRIGHT, ERNEST (ERNIE)—1941–49—officer, Cleveland White Sox, Cincinnati Buckeyes, Cleveland Buckeyes; vice-pres, NAL

WRIGHT, GEORGE—1906–12—ss, 2b, Quaker Giants, Brooklyn Royal Giants, Leland Giants, Chicago Giants, Lincoln Giants
WRIGHT, HENRY—1929–34—p, **Nashville Elite Giants,** Cleveland Cubs
WRIGHT, JOHN RICHARD—1937–48—p, Newark Eagles, Indianapolis Crawfords, Pittsburgh Crawfords, **Homestead Grays**
WRIGHT, ZOLLIE—1931–40—of, Memphis Red Sox, Monroe Monarchs, New Orleans Crescent Stars, Columbus Elite Giants, Washington Elite Giants, Washington Black Senators, New York Black Yankees
WYATT, ——— —1929—c, Detroit Stars
WYATT, DAVID (DAVE)—1896–1920—of, Chicago Unions, Chicago Union Giants; co-drafter, constitution of NNL
WYATT, RALPH—1942–46—ss, **Chicago American Giants,** Homestead Grays
WYLIE, ENSLOE—1944–47—p, Kansas City Monarchs, Memphis Red Sox
WYNN, CALVIN—1949—of, Louisville Buckeyes
WYNN, WILLIE—1944–50—c, **Newark Eagles,** New York Cubans

YANCEY, WILLIAM J. (BILL, YANK)—1923–36—ss, Philadelphia Giants, Hilldale, Philadelphia Tigers, Lincoln Giants, Darby Daisies, New York Black Yankees, Brooklyn Eagles, Philadelphia Stars
YOKELEY, LAMON—1926–38—p, Baltimore Black Sox, Bacharach Giants, Philadelphia Stars, Washington Black Senators
YORK, JIM—1920–23—c, Norfolk Stars, Hilldale, Bacharach Giants
YOUNG, ——— —1924—p, St. Louis Stars
YOUNG, BERDELL—1922–28—of, Bacharach Giants, Lincoln Giants
YOUNG, BOB—1950—inf, Cleveland Buckeyes
YOUNG, EDWARD (PEP)—1938–47—**c,** 1b, 3b, **Chicago American Giants,** Kansas City Monarchs, Homestead Grays
YOUNG, FRANK A. (FAY)—1939–48—sec, NAL
YOUNG, LEANDY—1944–45—of, Birmingham Black Barons
YOUNG, M. ——— —1927—p, Kansas City Monarchs
YOUNG, ROY—1942–45—umpire, NAL
YOUNG, T. J. (TOM)—1926–37—c, **Kansas City Monarchs,** St. Louis Stars, Detroit Wolves, New York Cubans, Pittsburgh Crawfords
YOUNG, W. H.—1949—officer, Houston Eagles
YOUNG, WILBUR—1945—p, Birmingham Black Barons
YOUNG, WILLIAM P. (PEP)—1919–34—c, Homestead Grays
YVANES, ARMANDO—1949–50—ss, New York Cubans

ZAPP, JAMES—1948–50—of, Birmingham Black Barons, Baltimore Elite Giants
ZIEGLER, WILLIAM —1927–29—of, Chicago Giants
ZIMMERMAN, GEORGE—1887—player, Pittsburgh Keystones
ZOMPHIER, CHARLES—1926–31—**2b,** 3b, ss, Cleveland Elites, Cleveland Hornets, Cleveland Tigers, Memphis Red Sox, Cleveland Cubs

INDEX